San Francisco

THE ROUGH GUIDE

P9-AOO-083

Other guides available in this series

Amsterdam
Australia
Barcelona & Catalunya
Berlin
Brazil
Brittany & Normandy
Bulgaria
California
Canada
Corsica
Crete
Cyprus
Czech & Slovak Republics
Egypt
England
Europe
Florida
France
Germany
Greece
Guatemala & Belize

Holland, Belgium &
  Luxembourg
Hong Kong & Macau
Hungary
Ireland
Italy
Kenya
Mediterranean
  Wildlife
Mexico
Morocco
Nepal
New York
Nothing Ventured
Pacific Northwest
Paris
Peru
Poland
Portugal
Prague
Provence

Pyrenees
Scandinavia
Scotland
Sicily
Spain
St Petersburg
Thailand
Tunisia
Turkey
Tuscany & Umbria
USA
Venice
Wales
West Africa
Women Travel
Zimbabwe & Botswana

Forthcoming titles

India
Malaysia & Singapore

Rough Guide Credits

Text Editor:	Greg Ward
Series Editor:	Mark Ellingham
Editorial:	Martin Dunford, John Fisher, Jonathan Buckley, Jules Brown, Graham Parker, Jo Mead, Samantha Cook
Production:	Susanne Hillen, Andy Hilliard, Gail Jammy, Vivien Antwi, Alan Spicer
Cartography:	Melissa Flack
Publicity:	Richard Trillo
Finance:	Celia Crowley, Simon Carloss
Administration:	Tania Hummel

DEBORAH would like to thank Debra Matsumoto at Chronicle Books for the usual mountain of reference books, and Deborah Parker Wong at Susie Biehler Associates for showing me the town and some exciting new discoveries. A special thanks to Bummer for giving me a reason to come home, and King Thomas who took care of him in my absence. But most of all this book is dedicated to the memory of Brett M Bennett, and, fortunately still with us, George Olson, the spirit of San Francisco.

JAMIE: For encouragement, help and hospitality, many thanks to Brando and Judah, Richard "skinny bones" Bardfield, Teri Buchanan, Molly Cahill, John Cunin, Agnes Ng, Merideth Post, Judy Rowcliffe and Dawn Stranne. For bravery in the face of calorific cuisine, my ongoing gratitude and affection to Catherine Robson.

Both authors owe a debt of gratitude to the many readers who wrote in with suggestions and corrections that proved a great help with the updating of the guide. These include: Gwen Brown; Carol Hamilton, Nick Smith and Tina Lefevre; Jonathan Lemon; Michael Lew; Katherine R Loo; Charles Masson; Ms A L Ranasinghe; Alison Rose; Ann Ross; I F Twohig; Richard Ullyett; and Sarah Wilson. Keep those cards and letters coming !

Thanks also to Ellen Sarewitz for proofreading and *Micromap Ltd* for map revisions.

This second edition published 1994 by Rough Guides Ltd, 1 Mercer Street, London WC2H 9QJ.

Distributed by the Penguin Group:

Penguin Books Ltd, 27 Wrights Lane, London W8 5TZ
Penguin Books USA Inc., 375 Hudson Street, New York 10014, USA
Penguin Books Australia Ltd, 487 Maroondah Highway, PO Box 257, Ringwood, Victoria 3134, Australia
Penguin Books Canada Ltd, 10 Alcorn Avenue, Toronto, Ontario, Canada M4V 1E4
Penguin Books (NZ) Ltd, 182–190 Wairau Road, Auckland 10, New Zealand

Originally published in the UK by Harrap Columbus Ltd.
Previous edition published in the United States and Canada as *The Real Guide San Francisco*.

The publishers and authors have done their best to ensure the accuracy and currency of all information in *The Rough Guide to San Francisco*; however, they can accept no responsibility for any loss, injury, or inconvenience sustained by any traveller as a result of information or advice contained in the guide.

Printed in the United Kingdom by Cox & Wyman Ltd (Reading).
Typography and **original design** by Jonathan Dear and The Crowd Roars.
Illustrations throughout by Edward Briant.
Excerpts in *Contexts* by permission.

British Library Cataloguing in Publication Data
A catalogue record for this book is available from the British Library.

ISBN 1-85828-082-6

San Francisco

THE ROUGH GUIDE

Written and researched by
Deborah Bosley and Jamie Jensen

With additional contributions by
Brett M Bennett

THE ROUGH GUIDES

Contents

List of Maps

Maps of Restaurants, Bars and Cafés

Introduction

The Bay Area is so beautiful, I hesitate to preach about
heaven while I'm here

Billy Graham

America's favorite city sits at the edge of the Western World, a location that lends even greater romance to its legend. Arguably the most beautiful, self-proclaimed the most liberal city in the US, **San Francisco** may well have had more platitudes heaped upon it than any other. But despite being the cozy favorite of the Californian tourist industry, with visitors bringing in over a billion dollars every year, it has changed remarkably little over the years, and remains a surprisingly small, almost provincial city, booming throughout the Eighties but still clinging to a few remnants of its radical past.

San Franciscans enjoy a rarefied kind of mutual appreciation, priding themselves on being the cultured counterpart to their philistine cousins in LA, as the last bastion of civilization on the lunatic fringe of America. If truth be told, apart from a progressive caucus in the gay community, it is a rather complacent and self-satisfied place nowadays, dominated by bumper-sticker-style politics that do little to address the city's undeniable – and growing – problems: drug use and violence are here, as elsewhere, on the increase, and the level of homelessness is a disgrace.

The narcissism of San Francisco is rooted in the sheer physical aspect of the place. The city is incredibly beautiful in parts, and with its switchback hills and rows of wooden Victorian houses, quite unique. It is also compact and approachable, one of the few US centers in which you can comfortably survive without a car: the majority of buildings are on a human scale, the neighborhoods inviting and secure, and open green spaces very much in evidence.

Climate and When To Go

The city of San Francisco emphatically does not belong to the California of monotonous blue skies and slothful warmth: flanked on three sides by water, it is regularly invigorated by the fresh winds that sweep across the peninsula. The **climate** is among the most stable in the world, with a daytime temperature that rarely ventures more than 5°F either side of a median 60°F, and can drop much lower. **Summer** does offer some sunny days of course, but it also

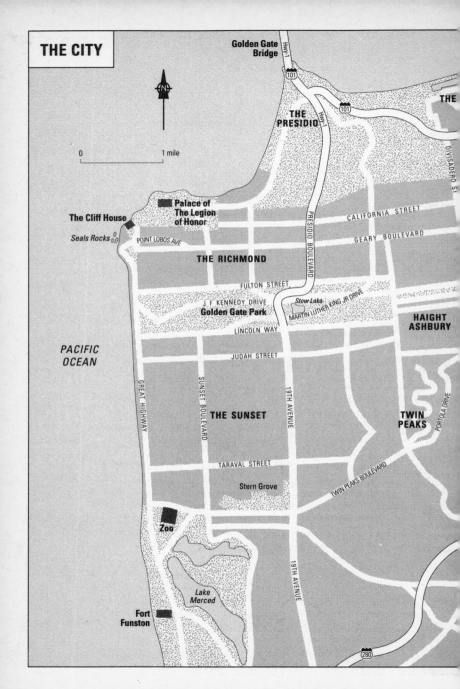

THE CITY

Golden Gate Bridge

Hwy-1

101

THE PRESIDIO

Hwy 101

THE

DIVISADERO ST

0   1 mile

The Cliff House

Palace of The Legion of Honor

Seals Rocks

POINT LOBOS AVE

CALIFORNIA STREET

GEARY BOULEVARD

PRESIDIO BOULEVARD

THE RICHMOND

FULTON STREET

J F KENNEDY DRIVE

Golden Gate Park

Stow Lake

MARTIN LUTHER KING JR DRIVE

HAIGHT ASHBURY

LINCOLN WAY

PACIFIC OCEAN

JUDAH STREET

GREAT HIGHWAY

SUNSET BOULEVARD

THE SUNSET

19TH AVENUE

TWIN PEAKS

PORTOLA DRIVE

TARAVAL STREET

Stern Grove

TWIN PEAKS BOULEVARD

Zoo

19TH AVENUE

Lake Merced

Fort Funston

280

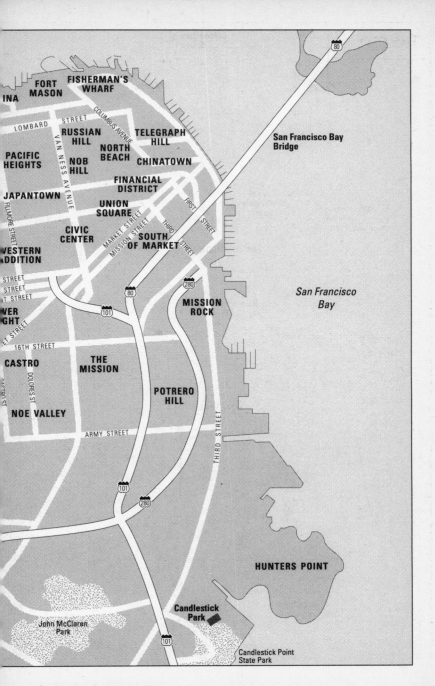

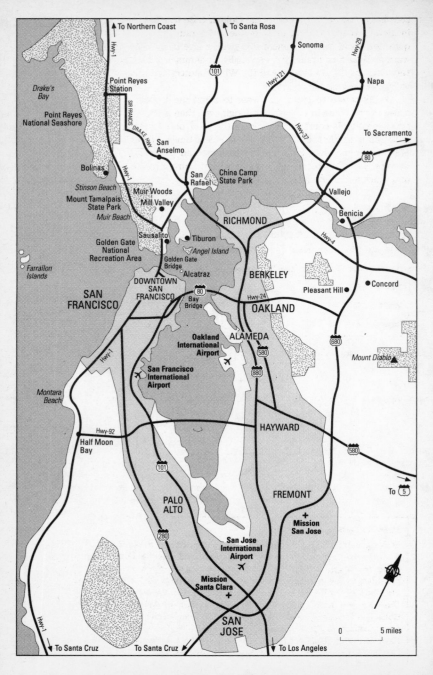

To Northern Coast

To Santa Rosa

Sonoma

Hwy-29

Napa

Hwy-121

Hwy-37

To Sacramento

80

Point Reyes
Station

Hwy-1

SIR FRANCIS DRAKE HWY

Drake's
Bay

Point Reyes
National Seashore

San Anselmo

China Camp
State Park

Vallejo

Benicia

Bolinas

Hwy-1

San
Rafael

Stinson Beach

Muir Woods

Mount Tamalpais
State Park

Mill Valley

RICHMOND

Hwy-4

680

Muir Beach

Sausalito

Tiburon

Golden Gate
National
Recreation Area

Angel Island

BERKELEY

Concord

Farrallon
Islands

Golden Gate
Bridge

Alcatraz

Pleasant Hill

SAN
FRANCISCO

DOWNTOWN
SAN
FRANCISCO

80

Hwy-24

OAKLAND

Bay
Bridge

ALAMEDA

Mount Diablo

Oakland
International
Airport

580

Hwy-1

San Francisco
International
Airport

880

Montara
Beach

HAYWARD

Hwy-92

580

Half Moon
Bay

To 5

101

FREMONT

PALO
ALTO

Mission
San Jose

280

San Jose
International
Airport

Mission
Santa Clara

N

SAN
JOSE

0   5 miles

Hwy-1

To Santa Cruz

To Santa Cruz

To Los Angeles

sees heavy fogs roll in through the Golden Gate to smother the city in gloom. **Winters** bring most of the city's rainfall, sometimes in quite torrential storms. Almost everywhere else in the **Bay Area** is warmer than San Francisco, especially in summer when the **East Bay** cities bask in sunshine, and the **Wine Country** and other inland valleys are baking hot and dry.

As for **when to go**, if you want to avoid the crowds it makes sense not to come in summer, although even then most of the tourist congestion is confined to a few of the most popular parts of the city, and is rarely too off-putting. The nicest times to visit are late May and June, when the hills are greenest and covered with wild flowers, or in October, when you can be fairly sure of good weather, and space in the hotels and restaurants.

Average Temperature (°F) and Rainfall (inches)

	Jan	Feb	Mar	April	May	June	July	Aug	Sept	Oct	Nov	Dec
Max °F	55	59	61	62	63	66	65	65	69	68	63	57
Min °F	45	47	48	49	51	52	53	53	55	54	51	47
Rainfall	4.7	3.8	3.1	1.5	0.7	0.1	0	0	0.3	1.0	2.5	4.4

Part 1

The Basics

Getting There from Britain and Europe

Though flying to San Francisco from Europe is pretty straightforward, choosing the best route can be more complicated than you might think, with prices fluctuating wildly according to how and when you go. Very few airlines have non-stop services from Britain – only *BA, Virgin* and *United* in fact – and the majority of options are so-called "direct" flights, which can land several times, waiting an hour or so at each stop; a flight is called direct as long as it keeps the same *flight number* throughout its journey. The first place the plane lands is your point of entry into the US, which means you'll have to collect your bags and go through customs and immigration formalities there, even if you're continuing on to San Francisco on the same plane. This can be a real pain after a ten-hour journey, so it's worth finding out before you book a ticket.

All international flights use the main **San Francisco International Airport** (SFO); for transportation details from there into the city, as well as from the two other Bay Area airports, see p.27.

Fares, Routes and Agents

The only scheduled airlines currently flying non-stop to San Francisco from London are *British Airways, Virgin* and *United*. Most of the direct flights offered by other carriers are via Los Angeles, though many fly via other US cities such as Minneapolis, Denver or Houston. The **non-stop flight time** is around eleven hours from London to San Francisco; add an hour at least for each stop in between on direct flights, twice that if you have to change planes. Following winds ensure that return flights are always an hour or two shorter than outward journeys. Because of the time difference between Britain and the West Coast (eight hours almost all year), flights usually leave Britain in mid-morning, while flights back from the US tend to arrive in Britain early in the morning.

The most expensive time to travel is **high season**, roughly between June and August and a week or so either side of Christmas. May and September are slightly less pricey, and any other time of year is considered **low season** and is consequently cheaper still. Weekend flights are almost always more expensive than those during the week. As for ticket types, **standby** deals (open-dated tickets which you pay for and then decide later when you want to fly – if there's room on the plane) are rare and usually offer little or no savings over the much more common **APEX** fares. APEX tickets must be purchased at least 21 days before your departure date, you have to stay for at least seven nights, and are liable to pay a hefty fee if you want to change your plans once the ticket has been issued. **Costs** for a return ticket range from around £300 in low season to over £600 for a weekend flight during the summer. Standard economy fares, if you haven't been able to book this far in advance, start at around £700 return.

Always shop around for the best price, either by scanning the travel ads in the Sunday papers, in London's *Time Out* or *Evening Standard,* or by contacting a travel agent or airline directly – we list phone numbers on p.4. As well as calling the

Flights to San Francisco

The following carriers operate **non-stop** or **one-stop flights** between London and San Francisco (all from Heathrow unless stated otherwise):

American Airlines daily via Dallas.

British Airways daily non-stop.

Continental daily from London Gatwick via Denver, Houston or Newark.

Delta daily from Gatwick via Atlanta.

Northwest four a week from Gatwick via Minneapolis.

TWA daily via Los Angeles.

United daily non-stop.

Virgin daily non-stop to San Francisco.

Airlines and Agents

Air India	☎ 071/493 4050	**Kuwait Air**	☎ 071/486 6666
Air New Zealand	☎ 071/741 2299	**Northwest**	☎ 0293/561000
American Airlines	☎ 081/572 5555	**TWA**	☎ 071/439 0707
British Airways	☎ 081/897 4000	**United**	☎ 081/990 9900
Continental	☎ 0800/776464		
Delta	☎ 0800/414767	**USAir**	☎ 0800/777333
Icelandair	☎ 071/388 5599	**Virgin Atlantic**	☎ 0293/747747

Toll-free phone numbers for airlines in the United States are listed on p.8.

Low Cost Flight Agents

Campus Travel
52 Grosvenor Gdns,
London SW1   ☎ 071/730 2101
Also many other branches around the country.

Council Travel
28A Poland St, London W1   ☎ 071/437 7767

STA Travel
86 Old Brompton Rd,
London SW7   ☎ 071/937 9971
Offices nationwide.

Travel Cuts
295 Regent St, London W1   ☎ 071/637 3161

Specialist Flight Operators

Falcon	☎ 071/221 6298	**Travel Express**	☎ 0273/835095
Globespan	☎ 0737/773171	**Unijet**	☎ 0444/458181
Jetsave	☎ 0342/322771		

Major Courier Firms

CTS Ltd	☎ 071/351 0300	**Polo Express**	☎ 081/759 5383
DHL	☎ 081/890 9393		

airlines to check on special deals you see advertised, ask about late availability; especially in February – certain dates get discounted at short notice, and considerable savings can be made. The details we've given are the latest available, but by the time you read them they're likely to have undergone at least subtle changes.

Travel agents will know all about the latest offers and, more importantly, will be aware of the many **restrictions** the airlines place on the fares;

contact a student/youth specialist such as *STA, Campus* or *Council* for the best deals for young people. **Specialist US flight agents** (listed above) offer discounted flights and also sometimes have cut-price seats on **charter flights** – excellent value, especially if travelling from **elsewhere in Britain**, although they tend to be hard to find in summer. *American Airplan*, for example, operates weekly flights from Stansted or Manchester to San Francisco for around £400 return.

If you're on a really tight budget you may be able to travel as a **courier**, carrying packages for one of the major firms. Normally you'll have to sacrifice your luggage allowances except for one carry-on bag, you may have to be ready to fly at a moment's notice, and your ticket may be restricted to a fortnight or so's validity, but going this way can bring the cost down to under £200. Again, we've listed some of the most likely courier companies opposite, though you'll need to call ahead to check on the latest arrangements.

Finally, if you've got a bit more time, or want to see a bit more of the USA, it's often possible to stop over in **another city** – New York especially – and fly on from there for little more than the cost of a direct London–San Francisco flight. Again, agents are the best source of cheap deals, especially to **New York**, on which carriers like *Air India* or *Kuwait Airlines* regularly have tickets for under £300 return, especially if you're a student or under 26. Also, with increased competition on the London–**Los Angeles** route, thanks to *Virgin Atlantic* among others, and price wars between US carriers, the cost of a connecting flight from LA to San Francisco has been brought down as low as £40. Many airlines also offer **air passes**, which allow you to fly between a given number of US cities for one discounted price. Package holidays and fly-drive deals are other options.

One word of **warning**: it's not a good idea to buy a **one-way** ticket to the States. Not only are they rarely good value compared to a round-trip ticket, but US immigration officials usually take them as a sign that you aren't planning to go home, and may refuse you entry.

Inclusive Holidays

Package holidays – fly-drive, flight plus accommodation, guided coach tours, or a combination of all three – can be a good way of ensuring a hassle-free trip, and are much cheaper than trying to sort things out on your own. The obvious drawbacks are the loss of flexibility and the fact that most schemes use hotels in the mid-range bracket, but there is a wide variety of options available. Any high-street travel agent should have stacks of brochures.

Fly-Drive

Fly-drive deals, which give cut-rate (and sometimes free) car rental when buying a transatlantic ticket, always work out cheaper than renting on the spot and give especially great value if you

intend to do a lot of driving. However, if you're planning to stay pretty much within San Francisco itself, having a car is a bonus but not strictly necessary. Though you can rarely get a deal if you're flying on a cheap ticket, competition between carriers and tour operators makes it worthwhile to phone them before approaching any car rental firm directly. Fly-drive deals can bring the cost of a week's car rental down to around £50 or less, usually including unlimited mileage – at a saving of perhaps 40 percent off standard rates. See "Getting Around" on p.29 for more about driving.

Flight and Accommodation Deals

There's really no end of combined **flight and accommodation deals** to San Francisco, and although you can often do things cheaper independently, you won't be able to do the *same* things cheaper; in fact, the equivalent room booked separately will normally be a lot more expensive. A handful of tour operators (see below) offer quite deluxe packages – seven nights in a fairly plush double room for two will set you back about £700 apiece, including the flights. *Trailfinders* can set up more basic packages for just over £500 each.

Touring and Adventure Packages

If you want to combine your stay in San Francisco with trips out into the rest of California, particularly the state's extensive wilderness areas, there are a number of tour operators you might want to contact. *Trek America*, *Contiki Travel* and *Top Deck* all offer trips, as does the more unconventional San Francisco-based *Green Tortoise* (see p.11). If you're interested in **backcountry hiking** to balance out a week in the city, the San Francisco-based *Sierra Club* offers a range of tours that take you into parts of the state that most people never see. Again, see the list below for addresses.

From Ireland

To get to San Francisco **direct from Ireland**, you're limited to flying *Delta*, which goes from Dublin six times a week via Atlanta. If you're under 26 or a student, *USIT* (Aston Quay, O'Connell Bridge, Dublin 2; ☎01/778117) has tickets for around IR£450; otherwise reckon on spending IR£600 on an ordinary APEX ticket. *Aer Lingus* (41 Upper O'Connell St, Dublin 1; ☎01/377 777 or 01/370191) has occasional special offers from Dublin and Shannon to gateway cities.

Specialist Tour Operators

AmeriCan Adventures
45 High St, Tunbridge Wells
Kent TN1 1XL ☎0892/511894

American Express
Phone Enquiries only ☎071/828-7411

Bon Voyage
18 Bellevue Rd, Southampton
Hants SO1 2AY ☎0703/330332

British Airways Holidays
Atlantic House, Hazelwick Ave
Three Bridges, Crawley
West Sussex RH10 1NP ☎0293/572704

Contiki Travel
Wells House, 15 Elmfield Rd
Bromley, Kent BR1 1LS ☎081/290 6422

Greyhound/Sun Trek
Sussex House, London Rd
East Grinstead
West Sussex RH19 1LD ☎0342/317317

Premier
Westbrook, Milton Rd
Cambridge CB4 1YQ ☎0223/355977

Thomson
Greater London House
Hampstead Rd
London NW1 7SD ☎071/387 6534

Top Deck
131 Earls Court Rd
London SW5 ☎071/244 8641

TransAmerica
3A Gatwick Metro Centre
Balcombe Rd
Horley, Surrey RH6 9GA ☎0293/774441

Trek America
Trek House, The Bullring
Deddington, Oxford OX15 0TT ☎0869/38777

Virgin Holidays
The Galleria, Station Rd
Crawley
West Sussex RH10 1WW ☎0293/617181

From Europe

Although the national airlines of all **European countries** have regular flights to the West Coast with connections to San Francisco, their prices are far in excess of anything you'll find in the UK, and you'll nearly always save money by booking a flight from London. The exceptions are the cut-price charter flights periodically offered in the major European cities; ask at a travel agent for details. In West Germany, look for deals which *United* may be offering from Frankfurt, their continental hub since taking over *Pan Am's* routes. For the best deals to New York from Brussels and Paris, contact **Nouvelles Frontières**, 66 boulevard St-Michel, Paris (☎46.34.55.30), and 21 rue de La Violette (Grand Place), Brussels (☎02/511 8013). Their London branch is at 1–2 Hanover St, W1 (☎071/629 7772).

Getting There from Australasia

Other than charter deals, seasonal bargains and all-in packages which may be on offer from high street travel agents, the cheapest way to fly to San Francisco from Australia and New Zealand is to use an APEX fare.

Round-trip tickets from Sydney to San Francisco cost around Aus$1320; *Continental* is often the best deal. From Auckland the return fare is around NZ$1599, though *Continental* sometimes has deals for slightly less. Fares to Los Angeles are usually slightly lower. If you do fly from down under, consider breaking your journey in Honolulu, Hawaii, where flights often stop anyway; you can usually stay over for as long as you like at no extra charge. Other airlines that serve the West Coast from Australia and New Zealand are *Air New Zealand, Qantas, Air France, United Airlines and Northwest.*

Australasian Agents and Airlines

Air New Zealand
Air New Zealand House
Queen St, Auckland — ☎ 09/357-3000

Anywhere Travel
345 Anzac Parade, Kingsford
Sydney — ☎ 02/663-0411

Brisbane Discount Travel
360 Queen St, Brisbane — ☎ 07/229-9211

British Airways
64 Castlereagh St
Sydney, NSW — ☎ 02/258-3300
Dilworth Building
Queen St/Customs St
Auckland — ☎ 09/367-7500

Budget Travel
PO Box 505, Auckland — ☎ 09/309-4313

Flight Centres
Circular Quay, Sydney — ☎ 02/241-2422
Bourke St, Melbourne — ☎ 03/650-2899
205–225 Queen St, Auckland — ☎ 09/309-6171
152 Hereford St, Christchurch — ☎ 03/379-7145
50–52 Willis St, Wellington — ☎ 04/472-8101

Northwest
309 Kent St, Level 13
Sydney NSW — ☎ 02/290-4455

Passport Travel
320b Glenferrie Rd, Malvern
Melbourne — ☎ 03/824-7183

Qantas
Qantas International Centre
International Square
Sydney, NSW — ☎ 02/236-3636

STA Travel
209 King St, New Town
Sydney, NSW 2000 — ☎ 02/519-9866
256 Flinders St, Melbourne — ☎ 03/347-4711
10 High St, Auckland — ☎ 09/309-9723
233 Cuba St, Wellington — ☎ 04/385-0561

Thai International Airways
Kensington Swan Building
22 Fanshawe St, Auckland — ☎ 09/377-0268

Topdeck Travel
45 Grenfell St, Adelaide — ☎ 08/410-1110

Tymtro Travel
Wallaceway Shopping Centre
Chatswood, Sydney — ☎ 02/411-1222

United
5th Floor, 10 Barrack St
Sydney NSW — ☎ 02/237-8888
7 City Rd, Auckland — ☎ 09/379-3800

Getting There from North America

Getting to San Francisco from anywhere else in North America is never a problem; the Bay Area is well serviced by air, rail and road networks. All the main airlines operate daily scheduled flights into San Francisco from across the country, and there are daily flights from Toronto and Vancouver as well.

Flying remains the best but most expensive way to travel; taking a train comes a slow second. Travelling by bus is the least expensive method, but again is slow, and is much less comfortable than either train or plane.

By Air

Beside the main **San Francisco International Airport** (known as SFO), two other airports, both in the Bay Area, may be useful – particularly **Oakland International** (OAK), across the bay but easily accessible. The third Bay Area airport, **San Jose Municipal** (SJO), forty miles south, is a bit out of the way but has good connections with the western US, LA especially. Both airports are well served by domestic carriers like *United, Continental, US Air* and *America West*. Transportation details for the various airports are given under "Points of Arrival" p.27.

As airlines tend to match each other's prices, there's generally little difference in the quoted fares. Barring another fare-war, round-trip prices start at around $350 from New York, slightly less from Midwest cities, slightly more from Toronto and Montréal.

What makes more difference than your choice of carrier are the conditions governing the ticket – whether it is fully refundable or not, the time and day and most importantly the **time of year** you travel. Least expensive of all is a non-summer-season midweek flight, booked and paid for at least three weeks in advance. While it's good to call the airlines directly to get a

---

Major Airline Numbers in the US

Air Canada	☎ 1-800/776-3000	KLM	☎ 1-800/374-7747
Aer Lingus	☎ 1-800/223-6537	Lufthansa	☎ 1-800/645-3880
Air France	☎ 1-800/237-2747	Mesa	☎ 1-800/933-6372
American Airlines	☎ 1-800/433-7300	Northwest	☎ 1-800/225-2525
America West	☎ 1-800/247-5692	SAS	☎ 1-800/221-2350
British Airways	☎ 1-800/247-9297	Southwest	☎ 1-800/435-9792
Canadian	☎ 1-800/426-7000	Tower Air	☎ 1-800/221-2500
Continental	☎ 1-800/231-0856	Trans World Airlines	☎ 1-800/221-2000
Delta	☎ 1-800/221-1212	United Airlines	☎ 1-800/241-6522
Iberia	☎ 1-800/772-4642	US Air	☎ 1-800/428-4322
Icelandair	☎ 1-800/223-5500	Virgin Atlantic	☎ 1-800/862-8621

Note that not all the above airlines fly domestic routes within the US.

Discount Agents in the USA and Canada
For travel agents in San Francisco, see p.43.

Council Travel Offices in the USA

Head office:

205 E 42nd St
New York, NY 10017 ☎212/661-1450

Other main offices at:

3300 M St NW, 2nd Floor
Washington, DC 20007 ☎202/337-6464

1153 N Dearborn St
Chicago, IL 60610 ☎312/951-0585

729 Boylston St, Suite 201z
Boston, MA 02116 ☎617/266-1926

2000 Guadalupe St, Suite 6
Austin, TX 78705 ☎512/472-4931

1314 Northeast 43rd St
Suite 210, Seattle, WA 98105 ☎206/632-2448

STA Travel Offices in the USA
nationwide information ☎1-800/777-0112

Main offices at:

48 E 11th St
New York, NY 10003 ☎212/477-7166

7202 Melrose Ave
Los Angeles, CA 90046 ☎213/934-8722

273 Newbury St
Boston, MA 02116 ☎617/266-6014

3730 Walnut St
Philadelphia, PA 19104 ☎215/382-2928

Travel Cuts Offices in Canada

Head Office:

187 College St
Toronto, ON M5T 1P7 ☎416/979-2406

Other main offices at:

MacEwan Hall Student Centre
Univ of Calgary
Calgary, AB T2N 1N4 ☎403/282-7687

12304 Jasper Ave
Edmonton, AB T5N 3K5 ☎403/488-8487

1613 rue St Denis
Montréal, PQ H2X 3K3 ☎514/843-8511

1 Stewart St
Ottawa, ON K1N 6H7 ☎613/238-8222

2383 Ch Ste Foy, Suite 103
Ste Foy, Quebec, PQ G1V 1T1 ☎418/654-0224

Place Riel Campus Centre
Univ of Saskatchewan
Saskatoon, SA S7N 0W0 ☎306/975-3722

501–602 W Hastings
Vancouver, BC V6B 1P2 ☎604/681-9136

University Centre
Univ of Manitoba
Winnipeg, MA R3T 2N2 ☎204/269-9530

---

sense of their official fares, it also worth checking with a reputable **travel agent** (such as the ones listed above) to find out about any **special deals** or student/youth fares that may be available.

In addition to the big-name scheduled airlines, a few lesser known carriers run no-frills flights, which can prove to be very good value, especially if you're only planning to buy a **one-way** ticket to the Bay Area. *Tower Air*, the New York-based charter operator, has a daily flight from New York to Los Angeles for $149; the onward flight (usually on *Southwest* or *United*) adds another $59 or so. If you're starting off from Denver and Salt Lake City, *Morris Air Service* has twice-daily flights to Oakland for $120 one way,

$204 round trip; they also have similarly low-priced flights from Seattle and Portland.

Travellers intending to fly from **Canada** are likely to find that, with less competition on these routes (*Canadian* flies to SF only from Vancouver; other routes are monopolized by *Air Canada*), fares are somewhat higher than they are for flights wholly within the US. You may well find that it's worth the effort to get to a US city first, and fly on to San Francisco from there.

By Train
If you have a bit more money and hanker after a few more creature comforts (all the trains have private cabins and dining cars) or simply have

Rail Passes for Overseas Travellers

Foreign travellers have a choice of four **rail passes** that include the Bay Area; the **Coastal Pass** permits unlimited train travel on the east and west coasts, but not between the two.

	15-day (June–Aug)	15-day (Sept–May)	30-day (June–Aug)	30-day (Sept–May)
Far West	$178	$158	$229	$209
West	$228	$188	$289	$259
Coastal	–	–	$199	$179
National	$308	$208	$389	$309

On production of a passport issued outside the US or Canada, the passes can be bought at *Amtrak* stations in the US. In the **UK**, buy them from *Destination Marketing*, 2 Cinnamon Row, York Place, London SW11 3TW (☎071/978 5212); in **Ireland**, contact *Eurotrain* (☎01/741 777); in **Australia**, *Walshes World* (☎02/232 7499); and in **New Zealand**, *Atlantic & Pacific* (☎071/978 5212).

the time and inclination to take in some of the rest of the US on your way to San Francisco, then an *Amtrak* **train** may be just the ticket for you. There's only one long-distance train per day from the north or east, and only a few from the south, but all three routes are among the most scenic on the entire *Amtrak* system.

The most spectacular train journey to San Francisco, the *California Zephyr*, runs all the way from Chicago but comes into its own during the ride through the Rockies west of Denver. After climbing alongside raging rivers through gorgeous mountain **scenery**, the route drops down the west flank of the Rockies and races across the Utah and Nevada deserts by night, stopping at Salt Lake City and Reno. The next day the train climbs up and over the mighty Sierra Nevada, following the route of the first transcontinental railroad on its way into Oakland, where you change to a bus for the ride into San Francisco.

A shorter but equally memorable route is the *Coast Starlight*, winding along the coast north from Los Angeles. The most incredible section is between Santa Barbara and San Luis Obispo, a 100-mile coastline ride during which it's not unusual to see seals, dolphins or even whales in the waters offshore. (The other LA-to-SF *Amtrak* routes head inland, by bus to Bakersfield then by rail north through the dull San Joaquin Valley. Avoid these if at all possible)

The final route to San Francisco, also called the *Coast Starlight*, is the southbound leg of the above journey. Starting out in Seattle, it runs south along the Puget Sound and across the Columbia

River to Portland, past the mountains and forests of the Pacific Northwest. Unfortunately, it passes through the prettiest stretch, around Mt Shasta, by night, but it's still a lovely ride.

Amtrak **fares** are generally on a par with flying, though off-peak discounts and special deals can make the train an economical as well as an aesthetic choice. One-way cross-country fares are around $250, though if you're travelling round-trip you can take advantage of what they call **"All-Aboard America"** fares, which are zone-based and allow three stopovers in between your origin and eventual return. This enables you to visit one or more additional cities without paying any extra. Travel within the West (from Denver to the Pacific) costs $189; within the West and Midwest (west of Chicago) costs $269; and for the entire USA the cost is $339.

While *Amtrak*'s basic fares are quite good value, if you want to travel in a bit more comfort the cost rises quickly. **Sleeping compartments**, which include small toilets and showers, start at around $100 per night for one or two people, including three meals a day.

For all *Amtrak* information, call ☎1-800/USA-RAIL.

By Bus

Bus travel is the most tedious and time-consuming way to get to San Francisco, and, for all the discomfort, won't really save you much, if any, money. *Greyhound* is the sole long-distance operator (toll-free information on ☎1-800/231-2222); their fares average around 10¢ a mile – which adds up to around $300 coast-to-coast. A one-way APEX ticket from New York to San Francisco, bought 14 days in advance, costs $79.50; purchased on the day of travel it's $125.

Note that *Amtrak* trains arrive in Richmond and Oakland across the Bay; they do not enter San Francisco itself. See pp. 27, 135 and 153.

The only reason to go *Greyhound* is if you're planning to visit a number of other places en route; *Greyhound's* **Ameripass** is good for unlimited travel within a certain time, and costs $250 for 7 days, $350 for 15 days and $450 for 30 days. **Foreign visitors** can buy Ameripasses before leaving home: in the UK, they cost £50 (4-day), £85 (7-day), £125 (15-day) or £170 (30-day). *Greyhound's* office is at Sussex House, London Road, East Grinstead, West Sussex RH19 1LD (☎0342/317317). Extensions can be bought in the US for the dollar equivalent of £12 a day.

By Car

Driving your own car gives the greatest freedom and flexibility, but if you don't have one (or don't trust the one you do have), one option worth considering is **driving for an automobile transporting company**. These companies operate in most major cities, and are paid to find drivers to take a customer's cars from one place to another. The company will normally pay for your insurance and your first tank of gas; after that, you'll be expected to drive along the most direct route and to average 400 miles a day. Companies are keen to use foreign travellers (German tourists are ideal, it seems) but if you can convince them you are a safe bet, they'll take something like a $200 deposit, which you get back after delivering the car in good condition. Availability varies greatly, and with the current economic slump, more cars have been leaving San Francisco than arriving. *Auto Driveaway*, 330 Townsend (☎415/777-3740), is

the main San Francisco company using drivers; look under "Automobile Transporters and Driveaways" in the Yellow Pages for your local branch office.

Though it's not really necessary if you're planning to stay in San Francisco itself, **renting a car** is the usual story of phoning your local branch of one of the majors (*Avis, Hertz, Budget, Thrifty*, etc – listed on p.29), of which *Thrifty* tends to be the cheapest. Most companies have offices at destination airports, and addresses and phone numbers are comprehensively documented in the Yellow Pages.

Also worth considering are **fly-drive deals**, which give cut-rate (and sometimes free) car rental when buying an air ticket. They usually work out cheaper than renting on the spot and are especially good value if you intend to do a lot of driving.

Package Tours

Many operators run all-inclusive **packages** which combine plane tickets and hotel accommodation with (for example) sightseeing, wining and dining, or excursions to tourist sites. Even if the "package" aspect doesn't thrill you to pieces, these deals can still be more convenient and sometimes even work out to be more economical than arranging the same thing yourself, providing you don't mind losing a little flexibility. With such a vast range of packages available, it's impossible to give an overview – major travel agents will have brochures detailing what's on offer.

Green Tortoise

One alternative to Long-Distance Bus Hell is the slightly counter-cultural *Green Tortoise*, whose buses, furnished with foam cushions, bunks, fridges and rock music, ply the major cities of the West Coast, running between Los Angeles, San Francisco and Seattle. In summer, they also cross the country to New York and Boston, transcontinental trips which amount to mini-tours of the nation, taking around a dozen days (at a current cost of around $279, not including contributions to the food fund), and allowing plenty of stops for hiking, river-rafting and hot springs. Other *Green Tortoise* trips include excursions to the major national parks (in 17 days for $399), and north to Alaska.

Main Office:		New York	☎212/431-3348
PO Box 24459,		Portland	☎503/225-0310
San Francisco,	☎415/821-0803	San Francisco	☎415/821-0803
CA 94124;	or 1-800/227-4766	Santa Barbara	☎805/569-1884
Seat Reservation Numbers		Santa Cruz	☎408/462-6437
Boston	☎617/265-8533	Seattle	☎206/324-7433
Eugene	☎503/937-3603	Vancouver	☎604/732-5153
Los Angeles	☎310/392-1990		

Disabled Travellers

Travellers with mobility problems or other physical disabilities are likely to find San Francisco – as with the US in general – to be much more in tune with their needs than any other country in the world. Steep hills aside, the Bay Area is generally considered to be one of the most barrier-free cities around, catering well to physically challenged travellers. All public buildings must be wheelchair accessible and have suitable toilets, most city street corners have dropped kerbs, and most city buses are able to kneel to make access easier and are built with space and handgrips for wheelchair users. Most hotels and restaurants (certainly any built in the last five years or so) have excellent wheelchair access.

Getting To and Around San Francisco

Most **airlines**, transatlantic and within the US, do whatever they can to ease your journey, and will usually let attendants of more seriously disabled people accompany them at no extra charge. The Americans with Disabilities Act 1990 obliged all air carriers to make the majority of their services accessible to travellers with disabilities within five to nine years.

Almost every **Amtrak train** includes one or more coaches with accommodation for disabled passengers. Guide dogs travel free and may accompany blind, deaf or disabled passengers in the carriage. Be sure to give 24 hours' notice. Hearing-impaired passengers can get information on ☎ 1-800/523-6590. On the ground, the major **car rental** firms can, given sufficient notice, provide vehicles with hand controls (though these are usually only available on the more expensive vehicles). **Amtrak** will provide wheelchair assistance at its train stations, adapted seating on board and a 15 per cent discount on

the regular fare, all provided 72 hours notice is given. **Greyhound**, however, is not to be recommended. Buses are not equipped with lifts for wheelchairs, though staff will assist with boarding (intercity carriers are required by law to do this), and the "Helping Hand" scheme offers two-for-the-price-of-one tickets to passengers unable to travel alone (carry a doctor's certificate).

The American Automobile Association (see p.18) produces the Handicapped Driver's Mobility Guide for **disabled drivers** (available from Quantum-Precision Inc, 225 Broadway, Suite 3404, New York, NY 10007). The larger car rental companies provide cars with hand-controls at no extra charge, though only on their full-size (ie most expensive) models; reserve well in advance.

Organizations

National organizations facilitating travel for the disabled include **SATH**, the **Society for the Advancement of Travel for the Handicapped** (345 Fifth Ave, #610, New York, NY 10016; ☎ 212/447-7284), a non-profit travel-industry grouping which includes travel agents, tour operators, hotel and airline management and people with disabilities. They will pass on any enquiry to the appropriate member; allow plenty of time for a response. **Mobility International USA** (PO Box 3551, Eugene, OR 97403; ☎ 503/343-1248) answers transport queries and operates an exchange programme for disabled people.

In San Francisco itself, the Mayor's Council on Disabilities puts out an annual guide for disabled visitors; write to them c/o Box 1595, San Francisco, CA, or call ☎ 554-6141. The Center for Independent Living, 2539 Telegraph Ave in Berkeley (☎ 841-4776), has long been one of the most effective disabled people's organizations in the world; they have a variety of counselling services and are generally a useful resource.

Entry Requirements for Foreign Visitors

Under the Visa Waiver Scheme, designed to speed up lengthy immigration procedures, British citizens visiting the United States for a period of less than ninety days only need a **full UK passport** (not a British Visitor's Passport) and a **visa waiver form**. This will be provided either by your travel agency, or by the airline during check-in, or on the plane, and must be presented to immigration on arrival. The same form can be used by citizens of most European countries, provided their passports are up-to-date, and covers entry across the land borders with Canada and Mexico as well as by air.

Prospective visitors from Ireland, Australia, New Zealand and all other parts of the world require a valid passport and a **non-immigrant visitor's visa**. To obtain a visa, fill in the application form available at most travel agents and send it with a full passport to the nearest US Embassy or Consulate. Visas are not issued to convicted criminals and anybody who owns up to being a communist, fascist or drug dealer.

Immigration Control

The standard immigration regulations apply to all visitors, whether or not they are using the Visa Waiver Scheme.

During the flight, you'll be handed an **immigration form** (and a customs declaration: see below), which must be given up at immigration control once you land. The form requires details of where you are staying on your first night (if you don't know, write "touring") and the date you intend to **leave** the US. You should be able to prove that you have enough money to support yourself while in the US – anyone revealing the slightest intention of working while in the country is likely to be refused admission – and may experience difficulties if you admit to being HIV positive or having AIDS. You stand the best chance of a problem-free entry if you happen to be English-speaking, white, well dressed and polite to the officials.

Part of the immigration form will be attached to your passport, where it must stay until you leave, when an immigration or airline official will detach it.

Customs

Customs officers will relieve you of your customs declaration and check whether you're carrying any fresh foods. You'll also be asked if you've visited a farm in the last month: if you have, you could well lose your shoes. The **duty-free allowance** if you're over 17 is 200 cigarettes and 100 cigars and, if you're over 21, a liter of spirits.

Canadian Visitors

Canadian citizens are in a particularly privileged position when it comes to crossing the border into the US. Though it is possible to enter the States without your passport, you should really have it with you on any trip that brings you as far as San Francisco. Only if you plan to stay for more than ninety days do you need a visa.

Bear in mind that if you cross into the States in your car, trunks and passenger compartments are subject to spot searches by US Customs personnel, though this sort of surveillance is likely to decrease as remaining tariff barriers fall over the next few years. Remember, too, that Canadians are legally barred from seeking gainful employment in the US.

As well as foods and anything agricultural, it's prohibited to carry into the country any articles from Vietnam, North Korea, Kampuchea or Cuba, obscene publications, lottery tickets, chocolate liqueurs or pre-Columbian artefacts. Anyone caught carrying drugs into the country will not only face prosecution but be entered in the records as an undesirable and probably denied entry for all time.

Extensions and Leaving

The date stamped on your passport is the latest you're legally allowed to stay. Leaving a few days later may not matter, especially if you're heading home, but more than a week or so can result in a protracted, rather unpleasant, interrogation from officials which may cause you to miss your flight. Overstaying may also cause you to be turned away next time you try to enter the US.

The only official way to get an **extension** is to go through the **US Immigration and Naturalization Service**, or INS, whose San Francisco office is at Room 200, 630 Sansome St (Mon–Fri 8am–4pm; ☎705-4411). They will automatically assume that you're working illegally and it's up to you to convince them otherwise. You'll also have to explain your change in plans: saying your money lasted longer than expected, or that a close (preferably well-heeled) relative is coming over, are both well-worked explanations.

Staying On

While San Francisco may be a great place to live, it's becoming increasingly difficult for foreigners to find **work** in the Bay Area.

Anyone planning an extended legal stay should apply for a **special working visa** at any US embassy at least six months *before* setting off for the States. There are a whole range of visas, depending on your skills and length of stay, but unless you've got relatives (parents or children over 21), or a prospective employer to sponsor you, your chances at best are slim. For details on finding long-term **accommodation**, see p.42.

US Embassy and Consulates in Canada

Embassy:	Complex Desjardins
100 Wellington St,	South Tower
Ottawa ON K1P 5T1 ☎613/238-5335	**Montréal, PQ** ☎514/281-1468
Consulates:	2 Place Terrace Dufferin
Suite 1050	**Québec City, PQ** ☎418/692-2095
615 Macleod Trail	
Calgary, AB ☎403/266-8962	360 University Ave
	Toronto, ON ☎416/595-1700
Suite 910, Cogswell Tower	
Scotia Square	1095 West Pender St
Halifax, NS ☎902/429-2480	**Vancouver, BC** ☎604/685-4311

US Embassies and Consulates elsewhere

UK	**Ireland**
	42 Elgin Rd, Ballsbridge
5 Upper Grosvenor St	Dublin ☎01/687122
London W1 ☎071/499 9000	
	Netherlands
3 Regent Terrace	Museumplein 19
Edinburgh EH7 5BW ☎031/556 8315	Amsterdam ☎020/310 9209
Queens House, 14 Queen St	**New Zealand**
Belfast BT1 6EQ ☎0232/328239	29 Fitzherbert Terrace, Thorndon
	Wellington ☎4/722 068
Australia	
Moonhah Place	**Norway**
Canberra ☎62/270 5000	Drammensveien 18
	Oslo ☎22 44 85 50
Denmark	
Dag Hammerskjöld Allé 24	**Sweden**
2100 Copenhagen ☎31/ 42 31 44	Strandvägan 101
	Stockholm ☎08/783 5300

Foreign Embassies and Consulates in the US

Great Britain

Embassy:
3100 Massachusetts Ave NW
Washington DC 20008 ☎202/462-1340

San Francisco Consulate:
1 Sansome St, #850
San Francisco, CA 94104 ☎415/981-3030

Australia
1601 Massachusetts Ave NW
Washington DC 20036-2273 ☎202/797-3000

San Francisco Consulate:
360 Post St ☎362-6160

Canada
501 Pennsylvania Ave NW
Washington DC 20001 ☎202/682-1740

Denmark
3200 Whitehaven St NW
Washington DC 20008 ☎202/234-4300

France
4101 Reservoir Rd NW
Washington DC 20007 ☎202/944-6000

Germany
4645 Reservoir Rd NW
Washington DC 20007 ☎202/298-4000

Ireland
2234 Massachusetts Ave NW
Washington DC 20008 ☎202/462-3939

San Francisco Consulate:
655 Montgomery St ☎392-4212

Netherlands
4200 Linnean Ave NW
Washington DC 20008 ☎202/244-5300

San Francisco Consulate:
601 California St ☎981-6454

New Zealand
37 Observatory Circle NW
Washington DC 20008 ☎202/328-4800

San Francisco Consulate:
360 Post St ☎362-6160

Norway
2720 34th St NW
Washington DC 20008 ☎202/333-6000

Sweden
600 New Hampshire Ave NW
#1200
Washington DC 20037 ☎202/944-5600

Work and Study

Illegal work, once quite easy to find, has become much more difficult to obtain in recent years, since the government introduced fines of up to $10,000 for businesses caught employing a foreigner without a **social security number** (which effectively proves you're part of the legal workforce). Understandably, most are now reluctant to employ travellers.

Any work you do find will be of the casual washing up/babysitting and farm-hand variety – traditionally low-paid cash work. Even restaurants can be reluctant to employ foreign waiters because of the visibility of the work. And remember, San Francisco is a small town with an economy to match – this is not the Los Angeles of work for anybody who wants it and success for those who can stick it.

Making up a fictitious social security number, or borrowing one from somebody else, is of course completely illegal, as are **marriages of convenience;** usually inconvenient for all concerned and with a lower succcess rate than is claimed.

Foreign students have a slightly better chance of a prolonged stay in San Francisco, especially if those who can arrange some sort of "year abroad" through their university at home. Otherwise you can apply directly to a Bay Area university: if they'll have you (and you can afford the painfully expensive fees charged to overseas students), it can be a great way to get to know the city, and maybe even learn something useful. The US grants more or less unlimited visas to those enrolled in full-time further education.

Another possibility for students is to get on to an Exchange Visitor Program, for which participants are given a J-1 visa that entitles them to accept paid summer employment and apply for a social security number. However, most of these visas are issued for jobs in American **summer camps**, which aren't everybody's idea of a good time; they fly you over, and after a summer's work you end up with around $500 and a month to blow it in. If you live in Britain and are interested, contact *BUNAC* (16 Bowling Green Lane, London EC1; ☎071/251 3472), or *Camp America* (37 Queens' Gate, London SW7; ☎071/589 3223).

Insurance and Health

Though not compulsory, travel insurance is *essential* for foreign travellers. The US has no national health system and you can lose an arm and a leg (so to speak) having even minor medical treatment.

Insurance policies can be bought through any high street travel agent or insurance broker, though the cheapest are generally *Endsleigh*, which charges around £35 for three weeks to cover life, limb and luggage (with a 25 percent reduction if you choose to forgo luggage insurance). Their forms are available from most youth/student travel offices (though their policies are open to all), or direct from 97–107 Southampton Row, London WC1 (☎071/436 4451). Another good option in Britain is *Touropa*, 52 Grosvenor Gardens, London SW1W 0NP (☎071/730 2101). Elsewhere in the world, get in touch with your nearest *STA* or *Travel Cuts* office (addresses on p.4, p.7 and p.9).

On all policies, read the small print to ensure the cover includes a sensible amount for medical expenses – this should be at least £1,000,000, which will cover the cost of an air ambulance to fly you home in the event of serious injury or hospitalization.

American travellers should find that their **health insurance** should cover any health charges or costs; if you don't have any you can get adequate coverage either from a travel agent's insurance plan or from specialist travel insurance companies such as *The Travelers*. If you are unable to use a phone or if the practitioner requires immediate payment, save all the **forms** to support a claim for subsequent reimbursal. Remember also that time limits may apply when making claims after the fact, so promptness in contacting your insurer is highly advisable.

If you have anything **stolen** (including money), register the loss immediately at the nearest police station (main addresses are given on p.25, or look under "Police" in the Emergency listings at the front of the phone book). They will issue you with a reference number to pass on to your insurance company – an accepted alternative to the full statement insurers usually require. Not surprisingly, however, few if any American health insurance plans cover against **theft** while travelling, though most **renter's or homeowner's insurance** policies will cover you for up to $500 while on the road.

Health Advice for Foreign Travellers

If you have a serious **accident** while in San Francisco, don't worry about being left to die on the sidewalk; emergency medical services will

---

Hospital Emergency Rooms open at all times

San Francisco General Hospital 1001 Potrero Ave near 22nd St in the Mission ☎821-8111	**Mount Zion Hospital** 1600 Divisadero St at Post St, Western Addition ☎885-7520
University of California Medical Center Parnassas Ave at Third Ave in the Sunset District ☎476-1037	**Pacific Medical Center** 2333 Buchanan St at Washington St, near LaFayette Park in Pacific Heights ☎923-3333

get to you quickly and charge you later. For emergencies or ambulances, dial ☎911 (or whatever variant may be on the information plate of the pay phone).

Should you need to see a **doctor**, lists can be found in the Yellow Pages under "Clinics" or "Physicians and Surgeons". A basic consultation fee is $50–75, payable in advance. Medications aren't cheap either – keep all your receipts for later claims on your insurance policy. For **dental care**, contact the *Dental Society Referral Service* (☎421-1435).

Many **minor ailments** can be remedied using the fabulous array of potions and lotions available in **drugstores**. Foreign visitors should bear in mind that many pills available over the counter at home need a prescription in the US – most codeine-based painkillers, for example – and that local brand names can be confusing; ask for advice at the **pharmacy** in any drugstore.

Travellers from Europe do not require **inoculations** to enter the US.

For advice on personal safety, and how to cope with emergency situations – including phone numbers to report lost checks or credit cards – see p.25.

Information and Maps

Information for prospective foreign visitors to the United States is supplied by the USTTA – United States Travel and Tourism Administration – which has offices all over the world, usually in US embassies and consulates. These serve mainly as clearing houses, stocking vast quantities of printed material, but are unable to help with specific queries. In Britain, you can only contact them by telephone, on ☎071/495 4466 (Mon–Fri 10am–4pm).

More advance information can be obtained by post from the **California Office of Tourism**, Suite 103, 1121 L St, Sacramento, CA 95814 (☎916/322-1396), though the best source of specific information on San Francisco is the **San Francisco Convention and Visitors Bureau**, Suite 900, 201 Third St, San Francisco, CA 94103 (☎974-6900), which publishes the handy eighty-page *San Francisco Book* and a very useful map, both of which they'll send to you for free.

Tourist Offices

Once in the Bay Area, there are a number of offices which dispense brochures and information to callers, though these can vary from indispensible to absolutely useless. Among the former is the main **San Francisco Visitor Information Center**, in Hallidie Plaza on the concourse of the Powell Street *BART/Muni* station (Mon–Fri 9am–5.30pm, Sat 9am–3pm, Sun 10am–2pm; ☎974-6900).

They have free maps of the city and the Bay Area, and can help with accommodation and travel information. The center also makes a good bench mark for getting your bearings, as it's centrally located and at the hub of city transit systems.

All the various **Bay Area regions** also have at least one main source of information, usually some kind of visitors' bureau, and almost every town will have at least an office operated by the very business-orientated local **Chamber of Commerce**. Where useful we've listed them under "Information" in appropriate sections of Part Three.

Maps

Most of the tourist offices we've mentioned can supply you with good **maps**, either for free or for a small charge, and, supplemented with our own, these should be enough for general sightseeing and touring. The best of the commercially available alternatives (obtainable in advance from specialist outlets like *Stanfords*, 12–14 Long Acre, London WC2; ☎071/836 1321) are the easy-to-read city plans published by *Rand-McNally* and *Gousha Publications* (£2.50 each), both of which have especially detailed sections on downtown, showing important buildings – very handy for keeping your bearings. They also do maps of Oakland and the East Bay, San Jose and the Peninsula, and Marin County. For the habitually lost, *Flashmaps* (£3.50) do a handbook on the city. The *American Automobile Association (AAA*; toll-free ☎1-800/336-4357), based at 1000 AAA Drive, Heathrow, FL 32746, provides free maps and assistance to its members, and to British members of the *AA* and *RAC*; they also have an office in San Francisco at 150 Van Ness Ave (☎565-2012), near the Civic Center, and at other locations all over the Bay Area.

For something more detailed, say for **hiking** purposes, it's best to wait till you're in San Francisco. Ranger stations in parks and wilderness areas all sell good-quality local hiking maps for $1–2, and camping stores generally have a good selection. Most bookstores will have a range of local trail guides, the best of which we've listed under "Books" in *Contexts*.

Map Outlets in the UK

London

National Map Centre
22–24 Caxton St SW1   ☎071/222 4945

Stanfords
12–14 Long Acre WC2   ☎071/836 1321

The Travellers Bookshop
25 Cecil Court WC2   ☎071/836 9132

Edinburgh

Thomas Nelson and Sons Ltd
51 York Place EH1 3JD   ☎031/557 3011

Glasgow

John Smith and Sons
57–61 St Vincent St ☎041/221 7472

Maps by **mail or phone order** are available from *Stanfords;* ☎071/836 1321

Map Outlets in North America

Chicago

Rand McNally
444 N Michigan Ave, IL 60611   ☎312/321-1751

Montréal

Ulysses Travel Bookshop
4176 St-Denis   ☎514/289-0993

New York

British Travel Bookshop
551 5th Ave   ☎1-800/448-3039
NY 10176   or 212/490-6688

The Complete Traveler Bookstore
199 Madison Ave, NY 10016   ☎212/685-9007

Rand McNally
150 East 52nd St, NY 10022   ☎212/758-7488

Traveler's Bookstore
22 West 52nd St, NY 10019   ☎212/664-0995

San Francisco

The Complete Traveler Bookstore
3207 Filmore St, CA 92123   ☎415/923-1511

Rand McNally
595 Market St , CA 94105   ☎415/777-3131

Seattle

Elliot Bay Book Company
101 South Main St, WA 98104   ☎206/624-6600

Toronto

Open Air Books and Maps
25 Toronto St, M5R 2C1   ☎416/363-0719

Vancouver

World Wide Books and Maps
1247 Granville St   ☎604/687-3320

Washington DC

Rand McNally
1201 Connecticut Ave NW 20036 ☎202/223-6751

Note: *Rand McNally* now has 24 stores across the US; call ☎1-800/333-0136 (ext 2111) for the address
of your nearest store, or for **direct mail** maps.

Map Outlets in Australasia

Adelaide
The Map Shop
16a Peel St, SA 5000   ☎08/231 2033

Brisbane
Hema
239 George St, QLD 4000   ☎07/221 4330

Melbourne
Bowyangs
372 Little Bourke St, VIC 3000   ☎03/670 4383

Sydney
Travel Bookshop
20 Bridge St, NSW 2000   ☎02/241 3554

Perth
Perth Map Centre
891 Hay St, WA 6000   ☎09/322 5733

Telephones and Mail Services

Because of the strong emphasis placed on business efficiency, and the fact that Americans in general demand excellent service, all forms of communication in the US *have* to be good – something that's especially true on the commercially important and comparatively far-flung West Coast.

Telephones

San Francisco **telephones** are run by *Pacific Telephone (Bell System)* – commonly abbreviated to *PacBell* – and linked to the nationwide *AT&T* network. Dial-phones are scarce: the vast majority are the push-button kind, emitting a different audio tone for each button pressed. Some numbers, particularly those of consumer services, employ letters as part of their "number", for example ☎788-BART, for information on the Bay Area Rapid Transit system. The letters are on the buttons. For help, call the **operator** (☎0).

The San Francisco **area code** – a three-figure number which must precede the seven-figure number if you're calling from another region – is ☎415. All San Francisco phone numbers are within this area code and we have in general omitted it from our listings; those numbers that are not – such as in Bay Area regions like the East Bay (☎510), the Wine Country (☎707) and San Jose (☎408) – are given with the relevant code. To phone one area code from another you have to dial a 1 before the code and number –

for example ☎1-707/963-9611 for *Robert Mondavi Winery* in the Napa Valley.

Public telephones invariably work and can be found everywhere – on street corners, in train and bus stations, hotel lobbies, bars, restaurants – and they take 25¢, 10¢ and 5¢ coins. The cost of a **local call** from a public phone (ie within the same area code) varies according to the actual distance being called (some area codes cover vast territories). Minimums are 20¢ for the first few minutes, plus a further amount if you talk for a long time; the operator – or a synthesized voice – will come on the line and ask you for the money.

Non-local calls ("zone calls") are more expensive – ie to numbers within the same area code but sometimes requiring you to dial 1 before the seven-digit number. Pricier still are **long-distance calls** (ie to a different area code), for which you'll need plenty of change – stuff it into the machine when the recorded voice tells you to. If you still owe money at the end of the call, the phone will ring immediately and you'll be asked for the outstanding amount (if you don't cough up, the person you've been calling will get the bill). Non-local calls and long-distance calls are far cheaper if made between 6pm and 8am, and calls from **private phones** are always much cheaper than those from public phones. Detailed rates are listed at the front of the **telephone directory** (the "White Pages", a copious source of information on many matters).

Making a telephone call from a **hotel room** is usually more expensive than from a payphone, though some budget hotels offer free local calls

Useful Numbers	
Emergencies	☎911
Ask to be connected with the appropriate emergency service: fire, police or ambulance.	
Local directory information	☎411
Operator	☎0
Long-distance directory information	☎1-(Area Code)/555-1212
Directory enquiries for toll-free numbers	☎1-800/555-1212

Main SF and Bay Area Post Offices

228 Harrison St CA 94101	☏ 550-6500
Chinatown, 867 Stockton St CA 94108	☏ 956-3566
North Beach, 1640 Stockton St CA 94133	☏ 956-3581
Marina, 3225 Fillmore St CA 94123	☏ 563-4673
Oakland Main, 1675 Seventh St CA 94607	☏ 874-8200
Berkeley Main, 2000 Allston Way CA 94704	☏ 845-1100

from rooms – ask when you check in. An increasing number of phones accept **credit cards**, while anyone who holds a credit card issued by an American bank can obtain an **AT&T charge card** (information on ☏ 1-800/874-4000 ext 359).

Many government agencies, car rental firms, hotels and so on have **toll-free numbers**, which always have the prefix ☏ 1-800. From within the US, you can dial any number which starts with those digits free of charge. Phone numbers with the prefix ☏ 1-900 are pay-per-call lines, generally quite expensive and almost always involving either sports or phone sex.

Mail Services

Post offices are usually open Monday to Friday from 9am until 5pm, and Saturday from 9am to 1pm, and there are blue **mail boxes** on many street corners. Ordinary **mail within the US** costs 29¢ for a letter weighing up to an ounce; the sender's address should be written on the envelope. The last line of the address is made up of an abbreviation denoting the state (California is "CA") and a five-figure number – the **zip code** – denoting the local post office. Letters which don't carry the zip code are liable to get lost or at least delayed. **Air mail** between the West Coast and Europe generally takes about a week. Postcards cost 40¢, aerograms are 45¢, while letters weighing up to half an ounce (a single thin sheet) are 50¢.

Letters can be sent c/o **General Delivery** (what's known elsewhere as **poste restante**) to:

Your Name
General Delivery
San Francisco, CA 94142
USA

Letters so addressed can be picked up at the post office at 101 Hyde St, in the Civic Center (Mon–Fri 9am–5.30pm, Sat 9am–3pm; ☏ 441-8329), but will only be held for thirty days before being returned to sender, so make sure there's a return address on the envelope. If you're receiving mail at someone else's address, it should include "c/o" and the regular occupant's name; otherwise it too is likely to be returned.

Rules on sending **parcels** are very rigid: packages must be sealed according to the instructions given at the start of the Yellow Pages. To send anything out of the country, you'll need a green **customs declaration form**, available from a post office.

International Telephone Calls

International calls can be dialled direct from private or public phones. You can get assistance from the **international operator** (☏ 1-800/874-4000), who may also interrupt every three minutes asking for more money, and again call you back for any money still owed immediately after you hang up. The **lowest rates** for international calls to Europe are between 11pm and 7am, when a direct-dialled three-minute call will cost roughly $6. In **Britain**, it's possible to obtain a free **BT Chargecard** (☏ 0800/800 838), using which all calls from overseas can be charged to your quarterly domestic account. To use these cards in the US, or to make a **collect call** (to "reverse the charges"), contact the local operator: *AT&T* ☏ 1-800/445-5667. To **phone anywhere outside North America** from San Francisco, dial ☏ 011 to get an international line, then the relevant international access code:

Australia	☏ 61	**Netherlands**	☏ 31
Denmark	☏ 45	**New Zealand**	☏ 64
Germany	☏ 49	**Sweden**	☏ 46
Ireland	☏ 353	**United Kingdom**	☏ 44

To call **TO San Francisco** from the rest of the world (excluding Canada), the US country code is always ☏ 1. Thus from the UK you dial ☏ 0101-415, followed by the seven-digit number.

Telegrams and Faxes

To send a **telegram** (sometimes called a *wire*), don't go to a post office but to a *Western Union* office (listed in the Yellow Pages). Credit card holders can dictate messages over the phone. **International telegrams** cost slightly less than the cheapest international phone call: one sent in the morning from the US should arrive at its overseas destination the following day. For domestic telegrams ask for a **mailgram**, which will be delivered to any address in the country the next morning.

Public **fax** machines, which may require your credit card to be "swiped" through an attached device, are found at photocopy centers and, occasionally, bookstores.

Costs, Money and Banks

To help with planning your San Francisco vacation, this book contains detailed price information for lodging (in Chapter 12) and eating (in Chapter 13). Naturally, as time passes, you should make allowances for inflation.

Your biggest single expense is likely to be **accommodation**. Few hotel or motel rooms cost under $30 – it's more usual to pay between $40 and $80 for anything halfway decent. Although dorm beds in hostels costing around $12–15 do exist, they are a bit thin on the ground, besides which San Francisco is not a city you want to do on the cheap.

As for **food**, fifteen dollars a day is enough to get you an adequate life-support diet, but, again,

the city is filled with wonderful restaurants and if you can manage $25 per day and upwards you should spend it and get the most out of this most cuisine-conscious of cities. Beyond this, everything hinges on how much sightseeing, taxi-taking, drinking and socializing you do – in San Francisco it's easy to get through a bank roll in a couple of days. The city seems to invite spending and having fun; above all, this is the place to come and **buy**.

Rates for travelling around using the MUNI system are very reasonable, but to make the most of the city, especially if there are two or more of you, renting a **car** can be a very good investment.

Sales Tax of 8.5 per cent is added to virtually everything you buy in stores, but it isn't part of the marked price.

Travellers' Checks

US dollar travellers' checks are the best way to carry money, for both American and foreign visitors; they offer the great security of knowing that lost or stolen checks will be replaced. You should have no problem using the better-known checks, such as *American Express* and *Visa*, in shops, restaurants and gas stations (don't be put off by "no checks" signs, which only refer to personal checks). Be sure to have plenty of the $10 and $20 denominations for everyday transactions.

Money: a note for Foreign Travellers

Even when the exchange rate is at its least advantageous, most foreign visitors find virtually everything – accomodation, food, gas, clothes and more – to be better value in the US than it is at home. However, if you're used to travelling in the less expensive countries of Europe, let alone in the rest of the world, you shouldn't expect to scrape by on the same miniscule budget once you're in the US.

Regular upheaval in the money markets causes the relative value of the US dollar against the currencies of the rest of the world to vary considerably. Generally speaking, one **pound sterling** will buy $1.40–1.80; one **Canadian dollar** is worth between 76¢ and $1;

one **Australian dollar** is between 67¢ and 88¢; and one **New Zealand dollar** is worth 55–72¢.

Bills and Coins

US currency comes in **bills** worth $1, $5, $10, $20, $50 and $100, plus various larger (and rarer) denominations. Confusingly, all are the same size and same green color, making it necessary to check each bill carefully. The dollar is made up of 100 cents in **coins** of 1 cent (known as a **penny**), 5 cents (a **nickel**), 10 cents (a **dime**) and 25 cents (a **quarter**). Very occasionally you might come across **JFK half-dollars** (50¢), **Susan B Anthony dollar coins**, or a **two-dollar bill**. Change (quarters are the most useful) is needed for buses, vending machines and telephones, so always carry plenty.

Each of the two main ATM networks operates a **toll-free** line to let customers know the location of their nearest machine;
Plus System is ☎1-800/THE-PLUS
Cirrus is ☎1-800/4CI-RRUS

Banks in San Francisco are generally open from 10am until 3.30pm or 4pm Monday to Thursday, and 10am to 6pm on Friday. Most major banks change dollar travellers' checks for their face value (not that there's much point doing this – and some charge for the privilege, so ask before you do), and **change foreign travellers' checks and currency**. Exchange bureaux, always found at airports, tend to charge less commission: Thomas Cook or American Express are the biggest names. Rarely, if ever, do hotels change foreign currency. **Emergency phone numbers** to call if your checks and/or credit cards are stolen are on p.26.

Plastic Money and Cash Machines

If you don't already have a **credit card**, you should think seriously about getting one before you set off. For many services, it's simply taken for granted that you'll be paying with plastic. When renting a car (or even a bike) or checking into a hotel you may well be asked to show a credit card to establish your creditworthiness – even if you intend to settle the bill in cash. **Visa**, **Mastercard** (known elsewhere as **Access**), **Diners Club**, **Discover** and **American Express** are the most widely used.

With *Mastercard* or *Visa* it is also possible to **withdraw cash** at any bank displaying relevant stickers, or from appropriate automatic teller machines (**ATMs**). *Diners Club* cards can be used to cash personal checks at *Citibank* branches. *American Express* cards can only get cash, or buy travellers' checks, at *American Express* offices (check the Yellow Pages) or from the travellers' check dispensers at most major airports. Most **Canadian** credit cards issued by hometown banks will be honored in the US.

American holders of ATM cards are likely to discover that their cards work in the machines of certain banks in other states (check with your bank before you leave home). Not only is this method of financing safer, but at around only a dollar per transaction it's economical as well.

Most major credit cards issued by **foreign banks** are accepted in the US, as well as cash-dispensing cards linked to international networks such as *Cirrus* and *Plus* – once again, check before you set off, as otherwise the machine may simply gobble up your plastic friend. Overseas visitors should also bear in mind that fluctuating exchange rates may result in spending more (or less) than expected when the item eventually shows up on a statement.

Emergencies

Assuming you know someone who is prepared to send you money in a crisis, the quickest way is to have them take the cash to the nearest **Western Union** office (information on ☎1-800/325-6000 in the US, or ☎0800/833833 in the UK) and have it instantaneously **wired** to the office nearest you, subject to the deduction of ten-percent commission. Their main office in San Francisco is at 697 Howard St in SoMa (daily 7am–midnight; ☎495-7301), and they're planning to have credit card facilities in the near future as well. **Thomas Cook** provides a similar service, which takes 24 hours and costs £25; their San Francisco branch is listed below. Both companies have several further locations in the Bay Area.

It's a bit less expensive to get a bank to transfer cash by cable, while if you have a few days' leeway, sending a postal money order, which is exchangeable at any post office, through the mail is cheaper still. The equivalent for foreign travellers is the **international money order**, for which you need to allow up to seven days in the international air mail before arrival. An ordinary check sent from overseas takes 2–3 weeks to clear.

British travellers in difficulties have the final option of throwing themselves on the mercy of the **British consulate**, 1 Sansome St (☎981-3030), who won't be at all pleased to see you but may deign to offer assistance. In worst cases only, they may repatriate you, but they will never, under any circumstances, lend you money.

Exchange Offices

American Express, 237 Post St (Mon–Fri 9am–5pm, Sat 10am–5pm; ☎981-5533).

Deak-International, 100 Grant Ave near Union Square (Mon–Fri 9am–5pm; ☎362-3452).

Thomas Cook, 425 Market St (Mon–Fri 9am–5pm; ☎995-2000).

Crime and Personal Safety

Though no one could pretend that San Francisco is trouble-free, by and large the worst areas for crime are also the most unusual places for tourists to visit, so you're unlikely to have to deal with any of the threatening environments of some other US cities. Most of the violent crime that does occur is drug-related and generally concentrated in deprived areas such as Hunter's Point, on San Francisco's southeast waterfront, or West Oakland. By being careful, you're unlikely to have problems even in these places, though you may well feel distinctly uncomfortable.

Street Crime

The biggest problem for most travellers is the threat of **mugging**. It's impossible to give hard and fast rules about what to do if you're confronted by a mugger. Whether to run, scream or fight depends on the situation – but most locals would just hand over their money.

Of course, the best strategy is simply to **avoid being mugged**. Following a few basic rules helps minimize the danger: *don't* flash money around; don't peer at your map (or this book) at every corner, thereby announcing you're a lost stranger; even if you're terrified or drunk (or both), *don't* appear so; *avoid* dark streets, especially ones you can't see the end of; and in the early hours stick to the roadside edge of the pavement so it's easier to run into the road to attract attention.

If **the worst happens** and your assailant is toting a gun or a knife, try to stay calm: remember that he (for this is generally a male pursuit) is probably scared, too. Keep still, don't make any sudden movements – and hand over your money. When he's gone you'll be shocked, but try to find a cab to take you to the nearest police station, or **phone** ☎ **911** and the police will send an officer to the scene, who'll take you to the nearest station. Here, report the theft and get a reference number on the report to claim insurance (see "Health and Insurance" above) and travellers' check refunds. For **more help**, ring the local *Travelers Aid* (☎781-6738) for sympathy and practical advice. For advice specifically for women in case of mugging or attack, phone the Rape Crisis Line (☎647-7273).

Stolen Passports

Needless to say, having bags snatched which contain travel documents is a big headache, none more so for foreign travellers than **losing your passport**. If the worst happens, go to the nearest consulate and get them to issue a **temporary**

Main SF and Bay Area Police Stations

San Francisco Police Dept 850 Bryant St, SoMa	☎553-1373
Central Station, 766 Vallejo St North Beach;	☎553-1532
Mission Station, 1420 Valencia St Mission District	☎553-1544
Northern Station, 841 Ellis St Western Addition	☎553-1563
Golden Gate Park Station Stanyan and Waller streets	☎553-1061
Potrero Station, 2300 Third St Hunter's Point	☎553-1021
Richmond Station 461 Sixth Ave	☎553-1385
Oakland Police Dept 455 Seventh St	☎874-8218
Berkeley Police Dept 2171 McKinley Ave	☎644-6743

passport, basically a sheet of paper saying you've reported the loss, which will get you out of America and back home. The only **British** consulate on the West Coast which (very grudgingly) issues passports under normal circumstances is in Los Angeles at 3701 Wilshire Blvd (☎213/385-7581); the San Francisco consulate, at 1 Sansome St downtown (☎981-3030), may help out, but only in real emergencies. If you can get to LA, things are reasonably straightforward; if not you need to ring them with an address where they can send an application form, and enclosing any ID you still have plus a $30 reissuing fee. Better than parting with your ID (especially if all you have left is a driving licence) is to send a *notarized* (ie specially stamped) photocopy of it. Most banks have a notary who'll do this at little or no charge. The passport issuing process can take six weeks; to speed things up, the consulate can telex record departments in Britain – but they won't do this until they've received a $10 telex fee.

Stolen Travellers' Checks and Credit Cards

Keep a record of the numbers of your **travellers' checks** separately from the actual checks; if you lose them, ring the issuing company on the toll-free number below. They'll ask you for the check numbers, the place you bought them, when and how you lost them and whether it's been reported to the police. All being well, you should get the missing checks reissued within a couple of days – and perhaps an emergency advance to tide you over.

Emergency Numbers

Mastercard (*Access*)	☎1-800/999-0454
American Express	
(TCs)	☎1-800/221-7282
(credit cards)	☎1-800/528-4800
Diners Club	☎1-800/234-6377
Thomas Cook	☎1-800/223-7373
Visa	☎1-800/227-6811

Getting Around the City

Getting around San Francisco is simple. In spite of the literally breathtaking hills, the city center is small enough to make walking a feasible way to see the sights and get the feel of things. In addition, the excellent system of public transportation is cheap, efficient and easy to use, both in the city and the more urbanized parts of the surrounding Bay Area – though to go any further afield you'd do well to rent a car. Cycling, and – outside the city center – mountain biking, is a good option too, though you'll need stout legs to tackle those hills.

Points of Arrival

The Airports

All international and most domestic flights arrive at **San Francisco International Airport** (SFO), about fifteen miles south of the city. Each of the many ways of getting into town from here is clearly signed from the baggage reclaim areas. The least expensive is to take a San Mateo County Transit (*SamTrans*) **bus**, leaving from the lower level of the airport. The #7F express takes around forty minutes to reach downtown (every 30min; $1.75); the slower #7B stops everywhere and takes over an hour (every 30min; 85¢); and a shuttle runs to the Daly City *BART* station (every 20min; 85¢). Bear in mind, though, that you're only allowed as much luggage as you can carry on your lap. The San Francisco **Airporter** bus ($6) picks up from outside each baggage claim area every fifteen minutes and travels to the downtown terminal on Ellis and Taylor Streets in about forty minutes. The blue **Supershuttle** and the **Yellow Airport Shuttle** minibuses, which cost a little more, are much quicker: they pick up every five minutes from outside the baggage claim area and will take you and other passengers to any city center destination for around $15 per head. Be ruthless, though – competition for these is fierce.

Taxis from the airport cost $30–35 (plus tip) for any downtown location, more for East Bay and Marin County, and are only worth considering if you can fill one. If you're planning to drive, there's the usual clutch of **car rental** agencies at the airport. All operate shuttle buses

that circle the top departure level of the airport road, and take you to their depot free of charge.

A number of domestic airlines (*America West* and *Continental* are two) fly into **Oakland International Airport** (OAK; see p.135 for details), across the bay. This airport is actually closer to downtown San Francisco than SFO, and efficiently connected with the city by the $2 *AirBART* shuttle bus from the Coliseum *BART* station. The third Bay Area airport, **San Jose Municipal** (SJO), also serves domestic arrivals, but is only worth considering if flights into the other two are booked up (see p.159 for more).

By Bus and Train

All San Francisco's **Greyhound** services use the **Transbay Terminal** at 425 Mission St (☎558-6789), south of Market St, near the Embarcadero *BART* station; the old Seventh Street Terminal was closed by the 1989 earthquake. **Green Tortoise** buses (☎285-2441) disembark behind the Transbay Terminal on First and Natoma. **Amtrak** trains stop across the bay in **Richmond** (with easy *BART* transfers) and continue to Oakland, from where free shuttle buses run across the Bay Bridge to the Transbay Terminal.

The main route **by car** from the east is I-80, which runs via Sacramento all the way from Chicago. The main north–south route through California, I-5, passes by fifty miles east, and is linked to the Bay Area by I-580. US-101 and Hwy-1, the more scenic north–south routes, pass right through downtown San Francisco.

Muni

The city's public transportation is run by the **San Francisco Municipal Railway**, or *Muni* (☎673-6864), and is made up of a comprehensive network of **buses**, **trolley buses** and **cable cars**, which run up and over the city's hills, and underground **trains**, which become **streetcars** when they emerge from the downtown metro system to split off and serve the suburbs. On buses and trains there's a flat **fare** of $1; $2 on cable cars. With trains, you must purchase tickets to get through the barriers before descending to the platforms; on the buses, correct change is required on boarding. Day passes, valid on all *Muni* services except the cable cars, cost $2.25.

If you're staying more than a week or so and need to rely heavily on public transportation, get a **Fast Pass**, which costs $32 and is valid for unlimited travel on the *Muni* system and *BART* stations (see below) within the city limits for a full calendar month. Fast Passes are available from most supermarkets and newsagents.

Muni trains run **throughout the night** on a limited service, except on the M-Ocean View line, which stops around midnight; buses, too, run all night, again at greatly reduced levels. For **more detailed information** pick up a *Muni* map ($1.50) from the Visitor Information Center or bookstores,

though it's unlikely that you'll need to be familiar with more than a few of the major bus routes, the most important of which are listed below. See also the route map overleaf, which details all major bus and *Muni* lines.

Other Public Transportation Services

A number of **other public transportation networks** run into San Francisco, though these are most useful as connections with the rest of the Bay Area. Along Market Street downtown, *Muni* shares the station concourses with **BART**, the Bay Area Rapid Transit system, linking major points in San Francisco with the East Bay and outer suburbs. The **CalTrain** commuter railway (their depot is at 4th and Townsend Streets, South of Market) links San Francisco with points along the Peninsula south to San Jose. **Golden Gate Ferry** boats leave from the Ferry Building on the Embarcadero, crossing the bay past Alcatraz to Marin County. For more details see the "Getting Around" sections of the various Bay Area chapters, Eight to Eleven.

Driving – Taxis and Cars

Taxis – as in most American cities, normally colored yellow – don't trawl the streets in San

---

Useful Bus Routes

#38 from Geary St via Civic Center, west to the ocean along Geary Blvd.

#5 From the Transbay Terminal, west along the north side of Golden Gate Park to the ocean.

#7 From the Ferry Terminal (Market St) along Haight St to the ocean.

#24 From Castro St north along Divisadero St to Pacific Heights and Marina.

#37 From Market St to Twin Peaks.

#30 From the CalTrain depot in SoMa, north to Fisherman's Wharf via North Beach and the Financial District.

#22 From the Mission along Fillmore St north to Pacific Heights.

#15 From 3rd St (SoMa) to Pier 39, Fisherman's Wharf, via the Financial District and North Beach.

#20 (Golden Gate Transit) From Civic Center to the Golden Gate Bridge.

Muni Train Lines

Muni N-JUDAH LINE From downtown west to Ocean Beach, via the Haight.

Muni J-CHURCH LINE From downtown to Mission and East Castro.

Muni L-TARAVAL LINE From downtown west to the zoo and Ocean Beach.

Muni K-INGLESIDE LINE From downtown to Balboa Park.

Muni M-OCEAN VIEW From downtown west to Ocean Beach.

Cable Car Routes

Powell–Hyde from Powell St along Hyde through Russian Hill to Fisherman's Wharf.

Powell–Mason From Powell St along Mason via Chinatown and North Beach to Fisherman's Wharf.

California St From the foot of California St in the Financial District through Nob Hill to Polk St.

Francisco the way they do in some cities. If you want one and you're not in a busy part of town or near a big hotel you'll probably have to telephone: try *Veterans* (☎552-1300) or *Yellowcab* (☎626-2345). Fares work out at approximately $3 for the first mile, $1.50 a mile thereafter.

You don't need a **car** to get around San Francisco, but if you're staying some way out from the center, it can make life easier – especially if you want to see something of the Bay Area while you're here. The only special rules to **driving** in the city are designed to contend with its often very steep gradients – you are obliged to turn your wheels to the curb when parking on hills. Bear in mind that **drink driving laws** (DWI – "Driving While Intoxicated") are very strict, and that all opened containers of alcohol in the vehicle are deemed illegal. If a police officer smells alcohol on your breath, he/she is entitled to administer a breath, saliva or urine test – and you can be fined up to $200 if you fail – or in extreme (or repeat) cases, to imprison you for thirty days.

It can be maddeningly difficult to find a place to leave the car, but don't lose your cool: **parking** restrictions in San Francisco are strictly enforced,

and traffic officers will cheerfully ticket you in a matter of seconds – which at an average of $30 per ticket can get expensive; worse, they'll sometimes tow your car away. A number of **parking lots** in the South of Market industrial area charge $5 per day; more central garages charge that much per hour. Of these, the best deals are to be had in the multi-storey garage at Sutter and Stockton, and the parking lots under Union Square downtown, under Portsmouth Square in Chinatown, and at Ghirardelli Square near Fisherman's Wharf.

If you **break down** in a rental car, call the emergency number that you'll find on your rental contract.

Driving for Foreigners

UK nationals can **drive** in the US on a full UK driving licence (International Driving Permits are not always regarded as sufficient). Fly-drive deals are good value if you want to **rent** a car (see p.5), though you can save up to 60 percent simply by booking in advance with a major firm. If you choose not to pay until you arrive, be sure you take a written confirmation of the price with you.

Car Rental Companies

Toll-free numbers for the big international **car rental firms** are listed below; all have outlets at the airport, and compete with bargain rates and special offers. **Unlimited mileage** is fairly standard, so you can plan long trips without fear of punitive mileage rates. Bear in mind that **insurance** (not obligatory but certainly advisable) is extra, and can add a hefty amount onto the daily rate.

San Francisco Offices

Alamo, 687 Folsom St ☎882-9440
Good daily rates, from as little as $21.95 per day.

Avis, 675 Post St ☎885-5011
Good week-long deals from $115.

Dollar, 364 O'Farrell St ☎771-5300
From $26.95 per day.

Enterprise, 1133 Van Ness Ave ☎441-3369
Small cars available from $23 per day.

Hertz, 433 Mason St ☎771-2200
Good weekly deals from $145.

Reliable, 349 Mason St ☎928-4414
$22 per day.

Thrifty, 299 Ellis St ☎673-6675
From $24 per day $130 per week.

National Toll-Free Numbers

Alamo	☎1-800/327-9633
Avis	☎1-800/722-1333
Budget	☎1-800/527-0700
Dollar	☎1-800/421-6868
Enterprise	☎1-800/325-8007
Hertz	☎1-800/654-3131
National	☎1-800/227-7368
Payless	☎1-800/729-5377
Rent-a-Wreck	☎1-800/535-1391
Snappy	☎1-800/669-4800
Thrifty	☎1-800/367-2277
Value	☎1-800/468-2583

UK Numbers

Alamo	☎0800/272 200
Avis	☎081/848 8733
Budget	☎0800/181 181
Europcar	☎081/950 5050
Hertz	☎081/679 1799
Holiday Autos	☎071/491 1111

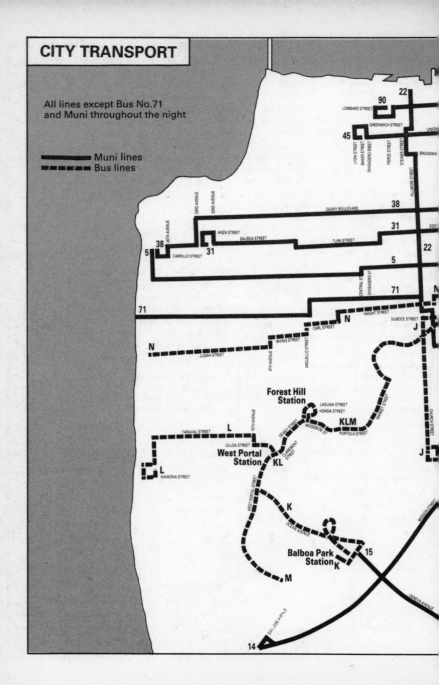

CITY TRANSPORT

All lines except Bus No.71
and Muni throughout the night

━━━━━ Muni lines
▬▬▬▬▬ Bus lines

Remember that it's safer not to rent a car straight off a long transatlantic flight, and that standard rental cars have **automatic transmissions**.

As for **rules of the road**, you must drive on the right and front-seat passengers must always wear seat belts. There are several **types of road** – the wide, straight and fast **Interstate Highways** (prefixed "I"); **State Highways** (eg Hwy-1); and **US Highways** (eg US-101) – though in San Francisco and the more built-up parts of the Bay Area most roads are better known by their local name. Hwy-1, for instance, is known as 19th Avenue. One rule that differs from the UK is that applied at junctions: you can turn right on a red light if there's no traffic approaching from the left except where prohibited, otherwise red and amber mean stop. The speed limit in the city and other built-up areas is 30–35mph; otherwise it's a maximum of 55mph. There are no **spot fines**, but if given a **speeding** ticket reckon on a fine of at least $75.

Cycling

In general, **cycling** is a cheap and healthy method of getting around San Francisco and the Bay Area, some parts of which have cycle lanes; local buses are often equipped to carry bikes strapped to the outside. In **country areas**, there's much scenic, and largely level, land, especially around the Wine Country. Bikes can be **rented** for $15–25 a day, $70–100 a week, from outlets usually found close to beaches, university campuses or simply in areas which are good for cycling; see the appropriate sections of the guide, or contact local visitor centers. Good-value city rental shops include **Park Cyclery**, 1865 Haight St (☎221-3777), which provides touring bikes for $18 per day, mountain bikes for $25 a day, and offer weekly rates from $75.

California Scooter, at 640 Stanyan St (☎751-4100), rents **scooters** for around $45 a day.

Organized Tours

If you've just arrived, you may want to orientate yourself by taking an **organized tour**. *Gray Line Tours* (☎558-9400) will whip you around the city in three fairly tedious hours, stopping at Twin Peaks and Cliff House, for around $25 a head. Skip it unless you're really pushed for time and want to get a general idea of the city's layout with minimal effort.

Excruciatingly expensive but spectacular **aerial tours** of the city and Bay Area in light aircraft are available from several operators, the cheapest of which is *Airship Industries Skycruise* (☎568-4101), which offers one-hour airship cruises for $150. Much cheaper is *Commodore Helicopters* (☎332-4482), which hover over the city for upwards of $70 per hour, with longer tours up and down the coastline available for considerably larger sums. You might prefer one of the more leisurely two-hour **bay cruises** operated by the *Blue & Gold Fleet* (☎781-7877) from piers 39 and 40 – though at $17 a throw these don't come cheap either, and in any case everything may be shrouded in fog.

For **tours of the Wine Country and other parts of the Bay Area**, see the relevant chapters in *Part Three*.

Walking Tours

Various excellent personalized **walking tours** explore San Francisco. The better ones usually have no more than five to a group and can often make an informative and efficient way to get to know a particular area of town. The Visitor Information Center will be able to give you a full list, but among those you might like to try are:

A.M. Walks, 1433 Clay St; ☎928-5965. If you can stand the early start (7am or 9am), you can take advantage of the cheapest downtown walking tour available. For only $12 San Francisco author John McCarroll will take you around Union Square, Chinatown and the Financial District on a two-and-half-hour witty, anecdotal trek.

Café Walks; ☎751-4286. Detailed walking tours of the Haight-Ashbury, a Mansion tour of Pacific Heights, and best of all a tour of North Beach and Russian Hill are available from $20 each. Tours last two to three hours and include a light lunch.

City Guides; ☎557-4266. The most extensive range of guided walks, sponsored by the San Francisco Public Library and all free.

Cruisin' the Castro, 375 Lexington St; ☎550-8110. The Supreme Champion of the walking tour circuit in San Francisco, Trevor Hailey, a resident of San Francisco's gay community for fifteen years, takes you on a fascinating tour of this small area. Her knowledge includes everything from politics to the best parties and she embellishes her three-and-a-half-hour tour with funny stories. $25 per person includes breakfast. Worth every cent.

Friends of Recreation and Parks, MacLaren Lodge, Stanyan and Fell streets; ☎221-1311. Tour Golden Gate Park with trained guides pointing out the park's flora, fauna and history.$15.

Helen's Walk Tour; ☎524-4544. Helen Rendon, a four-feet-ten-inch dynamo, leads you around the murals of the Mission with her personal brand of commentary and historical perspective. $20 per person includes a stop for coffee and pastries.

San Francisco Art Tours; ☎832-2421. Two-hour tours of either the downtown galleries, or (much better) the alternative art spaces South of Market. Traces the history of San Francisco's artistic community and discusses local artists. $15 per person.

San Francisco Discovery Walks, 1200 Taylor St; ☎673-2894. Four different tours highlighting major architectural sights. $15−20.

Travelling with Children

Visiting San Francisco with your kids is no more difficult than in any major city, but parents need to be aware that this is very much a place for adults – more so than, say, LA – and there aren't many things to occupy young ones. Mercifully, American restaurants being what they are, there is always something that children will want to eat – burgers, hot dogs, french fries and ice cream are in abundance. Hotels are more of a worry; only the larger (and more expensive) establishments will have facilities and play areas for children.

Activities

Of San Francisco's few specifically child-orientated attractions – all of which are listed in the relevant chapters of this book – the *Exploratorium* in the Marina District is excellent, as is the *Steinhart Aquarium* in Golden Gate Park, and the *Lawrence Hall of Science* in Berkeley will captivate any young mind. For more organized distractions, try the *Great America* amusement park in San Jose, or the animal-themed *Marine World/Africa USA* in Vallejo, accessible by transbay ferry. Young children will enjoy the *San Francisco International Toy Museum*, at 2801 Leavenworth St in the Cannery. It's a wonderland of building toys, stuffed animals, dolls, trains and 100,000 pieces of *Lego* that the children are encouraged to play with, and, best of all, that you don't have to clear up afterwards. For general child-entertainment, the **Golden Gate Park** is your best bet. As well as the above-mentioned *Steinhart Aquarium*, it holds the *Children's Playground* located on the Lincoln Avenue side of the park, which as well as the standard swings and climbing frames features the slide with the fastest ride in the West. Other traditional forms of amusement include the **San Francisco Zoo** (see p.126), where children can enjoy such hands-on exhibits as petting tarantulas and feeding the big cats. Finally, if you want to take your children on a **boat ride**, the best value is the *Golden Gate Ferry* to Larkspur or Sausalito, which departs from the Ferry Building at the foot of Market Street; children can ride for around $3.

Getting Around

On most international and domestic routes, children less than two years old are classified as "lap children". Provided they stay on your lap, they can fly for free. Discounts of up to fifty percent apply to children below the age of twelve, but over that the full standard fare is applicable.

For travelling around the city proper, the *MUNI* system is by and large clean, efficient and safe and children travel for a fraction of the cost of an adult ticket. If you want to travel beyond the city limits it is usually easier to bundle children into a car.

Gay and Lesbian San Francisco

San Francisco's reputation as a city for gay celebration is not new. It could even be outdated. This is undoubtedly still the gay capital of the world, but despite a high profile, the gay scene hasn't had much to celebrate in the last few years and there's been a definite move from the outrageous to the mainstream. It's unlikely that even AIDS will diminish the increasing number of gay activists in public office, but it has made them more conservative in approach, if not in policy. The exuberant energy that went into the posturing and parading of the 1970s has taken on a much more sober, down-to-business attitude, and these days you'll find more political activists organizing conferences than drag queens throwing parties. Things have changed.

From its beginnings as a Gold Rush town, when scores of men unaccompanied by their womenfolk came to San Francisco, an exclusively male culture has, not surprisingly, thrived. More significantly, the 1940s saw a big increase in the gay population, when a military purge of homosexual soldiers resulted in several thousand – who were serving in the South Pacific – being booted out at San Francisco; unable to return home with the stigma and shame of their expulsion, many stayed. Since that time gays have been coming here to make their homes away from the prejudice and isolation of the rest of the US, much of which still hasn't changed a great deal – 23 states still outlaw homosexuality, with penalties ranging from a $200 fine in Texas to twenty years' imprisonment in Georgia. San Francisco is still America's most liberal city for gay men *and* women, who, it's true to say, can genuinely enjoy their sexualities openly and without fear. However, the moral backlash caused by AIDS has inevitably awakened prejudice in San Francisco as it has everywhere. The basic principles of tolerance and support endure, though, and have even in some senses been reinforced. (It's interesting to note that on the same day the homophobic "clause 28" bill was being rushed through Parliament in Britain, San Francisco's former mayor, Art Agnos, rode through the streets of San Francisco in support of the Gay and Lesbian Freedom Day Parade.)

Certainly, post-AIDS, San Francisco's gay scene is a different way of life altogether. The Seventies were notorious for the bar and bathhouse culture and the busy and often anonymous promiscuity which went with it, but this toned down abruptly when AIDS first became a problem in the early 1980s. This wasn't a foregone conclusion by any means. Many men saw the closure of the bathhouses as an infringement on their civil liberties, and the rumor that AIDS is germ warfare by the US government has yet to disappear completely. Nowadays, however, the gay community has become a much more politicized grouping, directing its energies towards fundraising and programmes for AIDS patients.

Socially, San Francisco's gay scene has also mellowed, though in what is an increasingly conservative climate in the city generally, gay parties, parades and street fairs still swing better than most. Like any well-organized section of society, the gay scene definitely has its social season, and if you're here in June, you'll coincide with the Gay and Lesbian Film Festival, Gay Pride Week, the Gay Freedom Day Parade and any number of conferences. Come October, the street fairs are in full swing and Halloween still sees some of the most outrageous carrying-on.

Though the 1980s saw the flowering of a **lesbian** culture to rival the male 1970s upsurge, by the early 1990s, not a single women's bar remained. The explanation may lie in the words of one lesbian bartender, "All the dykes have dried out honey !". Sobriety has been a keen gay issue (in keeping with California society in general) since the advent of AIDS and is supposed to represent the much-vaunted new personal responsibility ethic. *Clean and Sober Clubs* are the informal partners of AA where ex-drinkers go to meet other ex-drinkers and congratulate each other once the initial grisly process of twelve-

Specifically **gay accommodation** is listed on p.206; the best of San Francisco's **gay and lesbian bars and clubs** are detailed under the relevant sections of Chapters Fourteen and Fifteen.

stepping has been completed. Fortunately, at exclusively female club nights around the city, good-humored lesbians can still be found drinking, dancing and carousing into the small hours (see p.239).

Neighborhoods and Publications

Traditionally, the area for gay men has been the **Castro**, together with a few bars and clubs around **SoMa** – though gay life these days is much less ghettoized and there are bars and clubs all over town. Rent boys and pimps prowl **Polk Street**, not the safest area at 2am but hardly a danger zone if you use common sense. Lesbian interests are more concentrated in the East Bay than the city, although women's activities thrive in the **Mission**.

New clubs and groups spring up all the time and you should keep an ear to the ground as well as referring to the many free gay publications available: *The Sentinel, Coming Up, The Bay Area Reporter* and *Gay Times* all give listings of events, services, clubs and bars in the city and Bay Area. Women should also keep an eye out in bookstores for *On Our Backs* and *Bad Attitude*, two magazines that often have useful pointers to lesbian organizations in town. Also useful for both men and women is *The Gay Book*, a telephone-cum-resource book that's available in gay bookstores. For a complete gay guide, you might try *Bob Damron's Address Book* (PO Box 422258, San Francisco, CA 94142; ☎1-800/462-6654 or 255-0404), again available from gay bookstores, which has complete listings of gay accommodation, bars, clubs and stores in California; the *Women's Traveller* provides similar listings for lesbians. But for something outrageous, you should get a copy of *Betty & Pansy's Severe Queer Review*, $7.95, from gay bookstores, a cult publication that pulls no punches in its assessments of San Francisco gay entertainment – hysterically funny and frank.

Gay Contacts and Resources

AIDS Hotline ☎863-2437
24-hour information and counselling.

Bay Area Bi-Sexual Network ☎654-2226
2404 California St; Referral service for support groups, social connections and counselling.

Dignity ☎584-1714
133 Golden Gate Ave; Catholic worship and services.

Gay Cocaine Counselling Service ☎1-800/262-2463

Gay Legal Referral Services ☎621-3900
PO Box 1983 SF; Enquiries regarding legal problems and legal representation.

Lesbian/Gay Switchboard ☎841-6224
24-hour counselling and advice. Contacts and activities referral service.

Gay Men's Group ☎750-5661
450 Stanyan St; Support group and advice on places to go, contacts, etc.

Gay Men's Therapy Center ☎673-1160
How to cope with AIDS issues and fears, grief counselling, etc.

Gay Therapy Center ☎558-8828
3393 Market St; Counselling and help with coming out.

SF AIDS Foundation ☎864-4376
25 Van Ness Ave; Referral service providing advice, testing, support groups.

Shanti Project ☎777-1162
525 Howard St; AIDS support group that offers care of PWAs, advice, testing and counselling.

SOL (Slightly Older Lesbians) ☎841-6224
Pacific Center, 2712 Telegraph Ave, Berkeley, CA 94705; a gathering-place and referral service for women over thirty.

Woman to Woman ☎939-6626
Confidential introductions.

Women's San Francisco

In contrast to the hostility you can experience in urban centers such as NY or LA, San Francisco has a friendly, non-threatening atmosphere that is particularly reassuring to travellers who are new to the city. Like any major city, it does of course have its trouble spots, but as these places have nothing you'd particularly want to see anyway, there is no need for undue caution.

Women in particular enjoy San Francisco; in the West Coast's most progressive city, women are treated with respect and courtesy almost everywhere and commonly hold positions of power and authority. The gains of the last twenty years are considerable and visible. San Francisco's large lesbian community is further proof that backward attitudes are hard to come by. Naturally common sense still applies; look as if you know where you are going, take taxis at night and **never** hitch – women travelling alone are not at all unusual but the successful ones learn to deal with any harassment firmly and loudly. Rape statistics are horrifically high, and while there is more chance of being mugged than raped, you may feel safer if you carry whistles, gas and sprays; useless in the event of real

Specific **accommodation** options for women are listed on p.206.

trouble but a confidence booster that can ward off creeps.

The flip side of San Francisco's gay revolution has in some women's circles led to a separatist culture, and women's resources and services are sometimes lumped together under the lesbian category. While this may be no bad thing, it can be hard to tell which organizations exist irrespective of sexuality. Don't let this stop you from checking out anything that sounds interesting, especially with regard to the bars and clubs listed in the Gay and Lesbian sections of Chapters Fourteen and Fifteen. Nobody is going to refuse you either entry or help if you're not a lesbian – support is given to anybody who needs it. Similarly, women's health care is very well provided for in San Francisco and there are numerous clinics you can go to for routine gynecological and contraceptive services: payment is on a sliding scale according to income, but even if you're flat-broke, you won't be refused treatment.

Women's Contacts and Resources

Bay Area Resource Center
318 Leavenworth St ☎ 474-2400
Services, information and clothing

Metropolitan Community Church
150 Eureka St ☎ 863-8843
A "women's spirit group" is held here each Wednesday at 7.30pm.

Radical Women
523A Valencia St ☎ 864-1278
Socialist feminist organization dedicated to building women's leadership and achieving full equality. Meetings held on the second and fourth Tuesday of each month.

Rape Crisis Line ☎ 647-7273
24-hour switchboard

Women's Building
3543 18th St ☎ 431-1180

Central stop in the Mission for women's art and political events. A very good place to get information also – the women who staff the building are happy to deal with the most obscure of enquiries. Don't be afraid to ask.

Women's Health Center No.1
3850 17th St ☎ 558-3908
Free contraception, AIDS testing, pregnancy testing and a well-women's clinic.

Women's Needs Center
1825 Haight St ☎ 221-7371
Low-cost health care and referral service.

Women's Yellow Pages
270 Napoleon St ☎ 821-1357
Call for a copy of this invaluable directory, with everything from where to stay to where to get your legs waxed.

Festivals and Holidays

Someone is always celebrating something in San Francisco, and while many of these are uniquely local affairs, most have their roots in the ethnic or national holidays of other countries, highlighting the region's diverse background. Street fairs and block parties take place all over the city throughout the summer months, and at the bigger events, like the Chinese New Year parade in February or Gay Freedom Day in June, it seems as if the entire city is joining in.

Festivals

The first big event in San Francisco's festival season is the **Chinese New Year** celebration, usually at the end of January or early in February, depending on the Chinese calendar. A week of low-key activities in and around Chinatown culminates in the Golden Dragon Parade, in which hundreds of people march through downtown leading a 75-foot-long dragon. To find out more, contact the *Chinatown Chamber of Commerce*, 730 Sacramento St (☎982-3000).

A month later, on March 17, the whole city dresses up in emerald hues to celebrate **St Patrick's Day**, which is marked by excessive consumption of green-tinted beer and by a lengthy parade through downtown.

Other celebrations continue the international flavor, starting with late April's low-key **Cherry Blossom Festival** in Japantown and picking up steam around the **Cinco de Mayo**, celebrating the Mexican victory at the battle of Puebla with a 48-hour party in the Mission over the weekend nearest to May 5.

June is the biggest party month, with the boisterous, music- and fun-filled **Festival on the Lake** on Oakland's Lake Merritt, followed by numerous San Francisco **street fairs** – the **North Beach Fair** and the **Haight Street Fair** to name two of the biggest – and the lively **Carnaval** happenings in the Mission. The month's main event is the **Lesbian and Gay Freedom Day Parade**, held on the last Sunday in June, when crowds of up to a quarter of a million pack Market Street for the city's biggest parade and party. The bands and dancers converge on City Hall afterwards for a giant block party, with outdoor discos, live bands and numerous craft and food stands.

Apart from the **4th of July** fireworks at Crissy Field in the Presidio, for the rest of the year the streets are comparatively quiet, except of course for the city's predominantly gay areas – the **Polk Street Fair** at the end of July, for example, which brings out the black leather brigades. Many of these celebrants resurface for the end-of-summer **Castro Street Fair**, early in October, and at the end of the month when there's one last burst of pre-winter activity on **Halloween** (October 31). Locals dress up and strut their stuff, promenading from bar to bar. Halloween also provides the basis for one of the Bay Area's most unexpected events, the **Pumpkin Festival** in Half Moon Bay, when local farmers open their fields to jack-o'-lantern hunters and host a range of pumpkin-based cooking and eating competitions.

Public Holidays

Banks and offices, and many but not all stores, will be closed for the full day on the following **public holidays**:

January 1 **New Year's Day**

January 15 **Martin Luther King's Birthday**

Third Monday in February **President's Day**

Easter Monday

Last Monday in May **Memorial Day**

July 4 **Independence Day**

First Monday in September **Labor Day**

Second Monday in October **Columbus Day**

November 11 **Veterans' Day**

Fourth Thursday in November **Thanksgiving Day**

December 25 **Christmas Day**

The Media

San Francisco is a bit of a media backwater compared to Los Angeles or New York City, but what it lacks in high-power status it makes up with in-depth coverage of local news and features. The provincialism of its daily newspapers – about half the stories in the main *San Francisco Chronicle* are straight reprints from other US papers – is a continual source of embarrassment, but there are dozens of free weekly newspapers, focusing in on the city or parts of the Bay Area, that are informative and entertaining. San Francisco's television is much the same as anywhere else in America, but the city's radio stations are excellent, offering an amazing range of music, the best of which is commercial-free, 24 hours a day.

Newspapers

San Francisco's major **daily newspapers** are the *San Francisco Chronicle* (50¢) in the morning, and in the afternoon, the re-vamped *San Francisco Examiner* (50¢), which is making great efforts to capture the liberal market with in-depth reporting, and, in the case of Hunter S Thompson, contro-versial columnists. On Sundays the two papers are published as a very large combined edition ($1), most of which can be discarded, with the exception of the very useful "Datebook" (also known as the "Pink Pages") which gives detailed listings of arts, clubs, films and forthcoming events. Perhaps the best daily paper for straight coverage of local, national and international events is the *San Jose Mercury-News* (25¢), based in the Silicon Valley but available all over the Bay Area.

There's also an abundance of **free publica-tions**, led by the *San Francisco Bay Guardian*, which has 100 pages of lively reporting and inva-luable listings every week. Other San Francisco freesheets to look out for (cafés and record stores are likely places) include the *SF Weekly* and the lesbian, gay and bisexual-orientated *Bay Times*, which has tons of listings and the best personal ads.

For listings of what's on in lively Oakland and Berkeley, and yet more voyeuristically interesting personal ads, the weekly *East Bay Express* is unsurpassed, while the Berkeley-based *Poetry Flash* has details of poetry readings, workshops and other literary events. If you're interested in more active pursuits, the monthly *City Sports* has rundowns of upcoming running and cycling and similar events in the Bay Area. There are dozens more locally based newspapers throughout the Bay Area, the best of which are listed in the "Information" sections of the relevant chapters.

TV

San Francisco **TV** is pretty much the standard network barrage, frequently interrupted by hard-sell commercials; game shows fill up most of the morning schedule; around lunchtime you can take your pick of any of a dozen daily soaps. Most hotels provide access to **cable networks** such as *CNN*, the round-the-clock news channel, and the mainstream pop of *MTV*.

San Francisco TV	
2 KTVU Fox	7 KGO ABC
4 KRON NBC	9 KQED PBS
5 KPIX CBS	

Radio

Bay Area **radio**, in contrast, is probably the best in the US, with some eighty stations catering to just about every conceivable taste. **AM** stations tend to be either all news, chat and phone-in shows or shit-kicking country-and-western tunes for truckers. A better option is the **FM** band, which is broadcast in stereo. The bulk of these stations are commercial, but by far the best are the dozen non-commercial stations, located at the far left end of the radio dial (88–92 FM). Most of these are affiliated with a college or university, and in the main their programming is anarchically varied, from in-depth current affairs discussions to mind-boggling industrial thrash.

San Francisco Radio

KSFO 560 AM Oldies music and Bay Area sporting events.

KCBS 740 AM News, talk-shows and excellent commentaries.

KGO 810AM News, and the most intense talk-shows.

KNEW 910 AM Country and western music.

KQED 88.5 FM Classical music, talk, community affairs.

KPOO 89.5 FM Community-based radio – blues, reggae, soul.

KUSF 90.3 FM Excellent college station with rock, news and off-beat issues.

KALX 90.7 FM Voted best US college station most years for its blend of anything-but-mainstream rock and reggae, though the UC Berkeley-based signal rarely makes it across the bay.

KCSM 91.1 FM Diverse but consistently high-quality programming, especially good for late-night jazz.

KJAZ 92.8 FM Mellow, laid-back style, good jazz.

KPFA 94.1 FM Long-running, listener-supported station known for its in-depth investigative reporting as well as arts programmes.

KSAN 94.5 Modern country and western music.

KKHI 95.7 FM Classical music.

KRQR 97.3 FM Album rock.

KBLX 102.9 FM "The Quiet Storm": soul, jazz and lots of house.

KFOG 104.5 FM Best of the rock stations with lots of oldies and the best of newies.

KMEL 106.1 Soul, house. Very funky.

KSOL 107.1 FM Dance music, with a good line in the latest rap.

Directory

ADDRESSES When pinpointing an **address** verbally, to a cab driver or when giving directions, San Franciscans always give the cross street rather than the number (eg Valencia and 18th), and you'd do well to follow their example. However, you may see numbered addresses written down (in this guide for example), in which case there is a formula for working out where it is on the city's very long thoroughfares. All streets work on blocks of 100 from their downtown source, which on north–south streets is Market Street, on east–west streets it is either Market Street, or, above here, the Embarcadero. For example, 950 Powell Street is on the tenth block of Powell north of Market; 1450 Post Street is on the fifteenth block of Post west of Market; 220 Castro Street is on the third block of Castro south of Market. Unlike many American cities, most streets have names rather than numbers, the only grid of numbered streets being that radiating into the docks area south of Market. Further out from downtown, in the Richmond and Sunset, the avenues all have their origin at the foot of the Presidio and travel south in increasing blocks of 100.

AIRPORT TAX $15, but always included in the price of your ticket.

APARTMENT HUNTING If you decide that you love San Francisco so much that you can't leave, be reassured that looking for somewhere to live is not the nightmare it is in New York or London: rented accommodation is plentiful and not that expensive, although the absence of housing associations and co-ops means that there is very little really cheap accommodation anywhere. Accommodation is almost always rented unfurnished so you'll have to buy furniture; in general, expect to pay $600 a month for a studio or one-bedroom apartment in the cheaper parts of town, anything up to $1100 for a nice neighborhood. 2–3 bedrooms will set you back something between $1000 and $1500, again depending on your neighborhood. Most landlords expect one month's rent as a deposit, plus one month in advance. Utilities, such as gas and electricity, are all charged monthly. To find a place, scour the *San Francisco Chronicle*, or, more usefully, the many free papers such as the *Bay Guardian* or the *East Bay Express* – and, for women, *Bay Area Women's News*. **Housing agencies** require two weeks' rent as a finding-fee.

BABY-SITTING *Bay Area Babysitting Agency* (☎ 991-7474).

CONSULATES See p.15.

CIGARETTES AND SMOKING Cigarettes are sold in virtually any foodstore, drugstore or bar, and also from vending machines on the outside walls of these establishments. You should be aware that smoking tobacco is greatly frowned upon in San Francisco: all movie houses and theaters are non-smoking, while restaurants are divided into non-smoking and smoking sections and some of the newer ones ban it altogether. Smoking is universally forbidden on public transportation and in elevators.

DATES In the American style, the date 1.8.95 means not August 1 but January 8.

DENTISTS Contact the *Dental Society Referral Service*, ☎ 421-1435.

DRUGS Possession of under an ounce of the widely consumed marijuana is a non-criminal offence in California, and the worst you'll get is a $200 fine. Being caught with more than an ounce, however, means facing a criminal charge for dealing, and a possible prison sentence. Other drugs are, of course, completely illegal and it's a much more serious offence if you're caught with any. Of the most widespread, crack and PCP ("angel dust") are confined to ghetto areas and the only contact you'll have with them will be if an addict tries to rob or kill you (statistically improbable). Ordinary cocaine, by contrast, is still the drug of the rich, though the sharp decrease in its street price means it's much more prevalent than it was. The fad for designer drugs such as Ecstasy, with which the Bay Area became associated for a while, has largely faded.

DRUG AND SUICIDE HOTLINE ☎752-3400.

ELECTRICITY 110V AC. All plugs are two-pronged and rather insubstantial. Some travel plug adapters don't fit American sockets.

EMERGENCIES Dial ☎911 for police, fire or ambulance services.

FLOORS The *first* floor in the US is what would be the ground floor in Britain; the *second* floor would be the first floor, and so on.

GRATEFUL DEAD HOTLINE ☎457-6388. Join the Deadheads and find out about upcoming gigs and other essential Dead facts.

ID Should be carried at all times. Two pieces should diffuse any suspicion, one of which should have a photo: driving licence, passport and credit card(s) are your best bets.

LAUNDRY All but the most basic hotels do laundry, for a wash and dry in a laundromat costs a lot less (about $1.50). *Brainwash,* 1122 Folsom St in SoMa, is a combo bar-and-laundromat; not a bad way to pass the time.

LEGAL ADVICE *Lawyer Referral Service* ☎764-1616.

MEASUREMENTS AND SIZES The US has yet to go metric, so measurements are in inches, feet, yards and miles; weight in ounces, pounds and tons. American pints and gallons are about four-fifths of Imperial ones. Clothing sizes are always two figures less what they would be in Britain – a British women's size 12 is a US size 10 – while British shoe sizes are one and a half below American ones.

PHARMACIES *Walgreen's,* 498 Castro St (☎861-6276), is open 24 hours every day.

POISONINGS *Poison Control Center,* ☎476-6600.

PUBLIC TOILETS There are no public toilets as such. Bars, and to a lesser extent restaurants and fast-food outlets, are your best bets, although technically you should be a customer.

TAX Be warned that sales tax is added to virtually everything you buy in a store, but isn't part of the marked price. In San Francisco and the Bay Area the sales tax is 7.5 percent, plus a 0.5 percent "earthquake" tax. Hotel tax will add 12 percent on to your bill.

TEMPERATURES Always given in Fahrenheit.

TICKETS For music, theater, sports and camping reservations, use a charge-by-phone agency, such as *BASS* (☎762-2277) or *MISTIX* (☎1-800/442-7275). For half-price theater tickets, try the *Tix Bay Area* booth on the Stockton Street side of Union Square (☎433-7827).

TIME The West Coast runs on Pacific Standard Time (PST), eight hours behind GMT in winter and three hours behind the East Coast. British Summer Time runs almost concurrent with US Daylight Saving Time – implemented between the last Sunday in April and the last Sunday in October – though there's a seven-hour time difference for two weeks of the year.

TIPPING Many first-time visitors to the US think of tipping as a potential source of huge embarrassment. It's nothing of the sort; tipping is universally expected, and you quickly learn to tip without a second thought. You really shouldn't depart a bar or restaurant without leaving a tip of *at least* 15 percent (unless the service is absolutely terrible). The whole system of service is predicated on tipping; not to do so causes a great deal of resentment, and will result in a short paypacket for the waiter or waitress at the end of the week. About the same amount should be added to taxi fares – and round them up to the nearest 50¢ or dollar. A hotel porter who has lugged your suitcases up several flights of stairs should get $3 to $5. When paying by credit or charge card, you're expected to add the tip to the total bill before filling in the amount and signing.

TRAVEL AGENTS *Council Travel,* 530 Bush St, Suite 700 (☎415/421-3473), and 2511 Channing Way, Berkeley (☎848-8604). *STA Travel,* 166 Geary St, Suite 702 , San Francisco (☎391-8407).

VENEREAL DISEASE HOTLINE ☎495-6463.

VIDEOS The standard format used for video cassettes in the US is different from that used in Britain. Recorded videos bought in the US are not compatible with video players bought in Britain, though blank tapes will work in video cameras.

The City

Chapter 1

Introducing The City

Surrounded on three sides by water, the land mass of San Francisco is scrunched up into the four dozen steep hills that give the city its beautiful setting, and serve as borders between its various sections. They also provide a good insight into San Francisco's class distinctions: as a general rule, geographical elevation is a stout indicator of wealth – the higher you live, the better off you are. Commercial square-footage is surprisingly small and is in any case mostly confined downtown.

However, San Francisco's undulations were not taken into account when its streets were laid out. Oblivious to topography, they follow a conventional grid, and thus will frequently climb straight up one side of a hill and then plummet down the other. In fact, Nob Hill, Russian Hill and Telegraph Hill, to name only the best known, are so steep that pavements often turn into stairways.

The best way to get a grip on what makes the city special is to walk. Armed with a good map you could plough through much of the city center in a day, although it's better to dawdle, unbound by itineraries: the most interesting districts, certainly, merit at least half a day each of just hanging about.

Downtown San Francisco, the obvious focus for your initial explorations, is examined in detail in our Chapter Two. This very compact area consists of three contradictory square miles crowded into the northeastern corner of the peninsula, between the hills and the bay. Situated to the north side of diagonal **Market Street**, the city's main commercial artery, its high-class stores and fancy hotels sit somewhat strangely between the poor, rather sleazy districts to the west and the exaggerated skyscrapers of the **Financial District** to the east (where the Transamerica Pyramid, for example, is clearly visible from almost anywhere in the city). Walk another block and you enter the more chaotic enclave of **Chinatown**, above which sits the otherworldly wealth of San Francisco's most famous peak, **Nob Hill**, from where the whole of downtown can be easily surveyed.

Chapter Three takes in something of a mixed bag, beginning just north of downtown, at the tip of the peninsula, with the old

See Chapters Twelve to Seventeen for comprehensive details of accommodation, restaurants and other facilities in San Francisco.

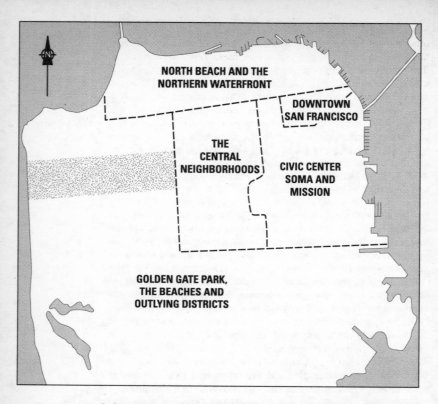

Italian enclave of **North Beach**. Despite gentrification, this popular neighborhood still harbors a vaguely bohemian population – a hangover from the days when the major Beat figures lived here. It's a good place for eating and drinking, with some of the city's best bars and restaurants. Further north, the hideous tat of **Fisherman's Wharf** is (for no good reason) the city's number-one tourist magnet, thronged by crowds jostling to cruise the bay, visit Alcatraz and buy cheap souvenirs and overpriced food. While by no means essential viewing, it does provide access to a lengthy bay-front promenade which takes you past exclusive, lofty neighborhoods such as **Pacific Heights** before leading into the vast expanse of cypress-lined avenues and windswept bluffs of the **Presidio**, ideal for long secluded walks and ocean-gazing across the orange spires of the **Golden Gate Bridge**.

Far from homogenized, San Francisco shocks every time you turn a corner: changes are abrupt and often unannounced. **Civic Center**, for example, a little way west of downtown and the starting point for Chapter Four, may be San Francisco's municipal and arts nucleus, holding some of the city's most grandiose architecture, but it's plonked awkwardly between the surrounding slums. Across the other side of Market Street, the **SoMa** (South of Market) neighborhood is renowned for its clubs and bars. Desolate during the daylight hours, it's neon-lit and buzzing by night. Further south and a whole lot funkier, you find yourself among the bars and restaurants of the vigorously Latin, non-stop **Mission** district.

Away from downtown and the commercial hubbub, San Francisco, not surprisingly, becomes more residential, made up of a patchwork of small and self-sufficient communities, largely defined by their distinct social and ethnic characteristics. Among the **Central Neighborhoods** explored in Chapter Five, the **Castro** has long been San Francisco's primary gay district – affluent, gentrified, and despite the sobering effects of AIDS still boasting an energetic bar scene and lots of good eating options. For voyeuristic strolling, the **Haight-Ashbury** is no less rewarding. Formerly the nucleus of San Francisco's 1960s counter-culture, its enduring air of radicalism is manifest in its left-wing bookshops, some tastefully tatty café society, and a smattering of residents still flying a slightly limp freak flag.

For an explanation of how to interpret addresses in San Francisco, see p.42

Finally, Chapter Six leads through the welcome tranquillity of **Golden Gate Park** – a gargantuan urban oasis that incorporates fine art museums, flower gardens and some convincingly bucolic open spaces – to some of San Francisco's most enthralling stretches of coastline, including the city's only **beaches**.

The 49-Mile Drive

If you have your own vehicle, you can orientate yourself – and see some of the best of San Francisco – by way of the **49-Mile Drive**, a route laid out around the city that takes in the most important scenic and historic points in about half a day. Marked by blue and white seagull signs, it circuits Civic Center, Japantown, Union Square, Chinatown, Nob Hill, North Beach and Telegraph Hill, before skirting Fisherman's Wharf and the Marina and Palace of Fine Arts – after which it passes the southern approach of the Golden Gate Bridge and winds through the Presidio. From here it sweeps along the ocean past the zoo and doubles back through Golden Gate Park, vaulting over Twin Peaks and dipping down to Mission Dolores and back to the waterfront for a drive by the Bay Bridge, Ferry Building and Financial District. Maps of the entire route are available (free) from the Visitor Information Center on Market Street at Powell where the cable cars turn around.

Chapter 2

Downtown San Francisco

S an Francisco spreads fairly evenly over most of its 49 square miles, but the greatest concentration of activity is in its oldest and easternmost plot, jammed between the waterfront and the steeply rising hills. It's difficult to draw clear borders, and the parameters shift according to who you ask, but most of what the locals call **downtown** is clustered within a square mile around the northern side of **Market Street** – San Francisco's main commercial and traffic drag, which bisects the northeastern corner of the peninsula. The area ends abruptly at the edge of the bay, where the vistas have been greatly improved by the recent tearing down of the Embarcadero Freeway.

In keeping with its quirky history, downtown San Francisco is a real mixed bag, conforming to no overall image: one block may be thronged with multinational banks and the young executives who work in them, another home to Chinese markets and sidewalk evangelists; turn the next corner and you'll find upscale department stores, private clubs and all the hallmarks of an affluent city.

The nearest thing to a center is **Union Square**, San Francisco's largest and liveliest urban space, populated in equal degree by high-style shoppers, eager street musicians and out-of-it tramps and beggars. As the city's main hotel and shopping district, and the junction of its major transportation lines, it makes a logical starting point for downtown wanderings. Leading off from the **Financial District** at the bottom of the hill (San Francisco's only real high-rise quarter), the most recently developed part of town is also the oldest – **Jackson Square** and the historic **Barbary Coast**, nestling inconspicuously in the shadows of the modern city. On the opposite side of the city center, and worlds away from the glitz and glamor, sits **Chinatown**, a dense and bustling warren of tacky stores and tasty restaurants that's home to the second largest Chinese community outside Asia.

As with most of central San Francisco, **walking** is the best way of seeing all this, though from Union Square you can hop on a cable car up the steep incline of **Nob Hill** to check out the grand mansions of old San Francisco's moneyed elite. It's possible, if exhausting, to cover the entire downtown area in a day; it's not particularly large. But unless you're on the tightest of schedules you'll get much more out of downtown (and indeed all of San Francisco) just mooching around.

Union Square and around

Though the area around **UNION SQUARE** may not top your list of places to see in San Francisco, it's home to most of the city's hotels, and some noteworthy bars and restaurants. As a result it's usually thronged with tourists and locals in equal numbers. During the lunch hour office workers spread out with a picnic to watch the street performers who gather. The square is also the heart of the city's shopping district, and draws a fairly ritzy crowd: limousines are bumper-to-bumper on the surrounding streets – Powell, Geary, Post and Stockton – and the well-heeled pop in and out of pricey department stores, in sharp contrast to the bums and winos from the nearby Tenderloin, and the increasing numbers of homeless people who sprawl across the open space's green patches, hoping to do a brisk trade panhandling from passing shoppers.

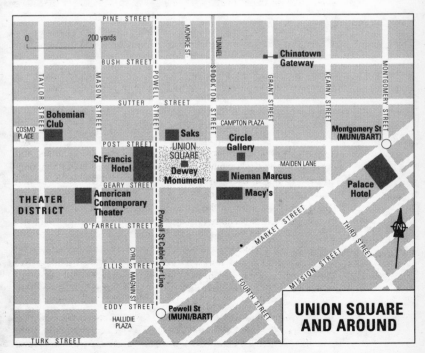

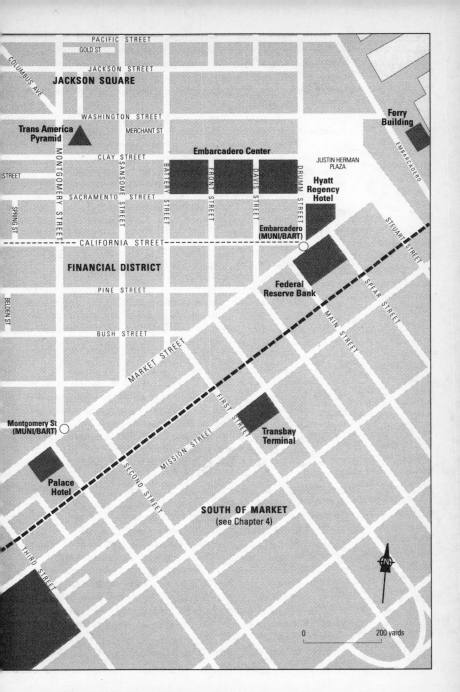

Union Square and around

Union Square takes its name from the mass meetings held here on the eve of the Civil War to pledge loyalty to the Union. The modern-day square also sees its fair share of protests, and, given its strategic commercial and transportation location, a well-organized demonstration (often by the gay community) can usually draw traffic to a halt. Drably landscaped, save a few palms, and mostly paved over, its main feature is the **Dewey Monument**, a pigeon-crowded Corinthian column in the center, topped by a miniature statue of winged Victory put up in 1904 to mark Admiral Dewey's naval successes in the Spanish-American War. More recently, in 1975, Union Square saw Sarah Jane Moore, a member of the Manson "family", attempt to assassinate President Gerald Ford outside the exclusive **St Francis Hotel** on Powell Street, facing the square – a regular temporary home to visiting dignitaries, changing its flags to honor the country of its more important guests. Nothing so flash for Queen Elizabeth II, who had to be put up at the tacky **Sir Francis Drake Hotel**, one block up Powell, when the Britannia broke down during a West Coast tour in the late 1970s.

The *St Francis* was a location in Francis Ford Coppola's paranoid post-Watergate film *The Conversation*, in which surveillance expert Gene Hackman spied on lovers strolling in the square from his hotel room. The hotel played a similar role in many of **Dashiell Hammett's** detective stories, as well as in his own life. In the 1920s Hammett worked there as an operative for the Pinkerton Detective Agency, investigating the notorious rape and murder case against the silent movie comedian Fatty Arbuckle. When Hammett later came to write *The Maltese Falcon* and other classic tales, he modelled many of the locations on the *St Francis*, though nothing in the hotel makes anything of the connection. One of surprisingly few ventures that does capitalize on the Hammett link is *John's Grill* at 63 Ellis St. It's been there since 1908 and looks it, with walls covered in Hammett memorabilia.

The sort of shady characters who inhabited Hammett's fictional world would today be more at home west of Union Square along Geary Street in what's optimistically called the **THEATER DISTRICT**. As in New York's Times Square, or London's Soho, the Theater District of San Francisco shares space with less rarefied entertainments, namely porn and prostitution, that spill over from the neighboring Tenderloin section near the Civic Center, and in fact the legitimate theater scene here is small and not highly rated (San Francisco has always been much better at the extremes – at the cutting edge of avant-garde performance, or in high-powered opera productions – than it has at mimicking Broadway). The flagship *American Conservatory Theater* playhouse at 415 Geary St has recently re-opened following a major restructuring to repair damage from the 1989 quake that almost rocked it to its foundations; the city's best theatrical space, its return was most welcome.

Music, theater and dance options are detailed from p.241 onwards.

Also part of this district, just north of the Square along Post and Sutter, are downtown's least visible landmarks – though the casual visitor might never suspect their existence, some fourteen private clubs are hidden away behind these discreet facades. Money isn't the only criterion for membership of these highly esteemed institutions, though being *somebody* usually is. Most notorious is the **Bohemian Club** at Post and Taylor. Better known for its *Bohemian Grove* retreat at the Russian River, where ex-presidents and corporate giants get together for masonic rituals and schoolboy larks, the club is housed in a Lewis Hobart Moderne-style building that includes a large theater, as well as more predictable amenities like a bar and good restaurant. Organized in the late 1800s by newspapermen and artists, it evolved into a businessmen's club with an arty slant (during its golden age, members included Frank Norris, Ambrose Bierce and Jack London), though these days the membership – all male – includes some of America's biggest political and business movers and shakers. A bronze cornerstone bears an owl (the club's emblem) and the motto "Weaving Spiders Come Not Here".

Union Square's claim to fame as **shopping** heaven is supported by the presence of large department stores such as *Macy's, Saks Fifth Avenue* and *Neiman Marcus* – the latter worth a look for its marvellous stained-glass rotunda, preserved from the old *City of Paris* store which stood on the site until Phillip Johnson did an uninspired job of designing the new store in 1982. The unlikely named *Gump's*, at 250 Post St, just off the square, is San Francisco's homegrown equivalent of *Liberty's* in London, specializing in Oriental fabrics and Art-Nouveau objects, and renowned for its museumworthy collection of jade figures. Elsewhere on this block you'll find the likes of *Gucci, Tiffany* and *Cartier*, though the most attractive place to window-shop is undoubtedly **Maiden Lane**, a chic little urban walkway that leads out of the square half a block south. Before the 1906 earthquake and fire this was supposedly one of the city's roughest areas, where homicides averaged around ten a month, and prostitutes displayed themselves behind open windows. Nowadays, aside from some prohibitively expensive boutiques, its main feature is San Francisco's only Frank Lloyd Wright building, the pricey little **Circle Gallery** at no 140 – a try-out for the Guggenheim in New York. Inside, a gently curving ramp rises towards the skylighted ceiling past some hugely expensive artwork, while in the cases on the lower floor fine china and crystal command equally high prices.

If you're moving on from Union Square, **cable cars** run along the Powell Street side of Union Square but are usually too packed to board. If you want to ride one up to Nob Hill – or on to the waterfront – try squeezing on a block or so up the hill, or line up with everybody else at the Market Street start, near the **Visitor Information Center**. Better still, wander east into the Financial District's looming forest of steel and glass towers.

The Financial District

The **FINANCIAL DISTRICT** is San Francisco's most highly charged neighborhood – and the city's phenomenal recent development is never more apparent than in these few small blocks, into which are crammed 38 million square feet of office space. Scattered among the banks and insurance companies are the copy centers and computer boutiques that serve the offices above, with an occasional restaurant of note – jam-packed at lunchtimes but otherwise deserted (and especially so at weekends). Sharp-suited workers clog the streets in well-mannered rush-hour droves, racing between the Montgomery *BART/ Muni* station on Market Street and their offices. As financial quarters go, San Francisco's is not unattractive, but there's not a great deal to come here for if you're not a high-rolling wheeler-dealer. However, it does constitute a virtually comprehensive library of architectural styles and periods, from Palladian piles to post-modern redoubts, though the old-style banking halls have been overshadowed since the frenetic building boom of the 1970s, when they became flanked by newer, taller structures. To avert the wholesale demolition of the area for more profitable towers, the city is nowadays directing new development to the south of Market Street.

The bars and restaurants of downtown San Francisco are detailed on the map on p.212.

Montgomery Street has been at the heart of San Francisco's business life since the Gold Rush, when it formed the young town's waterfront. To capture the trade of arriving prospectors, canny merchants built long wharves from their Montgomery Street warehouses across the mud flats which stretched out into the bay. Since then the shoreline has been filled in and built on. Many of the cross streets – Commercial, Clay and Washington – were simply constructed on top of the old docks, and today's steel and glass towers conceal the remains of over 100 wooden vessels abandoned in the haste to get to the mines. Nowadays tagged "the Wall Street of the West", Montgomery Street is still the main artery of the Financial District, but the contrast between generations is stark: the Ionic columns and robust stone details of the 1922 **Security Pacific Bank**, at Montgomery and California, are thoroughly overpowered by the ominous hulk of the former **Bank of America** headquarters across the street. Though not the tallest, this broad-shouldered monolith of dark red granite is surely the biggest thing on the San Francisco skyline, in the early 1970s challenging the city not only with its size, but also with the startling contrast of its hue – San Francisco used to be known as "a city of white". Ironically, the bank founded here in 1904 was forced to sell off the otherwise characterless tower in the early 1980s as a result of its over-zealous lending to developing countries. On the California Street side of the tower is a small plaza with a sleek granite sculpture grandly entitled *Transcendence*, though some San Franciscans have dubbed it *The Banker's Heart*.

The other widely hated Financial District monster is **101 California Street** between Front and Davis, a graceless structure – the biggest of Phillip Johnson's creations in the city and probably the least successful product of his post-modern dotage. This 48-storey serrated glass and granite cylinder rests, in all its bulk, upon a wedge and plaza. The lobby fancies itself as a greenhouse and has been rudely shoved between the tower's spindly legs. The potted

The Financial District

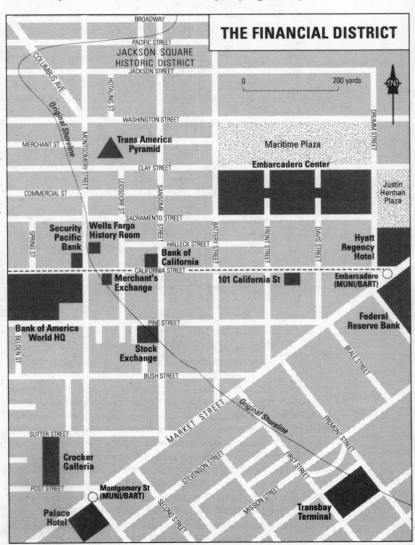

THE FINANCIAL DISTRICT

BROADWAY

PACIFIC STREET

JACKSON SQUARE
HISTORIC DISTRICT

JACKSON STREET

COLUMBUS AVE

Original Shoreline

HOTALING ST

WASHINGTON STREET

0   200 yards

N

DRUMM STREET

MERCHANT ST

MONTGOMERY STREET

Trans America
Pyramid

CLAY STREET

Maritime Plaza

Embarcadero Center

COMMERCIAL ST

LEIDSDORF ST

SANSOME STREET

Justin
Herman
Plaza

SACRAMENTO STREET

SPRING ST

Security
Pacific
Bank

Wells Fargo
History Room

HALLECK STREET

Bank of
California

BATTERY STREET

FRONT STREET

DAVIS STREET

Hyatt
Regency
Hotel

CALIFORNIA STREET

Merchant's
Exchange

101 California St

Embarcadero
(MUNI/BART)

Bank of America
World HQ

BELDEN ST

PINE STREET

Stock
Exchange

BUSH STREET

Federal
Reserve Bank

BEALE STREET

MARKET STREET

Original Shoreline

FREMONT STREET

SUTTER STREET

Crocker
Galleria

POST STREET

Montgomery St
(MUNI/BART)

STEVENSON STREET

SECOND STREET

FIRST STREET

MISSION STREET

Palace
Hotel

Transbay
Terminal

plants inside cry out for sunshine in the land of high-rise shadows and are removed regularly for therapeutic purposes. The people who work here are less fortunate.

Surprisingly, some fine **art** is tucked away in hidden corners of the district. Several blocks north, the **Merchants' Exchange Building** at 465 California St has a series of nineteenth-century marine paintings by Irish painter William Coulter. At the entrance of its **Grain Exchange Hall** are four huge columns, beyond which the six vast oil canvases depict the history of San Francisco as a seaport. This room was the original center of commercial life in the city, monitoring the comings and goings of every Pacific Coast ship. It was also the place where shippers, warehousemen and traders would gather to do their bidding.

If you want to get a better sense of San Francisco's historic importance as the financial center of the West, a handful of places deserve a quick look. The old **Stock Exchange** building at 310 Pine St is sadly closed to the public nowadays, but it's an impressive structure from the outside – not the original, but a 1930s Art-Deco monument fronted by musclebound figures. The **Wells Fargo History Room**, 420 Montgomery St (Mon–Fri 10am–5pm; free), details the origins of San Francisco's banking and financial boom with exhibits from the days of the Gold Rush. Mining equipment, gold nuggets, photographs and even an old stagecoach show the far-from-slick roots of the city's big money. The **Museum of the Money of the American West**, in the Bank of California at 400 California St (Mon–Thurs 10.30am–3pm; free), offers a similar range of gold nuggets and the like, and for a more hands-on grasp of the dynamics of modern finance, you should try the Economics Gallery in the **Federal Reserve Bank** (see below).

If negotiating the charging throngs down on the street is too much, you can always just gaze down on them from the rooftop garden of the **Crocker Galleria** at 1 Montgomery St. Skip the three floors of expensive boutiques and opt for a packed lunch with the office workers.

The Transamerica Pyramid

The landmark **Transamerica Pyramid**, indisputably the most memorable signature of San Francisco's skyline, serves as a useful dividing-point between the various downtown areas. Though the streets around it are oddly quiet considering the vitality of surrounding districts, the 855-foot tower, San Francisco's tallest, is a hinge marking the transition from the towers of the Financial District to the low-level tangle of North Beach and Chinatown. The pyramid arose amid a city-planning furore that earned it the name of "Pereira's Prick", after its LA-based architect William Pereira. However, since then it has been accepted as a notable addition, in these days of plump speculative buildings, as a rare example of an architecture which sacrifices the pragmatic to the symbolic. The 48-storey structure is capped by a colossal architectural ornament – a slender 212-foot hollow spire, lit from within. As the building tapers upwards, the floors that fetch the highest rents diminish in area; in other words, the pyramid, from a real estate perspective, would be far more valuable upside down.

Regular art exhibits are displayed in the lobby, and there's an observatory on the 27th floor, though this is fairly unremarkable, and you get the feeling that it should be higher. Nonetheless, it's free during business hours, and for that reason alone is worth a ride up in the elevator. Look in also on the small **redwood grove** on the east side of the building, landscaped with eighty redwoods from the Santa Cruz mountains, giving the building the appearance of an artificial mountain, with its own forest at its feet.

A brass plaque in the lobby is the sole reminder that this was once the site of San Francisco's prime literary and artistic crossroads, the **Montgomery Block**. From 1853, when it was built, until 1959, when it was torn down and made into a parking lot, the four-storey Montgomery Block was the city's most important meeting place. Though built as an office block for lawyers, doctors and businessmen, it was soon taken over by writers and newspapermen, and evolved into a live-in community of bohemian poets, artists and political radicals. Ambrose Bierce, Bret Harte and Joaquin Miller were frequent visitors to its bar and restaurant, and Mark Twain met a fireman named **Tom Sawyer** – who later opened a popular San Francisco saloon – in the basement steam baths. Later habitues included George Sterling, Maynard Dixon and **Sun Yat-sen**, who devised the successful overthrow of the Manchu Dynasty while running a local newspaper, *Young China*, from his second-floor office.

Jackson Square: the Barbary Coast

A century or so ago, the eastern flank of what is now the Financial District formed part of the "**Barbary Coast**", a rough-and-tumble waterfront district packed with saloons and brothels where hapless young male visitors were given "Mickey Finns" and "shanghaied" into involuntary servitude on merchant ships. The district centered on Pacific Street, which was known as "Terrific Street" until World War II, when its wicked reputation made it off-limits to military personnel. Many of the old dives died an inevitable death, but a few structures survived the 1906 earthquake and fire, and, during the 1930s, the Barbary Coast became a low-rent district that attracted artists and writers, including Diego Rivera, who had a studio on Gold Street at the height of his fame as the "communist painter sought after by the world's biggest capitalists". Most of these old structures have since been restored and preserved as the **Jackson Square Historic District** – not in fact a square, but a rectangle formed by Jackson, Montgomery, Gold and Sansome streets, making up a few dense blocks of low-rise, mostly brick buildings that now house the offices of advertising agencies and design firms, as well as some fairly ritzy restaurants and watering holes that feed the style-conscious workers therein.

It's more a place for aimless wandering – **Gold Street** and **Hotaling Place**, the narrow alleys off Jackson Street, are best – than for searching out specific highlights, but it does hold a few noteworthy sights. Now an office block, 415 Jackson St was the original Ghirardelli chocolate factory, later moved north to what's now Ghirardelli Square, close by Fisherman's Wharf. At the heart of the district, the survival of **Hotaling's Whisky Distillery** at 455 Jackson inspired this post-earthquake poetic ditty:

> *If, as they say, God spanked the town*
> *for being over frisky*
> *Why did He burn His churches down*
> *and save Hotaling's Whisky?*

Pacific Avenue, originally Pacific Street, the old heart of the Barbary Coast, is now perhaps the most anodyne stretch of the Jackson Square district, though Montgomery Street, at its western edge, holds a number of handsome facades, many with further literary and libertine associations.

Just down from Jackson Street, 732 Montgomery St was the home of San Francisco's first literary magazine, the *Golden Era*, founded in the 1850s, which helped launch the careers of Bret Harte and Mark Twain. Writers John Steinbeck and William Saroyan later spent many a night drinking in the vanished *Black Cat Café* down the street. In the middle of the block, **722–728 Montgomery Street**, where Oscar Wilde paid a visit to the artist Jules Tavernier during his whirlwind visit to San Francisco in 1882, has had its original stucco stripped and been done up in overwrought Victorian mode. In its time, the building has been a theater, Turkish bath, tobacco warehouse and auction room; today you can peer through the windows and see the fascinating, if excessive, clutter and career mementoes of flamboyant San Francisco lawyer, Melvin Belli, which fill the place.

The Embarcadero

At the northeastern edge of the Financial District, the small waterfront district known as **THE EMBARCADERO** separates the city from the bay. Before the building during the 1930s of the bridges that connect the city to Oakland and Marin County, the Embarcadero was the main point of arrival for 50,000 cross-bay commuters daily. It's still a transportation hub, but the main focus of the area is now a satellite city of offices, hotels and stores housed in four huge modern blocks, recently freed from the shadow of the contentious freeway that shared its name.

The Embarcadero Freeway was badly weakened during the 1989 earthquake. Its subsequent fate aroused passionate debate between the traders who relied on its capacity to move traffic around town, and the aesthetes who thought it spoiled the view of the bay. There was never any question about its efficiency, and driving across it at night, approximately level with the tenth floor of the skyscrapers, was something of a thrill. But typically the citizens of San Francisco put beauty before progress; after some fierce debating, down it finally came in 1992.

Commuters from Marin County still arrive at the **Ferry Building** at the water's edge, at the foot of California Street. Modelled on the Moorish cathedral tower in Seville, this small-scale dignified structure is positively dwarfed by the looming structures of the Financial District; and although recently freed from the obscurity imposed by the Embarcadero Freeway, there is not much to suggest its former importance.

North and south from the foot of Market Street (which focuses on a fine view of Twin Peaks) stretches San Francisco's once-vital five-mile-long **waterfront**. Now deathly quiet, it was alive during the first half of the century to the sights and sounds of huge ships loading and unloading cargo at what was still the main point of arrival for goods and people to the city. It was also the site of one of the more notorious episodes of twentieth-century San Francisco, when, on the eve of America's involvement in World War I, on July 22, 1916, ten members of a massive pro-war demonstration were killed by a bomb. Though there was no tangible evidence of any link, opposition to US intervention in the war led to the city's union leaders being held responsible for the attack, and charged and found guilty (on perjured testimony) of murder. Tom Mooney, a prominent longshoremen's activist, was sentenced to death, and it took twenty years of lobbying and protest (by Emma Goldman among others) before he was freed and his name cleared. His alleged co-conspirator, Warren Billings, spent most of his life behind bars before being pardoned in 1961. The site of the bombing is now filled by the brick fortress headquarters of the **Southern Pacific Railroad Corporation**.

Across the street, you can wander inside the angular **Hyatt Regency** hotel and gaze up into its twenty-storey-high atrium lobby, filled with pot plants, trees and a fountain/sculpture set in a reflecting pool. An amusing novelty is the rooftop *Equinox* revolving bar. The hotel is part of the enormous **Embarcadero Center** development, sponsored by the celebrated eastern Rockefeller family and originally to have borne their name. Somehow "Rockefeller Center West" was an appellation that didn't sit so well on the Barbary Coast: San Francisco sees itself in no sense as subordinate to the Big Apple and is only begrudgingly part of the same state as the Big Orange. The four tower-slabs of the Center rise from a multi-level base of offices, stores and cafés that

The bars and restaurants of downtown San Francisco are detailed on the map on p.212.

stretch for several blocks east around the **Justin Herman Plaza**. A large paved space, this is largely unused except for the skateboarders who alone can appreciate such vast stretches of concrete, although it did see some excitement when U2 staged an unannounced concert here in February 1988. For the best part of the day the city came to a standstill as people left their offices and abandoned their shopping, hoping to catch a glimpse of the visiting megastars. Someone hung a banner from an office window that read "SF loves U2" – lead singer Bono misinterpreted the SF for Sinn Fein and after a vitriolic outburst threatened to cancel the gig. Whoops.

Nearby at 101 Market St, the **Federal Reserve Bank** (Mon–Fri 10am–4pm; free) is an unbeatable amusement if you're at all interested in the machinations of money in the city. Computer games allow you to engineer your own stock-market disasters, while gallery exhibits detail recent scandals and triumphs in the financial world.

Outside the bank is the starting point of the California Street cable car line, which leads you out of the Financial District, past Chinatown and up to Nob Hill.

Nob Hill

Nob Hill, the hill of palaces, must certainly be counted the best part of San Francisco. It is there that the millionaires are gathered together vying with each other in display. From thence, looking down over the business wards of the city, we can decry a building with a little belfry, and that is the stock exchange, the heart of San Francisco: a great pump we might call it, continually pumping up the savings of the lower quarter to the pockets of the millionaires on the hill.

Robert Louis Stevenson

If the Financial District is where money is made in the city, the posh hotels and masonic institutions of **NOB HILL**, just above, are where it is shown off. In a city famous for its hills, this one tops the lot. It is, as Joan Didion wrote, "the symbolic nexus of all old California money and power", and remains San Francisco's most revered address, its mansions, exclusive hotels and restaurants looking snootily down over the lower areas of the city. Traditionally, San Francisco's moneyed elite preferred level streets, and it was the invention of the cable car in the 1870s that turned this from an inaccessible backwater into a slice of prime real estate. At its summit, the hill is 338 feet above sea level, offering fantastic views of the city below.

While the Nob Hill area may hold very few real sights as such, just nosing around, or calling into the grand hotels for a drink in their rooftop bars, is pleasant enough, taking in the aura of privilege and luxury that distinguishes the neighborhood and enjoying the views over the city and beyond.

When the transcontinental railroad barons made their fortune, they had no doubts about where to invest it. Originally called the California Street Hill, the area became known as Nob Hill after the **Big Four** robber-baron industrialists, Collis P Huntington, Charles Crocker, Mark Hopkins and Leland Stanford, who had made millions on the Central Pacific Railroad, and the bonanza kings of the silver mines of the Comstock Lode, built their mansions here in the 1880s. Sadly, only one of these ostentatious piles survived the 1906 fire, the brownstone mansion of James C Flood, which cost a cool million dollars in 1886 – now the **Pacific Union Club**, a private retreat for the ultra-rich on California Street at Mason. Behind the club sits **Huntington Park**, not the finest of San Francisco's small parks but a good place to watch nannies push the power-brokers of the future around in their prams. The mansions of other millionaires were not so fortunate, and their former sites now hold some of San Francisco's grandest **hotels**: along California Street, the *Mark Hopkins*, with its spectacular rooftop bar, the *Stanford Court*, the elegant *Huntington* and the strikingly-lobbied *Fairmont* all quietly compete for the top-dollar trade.

Impressive though they are, none of these buildings can compete for effect with the hill's biggest hunk of aspirational architecture, the mock-Gothic **Grace Cathedral** across Huntington Park from the Pacific Union Club (daily 7am–6pm, with free tours Mon–Fri 1–3pm, Sat 11.30am–1.30pm & Sun 12.15–2pm – the highlight is definitely the choral service on Sundays at 11am with a coffee hour afterwards). Originally, the block the cathedral stands on was occupied by the homes of the Crocker family, who donated the site to the Episcopal Church after losing their houses in the 1906 fire. Construction began soon after, though most of it was built of faintly disguised reinforced concrete in the early 1960s. The interior shelters an eleventh-century French altar and Renaissance reredos, but the carillon in the bell tower is a contemporary addition from Croydon, England. One part that's worth a look is the entrance, adorned with faithful replicas of the doors of the Florence Baptistry; study, too, the allegorical stained glass around the cathedral walls.

Chinatown

Hemmed in by moneyed neighbors, plumb at the foot of Nob Hill and just three blocks from Union Square, the two dozen square blocks of constant chaos that make up **CHINATOWN** are completely distinct from any other neighborhood in the city. The gateway arches that mark Chinatown's borders seem barely able to contain the district, and it's by far the city's most thickly populated quarter, with over 80,000 residents in a quarter-mile area. Though home to the second largest community of Chinese outside Asia, it's no longer solely Chinese: Vietnamese, Thais, Filipinos and Koreans

Chinatown

have all made inroads over recent years, further adding to the dynamism of the neighborhood. Noisy, smelly, colorful and overcrowded, Chinatown manages to retain a degree of genuine autonomy, despite its obvious reliance on the tourist dollar, with its own schools, banks and newspapers alongside the predictable morass of souvenir stores. Fortunately, most of the tourist pandering goes on along the main street, Grant Avenue, off which dark, gloomy alleyways thread between buildings that house the real Chinatown of grocery stores, laundries, temples and bakeries. Looming ominously and casting tall, dark shadows over the small, often unkempt buildings are the massive gleaming monoliths of the Financial District. Contrasts don't come much cruder.

The first Chinese arrived in Northern California in the late 1840s, many of them fleeing famine and the Opium Wars at home and seeking the easy fortunes of the Gold Rush. Later, in the 1870s, thousands more came across to build the Transcontinental Railroad. At first the Chinese, or "coolies" as they were called (taken from the words *ku li*, meaning "bitter toil"), were accepted as hard-working laborers, but as the railroad neared completion and unemployment rose, many moved to San Francisco, swelling what was already a sizeable community. The city didn't extend much of a welcome: jingoistic sentiment turned quickly into a tide of racial hatred, manifest in sometimes vicious attacks that bound the Chinese defensively into a solid, homogenous community.

The population stagnated until the 1960s, when the lifting of the anti-Chinese immigration restrictions swelled numbers to close on 160,000. Nowadays the Chinese are the city's most affluent ethnic group: by day the area seethes with activity and congestion; by night the traffic moves a little easier, but the blaze of neon and marauding diners gives the feeling that it just never lets up. Overcrowding is compounded by a brisk tourist trade, and Chinatown boasts some of the most egregiously tacky shops and facades in the city. Genuine snatches of ethnicity are sullied by pseudo-Chinese Americana at every turn.

You can approach Chinatown from all sides: Nob Hill drops down to its center, North Beach blends into its upper reaches and the Financial District flanks it to the east. Coming from the south and Union Square, you enter through the large **dragon-clad archway** that crosses the intersection of Bush Street and **Grant Avenue** – a gift from the Government of Taiwan and, judging by the look of it, not one that broke the bank. Once through here, Grant Avenue seems suddenly much narrower, crowded with gold-ornamented portals and brightly painted balconies which sit above the souvenir stores and restaurants. Plastic buddhas, floppy hats and chopsticks assault the eye from every doorway. The least obviously Chinese of these false fronts, a horseshoe-shaped funnel at 916 Grant Ave, marks one of the very few **bars** in Chinatown – *Li Po's*, named after the great Chinese poet and still something of a literary hang-out. Some of the **restaurants**, too, are historical landmarks, none more so than *Sam Woh's* at 813 Washington St – cheap and churlish exhaunt of the Beats and still a popular late-night hang-out in which, legend has it, Gary Snyder taught Jack Kerouac to eat with chopsticks and had them both thrown out for his loud and passionate interpretation of Zen poetry.

Chinatown's restaurants are listed on p.213.

Before the days of all-consuming tourism, Grant Avenue was known as Dupont Street, an ensemble of opium dens, bordellos and gambling huts terrorized by *tongs* – **gangs** who took it upon themselves to police and protect their district in any (usually violent) way they saw fit. Their original purpose was to retaliate against racial hooliganism, but they developed quickly into Mafia-style familyfeuding – as bloody as any of the Chicago gangland wars. These days there isn't much trace of them on the streets, but the mobs continue to operate, battling for a slice of the lucrative West Coast drug trade.

Parallel to Grant, **Stockton Street** is closer to the real thing – Chinatown's main street, crammed with exotic fish and fruit and vegetable markets, bakeries and spice stores; your dollar will go further here than anywhere else in the neighborhood and your search for the authentic face of Chinatown will be better rewarded, especially if you can manage an early rise. Between Grant and

Chinatown

Stockton, at the center of Chinatown, jumbled alleys hold the most worthwhile stops in the area. The best of these is **Waverly Place**, a two-block corridor that was lined with brothels before the 1906 catastrophe and is now the site of most of Chinatown's many family associations and community support groups. It's also home to two opulently decorated but skilfully hidden **temples** (nos 109–11 and 123–129), their interiors a riot of black, gold and vermillion. They're still in use today and open to visitors, but the variable opening times mean you'll have to take pot luck to get in. Nearby, Chinatown's history is well documented in the **Chinese Historical Society of America** at 650 Commercial St (daily 9am–4pm; donations), which traces the beginnings of the Chinese in the US and has a small but worthy collection of photographs, paintings and artefacts from the pioneering days of the last century.

Another, more accessible, point of interest is the **Buddha's Universal Church** at 720 Washington St, where America's largest Zen sect give tours on the second and fourth Sunday of each month. This five-storey building was painstakingly built by the sect-members from an exotic range of polished woods, adorned everywhere by mosaic images of the Buddha. Across the street at 743 Washington, the triple-tiered pagoda of the **Bank of Canton** once housed the multilingual operators of the Chinatown telephone exchange, and the site was earlier the home of the *California Star* newspaper – the city's first daily, and the one that announced the discovery of gold in 1848. Not as rich with history, the **Chinese Cultural Center**, tucked away inside the *Holiday Inn* at 750 Kearny St (Tues–Sat 10am–4pm), nonetheless has a regular programme of art shows, mostly contemporary, that give much needed exhibition space for the Chinese artistic community. A concrete footbridge connects the *Holiday Inn* and the Cultural Center with the larger of Chinatown's two green spaces, **Portsmouth Square**. This was the old center of the city, and the place where Sam Brannan announced the discovery of gold – an event that transformed San Francisco from a sleepy Spanish pueblo into a frontier town. Though not the most attractive of parks these days – like Union Square, it's built on top of a multistorey car park – it's nonetheless an oasis in a very cramped part of town. Old men come to play chess while younger ones fly past on skateboards. In the northwest corner there's a statue of the galleon *Hispaniola* from *Treasure Island*, a monument to Robert Louis Stevenson – who, while waiting for his lover's divorce to come through in 1879, used to come here and write. The other, smaller park, **St Mary's Square**, two blocks south, is dwarfed by a wall of Financial District skyscrapers and marks the western edge of their permissible development. The square holds a bold, modernist sculpture of Sun Yat-Sen, founder of the Chinese republic. Its modern lines would look misplaced anywhere in the neighborhood, but do so particularly here, where the little old ladies do their modest Tai Chi routines of a morning.

Chapter 3

North Beach and the Northern Waterfront

rom the highly exclusive to the downright offensive, San Francisco's **NORTHERN WATERFRONT** gives you the best and the worst of the city. Before the area came to rest on landfill, the original waterfront was the aptly named **North Beach**, a sunny neighborhood in a wind-sheltered valley between two hills in the northeastern corner of the peninsula, which despite gentrification has managed to weather the changes with its Italian foundations intact. As one of the city's oldest neighborhoods, it has an appealing worn-in feeling; it's a wonderful area for just hanging around cafés and bars and weaving through its gently sloping streets.

Within walking distance, flanking either side of North Beach, **Russian** and **Telegraph hills** are more residential in flavor, though they, too, are good for strolling and taking in the views of the waterfront – an attractive stretch on the whole, apart from the eyesore that is **Fisherman's Wharf**. As the major focus of tourist activity, you'll have to plough through a lot of overpriced tat and commercial gimmicks here to find what remains of the almost obsolete fishing industry: thronged by hundreds of dollar-dropping visitors, it is as crowded as it is unappealing.

As you move west from the Wharf, things start to improve: **Aquatic Park** is a small **beach** that draws a few hardy bathers, though better known as the home of the **Maritime Museum**. It's used as a walk-through on the way to **Fort Mason** – an old military installation that was rescued from the clutches of development and now has an impressive grouping of small museums, workshops, theaters and an excellent youth hostel. Continuing west, the waterfront becomes a focus for the fancy yacht clubs that make up the northernmost tip of the **Marina** district, with its neighbor **Pacific Heights**, a desirable district that thrives on its exclusivity and has little to offer the visitor beyond a mild envy and the distinctive

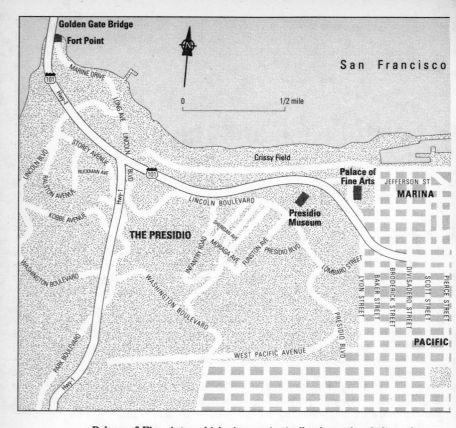

Palace of Fine Arts, which rises majestically above the skyline of
expensive homes. If you're a keen walker, you may want to trudge
the extra mile to the sizeable chunk of open green space that covers
the remainder of the northern waterfront. **The Presidio** is a former
army base that has been turned over to public use. There's not an
awful lot there, but its eucalyptus groves provide an inspiring
approach to the orange spires of the city's most famous landmark,
the **Golden Gate Bridge**.

North Beach

Starting from the base of the Transamerica Pyramid, **Columbus
Avenue** cuts diagonally through the heart of one of San Francisco's
most wanderable quarters, **NORTH BEACH**. This was indeed a
beach before landfill pushed back the bay; nowadays, resting in the
hollow between Russian and Telegraph hills, North Beach likes to

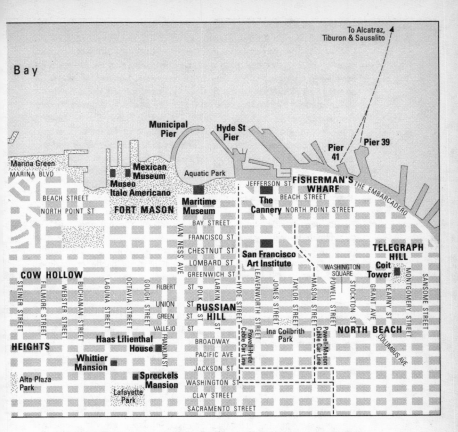

Bay

To Alcatraz, ◢
Tiburon & Sausalito

Municipal Pier
Hyde St Pier
Pier 39
Pier 41

Marina Green
MARINA BLVD

Mexican Museum
Aquatic Park
FISHERMAN'S WHARF
THE EMBARCADERO

Museo Italo Americano
JEFFERSON ST
BEACH STREET

BEACH STREET
NORTH POINT ST
FORT MASON
Maritime Museum
The Cannery
NORTH POINT STREET

BAY STREET

FRANCISCO ST

VAN NESS AVE
CHESTNUT ST
San Francisco Art Institute
TELEGRAPH HILL

LOMBARD ST
Coit Tower

COW HOLLOW
GREENWICH ST
WASHINGTON SQUARE

STEINER STREET
FILLMORE STREET
WEBSTER STREET
BUCHANAN STREET
LAGUNA STREET
OCTAVIA STREET
GOUGH STREET
FILBERT ST
POLK ST
LARKIN ST
HYDE STREET
LEAVENWORTH STREET
JONES STREET
TAYLOR STREET
MASON STREET
POWELL STREET
STOCKTON STREET
GRANT AVE
KEARNY ST
MONTGOMERY STREET
SANSOME STREET

UNION ST
GREEN ST
VALLEJO ST
RUSSIAN HILL

Powell/Hyde Cable Car Line
Ina Coolbrith Park
Powell/Mason Cable Car Line
NORTH BEACH
COLUMBUS AVE

HEIGHTS
Haas Lilienthal House
BROADWAY

PACIFIC AVE

Whittier Mansion
JACKSON ST

Alta Plaza Park
Spreckels Mansion
WASHINGTON ST

Lafayette Park
CLAY STREET

SACRAMENTO STREET

think of itself as the happening district of San Francisco. Originally
it was the city's Italian quarter, with, at its peak during the 1940s,
some 60,000 mostly northern Italians living within its boundaries.
With the increased prosperity and mobility that followed the war,
many left the area, and as rents came down the disenchanted
children of postwar America moved in. Since this migration of the
1950s, when the more prominent figures of the **Beat movement**
gathered here, it has been among the city's most sought-after
sectors for anyone vaguely alternative. It still has a certain Italian
slant, and is home to some of the city's best bars and restaurants,
but rocketing real estate prices are inevitably bringing about
change, and die-hard free-thinkers wrestle to maintain their territory
amidst the growing numbers of suave young professionals slumming
it at North Beach's traditionally scruffy cafés. That said, there's still
a solid core, and the anecdotes connected with North Beach remain
legion – get chatting to any barfly over fifty, they seem to know
them all.

The bars and restaurants of North Beach are detailed on the map on p.215.

North Beach

The southern edge of the district is visually anchored by the green flatiron **Columbus Tower**, situated on the island formed by Columbus, Kearny and Jackson streets and looking somewhat surreal against the corporate backdrop of the downtown skyline. Developers have been trying to knock this down for years, but the efforts of its owner, San Francisco-based filmmaker Francis Ford Coppola, have so far ensured its survival. Across Columbus, the now defunct *Purple Onion* nightclub, and the *Hungry i* down Jackson Street, hosted some of the biggest names of the 1950s San Francisco scene. Politically conscious comedians like Mort Sahl, Dick Gregory and the legendary Lenny Bruce performed here, as did San Francisco author Maya Angelou, in her earlier guise of singer and dancer. These landmarks have now closed or changed beyond recognition, but the district still trades on a reputation earned decades ago.

For more on the City Lights, *see* *p.260.*

Another North Beach literary landmark, the **City Lights Bookstore**, stands two blocks up Columbus. The nation's first all-paperback bookstore, established in 1953 and still owned by the poet and novelist Lawrence Ferlinghetti, it's open until midnight seven days a week, and its vast collection of avant-garde, contemporary and Beat writings keep it very much at the core of the San Francisco literary scene. To encourage the creative juices, almost every local with literary aspirations has spent some time at **Vesuvio's**, handily placed next door. The likes of Dylan Thomas and Jack Kerouac regularly got loaded here, and while times have changed considerably since then, it remains a haven for the lesser-knowns to get ploughed with impunity and pontificate on the state of the arts. On the other side of Columbus two other Beat bars, *Spec's* and *Tosca's*, should satisfy all but the most unquenchable thirst.

Assuming you leave any of these places with your senses intact, you'll find yourself at the crossroads of **Columbus and Broadway**, where poetry meets porn in a raucous assembly of slowly dying strip joints, rock clubs and drag queens. Most famous of these is the *Condor Club*, where the sight of Carol Doda's silicone-implanted breasts thrilled a decade of voyeurs before she quit the stage for a quieter life. Her nipples, once immortalized in neon above the door as a tribute to the years of mammary fascination, have ceased to flash with the conversion of the club into a café, signalling lean times for the other clubs along the strip and what seems to be the long death of the sex-club era. Beat tourists will want to stop for a look at the building two blocks down, on the northeast corner of Broadway and Montgomery, where Allen Ginsberg lived during 1955 when he wrote the definitive Beat poem, *Howl*.

Continuing north on Columbus the bright lights fade and you enter the heart of the old Italian neighborhood, an enclave of restaurants, cafés and delicatessens set against a background of narrow streets and leafy enclosures. **Fugazi Hall** at 678 Green St, between Columbus and Powell, is the neighborhood's grandest symbol of Italian pride. Donated to the community in 1912 by their most prominent figure, John Fugazi, a banker who founded the Transamerica Corporation, this elaborate terracotta ornamented building is now host to San Francisco's longest running show, *Beach Blanket Babylon*. An upper-floor room holds photographs depicting the history of the local Italian community.

A couple of hundred yards along, at Columbus Avenue and Union Street, **Washington Square Park** is not, with its five sides, much of a square; neither, thanks to urban overcrowding, is it much of a park. However, it's big and green enough for the elder Italians to rest on

North Beach

For more on Beach Blanket Babylon, *see p.249.*

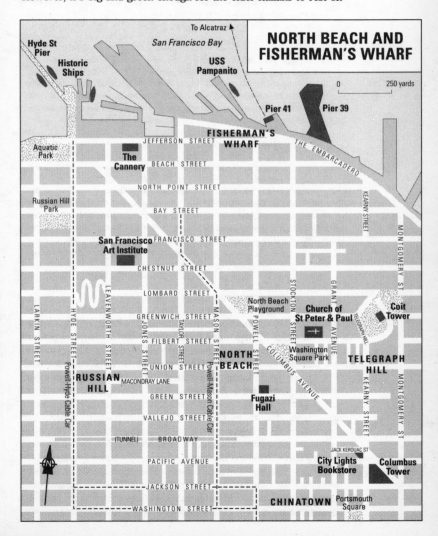

NORTH BEACH AND FISHERMAN'S WHARF

North Beach

the benches and the neighboring Chinese to do their Tai Chi routines here on a Sunday morning. On the north side of the park the lacy spires of the **Church of St Peter and Paul**, where local baseball hero Joe DiMaggio married Marilyn Monroe, dominate the neighborhood. The statue of Benjamin Franklin in the center of the park was donated by an active prohibitionist, who installed taps at the base of the monument in the unlikely hope that people would drink water from them rather than try to get their hands on bootleg liquor.

A quick diversion along any of the side streets – Grant is one of the best – will lead you to small landmarks such as the *Café Trieste*, on Grant and Vallejo, a literary waking-up spot since the days of the Beats and still a reminder of more romantic times. On Saturday mornings the owners treat customers to renditions of their favorite opera classics; at other times the café packs in a heavy-duty art crowd, toying with their cappuccinos and browsing through slim volumes of poetry. *The Lost and Found Saloon,* half a block up Grant next to the ancient *Fugazi Hardware Store,* is another survivor: except for a name-change it's much the same as it ever was, still a favorite with the jazz-and-poetry brigades. There are dozens of bars and cafés jumbled throughout the neighborhood, the best of which are listed in Chapters Thirteen and Fourteen, *Eating* and *Drinking.*

Before you enter the movement of Market Street again, stop at the **Tattoo Museum,** 841 Columbus, and check out Lyle Tuttle's bizarre collection of the flesh canvases that have fallen under his needle. This is in fact a working tattoo parlor, where the renowned tattooist is happy to execute your own designs.

Russian Hill and Telegraph Hill

The two hills that rise steeply to either side of Columbus Avenue are where the bar- and café-hoppers go home to. To the west of Columbus Avenue, **Russian Hill** is known to some for Lombard Street – the much-photographed "Crookedest Street in the World" – and to others as the home of writer Armistead Maupin's *Tales of the City* crew. To the east, the narrow alleys and eclectic architecture of **Telegraph Hill** – named after an old communications station that once stood here, and now capped by Coit Tower – are perched on 45-degree inclines. Both hills have the lion's share of the city's most desirable, if not most prestigious, residences, and if you've got strong legs the network of enticing paths, leafy alleys and stairways that climb their heights can make for a great afternoon's wander.

Russian Hill

Bounded by North Beach to the east and Nob Hill to the south, **RUSSIAN HILL** is an immaculately maintained residential neighborhood of steep slopes and small parks, whose population could be termed the high-end of bohemia. Its western edge is the lively Polk Street strip of movie houses, cafés and small off-beat stores which start out quite smart at the northern end and degenerate as you move south toward the rent-boy hangout approaching Civic Center.

The hill takes its name from a mysterious legend that tells of a group of Russian sailors who died and were buried here during a fur-trading expedition in the early 1800s. Excavations carried out some years ago uncovered some unidentified graves, but no tangible proof exists either to deny or confirm the story. At its summit, the hill is some 295 feet high and no houses were built until cable car lines crossed it during the 1880s. Since that time, it has had an artistic reputation supported only by a few literary inhabitants – Jack Kerouac, Ambroce Bierce, Joaquin Miller, Frank Norris and California's first Poet Laureate, Ina Coolbrith – and its art institute. For the most part it's a quiet, fairly wealthy enclave in a crowded corner of town: figuratively, and literally, above it all. A sensible city ordinance prohibits tour buses, and the most you'll see of other visitors will be those hanging off the Powell–Hyde cable car that traverses Russian Hill on its way to Fisherman's Wharf.

Whether you tour the area by day or night, **Hyde Street** makes a sensible point of reference. It's central to anything you might want to see as well as being well served from downtown and the waterfront by cable cars. Come before nightfall, if only to visit the **San Francisco Art Institute** at 800 Chestnut St (galleries open Tues–Sat 10am–5pm; free) on the eastern slope. As the oldest art school in the Western United States, the institute has been central to the development of the arts in the Bay Area. Housed in a hybrid structure, one part Mission-style from the 1920s and another part concrete brutalism from the 1960s, it has four galleries, three dedicated to painting and one to photography, mainly exhibiting the work of the students and rotated on a regular basis. The highlight of the institute is unquestionably the **Diego Rivera Gallery**, which has an outstanding mural done by the painter in 1931 at the height of his fame. The **cafeteria** on a deck at the back of the building is a cheap place to refresh yourself and enjoy the great views of North Beach, Telegraph Hill and the bay.

Two blocks away on the 1000 block of Lombard at Hyde, you'll run into the cars lining up to drive down the "Crookedest Street in the World" – a narrow, tightly curving street with a 5mph speed limit to make descending its steep gradient less than hazardous. It's featured as often as the Golden Gate Bridge in publicity shots for the city, and is usually surrounded by camera-wielding tourists by day – better to see it at night after they're gone and city lights twinkle below. Its contours make for a thrilling descent by car. At the top of the street is the tiny but immaculate **Alice Marble Park**, good for taking a breather and stretching out in the sun. To continue on from here, head south to Union Street and then one block east until you come to **Macondry Lane**, a walkway made famous as "Barbary Lane" in Armistead Maupin's *Tales of the City*. The lane's leafy enclosure makes for a pleasant stroll across the cobbles, leading to a rickety old staircase that descends to the intersection at Taylor Street, also featured prominently in Maupin's narrative.

From here it's a demanding two-block uphill walk to **Russian Hill Place**, off Vallejo between Jones and Taylor. After ascending the steep staircase at the summit of the hill, you're rewarded with a 180° view of the city that includes the skyscrapers of the Financial District, the candy-colored houses of North Beach and Telegraph Hill, the Bay Bridge, and, of course, the shimmering bay. After all the climbing you'll probably be eager to get back to Hyde and recover on a cable car, but before leaving you should take a walk down **Russell Street**, a small lane west of Hyde between Grant and Union. Check out the modest (by San Francisco standards) little house at no 29, in the attic of which Jack Kerouac lived for six months in 1952 with Neal and Carolyn Cassady. It was here, with Neal's encouragement, that Kerouac began an affair with Carolyn that endured for many years. Kerouac produced some of his best work during this period, inspired by tape-recorded sessions with Neal Cassady, and went on to write *Doctor Sax, Visions of Cody* as well as revising earlier versions of *On the Road*. Carolyn Cassady's own rich memoir, *Heartbeat*, chronicles this period, with some vivid physical descriptions of the city itself.

The prolific turn-of-the-century San Francisco architect **Willis Polk** lived nearby, at the head of the Vallejo Street staircase between Jones and Taylor, in an attractive, shingled house of his own design. Not the work of Willis Polk, but worth a peek, is the 1000 block of Green Street, where one of the city's few remaining octagonal houses survives thanks to the *Colonial Dames of America*. The **Feusier Octagon House**, built in the 1870s, is not open to the public. An alternative to taking the Hyde Street cable car back downtown is to walk a couple of blocks east to the Powell–Mason cable car line, passing on the way the **Ina Coolbrith Park**, another postage stamp piece of greenery, but quiet and pretty enough for a sit-down before negotiating the crowds.

Telegraph Hill

Once an extension of the wilder North Beach territory, but now a firmly settled community in its own right, the pastel clapboard homes of **TELEGRAPH HILL** dangle precipitously from the steep inclines. Apart from the stiff walk, there's no easy way up, unless you're willing to sit on *Muni* bus #39 while it makes the slow climb through the usually packed tourist traffic, and anyway the walk may make you appreciate the dramatic panorama, from the Golden Gate Bridge in the west to the hills of Berkeley across the bay to the east.

The most direct path to the top of the hill is to take **Filbert Street**, a steep climb from Washington Square Park past the flowery gardens of a line of cottages, up to Telegraph Hill Boulevard. The best viewpoint is from the top of **Coit Tower** (daily 10am–5pm; $3), a phallic concrete monument to the firefighters who doused the flames of 1906, designed by Arthur Brown, the architect of City Hall.

While waiting for the lift to the top of the tower, check out the marvellous social realist WPA **murals**, inspired and supervised by Diego Rivera. All the frescoes are thematically linked, though the style varies greatly. One section depicts musclebound Californians working on the land; another shows a man reading Marx in front of a wall of books by left-leaning authors like Upton Sinclair and Jack London, while others contemplate apocalyptic newspaper headlines. The murals were completed in 1934, during a longshoremen's dispute that escalated into a general strike after two union members were killed by police during demonstrations. When rumors about the "subversive" frescoes reached the authorities, the Art Commission ordered that a hammer and sickle be removed from one and even tried to close the tower until tempers had cooled. A picket of the tower was mounted by local unions, keeping it in the headlines until the authorities gave in and allowed it to open several months later.

Heading back down you may feel more able to stop and savor the subtle charms of the hill's many fine houses, and there are a few places you definitely won't want to miss. The fine Art Moderne apartment block in which Lauren Bacall lived in the classic Bogart and Bacall film *Dark Passage* still stands just down from Coit Tower on the eastern side of the hill at 1360 Montgomery St. From Montgomery the beautifully landscaped **Filbert Steps** drop steeply down, looking out over the Bay Bridge and giving access to narrow footpaths such as **Darrell Place** and **Napier Lane** that cut off to either side. Napier Lane is one of the few remaining boardwalks in the city, lined with cottages and overflowing greenery.

Fisherman's Wharf and Alcatraz

On the whole, San Francisco seldom goes dramatically out of its way to please the tourist, but **FISHERMAN'S WHARF** is a rare exception, pulling in millions of visitors each year with its crowded and hideous ensemble of waterfront kitsch and fast-food stands. A series of refurbished piers have been converted into souvenir complexes and places to pick up a pleasure cruise around the bay; stalls selling sweatshirts and baseball caps crowd out the few places of any real interest; and all in all it makes for a sad spectacle – and a rather misleading introduction to San Francisco.

Restaurants in the Fisherman's Wharf area are reviewed from p.214 onwards.

It may look like it has taken a hundred years of steady endeavor to make the place so awful, but in fact the Wharf (as it now stands) is only thirty years old. Though it might seem hard to believe now, this was originally a serious fishing port, trawling in real crabs and not the frozen sort now masquerading as fresh fish on the stands. The few fishermen that can afford the exorbitant mooring charges these days are usually finished by early morning, and get out before the tourists arrive. The stores and bars here are among the most overpriced in the city and crowd-weary families do little to add to the ambience. There are a few good seafood restaurants and a hand-ful of mildly interesting spots, but, frankly, the best thing you can do with the Wharf is skip it altogether.

Details of bay cruises can be found on p.32.

At the eastern edge of the Wharf, **Pier 39** marks the beginning of a high-volume strip that continues for eight blocks west. You can take a boat from here and cruise the bay, but the central focus is a large complex of stores and restaurants, not all awful but certainly all expensive and usually swarming with people.

A cluster of exorbitantly priced museums and exhibitions west along Jefferson Street – known as the **Amusement Zone** – are designed to relieve you of more money: a **Wax Museum** (daily 9am–10.30pm; $7.95) with laughable replicas – the one of Cleopatra is uncannily like that of Elizabeth Taylor; **Ripley's "Believe It or Not" Museum** (Sun–Thurs 10am–10pm, Fri & Sat 10am–midnight; $6); even a **Guinness World of Records Museum** (daily 10am–10pm; $5.95). Sadly, even for people with kids to amuse, none are really worth the expenditure of very much energy or money. Better to walk to **Pier 45** at the foot of Taylor Street to see the last vestiges of the working wharf. It still pulls in some twenty million pounds of fish a year, although up to ten times that amount arrives by truck to serve the restaurants of the Bay Area. Unless you're there early morning, you won't see much action, but the boats and storage sheds are there to poke around in. At the very end of the pier is the **USS Pampanito** (daily 9am–9pm; $5), a submarine that sank five Japanese ships during its operation in World War II. While hardly a must, it rates highly as an attraction compared to other sights in the area.

Of the Wharf's two refurbished **shopping complexes**, the first, **The Cannery** on Jefferson Street at Leavenworth, was a fruit-packing factory that was done up in the 1960s when the tourism drive really took off. Escalators take you up and around the three floors of shops. **Ghirardelli Square** at 900 N Point St marks the western edge of the Wharf, a boutiquey mall that is a far cry from its days as a chocolate factory, its red neon sign a consumer landmark for miles around. A little more upmarket than The Cannery, its careful refurbishment took six years, and to its credit contains some very good restaurants and one thing you don't need money to enjoy. The non-profit **California Crafts Museum** (daily noon–6pm; free) is better than its name suggests. A far cry from the batik and macramé knick-knacks you might expect, it has some innovative stuff, exhibiting work in media (wood, metal, glass and clay) that are often unrecognized by galleries. In addition to the more traditional ceramics and suchlike, you'll be able to see some designer furniture and unusual sculpture. To travel back downtown, either wait in line at the cable car turnaround in **Victorian Park**, at Hyde and Beach, or catch the downtown loop bus #19 at the same junction.

The **Maritime Museum**, at the foot of Polk Street (daily 10am–6pm; free), is housed in a former casino known as the "Boathouse" – a bold, Art-Deco, streamlined imitation of a luxury liner, with three curving levels, steel railings and porthole windows. Permanent exhibits inside trace the saga of the people and merchant ships that shaped the development of the city back in the days of the Barbary Coast. Hundreds of artefacts, photographs and documents chart San Francisco's seafaring history, but the most interesting item is Hilaire Hiler's 1939 **mural** in the main room, symbolizing the lost continent of Atlantis in 37 individual hallucinogenic panels.

Russian Hill and Telegraph Hill

The Mandarin, *a top-quality Chinese restaurant in Ghirardelli Square, is reviewed on p.217.*

More seafaring vessels are on display at the **Hyde Street Pier** at the foot of Hyde Street (daily 8am–5pm; $3). Originally the pier was used to serve the Sausalito ferries before the opening of the Golden Gate Bridge; today it boasts a collection of five historic ships, three of which are open to the public. The *Balclutha* is the most interesting, a hard-working ship of the late 1800s that journeyed round the Cape Horn, returning with wine and spirits from London, coal from Wales and hardware from Antwerp. She was put into retirement in the 1930s, to be dragged out and done up for bit parts in such films as *Mutiny on the Bounty*, before her current job as a showboat. The *Eureka*, once the largest passenger ferry in the world, is now loaded with a fleet of vintage cars and trucks; the *Alma* is a flat-bottomed workhouse that used to carry hay and lumber around the bay.

Alcatraz

Boats to Alcatraz leave hourly from Pier 41, from 8.15am onwards; the last boat back leaves at around 6pm ($8 per person).

Visible from the waterfront, its beacon flashing eerily in the fog, the prison island of **Alcatraz** is commonly known as "The Rock" – a craggy little islet rising out of the bay that was originally home to nothing more than thousands of pelicans ("Alcatraz" means pelican in Spanish). In the late nineteenth century the island became a military fortress, and in 1934 it was converted into America's most dreaded high-security prison, in an attempt to restrain the hitherto uncontrollable heavyweights of the penal system. Surrounded by freezing, impassable water, it was an ideal place for a jail, and safely kept some of America's most wanted criminals behind bars – Al Capone and Machine Gun Kelly were just two of the villains imprisoned here, and Robert "Bird Man" Stroud had a film made about him and his time here.

The conditions were about as inhuman as you'd expect: most inmates were kept in solitary confinement, in cells no larger than five by nine feet, some without light; they were not allowed to converse with the guards, read newspapers, play cards or even talk to the other inmates; relatives were allowed to visit for only two hours per month. The psychological toll it took on the prisoners is said to have been devastating. Frustration culminated in several riots, including one particularly bloody affair that ended in the deaths of several guards and inmates. Despite many ingenious attempts, no successful escape was ever verified; of the 36 men who tried, some were shot, most were captured in the water and five vanished, presumed dead.

For all its usefulness as a jail, however, the island turned out to be a fiscal as well as penitential nightmare, and after years of generating massive running costs, not to mention whipping up a storm of public protest when it started to imprison petty criminals, it closed in 1963. The remaining prisoners were distributed among decidedly less horrific detention centers, and the island remained abandoned until 1969, when a group of Native Americans staged an occupation as part of a peaceful attempt to claim it for their people

– citing treaties which designated all federal land not in use as automatically reverting to their ownership. Using all the bureaucratic trickery they could muster, the government finally ousted them in 1971, claiming the operative lighthouse qualified Alcatraz as active. Nowadays the island's sole function is as a tourist attraction. You can wander about on your own if you wish, but many of the annual 750,000 visitors join the excellent hour-long audio-tours ($5) of the abandoned rows of cells. On the tape are sharp anecdotal commentaries by several of the surviving inmates, recalling the horror and desperation of their time and the conditions of the prison. The area around the main prison building is, in parts, quite pretty, and the views of the city from the island are impressive. Speculation about the future of the island has included plans to turn it into an offshore gambling haven (gambling is illegal in California), although the latest proposal – and one that looks set to stick – is a scheme to let the island revert to its natural state and develop a series of hiking trails.

Fort Mason and the Golden Gate National Recreation Area

A little way west of Fisherman's Wharf, the area known as the **Golden Gate National Recreation Area** was organized in 1972 to provide much-needed central park space for the city by pulling together vacant parts of the waterfront. It encompasses almost seventy square miles of waterfront property, from the beach areas to the south, right up to the cliffs of Marin County on the other side of the Golden Gate Bridge. By claiming this property for public use, commercial enterprise has been pushed back, and the waterfront feels very much on the fringes of the city. Just a few blocks can take you from urban density to seafront openness.

At the foot of Hyde Street, **Aquatic Park** holds a small **beach** and an impressively long, windy pier. Few brave the choppy waters of the bay, however, and most use the beach as a sunny spot to walk dogs, take picnics and generally laze about. At weekends, salsa and reggae bands set up on the broad semicircle of steps above it and entice crowds away from the congestion of the Wharf. The three-and-a-half-mile scenic walk that begins here – the **Golden Gate Promenade** – wraps along the waterfront to the Golden Gate Bridge, passing through attractive spots like Marina Green and the Palace of Fine Arts (see below).

Fort Mason, adjacent to the park, can be reached by car via Bay and Franklin streets, or by climbing a spectacular flight of stairs up to the bluff from the foot of Van Ness Avenue. This military site, dating originally from the late 1700s, was maneuvered into public hands in 1972, when a powerful congressman and environmentalist, Philip Burton, blocked plans to turn the land over to private

Fort Mason

For details of Fort Mason's hostel, see p.207.

speculation. Initially used by Spanish soldiers from the Presidio in 1797, it came under the auspices of the US Army in 1850, but failure to occupy the land immediately led squatters to build homes here. The squatters took thirteen years to evict, in a gradual programme of building, but the Fort was to shelter the homeless again as a refugee center after the 1906 earthquake and fire. It saw its greatest action during World War II, when 1.6 million soldiers passed through on their way to the Pacific War Zone, and again in the early 1950s during the Korean War, when it was a logistical support center.

Today Fort Mason is known locally as "Fort Culture", its old shed-like buildings housing an assortment of arts organizations known collectively as the **Fort Mason Center**. The fruit of pressure for free or low-cost cultural activities in the city, the complex has grown tenfold since its opening in 1976. It also holds a **hostel**, workshops, a few stores and several **museums** staging a mixture of permanent and temporary exhibitions.

With minimal exhibition space, not much larger than the average schoolroom, the little-known **Mexican Museum** in Building D (Wed–Sat noon–5pm; $4, free the first Wed of each month) nonetheless manages to pack in rare pieces of Hispanic, colonial and folk art. Originally intended to represent the talents of local Mexican artists, the museum also occasionally scores coups over the larger museums, and displays works by such artists as Diego Rivera and Frida Kahlo. Proceeds from the sale of postcards, prints and a limited selection of Mexican hand-made crafts in the small shop go towards maintaining the museum.

A short walk from here, the **Museo Italo Americano** in Building C (Wed–Sun noon–5pm; free) is similar in conception, if vastly different in proportions. Over 5000 square feet of gallery space are dedicated to mainly temporary installations showing the works of local Italian/American artists and sometimes more prestigious travelling shows. Styles vary with the exhibitions, but you can usually rely on the accent being heavily contemporary. Much of the collection is geared towards an understanding of Italian architecture and culture and is more broadly based than the other ethnic museums at the Fort. If you can stand another museum in one day, the **African American Historical and Cultural Society** in Building C (Wed–Sun noon–5pm; free), is dedicated to preserving the history of black Americans. As well as a library, gift store and meditation room, a **gallery** shows excellent work by new and master artists of African-American descent, and a rather academic **museum** holds specialist artefacts and archival materials.

For more on the Magic Theater, see p.249.

Though the Fort is predominantly a daytime attraction, crowds come here by night for performances at the acclaimed **Magic Theater**, one of the oldest and largest theater companies on the West Coast. At night, the Fort's always pretty bluff becomes one of the most irresistibly romantic spots in the city.

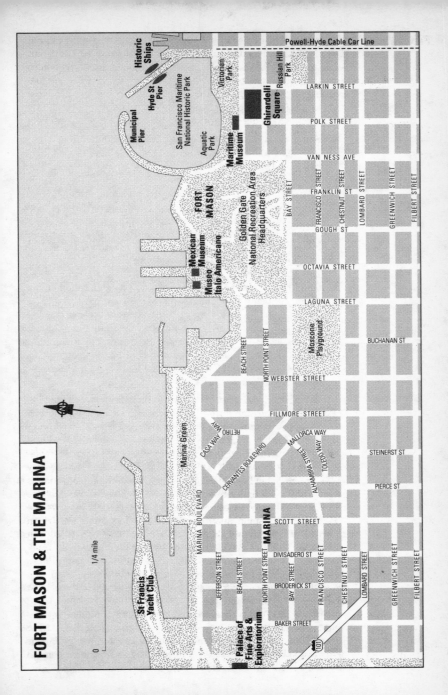

FORT MASON & THE MARINA

0   1/4 mile

Powell-Hyde Cable Car Line

Historic Ships

Hyde St Pier

Municipal Pier

San Francisco Maritime National Historic Park

Victorian Park

Russian Hill Park

LARKIN STREET

Ghirardelli Square

POLK STREET

Aquatic Park

Maritime Museum

VAN NESS AVE

FRANCISCO STREET

CHESTNUT STREET

GREENWICH STREET

FILBERT STREET

BAY STREET

FRANKLIN ST

FORT MASON

Golden Gate National Recreation Area Headquarters

GOUGH ST

LOMBARD STREET

Mexican Museum

Museo Italo Americano

OCTAVIA STREET

LAGUNA STREET

Moscone Playground

BUCHANAN ST

BEACH STREET

NORTH POINT STREET

WEBSTER STREET

Marina Green

FILLMORE STREET

CASA WAY

RETIRO WAY

MALLORCA WAY

STEINERST ST

CERVANTES BOULEVARD

ALHAMBRA STREET

TOLEDO WAY

PIERCE ST

MARINA BOULEVARD

SCOTT STREET

MARINA

St Francis Yacht Club

JEFFERSON STREET

BEACH STREET

NORTH POINT STREET

DIVISADERO ST

BAY STREET

FRANCISCO STREET

CHESTNUT STREET

LOMBARD STREET

GREENWICH STREET

FILBERT STREET

BRODERICK ST

Palace of Fine Arts & Exploratorium

BAKER STREET

101

The Marina, Palace of Fine Arts and Union Street

Perched prettily on the edge of the bay, with its tastefully arranged Mediterranean revival houses and shops, the **MARINA** is a fitting neighborhood for the young, image-conscious, money-no-object sort of professionals who inhabit it. Flanked by the Presidio to the west and Fort Mason to the east, it's one of the city's greenest districts, and its prestigious yacht club, joggers and kite-flyers all add to the ambience of a neighborhood that would rather be a resort. Ironically, the Marina, built specifically to celebrate the rebirth of the city after the massive earthquake of 1906, was the worst casualty of the earthquake of 1989 – tremors tore through fragile landfill and a good number of homes collapsed into a smouldering heap. Rebuilding was immediate, however, and the only reminders of the destruction are the obviously new structures that went up to replace the lost dwellings. Even disaster was not enough to bring rents down, and the Marina remains, despite its hazardous foundations, home to a well-heeled and very smart young set.

The Marina's commercial center runs along **Chestnut Street** between Broderick and Fillmore streets. As a neighborhood, it has a reputation for being something of a haven for swinging singles: the local watering holes are known as "High-intensity breeder-bars" and even the local *Safeway* has been dubbed "The Body Shop" because of the inordinate amount of cruising that goes on in the aisles. Union Street (see below) is better for ordinary shopping, but Chestnut is just the job if you all you want to do is grab a bite to eat, have a drink and look at the locals.

Before the 1915 Panama Pacific International Exhibition to commemorate the rebuilding of the city after the 1906 earthquake and fire, the Marina didn't exist at all. On the bay north of Pacific Heights, a sea wall parallel to the shoreline was built and the marshland in between was filled in by pumping up sand from the bottom of the ocean. Dredging left enough deep water for the creation of the **St Francis and Golden Gate Yacht Clubs**, which occupy a prestigious spot at the foot of Baker Street. Slightly to the east is **Marina Green**, a large stretch of turf frequented for the most part by fitness fanatics. For less strenuous exercise, walk the **Golden Gate Promenade** which runs parallel to Marina Boulevard and runs for a couple of miles before reaching the bridge.

The Palace of Fine Arts and Exploratorium

Marking the westernmost point of the neighborhood is the Marina's most notable landmark, the magnificent **Palace of Fine Arts** at Baker and Beach. It is not, as the name suggests, a museum, but a huge, freely interpreted classical ruin by Bernard Maybeck, whose dream-like columns and rotunda were also created for the Panama Pacific Exhibition in 1915. The weeping figures on the colonnade, by sculptor Ulric Ellerhusen, are said to represent the melancholy of life without art. Whatever the implicit message, the lachrymose ladies are the ultimate decorative detail on a structure conceived out of great optimism for post-earthquake San Francisco. It was saved from immediate demolition after the exhibition by sentimental San Franciscans, and crumbled with dignity until the late 1950s when a wealthy resident put up the money for its reconstruction. It's the sole survivor of many such triumphal structures built for the Exhibition, which stretched from here all along the waterfront to Fort Mason. Surrounded by Monterey cypresses, a swan-filled lagoon and other nice touches of urban civility, it beats Marina Green hands down as a picnic spot and makes for the best idling in the neighborhood.

Like the Palace of Fine Arts, the rather unsightly hangar-like **Exploratorium** next door (Wed 1–9.30pm, Thurs & Fri 1–5pm, Sat & Sun 10am–5pm; $5), is a product of high ideals, founded in 1969 on the idealistic premise that a better understanding of the sciences is the key to solving the world's problems. More than 500 exhibits explore light and color, sound and music, patterns of motion, language and other natural phenomena. Each year over half a million people come to peer through lenses, look in mirrors, stare through filters, experiment with magnets and electricity, spin wheels, swing pendulums and supposedly, in the process, "learn more about their environment and themselves". It makes a good pacifier for restless children, although some of the exhibits can be a bit tedious for anybody with an elementary grasp of science.

Union Street

Known by some as **COW HOLLOW**, Union Street is the busy commercial strip which rests between the Marina and its slightly wealthier neighbor, Pacific Heights, to the south. It takes its name from the days when cows rather than shoppers grazed the valley between Russian Hill and the Presidio, and washerwomen would bring their loads to what was one of the very few sites of fresh water in the city. Problems with open sewage, and complaints from the neighbors up on Pacific Heights about the stench from the cows, brought its pastoral days to an end, and these days cattle markets of an altogether different variety set the tone: Union Street, like the Marina, is quite the place for single straight people come sundown, the bars full of well-paid young professionals, dressed to death and very expectant, slinging down cocktails and waiting for their luck to change.

Indeed, despite stumbling across some attractive flower-filled courtyards, shopping and bar-hopping is what Union Street is all about. Second only to the downtown area, the seven-block stretch between Fillmore and Franklin is crammed with boutiques, fancy restaurants, antique stores, cafés and bars. Even the most faint-hearted consumer will find it hard to ignore the bookstores and classy Italian designer stores.

Pacific Heights

Sharply defined by California Street to the south, Van Ness Avenue to the east, the Marina to the north and the hulking green landmass of the Presidio to the west, **PACIFIC HEIGHTS** is a beautifully poised millionaires' ghetto. It's a common source of amusement that when the bright young things of the Marina grow up and have kids, they climb the hill to Pacific Heights and look down on all the fun they used to have. Even when these were bare hills back in the 1860s, their panoramic views of the ocean earmarked them as fashionable territory as soon as the gradient-conquering cable cars could link them with downtown. Lavishly proportioned mansions teeter precipitously atop hills that are the chosen domain of the stockbroker, business magnate and the odd best-selling novelist. Erle Stanley Gardner, the creator of Perry Mason, set up his one-man fiction-factory here, producing 82 novels that sold some three hundred million copies.

The neighborhood is neatly divided by Fillmore Street: to the west are the large dwellings that earned the neighborhood its reputation; to the east swanky Art-Deco apartment buildings that do little to damage it. Known as the **Upper Fillmore**, the stretch of Fillmore Street above California Street is where locals go to shop, dine and generally lash their cash – a street that merits your exploration if you're to get a clear idea of exactly the kind of people who can afford to live here. Approaching the area from the south where California crosses Fillmore, you should ascend the latter through the maze of fancy pet stores, florists and restaurants towards the more residential territory to the north, taking in the air of casual wealth and sophistication. The stores, while pricey, are not that remarkable, and unless you're a shophound, skipping the boutiques and heading straight for a walk around the mansions would not constitute a loss.

The western portion of the neighborhood is centered around the quiet and restful **Alta Plaza Park**, one block west of Fillmore at Clay and Steiner. A lovely piece of urban landscaping, this is where local dogwalkers earn their keep, exercising the pretty pooches, and you can enjoy the good views of St Mary's Cathedral and Civic Center from its crest. Streisand fans will recognize the park as the site of the famous scene in *What's Up Doc?*, in which she drives the car down the steps on the south side of the park. Close inspection reveals cracks left in the steps after shooting the scene. North of the park, the territory becomes solidly residential, home to well-tended gardens around immaculately maintained houses, apart from one rogue structure on the southwestern corner of Baker and Broadway. This Italian Renaissance Palace, probably built around the turn of the century, is in a romantic stage of decay and from its fancy perch overlooks the Getty Mansion down the street. One block over, at the intersection of Broadway and Lyon, you'll reach the fenced-off Presidio and won't be able to go any further west. From here, a set of steps leads south down a steep incline and out to the water's edge, passing grandiose homes and presenting a magnificent view of the Palace of Fine Arts and the bay.

To do anything other than mooch about, you'll need to cross Fillmore and explore the eastern side of the neighborhood, filled for the most part with luxury apartment buildings that replaced the great Victorian piles the modern rich found too gloomy to live in. There are, however, still a couple where you can actually get a look around the inside. The **Whittier Mansion**, 2090 Jackson St (Wed, Sat & Sun 1.30–3pm; free) is home to the *California Historical Society* and has a good collection of nineteenth-century Californian art and immaculate Queen Anne furniture. One block east, the **Haas-Lilienthal House**, 2007 Franklin St (Wed noon–4pm, Sun 11am–4.30pm; $3), is the headquarters for the *Foundation for San Francisco's Architectural Heritage* – a fully furnished Queen Anne-style house. The unchallenged star, but unfortunately one you can't venture inside, is the **Spreckels Mansion** at Gough and Washington, whose ostentatious faded elegance, grand in every detail, is as unrestricted in its design as in its decay. Follow the house around to its lovely sloping back garden and look at it in its entirety – pulp-romance writer Danielle Steele took over the empty mansion several years ago, and despite a spending programme on the inside that made her the darling of the interior design industry, the outside has mercifully yet to be tackled and crumbles gracefully on its majestic perch.

The Presidio

Occupying most of the northwest tip of the San Francisco peninsula, the **PRESIDIO** covers some 1600 acres and is home to 75 miles of forested roads. After a hundred years of sporadic military use, it is progressively being handed over to the public, though the Army will continue to maintain a small presence. No one has ever been denied access to this beautiful corner of the city, but it's never offered much to do other than taking a drive through its eucalyptus-scented highways or choosing a section to hike through. Also a favorite spot with cyclists, the Presidio lacks the congestion of Golden Gate Park, and makes for a pleasant, if lengthy, stroll on the way to the beaches.

San Francisco's beaches are covered in Chapter Six.

In the 1770s the Presidio was founded as a frontier station for the Spanish Empire, which garrisoned the distant peninsula to forestall British and Russian claims on the San Francisco Bay. In 1822 it became the northernmost outpost of the new Mexican republic. After the Americans took over in 1846, the US Army started to develop the inherited adobe structures, but the Presidio didn't take on its present appearance until the 1880s, when an environmentally minded major initiated a programme of forestation that changed it from a windswept, sandy piece of coastline into the dense thicket it is today. Afterwards it served mainly as a medical and administrative army base; the only time its harbor defences were activated was for a brief period during World War II.

The main entrance to the Presidio is by way of Lombard Street, west of Pacific Heights and the Marina. A huge gate bearing the figures of Liberty and Victory leads you inside to the main quadrangle of buildings that functioned as the military headquarters. There's a small chapel and adobe officers' mess, but the only thing you can actually visit is the **Presidio Museum**, on Lincoln Boulevard and Funston Avenue (Tues–Sun 10am–4pm; free) – the original hospital building, converted into exhibition space. In addition to military history, detailed models and maps trace how San Francisco's appearance has changed over the centuries, showing which parts of the city were wiped out by the 1906 earthquake.

You may recognize Fort Point as the site of Kim Novak's suicide attempt in Alfred Hitchcock's Vertigo.

The Presidio's (and perhaps even San Francisco's) most dramatic location is the **Fort Point National Historic Site**, a brick fortress built in the 1850s to guard the bay. From here, where the surf crashes and the Pacific stretches interminably, you get a good sense of the place as the westernmost frontier of the nation. It was originally to have been demolished to make way for the Golden Gate Bridge, but the redesign of the southern approach left it intact. It's a theatrical site, with the ocean pounding away beneath the great span of the bridge high above. Supposedly, the water here makes for one of the best (if most foolhardy) local surfing spots.

The Golden Gate Bridge

The orange towers of the **Golden Gate Bridge** – probably the most beautiful, certainly the most photographed, bridge in the world – are visible from almost every point of elevation in San Francisco. As much an architectural as an engineering feat, the bridge took only 52 months to design and build and was opened in 1937. Designed by Joseph Strauss, it was the first really massive suspension bridge, with a span of 4200 feet, and until 1959 ranked as the world's longest. It connects the city at its northwesterly point on the peninsula to Marin County and Northern California, rendering the hitherto essential ferry crossing redundant, and was designed to withstand winds of up to a hundred miles an hour and swing as much as 27 feet. Handsome on a clear day, the bridge takes on an eerie quality when the thick white fogs pour in and hide it almost completely.

You can either drive or walk across. The drive is the more thrilling of the two options as you race under the bridge's towers, but the half-hour walk across it really gives you time to take in its enormous size and absorb the views of the city behind you and the headlands of Northern California straight ahead. Pause at the midway point and consider the seven or so suicides a month who choose this spot, 260 feet up, as their jumping-off spot. Monitors of such events speculate that victims always face the city before they leap. Perhaps the best-loved symbol of San Francisco, in 1987 the Golden Gate proved an auspicious place for a sunrise party when crowds gathered to celebrate its fiftieth anniversary. Some quarter of a million people turned up (a third of the city's entire population); the winds were strong and the huge numbers caused the bridge to buckle, but fortunately not to break.

Chapter 4

Civic Center, South of Market and The Mission

While much of San Francisco is depicted as some kind of urban utopia – not always erroneously – the districts of **Civic Center**, **South of Market** and **The Mission** reveal a city of harsh realities. Pretty tree-lined streets, hills and stunning views are conspicuously absent down here, and for the most part these areas are a gritty, blue-collar reminder that not everybody in San Francisco has it easy. **Civic Center**, supposedly the bastion of civic pride, has big problems. The offices of the mayor overlook a park that for several years, between evictions, has been the chosen abode of hundreds of homeless people, much to the embarrassment of City Hall. Immediately north of Civic Center, **Polk Gulch** on the other hand thrives on its slightly seedy edge, a flourishing commercial strip of bars, theaters and shops that nicely balances the comparatively staid nature of gay life in the Castro. Running parallel to Polk Gulch, north of Civic Center, the main north–south city artery of **Van Ness Avenue**, a traffic-swarmed stretch of Highway 101, runs along the westernmost edge of downtown and makes the clearest division between San Francisco's commercial and residential districts.

Tucked between the southern end of Van Ness Avenue and downtown, the **Tenderloin** is San Francisco's most notorious neighborhood. Despite attempts at gentrification it remains a stronghold of low-rent dwellings, the homeless, and the soup kitchens and shelters that sustain them. **South of Market** (SoMa), the large chunk of land that takes its name from its position immediately south of Market Street, has responded rather better to recent investment: an industrial wasteland turned hip club turf whose now fairly empty blocks will no doubt be changed beyond recognition by the massive forthcoming commercial and housing development programme. When the new **Museum of Modern Art** opens in January 1995 it will become a different area entirely. The last part to change will be the old docklands around **Mission Rock** and **China Basin** – still romantically desolate, save the odd waterfront location for a beer and burger. In sharp contrast, the large, lively, low-rent **Mission** has long been the city's first stop for immigrants. Home to many different nationalities over the years, for the last couple of decades it has been solidly and increasingly Hispanic. Nestling in a hilly corner west of the Mission, **Potrero Hill** couldn't be more different, a small enclave of brightly painted houses on slopes offering panoramic views of downtown and the waterfront, determinedly village-like and resistant to change.

Civic Center

Born out of a grand, celebratory architectural scheme, **CIVIC CENTER**, a little way southwest of the downtown area, is an impressive layout of majestic Federal and municipal Beaux Arts buildings focusing on the grand dome of City Hall, designed by Arthur Brown and completed in 1915 just in time for the Panama Pacific International Exhibition. The surrounding complex is a watered-down version of planner Daniel Burnham's ambitious schemes for the city, which would have seen grand avenues fanning out across San Francisco, including one extending to the Panhandle of Golden Gate Park. Drawn up with the help of architect Willis Polk, the plans won the wholehearted approval of city leaders, only to be delayed by the massive earthquake and fire of 1906. Political difficulties after the quake delayed the project further, and although Burnham doggedly pursued his vision of a "City Beautiful", the project was only finished after his death. He no doubt would be saddened by the complex today: it's still a fine collection of buildings, but the elegant layout has become the focus of San Francisco's most glaring social problem – the homeless. Periodically police evict the hundreds of streetpeople who set up makeshift homes on the plaza opposite City Hall and on the grass verges around the quadrangle, moving them to temporary shelters in response to a growing rage at the lack of decent public housing in the city. Being San Francisco's center for the performing arts – by night, beautifully lit and swarming with dinner-suited San Franciscans heading in and out of the opera, ballet and symphony – the problem was not one that could be easily hidden, and although the authorities have since established a number of shelters, Civic Center, along with the adjacent Tenderloin, remains the most intensely down-and-out area of town.

Using the Civic Center *Muni* and *BART* station as your starting point, you'll emerge from underground facing the **United Nations Plaza** just south of the main quadrangle. Built to commemorate the founding of the UN here in 1949, it is an attractive design with fountain and flags which has become the largest public urinal in the city – if the stench doesn't deter you, the characters who hang around it will. Wednesdays are the exception, when the site serves as the city's largest and most inexpensive fruit and vegetable market. Moving

see Downtown San Francisco Chapter

FINANCIAL DISTRICT

SACRAMENTO STREET
CALIFORNIA STREET
PINE STREET
BUSH ST
SUTTER ST
POST ST
GEARY STREET
O'FARRELL STREET
ELLIS STREET
EDDY STREET
TURK STREET
GOLDEN GATE AVENUE

BUCHANAN STREET
LAGUNA STREET
GOUGH STREET
FRANKLIN STREET
VAN NESS AVENUE
POLK STREET
LARKIN ST
HYDE STREET
LEAVENWORTH STREET
JONES STREET
TAYLOR STREET
MASON STREET
POWELL STREET
STOCKTON STREET
GRANT AVENUE
KEARNY STREET
MARKET STREET

Montgomery St (MUNI/BART)

Transbay Terminal

Powell St (MUNI/BART)

Pacific Telephone Exchange

TENDERLOIN

Old Mint

Moscone Convention Center

SOUTH OF MARKET

Public Library

UNITED NATIONS PLAZA

Civic Center (MUNI/BART)

Veterans Building

Opera House

Symphony Hall

City Hall

CIVIC CENTER

MCALLISTER STREET
FULTON STREET
GROVE STREET
HAYES STREET
FELL STREET
OAK STREET
PAGE STREET
HAIGHT STREET

MISSION STREET
SIXTH STREET
HOWARD ST
SEVENTH STREET
FOLSOM STREET
HARRISON STREET

FIFTH STREET
FOURTH ST
THIRD STREET
SECOND STREET

Van Ness (MUNI)

EIGHTH STREET
NINTH STREET
10TH STREET
11TH STREET
12TH STREET

BRYANT STREET
BRANNAN STREET
TOWNSEND STREET
KING STREET
BERRY STREET

101

GOUGH ST
MCCOPPIN ST

MARKET STREET

DUBOCE AVE.

Church St (MUNI)

Levi Strauss Factory

14TH STREET

80

101

HOOPER ST
IRWIN ST
HUBBELL ST

15TH STREET

16th St (BART)

16TH STREET

17TH STREET

Mission Dolores

CHURCH STREET
DOLORES STREET
GUERRERO STREET
VALENCIA STREET
MISSION STREET
CAPP STREET
SOUTH VAN NESS AVE.
FOLSOM STREET
HARRISON STREET
BRYANT STREET
HAMPSHIRE STREET
POTRERO STREET
KANSAS STREET
RHODE ISLAND STREET
DE HARO STREET
CAROLINA STREET
WISCONSIN STREET
ARKANSAS STREET
MISSOURI STREET
TEXAS STREET

MISSION

18TH STREET

Women's Building

19TH STREET

Dolores Park

20TH STREET

POTRERO HILL

21ST STREET

22ND STREET

23RD STREET

24th St (BART)

24TH STREET

Civic Center

Once the new library next door is completed, the old building will house the Asian Art Museum, now in Golden Gate Park – see p.120

north, you enter the main square of Civic Center, where, on McAllister and Larkin, the **San Francisco Public Library** is three floors of regal turn-of-the-century architecture. The classical columns adorning the entrance guard a fairly standard collection of reading material, although the **San Francisco History Room and Archives** on the third floor is excellent (Tues–Sat 10am–6pm; free). In this quiet, crowd-free space, used mainly as a research library, the books are primarily of scholarly interest, but some fascinating glass cases are packed with bits and pieces evoking the history of the city – newspaper cuttings, old coins, photographs and paraphernalia from the Gold Rush years.

Dominating the quadrangle at its far end on Polk Street, **City Hall** is arguably the best-looking building in town. Modelled on St Peter's Cathedral in Rome, this grandiose green-domed baroque structure of granite and marble forms the nucleus of Civic Center. The interior is as grand as its facade: a large baroque marble staircase dominates the center, which you should ascend after gazing up into the gold-inlaid dome, and wander beneath the opulent arches. It

For more on the assassination of Harvey Milk, see p.108.

was here in 1978 that Dan White got past metal-detecting security by climbing through a basement window and assassinated Mayor George Moscone and gay Supervisor Harvey Milk. Later, when White was found guilty of manslaughter (not murder), it was the scene of violent demonstrations, as gay protesters set fire to police vehicles and stormed the doors of City Hall – an event that has come to be known as the "White Night Riot".

Directly behind City Hall on Van Ness Avenue are San Francisco's cultural mainstays, most elegant of which is the **War Memorial Opera House**, home to the *San Francisco Opera* and

See p.248 for details of ballet and opera performances.

Ballet. A suitably refined structure, its understated grandeur puts to shame the giant fishbowl of the **Louise M Davies Symphony Hall** next door. Built in 1980 at a cost of almost 35 million dollars, the symphony hall has none of the restraint of its dignified neighbor, and, despite having fans in the Modernist architecture camp, the consensus is that it's a blight on the otherwise tastefully harmonious scheme of Civic Center. Both buildings enjoy a healthy patronage, and come nightfall the formally dressed arrive by the busload. Sadly, few performances are subsidized, so prices remain generally high.

If your budget doesn't stretch to a night at the opera, you can at least get a sense of its history and successes at the **San Francisco Performing Arts Library and Museum**, 399 Grove St (Mon–Fri noon–5pm; free), around the corner between the opera house and symphony hall. Housing the largest collection of performing arts material outside of New York, the museum has over a million painstakingly collected programmes, photographs, posters and press clippings concentrating on music, dance, theater and opera. Performing arts fans could spend hours raking through the memorabilia, the highlight of which is the Isadora Duncan collection, focusing on the influential dancer who was born in the city in 1877.

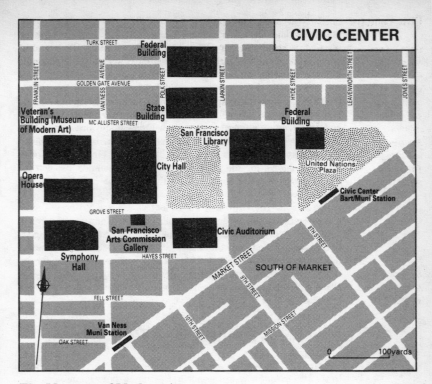

The Museum of Modern Art

The Civic Center's biggest crowd-puller is the undeniably excellent
Museum of Modern Art, for the moment occupying the top two
floors of the Veteran's Building on Van Ness Avenue at McAllister
(Tues–Sat 10am–4pm; $4, free on Tues). The first museum on the
West Coast devoted solely to twentieth-century art, it opened in
1935, but failed to achieve any international prestige until the
mid-1970s when new leadership shook up the collection. It is
currently scheduled to move to a bold new home South of Market,
designed by Swiss architect Mario Botta (thereby doubling its
exhibition space and enabling it to pull in the bigger travelling
exhibits it hitherto has had to decline). In its present limited space,
it has never ranked as a big-league gallery, but the material it does
have is well chosen and representative of a diversity of media and
styles – and its compact size enables you to take the whole
collection in at once. Small but bold, this was the first California
museum to set up an architecture and design department, and has
recently widened its net further and started exhibiting video
installations – an art form to which most established museums have,
at best, been lukewarm.

The permanent collection is distinguished by some major paintings from the **American Abstract Expressionist** school, most notably Clyfford Still, Jackson Pollock and Philip Guston. Other strong areas include **German Expressionism, Fauvism** and **Mexican Painting** by Frida Kahlo and Diego Rivera. There's a smattering of works by Dali, Matisse, Picasso and Kandinsky, but by no means their best, and the museum excels most with its collection of twentieth-century **photography**, which includes work by both European and American photographers – Cartier-Bresson and Brassai, as well as Man Ray and Ansell Adams, all get a look in. By appointment, there's also access to an exhaustive **Fine Arts Library** with over 12,000 volumes for the committed archivist, though most will be happy with the **bookstore**'s exhaustive stock of posters and art-related literature.

Nearby at 155 Grove St, the gallery of the **San Francisco Arts Commission** is the foremost exhibition space for up-and-coming artists in the Bay Area. Less prestigious but worth a look is the **San Francisco Women Artists Gallery** at 370 Hayes St, concentrating mostly on photographs, alongside some paintings and crafts. By far the most superior commercial gallery is the **Vorpal Gallery** at 393 Grove St – a large space with fine contemporary work that merits at least half an hour's browse.

Van Ness Avenue and Polk Street

Running parallel to each other from Market Street near Civic Center to the waterfront way to the north, the major thoroughfares of **Van Ness Avenue** and **Polk Street**, though no more than a block apart, have quite distinct characters. Clearly separate, too, from the affluent neighborhoods that use them (Russian and Nob hills), each has enough movie houses, restaurants, bars and stores to count as an autonomous strip, and strict social distinctions can be made between those who shop and dine on one as opposed to the other. They may not be at the top of your sightseeing list, but you'll certainly use them at some point to traverse the city.

Van Ness, by far the busier of the two, is the widest street in the city, and the major carrier of northbound traffic headed for the Golden Gate Bridge and beyond. It rarely sees a quiet moment; traffic flows pretty much 24 hours per day, and the street is not recommended for casual strolling. Though it seems hard to believe now, when originally laid out in 1854 this was a quiet, prestigious boulevard of graceful mansions, though these were dynamited in 1906 to ebb the fire that had raged through downtown and would have consumed the city had the firefighters not managed to stop it here. The few surviving houses were used as temporary retail outlets during the rebuilding of downtown, and apart from a couple of condominium complexes, the avenue has not been residential since.

During the 1920s a stately row of luxury car showrooms were built and these remain today as the places to shop for Rolls Royces, Jaguars and Cadillacs. Most interesting is the Cadillac showroom at **901 Van Ness Avenue**, designed by Bernard Maybeck in 1928 and a temple-like construction for the worship and consumption of luxury automobiles. It's doubtful that you'll find yourself car-shopping, however; more likely you'll be here at night to eat in one of Van Ness's many restaurants or take in a movie at one of its theaters.

Van Ness restaurants such as Enoteca Lanzone *and* Star's *are reviewed on p221.*

While Van Ness is a place to pass through, **Polk Street** is more a place to pause, and can make a refreshing contrast to some of the city's stuffier neighborhoods. It improves the further north you go, especially on the southwestern side of Russian and Nob hills, close to the junction with California Street at the end of the cable car line – an area better known as **POLK GULCH**. For years Polk Street has been home to the sleazier side of the city's gay culture, but apartment prices here are beginning to rival the most expensive in the city, and the strip looks set for big changes.

Polk Gulch is still a center for interesting and affordable small shops, several good movie theaters, San Francisco's best oyster bar and some rollicking good drinking holes. The characters who hang out here are far from dull – the poet John Wieners wrote the *Hotel Wentley* poems in Polk Gulch, and Frank Norris lived here for a while and now has a small side street off the strip named after him – and it still nurtures a small contingent of poets in its diners and coffee shops, muttering at their notebooks. Go by day for inexpensive snooping around its bookstores and clothing shops, but Polk Street is best appreciated at night when the streets fill up with people eating on the cheap, going to the movies, or visiting the neighborhood's **gay bars**, which have a raw (though not inhospitable) edge that's a far cry from the down-home feel of the Castro's watering spots, and still rock to a beat more reminiscent of the free-wheeling 1970s. It's hardly intimidating, but if the thought of open solicitation bothers you, you're probably better off giving it a miss.

If you're here at the end of June or beginning of July, make an effort to attend the **Polk Street Fair**, possibly the largest assembly of leather-clad gay men you're ever likely to see (see "Festivals and Parades" on p.38) as they gather for a weekend of gay celebration and high-spirited revelry.

The Tenderloin

The **TENDERLOIN**, squashed on the north side of Market Street between Union Square's Theater District and Civic Center, is a small, uninviting area measuring no more than four blocks by five. Despite its prime location beneath Nob Hill, this remains one of the shabbiest – and poorest – spots in the city. The streets are the dirtiest and most litter-strewn in the whole city, and form a kind of base

The Tenderloin

for increasing numbers of homeless, who cram the local soup kitchens and flophouses, while between the poorhouses and the porn shops, prostitutes do a brisk trade. Despite complaints from the recent wave of Vietnamese and Laotian immigrants who have moved in with their young families, nothing seems likely to change, at least in the immediate future. That's a pity, as the Tenderloin holds some of San Francisco's least expensive hotels, and many travellers on limited budgets find themselves staying here. If you are among them, it's best to treat this area simply as a place to sleep, and move on to the more interesting parts of town for your entertainment.

For columnist Herb Caen's account of the Tenderloin, see p.282.

Smack in the middle of town, the Tenderloin is at least convenient, and most things you'll want to see will be within walking distance; also, thanks to the Vietnamese immigrants, there are several places for ultra-cheap food-on-the-run. There are some lively if grimy bars a few blocks away in the Theater District. Partly as an attempt to spruce the area up for the immigrant influx, the city has gone to great lengths to design a "bum-proof" park on Jones and Eddy, replete with every imaginable barrier to dissuade the locals from establishing residence – on a good day, and with heavy patrolling by local police, it can claim to be a success.

Efforts to dignify the strip of **Taylor** around **Eddy** and **Turk** have been less successful; despite the constant police patrols, and city programmes to make the streets safer, drug dealers and prostitutes have made this their territory and lingering is not recommended.

South of Market

As Market Street bisects the city, the division it makes is more than simple geography. Its north side, with perhaps the exception of the the Tenderloin, is affluent, bristling and lively; the south side, from Embarcadero to about 12th Street, is a half-used industrial and transportation area that, on the face of things, is among the city's least appealing quarters. This is **SoMa** (South of Market), a district of old factory spaces that have been converted into galleries, fashionable restaurants and nightclubs. The first factories and foundries appeared as early as the 1850s, but the area boomed as an industrial base in the 1940s after World War II, and, with its extensive docks and railyards, became the largest transportation hub on the West Coast. The decline of shipping and the rail freight system in the 1960s left much of the area desolate, but in the last ten years or so SoMa has experienced a dramatic renaissance, and is nowadays the only place any serious San Franciscan night owl will be seen after dark. It's reminiscent, in a way, of New York's SoHo, and while by day it can seem a bleak expanse of largely deserted warehouse spaces, by night it can fairly claim to be the epicenter of San Franciscan nightlife.

SoMa's bars and restaurants are detailed on the map on p.219.

SoMa divides into three areas: the increasingly developed area around the **Transbay Terminal**; the nightclub plexus around 11th and Folsom; and the as yet undeveloped dockland areas of **Mission Rock and China Basin**. The area has been through several sporadic periods of decline and recovery, particularly the 1980s when a construction ban in the Financial District pushed development south. The massive redevelopment came in the wake of major projects like the **Moscone Convention Center** – named after the mayor who was assassinated along with Harvey Milk – where Walter Mondale was nominated as the Democratic Party candidate for president in 1984, and the **Yerba Buena Center**, an enormous project of offices and condominiums. Of all the planned buildings, the most exciting will be the new home of the **Museum of Modern Art** designed by Mario Botta, which will more than double the current exhibition space and – optimists predict – make San Francisco a foremost center for contemporary art on the West Coast when it opens early in 1995.

The Transbay Terminal and around

The corner of SoMa closest to the Embarcadero holds a large concentration of buildings that were prohibited residence in the Financial District. The densest part of SoMa, this includes the **Transbay Terminal** at First and Mission, swarming twice daily with commuters, and the first in a proposed series of yuppie housing developments, **Bayside Village**. City ordinances state that any commercial downtown developer must make funds available for medium- to low-cost housing for the extra workforce that is drawn to the city. With rents starting at $1000 per month, it's a questionable definition of low-cost housing, though terrifically handy for the Financial District whizz-kids who have only a ten-minute walk to work. Recently the area has spawned a few lively bars and restaurants, which help to minimize its desolate feeling by night.

The **Rincon Center**, 101 Spear St, is worth a look, not for architectural interest but for the permanent exhibition of murals by Anton Refregier. In all, 27 murals depict life during the Depression and industrial themes; they were inspired by Diego Rivera, who left his mark in several sites around the city during the 1920s and 1930s. Walking west from the Rincon Center along Mission you hit the 200 block of New Montgomery Street and the **Pacific Telephone Building**, a product of architecture's golden age in the 1920s: it's a gently tapered, subtly shadowed mountain, detailed in terracotta – really just another office building, but one that aspires to greatness. A couple of blocks over, the **Cartoon Art Museum**, 665 Third St (Mon–Fri 10am–5pm; free), shows the original artwork – sketches and separations – from which cartoons are made, including examples of newspaper cartoons, magazine panels, comic book illustration and animation art.

Though most people only visit at night, a daytime stroll will reveal some interesting, if unexpected, corners of SoMa. Nestled

South of
Market

The South Park
Café *is
reviewed on
p.222.*

between Brannan and Bryant, Second and Third, **South Park** is an
odd fish in the heavy industrial landscape, a small open space
designed by an English architect to mimic the squares of London.
The few surviving bits have been recently rediscovered and increasingly house the offices of architects and designers, who can be seen
lunching at the chic and genuinely French *South Park Café* on the
square. Around the corner, where Third Street meets Brannan, a
plaque marks the birthplace of *Call of the Wild* writer Jack London,
though he soon escaped what were then pretty mean streets, enjoying his better days in Oakland and the valleys of Sonoma.

Folsom Street

Folsom Street between Seventh and Eleventh streets is the main
artery of clubland. A former gay strip, it was once the center for
much lewder goings on than the now respectable Castro. A few gay
clubs and bars remain, but for the most part the mix is pretty diverse
and you should expect to find everything except the very tame. The
kernel of activity is around Folsom and 11th, where the largest
grouping of clubs and bars draws crowds who don't mind the long
waits at weekends. Comparatively little traffic uses this intersection
during the day, and it comes as a surprise to see the bumper-to-
bumper and double-parked vehicles after midnight. If you find yourself here during the day and want to check out the area, take a walk
along Folsom to the block between Seventh and Eighth: *Brainwash*
at 1122 Folsom is the epitome of SoMa, a café where you can also do
your laundry; opposite, *Buster's Newsstand* has an exhaustive
collection of magazines and guides to SoMa and the nightlife scene.
A handful of small local galleries includes the interesting **Artspace** at
Ninth and Folsom – an avant-garde space for the exhibition of
unusual works and video installations.

Rising impressively out of the desolation of the area, the **Old
Mint Museum**, Fifth and Mission (Mon–Wed 10am–4pm; free), is an
unexpected sight. Classically styled from brick and stone, the building is no longer used as a mint, but a stroll around still allows you to
glimpse an awful lot of money. As well as a million dollars' worth of
gold bars stacked in a pyramid, there's a million-dollar coin collection and lots more valuables besides.

Mission Rock and China Basin

With all the new development in progress, it can be hard to imagine
what SoMa looked like before. But the real spirit of blue-collar, industrial San Francisco can still be found around the abandoned docks
and old shipyards known as **Mission Rock** and **China Basin**. They
cover a large area on the eastern edge of the peninsula, and unless
you're wildly energetic you'll probably need a car to get the best out
of them. Deserted apart from a few spots along the water, it's strange
to think that this was once the busiest port along the West Coast,

employing thousands of men, most of whom were members of San Francisco's radical Longshoremen's Union. Few of the docks are operational now, and the most the area is good for is an indolent stroll, taking in the views of the East Bay across the water and stopping off for a drink at the couple of places along the shoreline.

The easiest way to reach the district is to follow Third Street south from Market as it curves round to meet the dock area. Starting at the **switchyards** where the drawbridge crosses China Basin Channel at Third Street, you'll see a small hut-like building on the south side of the bridge – formerly *Blanche's*, a tiny café that drew attention to the problems of development here when the city tried to get Blanche to move. Despite having her trading licence taken away, she opened up the small pier, which juts out over the channel switchyards, for all-comers to bring their sandwiches and wine at lunchtime and look at her collection of antiques from the mills of San Francisco's boomtown days. Sadly, financial deprivation pushed Blanche into retirement and the site has now been taken over by a Vietnamese family who can never quite capture Blanche's ambience. It was on the switchyards below that Jack Kerouac worked as a brakeman in the 1950s for Southern Pacific, at the same time writing the material that was later to appear in *Lonesome Traveller*, detailing scenes of SoMa skid row hotels, drunks and whores.

A short walk south takes you to the heart of China Basin, the old water inlet, and Mission Rock – the old Pier 50 that juts out into the bay. This was the focus of the old port where freight ships used to dock from Asia. Occasionally the odd ship will sail by, but these days military ships from the Oakland Naval Base are more likely to be cruising the bay than the freight liners that once jammed the waterways. A few small boat clubs have sprung up along the waterfront, but most people come to visit the *Mission Rock Resort* or *The Ramp* – two creaky wooden structures that are local landmarks. *The Ramp* in particular is quite the place to be on Sundays when people gather to hear live jazz on the small pier. Locals are determined that these two places should not be sacrificed in the rush for development, but frankly their chances of survival are slim once the Mission Bay Project picks up steam.

For more on
The Ramp, *see*
p.244.

The Mission

Low-rent, hip, colorful, occasionally dangerous and solidly working-class, the **MISSION** is easily San Francisco's funkiest neighborhood. Positioned way south of downtown, it is also the city's warmest, avoiding the fogs which blanket most of the peninsula during the summer. Stretching from the southern end of SoMa down to Army Street in the south, the Mission is a large district, although with *BART* stations at each end, getting here isn't a problem. Most of the action takes place in the eight blocks between the two *BART* stations

The Mission

(16th and 24th St), along Mission, Valencia and Dolores. The streets are lined with thrift stores, bookstores, cafés and bars in which it isn't difficult to empty your pockets. Overall, it's a noisy melange of garages, furniture and junk stores, old movie houses and parking lots: inexpensive food, and a fair concentration of lively nightspots, make the Mission a good base if you're staying in the city for any length of time.

The bars and restaurants of the Mission (and the Castro) are detailed on the map on p.220.

As a first stop for arriving immigrants to the city, the Mission is something of a microcosm of the history of San Francisco. It was first inhabited by the Scandinavians and Germans, later the Irish, then the Italians, and most recently and significantly, it has been the home of San Francisco's Hispanic population. There's a marked political edge to the area, with active Hispanic campaigning and a multitude of **murals** depicting aspects of the Latin American struggle. Sadly, it is also one of the few areas in town where women are likely to encounter the cat-calling and hissing of Latin men, and perhaps as a defiant result of this it has become a lesbian stronghold, with feminist bookstores and meeting places dotting the streets. There is, too, a flourishing arts scene – theater groups, cultural centers and a thriving Latin literary network, possibly San Francisco's most vibrant since the Beats, that feels far away from the middle-class complacency of much of the rest of the city.

The district takes its name from the **Mission Dolores** on 16th and Dolores (daily 9am–4pm; $2), San Francisco's oldest building – its fragile adobe structure survived the earthquakes of 1906 and 1989. Founded in 1776, it was the sixth in a series of Spanish missions built to consolidate Spain's claim to California. Distorted as it is in pious romanticism, the true story of California's Mission period is often hard to uncover. Tales of kindly Franciscan friars coming to save the native peoples are misguided fantasy, and in reality the Spanish Franciscans all but obliterated the Native Americans in San Francisco and indeed California. The eerie, still, cool interior of the mission is filled with paintings, with an old Mexican statue of Saint Francis tucked away in one corner. Few reminders remain of the Costanoans who were enslaved here, and little in the adjoining cemetery indicates that over five thousand of them are buried here. As well as the Costanoans, the gravesites are occupied by Spanish, Mexican and Yankee pioneers, California's first governor and San Francisco's first mayor. The **Basilica** adjacent to the mission is hardly worth entering, but its Churrigueresqe Revival design makes it one of the most beautiful block-fronts in town.

Dolores Street itself is an attractive boulevard divided by a line of palm trees along the western border of the neighborhood. High on a hill, **Dolores Park** commands the best view of the downtown skyline – a pretty, quiet place to rest during the day, plagued though it is with children on BMX bikes and defecating doggies. By night it's a little more sinister and has a reputation for being one of the central exchanges for San Francisco's drug trade.

Valencia Street is a curious mix of housing projects, groovy bars, chronically low-profit progressive **bookstores** and restaurants. There are few sights proper along here, but the **Levi Strauss & Co Factory** at 250 Valencia St (Mon–Fri 10am–5pm; tours Wed & Fri only, reserve on ☎565-9153), where you can see how the world's most famous jeans are made, is definitely worth a visit. The Levi Strauss empire started in the Gold Rush days when leftover tent material was used to make work jeans, and has gone on to become the biggest manufacturer of jeans in the world. Tours of the plant include a look at the cutting and sewing operations, and advice on how to "stonewash" your new pair to make them look old.

Two blocks up at 446 Valencia, **Intersection for the Arts** is a non-profit organization that hosts cultural and theatrical events. The programme changes constantly, but occasionally they have good exhibitions of local artists and it's worth popping in just to see what's on. Similarly the **Women's Building** at 18th and Valencia supports gay, lesbian, peace and progressive groups and often has interesting lectures and exhibitions. Across the first floor of the building a mural depicts local feminist heroines.

Mission Street is a slightly more congested version of Valencia and unless you're bargain hunting in the thrift stores (see p.257) or hanging around its bars, you should take it as far as **24th Street** – the axis of Latino shopping, with Nicaraguan, Salvadorean, Costa Rican, Mexican and other Latin American stores and restaurants. Apart from being the most authentic Latin street in the neighborhood, it's a good place to start a self-guided tour of the Mission's 200-odd **murals**, the fruits of a City Hall scheme to occupy the creative talents of the Mission's poor and not unusually disaffected youth before their energies were channelled into criminal activities. Now the major attraction in a neighborhood that until recently rarely saw tourists, hundreds are peppered all over the Mission. The biggest concentration is along 24th Street between Mission and South Van Ness. The largest is a tribute to local hero **Carlos Santana**, adorning three buildings where 22nd Street meets South Van Ness; for more controversial subject matter take a walk down **Balmy Alley** between Folsom and Harrison off 24th Street, where every possible surface is covered with murals depicting the political agonies of contemporary Central America. It was started in 1973 by a group of artists and community workers and has become the most quietly admired public art in San Francisco. Several organizations conduct walking tours of the Mission, but none more amusing or authentic than the four-foot-ten dynamo who runs *Helen's Walking Tours*.

More Latin artwork is on display at the **Mission Cultural Center**, 2868 Mission St (daily 10am–6pm; ☎821-1155), founded in 1977 with the aim of preserving and promoting Latino cultural arts. As well as theatrical productions, poetry readings and classes, there is a large exhibition space for the changing contemporary exhibitions of local paintings and drawings.

The Maelstrom *and* Modern Times *bookstores on Valencia Street are reviewed on p.261.*

Helen's Walking Tours *are detailed on p.33.*

Potrero Hill

Cut off from the rest of the Mission by the freeway, rising above San Francisco General Hospital, **POTRERO HILL** is a tiny community that's easy to miss. Its quiet streets and brightly painted houses sit high on a hill overlooking the Mission to the west and the SoMa docks to the north. Unpretentious and solidly residential, it's a peaceful neighborhood that prides itself on its isolation, a lack of tourist traffic and a pace more evocative of a country village than a major city; it even has its own weekly newspaper. There's precious little to do, but its leafy streets are perfect for a morning stroll, taking in the views of downtown and the docks and pausing for a coffee; there are also several excellent **restaurants** in the area.

Chapter 5

The Central Neighborhoods

Residential, well tended and, for the most part, almost anodyne in their pleasantness, San Francisco's **CENTRAL NEIGHBORHOODS** don't have the cachet or excitement of downtown, nor, on the whole, the hip qualities of North Beach or South of Market, but they're most of the reason San Franciscans find their city so easy to live in. Self-sufficient and independent, each of these inviting hamlets has its own distinct ethnic and social identity, the result of years of immigrant waves and political activity. Bounded by the fancy reaches of Pacific Heights and the Presidio to the north, and stretching from the Civic Center to the Pacific Ocean beaches, they sit snugly in a series of sunny valleys and gentle slopes that makes up the core of living space in San Francisco, their ornate Victorian architecture, interspersed with open spaces and parks, sidewalk cafés and small stores, revealing something of the city's true identity as a remarkably civilized place to live.

The area as a whole is definitely on the way up. The largest and most depressed neighborhood, the **Western Addition** is shrinking rapidly, as money from Pacific Heights trickles down in the search for real estate, its borders being redefined by a gentrification boom that shows little sign of slowing even in the throes of a strident recession. In its northern reaches, the pristine enclave known as **Japantown** has been spruced up by affluent Japanese families who have bought up lots, opened stores and transformed the streets. South of here, dilapidated housing estates give way at Haight Street to the eponymous **Lower Haight**, another recently poor but now terminally trendy neighborhood that threatens to overshadow its famous neighbor to the west, the **Haight-Ashbury**.

The Haight is long past its 1960s heyday of druggy hedonism, but traces of its anti-Establishment past linger in bookstores and cafés that continue to draw a steady subculture. The Haight's

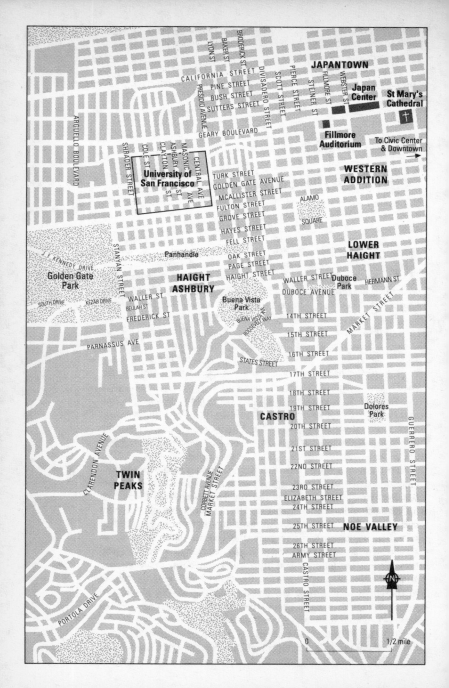

biggest appeal, apart from its bars and hstory, is perhaps its proximity to the urban idyll of **Golden Gate Park**, which stretches west for two miles as far as the ocean.

The **Castro**, southeast of the Haight and at the far end of Market Street from downtown San Francisco, is perhaps the city's most distinctive neighborhood, though more for its people than for any great sights. As the focus of San Francisco's gay community, it has been through the struggles of the 1960s which culminated in widespread recognition and acceptance in the freewheeling 1970s, only to be knocked off its feet by the advent of AIDS in the 1980s. Gay pride is starting to re-emerge and a radical caucus among the younger men is in evidence, but the neighborhood's outrageous days are clearly over. In a sunny valley over the hill from the Castro, **Noe Valley** is a restful, attractive district that has changed little over the years – family-orientated, with a rooted suburban feel. **Twin Peaks**, the city's most distinctive summit, looms over Noe Valley and the Castro, offering fresh air and unbeatable 360° views over the city below.

The Western Addition, Japantown and the Lower Haight

Looking at any map of San Francisco, you'll see several blocks labelled the **WESTERN ADDITION**, smack in the middle of the peninsula – a central position which belies its status as one of the city's most relentlessly poor neighborhoods. Also known as "the Fillmore" after its main thoroughfare, the large, mostly black area spreads both sides of Fillmore Street from Geary Boulevard south to around Haight Street, marked by block after block of semi-abandoned and low-rent dwellings where unemployment, drugs and violence are tangible indications that the community does not share in the prosperity of the rest of the city.

Over the last few years the city has taken steps to improve conditions here, though only by moving the problem elsewhere. Whole blocks of the Western Addition have been demolished and crime-infested housing projects ripped out and replaced with new structures. These new apartment buildings have been constructed with some architectural sympathy for those who will inhabit them, but whether they manage to avoid the deterioration that blighted their predecessors remains to be seen. In an effort to reform the area, private blocks are being sold on the basis of their proximity to the Civic Center and downtown areas. They're built, claim officials, for middle-income families, though they're more likely to be snatched up by the increasing tide of well-to-do professionals, which leaves the city with a bigger social problem than the one it's trying to cure, with poor, dispossessed and now homeless black families inevitably being squeezed out.

The Western
Addition,
Japantown
and the
Lower
Haight

The most obvious changes have been taking place in the northern parts of the district, where **JAPANTOWN** fills the area between Fillmore and Webster streets, with Geary Boulevard marking its southern border and Pine Street separating it from Pacific Heights. Japanese immigrants first came to the area via Hawaii, where they worked on the sugar plantations at the turn of the century. Slowly, the businesses they built up in the Western Addition grew to occupy some forty blocks, but the Japanese were obliged to sell their property, reluctantly and in haste, when anti-Japanese hysteria swept California in response to the Pearl Harbor bombing. Several years later, some Japanese drifted back and tried to pick up the threads, but found their old neighborhood occupied by the black community who now inhabit most of the area. Today, divided from the rest of Western Addition by the Geary Boulevard expressway, Japantown occupies only six blocks and doesn't look set to expand any further.

In contrast to the old, ad hoc and concentrated development of Chinatown, Japantown is well tended and new – and really quite American. It's something of a misnomer for what is basically a shopping center – the Japanese Cultural and Trade Center (*Nihonmachi*) – albeit one with a distinctly Eastern flavor and a five-tiered, 100-foot pagoda at its heart. Better known as the **Japan Center**, it's the home of a few Japanese restaurants and stores, the Japanese Consulate and, more interestingly, the excellent **Kabuki Complex** – an ultra-modern industrial design in glass with eight movie screens. For most of the year these show current-release and popular films, but at the beginning of May they host the **San Francisco Film Festival** which runs for about three weeks. The Japan Center's other main highlight is the **Kabuki Hot Springs** (1750 Geary Blvd, ☎922-6000; 10am–10pm). These genuine community baths offer shiatsu massage, steam baths and other luxuriating facilities for around $35 a session.

*There's more
on San
Francisco's
Festivals on
p.38.*

Away from the Japan Center complex there are some signs of a more traditional Japanese lifestyle working alongside the new. Over on Pine Street at Octavia, the **Buddhist Church of San Francisco** has a multiracial congregation and offers services in both English (Sun 10am) and Japanese (Sun 1pm) to cater to the diversity of San Franciscans who have chosen Buddhism as their faith. The plainness of the building itself gives little indication of the sumptuous temple inside, filled with what are claimed to be relics of the Buddha, donated by the King of Siam in 1935. Two blocks over, where Geary meets Gough, is the monumental **St Mary's Cathedral**. Visible from the heart of downtown, St Mary's is San Francisco's newest Roman Catholic cathedral, built in 1971 – elaborate and ostentatious, with a comparatively functional, modern interior. Take a walk around the inside and look up into the 190-foot dome.

Another, much more sinister quasi-religious relic once stood on the now-empty lot six blocks to the west, on Geary between Scott and Steiner. This was the site of the **People's Temple**, in which, during the 1970s, the Reverend Jim Jones established the cult that was later to go and live in "Jonestown", Guyana – an attempted utopia of common-living and egalitarian principles. The mass suicide in 1978 that came to be known as the "Jonestown Massacre" involved mainly San Franciscans, devastating the city just as it was trying to come to terms with the recent assassination of George Moscone and Harvey Milk. Today there is little reference to Jones in San Francisco, and rumors that the old temple was jinxed seem to have had some supporting evidence. Several years after the Jonestown Massacre, a wealthy, anonymous man filled the temple with riches, priceless antiques and artwork that the public could visit free of charge. After a series of small mishaps and accidents, a mysterious fire burned it to its foundations several years ago – no great loss for superstitious San Franciscans.

The Western
Addition,
Japantown
and the
Lower
Haight

Other local landmarks have been luckier. The **Fillmore Auditorium**, the large three-storey yellow brick building at the southwest corner of Fillmore and Geary, saw some of rock music's biggest heroes at its zenith in the mid-1960s. The first official home of psychedelia, it was in this small (1000 capacity) ballroom that Bill Graham staged weekend dance concerts featuring the acid-drenched sounds of the Grateful Dead, Jefferson Airplane and Janis Joplin, sometimes all on the same bill – and the now legendary light shows that went on to become a major component of the psyche-delic experience during the "Summer of Love".

Heading south on Fillmore Street through the heart of the Western Addition (*Muni* bus #23 runs all day and night), you pass through one of the few parts of San Francisco that survived the 1906 earthquake and fire. For a few years afterwards, Fillmore Street was the city's main commercial stretch, with houses turned into hotels and front rooms converted into banks and grocery stores. However, as the rest of San Francisco returned to normal, the Fillmore area was abandoned, a state of things which has continued more or less to the present day. But despite the general shabbiness it's safe enough to walk through – during the day, at least. Should you do so, divert a block west of Fillmore along Fulton Street to **Alamo Square**. This small gem of a park is quiet, pastoral and at its peak has one of the city's nicest views: sit on the crest and look east across Steiner Street at the multicolored **Painted-Ladies** – six identical, marvellously restored 1894 Victorian houses set against the skyline of the Financial District, which feature in most brochures on San Francisco. Though you might take the presence of these houses as a sign of yet more impending gentrification, they've been in good shape for a number of years, while the surrounding area remains one of the city's least cared for. A number of similar houses nearby have been done up recently, but with such a large stock of public housing in its environs, a total yuppie invasion looks unlikely.

The Western Addition, Japantown and the Lower Haight

Lower Haight is home to some of the city's best bars and meeting places – see p.236.

The few newcomers, particularly around the junction of Fillmore and Haight, have had an effect, but have so far managed to strike the right balance of bringing better stores and restaurants to the area without evicting its residents or radically changing its character. Nowadays the area, known as the **LOWER HAIGHT**, is in a period of transition and has become a major stomping-ground of the sort of fashion victims usually spotted hanging out South of Market. There's a growing mix of ethnic restaurants, and, given its good access to downtown and proximity to the Castro and Haight-Ashbury, its desirability as a place to live for good-time boys and girls on a budget is undeniable – a fine place to get a cheap breakfast, browse the bookstores, rake through vintage clothing stores and drink yourself silly.

The Castro

The bars and restaurants of the Castro (and the Mission) are detailed on the map on p.220.

Arguably San Francisco's most progressive, if no longer most celebratory, neighborhood, **THE CASTRO** is the city's avowedly Gay Capital and, as such, the best barometer for the state of the AIDS-devastated gay scene. People say many things about the changing face of the Castro – some insist it still ranks as one of the wildest places in town, others reckon it's a shadow of its former self. But all agree that things are not the same. As a district, the Castro occupies a large area stretching from Market Street as far south as Noe Valley (see below), but in terms of visible street life the few blocks from Market to 20th Street contain about all there is to see. These streets, once brimming with gay emancipation, have sobered into restraint and resolution. A walk down the Castro ten years ago would have had you gaping at the non-stop revelry, and while most of the same bars and hangouts still stand, these days they're host to an altogether different, younger and more conservative breed. It is still undeniably the province of the gay man, and dignity and determination have survived, but the energy that was once invested in hard-won, open hedonism has been squarely diverted to the formation of AIDS support groups, care for the sick, and enough political dexterity to maintain their mainstream influence in the city's political arena.

The Castro *Muni* station at Market Street is about the best place to begin a tour, at **Harvey Milk Plaza**, dedicated to the extremely popular gay city Supervisor who before his assassination in 1978 owned a camera store on Castro Street and was the community's most prominent figure. Milk's and Mayor George Moscone's assailant, Dan White, was a disgruntled ex-Supervisor who resigned when the liberal policies of Moscone and Milk didn't accord with his conservative views. A staunch Catholic, White was a spokesman for San Francisco's many blue-collar Irish families and, as an ex-policeman, saw himself as the vanguard of the family values he believed gay rights were damaging. He later tried to get his post back but was refused by Moscone, and soon after climbed through a basement window in City Hall, sauntered into their offices and shot them both dead. At the trial, during which the prosecution never once used the word "assassination" or recognized a political motive for the killings, White pleaded temporary insanity caused by harmful additives in his fast-food diet – a plea which came to be known as the "Twinkie defence" – and was sentenced to five years' imprisonment for manslaughter. The gay community reacted angrily to the brevity of White's sentence and the riots that followed were among the most violent San Francisco has ever witnessed, protesters marching into City Hall, turning over and burning police cars as they went. White was released in 1985 and moved to Los Angeles, committing suicide shortly afterwards. The anniversary of the murders, **November 27**, is marked by a candlelight procession from the Castro to City Hall.

Before heading down the hill into the heart of the Castro, take a short walk across Market Street to the headquarters of the **Names Project** at 2362 Market St (daily 10am–7pm). The organization was founded in the wake of the AIDS crisis and sponsored the creation of "The Quilt" – a gargantuan patchwork composed of panels, each 6ft x 3ft (the size of a gravesite) and bearing the name of a loved one lost to the disease. Made by their lovers, friends and families, the panels are stitched together and regularly toured around the country; it has been spread on the Mall in Washington DC several times to bring the impact of the epidemic home to the government. Sections of the quilt, too large to be exhibited in any one place in its entirety, continue to tour the world to raise people's awareness of the tragedy, and funds to help keep the care programmes alive. Inside the showroom are the thousands of panels stored on shelves: some are hung up for display and machinists tackle the endless task of stitching the whole thing together. Sharing space with the *Names Project*, **Under One Roof** is a shop that has been set up as an additional fund-raising aid for the fifty or so participating Northern California AIDS service organizations, selling books, t-shirts and gift items.

Back on Castro Street, one of the first things you see is the **Castro Theater**, self-described as "San Francisco's landmark movie palace" and undeniably one of San Francisco's better (if not best) movie houses, as popular for its pseudo-Spanish baroque interior as it is for its billing, which includes revival programmes, twenty-minute performances on a Wurlitzer organ and plush velvet surroundings.

For more on the Castro Theater, see p.251.

Half a block down the hill, the junction of **Castro and 18th streets**, known as the "gayest four corners of the earth", is the heart of the Castro, and the site of much political activity, particularly at weekends, when people set up petition stands, canvas for votes and the bums hang out capitalizing on the throng. **The Sisters of**

The Castro

*See p.261 for
more on the
Castro's
noteworthy gay
and lesbian
bookstores.*

Perpetual Indulgence, a now world-famous group of local figures who won their notoriety by dressing up as nuns and roaring about on motorbikes and roller skates, spend a lot of time at this junction canvassing for some cause or other, usually in full regalia and always surrounded by an amused crowd. Cluttered with bookstores, clothing stores, cafés and bars, this junction is as dense as the neighborhood gets and a sure sign that, despite the losses of the last few years, the survival of the community is assured.

Noe Valley

NOE VALLEY, immediately south of the Castro, is remarkable only for its insignificant status in the pantheon of San Francisco neighborhoods; in fact, so good is it at failing to capture imaginations that it has been fondly tagged "Noewhere Valley". Sitting snugly in a sunny valley, the main vein of which runs along 24th Street from the borders of the Mission, its air of rugged unfashionableness is manifest in clean streets, visible signs of family life, blue-collar sports bars, small human-scale stores and a noticeable lack of street crime and vagrancy – in some degree refreshing after the artificiality and sleaze of the Haight, Mission or SoMa.

A good balance of commercial activity along 24th Street gives you reason enough to spend an afternoon wandering in and out of the book and record stores, good delicatessens and clothing stores. The neighborhood is served by the J-Church streetcar, which, from downtown, winds prettily past Dolores Park and around leafy, curving hills before stopping at Church and 24th Street. It is surprisingly close to the center of town, and with San Francisco real estate prices climbing way beyond the means of most, it's perhaps a matter of time before the rents squeeze out the families to make room for wealthy professionals.

As well as the 24th Street strip, Church Street between 24th and 30th has an unusual (and thankfully uncrowded) hotch-potch of weird little junk stores, nail parlors and hair salons. Noe Valley is *the* place to get your appearance sorted out: there are about seven hairdressers between 24th and 30th alone, and all along 24th Street beauty salons vie for your business with some pretty cut-throat prices. There's even a **hot tub** and sauna place called *Elisa's Health Spa* (4026 24th St), where you can get half an hour in an outdoor hot tub for $7.50 and half an hour's shiatsu massage for $20.

Diverting slightly onto Sanchez Street, the **Noe Valley Ministry** (1021 Sanchez) is a place to look out for. Originally built in the late nineteenth century as a Presbyterian Church, this attractive Gothic-style building now serves as the neighborhood community center and, in addition to providing a forum for worship, lectures and a nursery school, hosts a good programme of concerts each Saturday, ranging from classical and chamber choir to modern jazz and soul.

Twin Peaks

Real estate prices in San Francisco are gauged in part by the quality of the views, so it's no surprise that the curving streets that wind around the slopes of **TWIN PEAKS** hold some of the city's most outrageously unaffordable homes. If the peaks themselves were up for sale they'd command millions, but fortunately they're among the few hills in San Francisco that have been saved from being entirely covered with houses, and so offer spectacular, 360-degree views that you should make every effort to see.

It's a stiff but rewarding climb or bike-ride up Twin Peaks Boulevard from the top of Market Street (*Muni* bus #37 saves most of the work), or you can join one of the many guided **bus tours** of the city – they all stop here. It makes a beautiful drive by night as well, though it can get terribly cold and windswept.

Before the skyscrapers went up downtown, Twin Peaks was San Francisco's most distinctive landmark – Market Street was laid out expressly to focus sightlines on its voluptuous symmetry. Before that, local Native Americans related that they were created when a married couple argued so violently that the Great Spirit separated them with a clap of thunder; they were later tagged "Breasts of the Indian Girl" by Spanish explorers but Americans finally settled on the more literal name of Twin Peaks. Architect Daniel Burnham spent time here in 1905 working on a master plan for the city that would have replaced the relentless urban grid with more curving streets and broad parkways. Despite the opportunity offered by the earthquake and fire of the following year, commercially minded civic authorities lacked the vision to carry it out, and the ideas were largely forgotten, except for his plans for Civic Center.

Haight-Ashbury

Two miles west of downtown San Francisco, the **HAIGHT-ASHBURY** neighborhood lent its name to an era, giving it a fame that far outstrips its size. Small and dense, "The Haight" spans no more than eight blocks in length, centered around the junction of Haight and Ashbury streets. Since it emerged in the Sixties as the mecca of the counter-cultural scene, it has gone slightly upmarket, but this remains one of San Francisco's most racially and culturally mixed neighborhoods, with radical bookstores, laid-back cafés, record stores and second-hand clothing boutiques recalling its days of international celebrity.

Until 1865, the Haight was no more than a pile of sand dunes, claimed in part by squatters. Then a forward-thinking Supervisor called Frank McCoppin spearheaded the development of the dunes into the area now known as Golden Gate Park. The landscaping of the Panhandle that leads into the park, the creation of a cable car line along Haight Street, and an amusement park drew people out to the western edge of town – development continued and by the 1890s the Haight was a thriving middle-class neighborhood. After the 1906 earthquake, new building gathered pace and the neighborhood's desirability grew. That was checked by the 1930s Depression, which turned many of the respectable Victorian homes into low-rent rooming houses. The 1950s saw inroads of students from the then nearby San Francisco State College, and a youth culture began to develop that later blossomed into Flower Power, the hippies and the Summer of Love.

The first hippies were an offshoot of the Beats, many of whom had moved out of their increasingly expensive North Beach homes to take advantage of the low rents and large spaces in the run-down Victorian houses of the Haight. The post-Beat bohemia that subsequently began to develop here was a small affair at first, involving the use of drugs and the embrace of Eastern religion and philosophy, together with a marked anti-American political stance. Where Beat philosophy had emphasized self-indulgence, the hippies, on the face of it at least, attempted to be more embracing, emphasizing such concepts "universal truth" and "cosmic awareness". The use of drugs was crucial and seen as an integral, and positive, part of the movement – LSD especially, the effects of which were just being discovered, despite an esoteric following in psychoanalytical circles for decades before.

Hunter S Thompson's seminal 1967 article The "Hashbury" is the Capital of the Hippies *is reprinted on p.284 of this book.*

Naturally it took a few big names to get the ball rolling, the pivotal occasion coming in January 1966 when Ken Kesey and his Merry Pranksters hosted a Trips Festival in the Longshoremen's Hall at Fisherman's Wharf. Attended by thousands, most of whom had dropped acid, it set a precedent for wild living, challenging authority and dropping out of the social and political establishment. At the time LSD was not illegal and was being hyped by groups like the Pranksters as an avant-garde art form, consciousness-raising in its effects. Pumped out in private laboratories and promoted by the likes of Timothy Leary with the prescription "Turn on, tune in, drop out", LSD galvanized a generation into believing that it could be used to raise the creativity of one and all. Before long, life in the Haight took on a theatrical quality: Pop Art found mass appeal, light shows became legion, dress flamboyant and behavior untethered from any notion of respectability. The Grateful Dead, Jefferson Airplane and Big Brother and the Holding Company began to make names for themselves, and, backed by the business weight of Bill Graham, the psychedelic music scene became a genuine force nationwide.

It wasn't long before large numbers of kids from all over America started turning up in the Haight for the free food, free drugs . . . and free love. Money became a dirty word, the hip became "heads", the others "straights", and by the time of the massive "Be-In" in Golden Gate Park in 1966 and the so-called "Summer of Love" the following year, this busy little intersection

had attracted no fewer than 75,000 transitory people in its short life
as the focus of alternative culture.

But along with all the nice middle-class kids who simply wanted
to get stoned, came the outcasts, the crazies and the villains.
Charles Manson recruited much of his "family" in the Haight and the
enormous flow of drugs through the neighborhood made it inviting
prey for organized crime. Hunter S Thompson, too, spent his time
here researching and writing his book *Hell's Angels*, and was
notorious for inviting Angels to his apartment on Parnassus Street
for drinking and drug-taking sessions which were noisy, long and
sometimes – given Thompson's penchant for firearms – even
dangerous.

The Haight today has few real sights, relying instead on the
constant turnover of hip clothing stores, popular cafés and bookstores to sustain its legend. Two blocks east of the Haight-Ashbury
junction, **Buena Vista Park** is a mountainous forest of Monterey
pines and California redwoods, used by dogwalkers and other
people who go to enjoy the stunning views of the city, but come
nightfall the locale of much sex-in-the-shrubbery. Around the park
are examples of some of the most lavish Victorian architecture to be
found in the city, many decorated to death with turrets, false gables,
columns, corner towers and elaborate window design; indeed for all
its hipness and supposed disdain for bourgeois living, the Haight
has all the makings (or at least the architecture) of an exclusive,
chi-chi community.

Some determinedly psychedelic outposts do remain. For example, the **Holos Gallery**, at 1792 Haight St, has the largest collection
of holograms in California: a dimly-lit affair that could be said to
encapsulate the 1960s – trashy and ultimately empty, but a good
idea at the time. A more worthwhile hangover is the **Haight-
Ashbury Free Clinic** at 558 Clayton St. By American standards, it's
quite a phenomenon, providing free health care since the 1960s
when drug-related illnesses became a big problem in the Haight. It
survives – barely – on contributions and continues to treat drug
casualties and the poor, both disproportionately large groups in this
part of the city.

Otherwise, stroll along the Haight and take advantage of what is
still one of the best areas in town to **shop**. It shouldn't take more
than a couple of hours to update your record collection, dress yourself up and blow money on good books. If you're looking for food,
some interesting restaurants are starting to appear along Haight
Street, although there's still a better line in bakeries, cafés and
lunch-type places. Moving west along Haight Street things get
livelier the nearer you approach to the **Panhandle**, the finger-slim
strip of greenery that eventually leads to Golden Gate Park but is
generally considered to be part of the Haight. The Panhandle was
landcaped before the rest of the park back in the 1870s, and for a
while was the focus for High Society carriage rides, where the

Haight-Ashbury

well-dressed would go to look and be looked at. In post-quake 1906 it became a refuge for fleeing families, with some thirty thousand living in tents. During the 1960s it was the scene for outdoor rock concerts which caused considerable wear and tear on the delicate landscape. Today it's rather seedy: home to vagrants and the few guitar-strumming hippies that remain.

Chapter 6

Golden Gate Park, The Beaches and Outlying Districts

Beyond downtown and the central neighborhoods, San Francisco's **Outlying Districts** lack much of the character that has helped define the city – peripheral areas that resemble the suburbs common to so many American cities. What they do provide is a feeling of openness and room to breathe and, although often shrouded in fog, a magnificent shoreline at the edge of the Pacific Ocean that is a mere twenty-minute drive from downtown. The area also benefits from an abundance of large green spaces, most famous of which is the magnificent **GOLDEN GATE PARK**: its museums, gardens and lakes something of an oasis for San Franciscans struggling to find relief from the congestion of their city. Beautifully landscaped and immaculately maintained, its vast grounds have room aplenty for the joggers, bike-riders and busloads of tourists who flock here.

As you'd expect, the area around the park is predominantly residential, inhabited by families and those who either can't afford – or don't care – to live in the city proper. Whichever way you look at it, it's unlikely to be at the top of your agenda on a short visit; and public transportation connections can be irksome. If you have the time, explorations reveal some of the city's best **beaches**. The most popular of these, **Baker's Beach**, and the less-visited **China Beach**, are easily accessible from downtown, curving around the peninsula from the Golden Gate Bridge to meet **Lands End** – a usually uncrowded set of hiking trails and cliffs above the shoreline that make for a perfect break from the city. A little way inland, the **Palace of the Legion of Honor**, San Francisco's finest arts museum, stands in majestic isolation on a bluff near the ocean. The least patronized of all the city's museums, its high-caliber collection merits an unhurried half-day's browsing, free from jostling crowds.

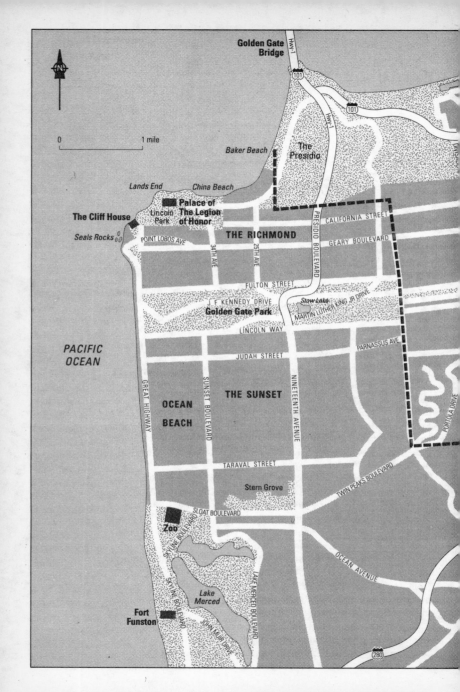

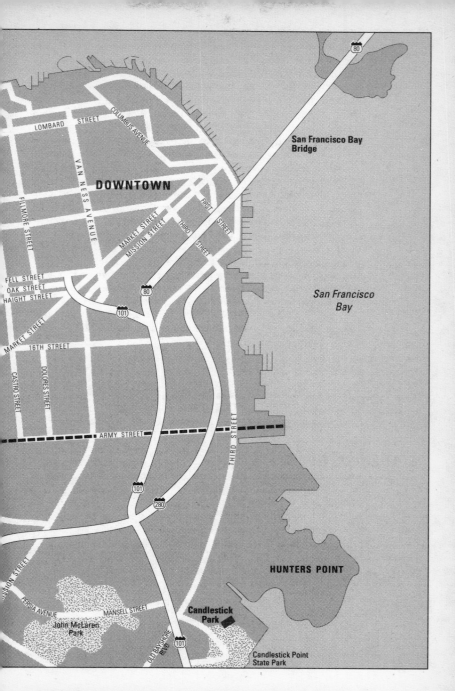

Around Point Lobos, the peninsula's westernmost tip, parked tour buses and camera-toting tourists signal arrival at the **Cliff House**, **Sutro Baths** and **Seals Rocks** – a trio of seaside attractions that forms the busiest point along the coast. Stretching for miles from here is the vast expanse of **Ocean Beach**: better suited to dog-walking than sun-worship, it's not a crowd-puller and is used mostly by the residents of the often fog-bound **Richmond** and **Sunset** neighborhoods that hug the ocean's edge nearby.

Further south, the city's prettily landscaped **zoo** and the leafy ravine of **Stern Grove**, are both good options for restless children, either to see the animals or just kick a ball about. Similarly **Lake Merced**, a little further south, is a fine place to stop for lunch, take a boat out or sit around waiting for the fog to lift. Better still, head west to reach the beautiful cragginess of **Fort Funston**, San Francisco's southernmost and probably most attractive stretch of beach. You're considerably less likely to visit notorious **Hunter's Point**, over on the southeastern edge of the peninsula near a massive US Navy shipyard – a run-down neighborhood with some of the city's worst urban problems – though you may find yourself travelling through on your way to **Candlestick Park**. This is the city's main outdoor sports arena, where local heroes the *San Francisco 49ers* (football) and their baseball equivalents, the *San Francisco Giants*, keep the city's sporting morale intact with regular strings of victories.

Golden Gate Park

Unlike most American cities, San Francisco is not short on green space, but **GOLDEN GATE PARK** is its largest, providing a massively bucolic antidote to the center of town. Despite the throngs

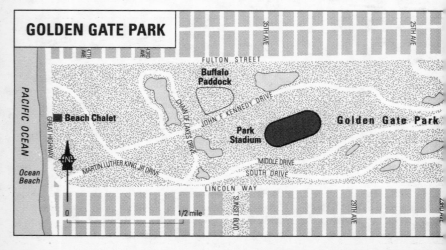

of joggers, polo players, roller-skaters, cyclists and strollers it never gets overcrowded, and you can always find a spot to be alone. Inspired by Frederick Law Olmsted, creator of Central Park in New York, and designed by park engineer William H Hall in 1871, it's one of the most beautiful and safest corners of the city, with none of the menace of New York's park. Spreading three miles or so west from the Haight to the Pacific, it was constructed on what was then an area of wild sand dunes buffeted by the spray from the nearby ocean, with the help of a dyke to protect the western side from the sea. John McLaren, the Scottish park superintendent for fifty-odd years, planted several thousand trees here, and it's nowadays the most peaceful – and most skilfully crafted – spot to relax in the city.

Exploration of all the corners of this huge park could take days of footwork, though it's best to wander aimlessly, getting lost and seeing what you can stumble across. Sloping gently from east to west, it divides roughly into two sections: the eastern side, nearest the Haight, has all the main attractions – art and science museums, horticultural palaces, tea gardens and bandstands. The west is fairly isolated, with more open space and a less sculpted landscape better suited to horse riding and other outdoor activities.

Fell Street runs along the side of the Panhandle, becoming John F Kennedy Drive where it enters the park. Follow this for half a mile to reach the busiest section, near the **museums**. The largest of these, the **M H de Young Memorial Museum** (Wed–Sun 10am–5pm; $4, free Sat mornings and first Wed of month), is the city's most diverse; its permanent collection of American art, from colonial times to the twentieth century, is rated among the best on the West Coast. The museum had its origin in the California Midwinter International Exposition of 1894, a venture that was so successful that the Fine Arts Building (around which the current museum was built) was

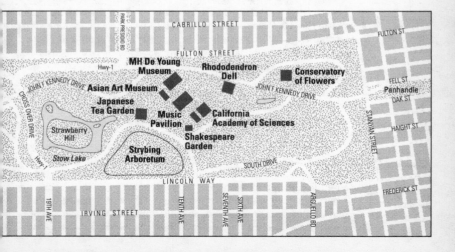

turned over to newspaper publisher M H de Young with the purpose
of establishing a permanent museum. Overall the collection is very
impressive, in particular the core of over a hundred paintings from
the collection of Mr and Mrs John D Rockefeller III that features
works by John Singleton Copley, Rembrandt Peale and John Singer
Sargent. The works in the new British Galleries date from the reign
of George III in the latter half of the eighteenth century and continue
into the early years of the nineteenth – an era of potent achievement
in the Neoclassical and Rococo periods. Major painters represented
include John Constable, Sir Joshua Reynolds, Thomas Gainsborough
and Henry Raeburn. Least interesting is the museum's showing of
the traditional arts of Africa, Oceania and the Americas, with the
ancient arts of Egypt, Greece and Rome slightly better represented.

*The Asian Art
Museum is
scheduled to
move in 1994;
see p.92.*

Next door, the **Asian Art Museum** (Wed–Sun 10am–5pm; $4,
free Sat mornings and the first Wed of each month) opened in 1966
after Avery Brundage, long-time head of the International Olympic
Committee, donated his world-famous collection to the city of San
Francisco. Its sheer size precludes the display of the whole lot at
once; instead works are rotated periodically. Highlights include the
Jade Room, in which the pieces date back as far as 3500 years, and
the oldest-known **Chinese Buddha** image (338 AD). The addition of
a new **Indian Gallery** has done much to improve the museum, with
over twenty miniature paintings, heavy stone sculptures from the
Jain period, and textiles.

Opposite is the **California Academy of Sciences** (daily 10am–
5pm; $5, children under 6 free), perfect for inquisitive children. The
natural history museum holds a thirty-foot skeleton of a 130-million-
year-old dinosaur and life-size replicas of humans throughout the
ages, but the show stealer is the collection of 14,500 specimens of
aquatic life in the **Steinhart Aquarium** (same times and ticket). The
feeding of the seals and dolphins at 10.30am is always worth seeing,
as is the doughnut-shaped tank known as the Fish Roundabout: the
viewing area is in the center of this 200-foot-circumference tank and
the impression of being underwater with the fish swimming all about
you is uncanny. Reptile fans will enjoy watching the scaly beasts in
The Swamp – a simulated habitat for lizards, alligators and tortoises.
Adults will get more out of a trip to the Academy of Sciences if they
can catch the **Morrison Planetarium** (schedule varies; ☎387-6300)
at the right time. Laser light shows and rock music often draw an
acid-crazed crowd for the evening performances.

*Despite the
widely
prevalent belief
that fortune
cookies are
Chinese, they
were in fact
invented by the
Hagiwara
family.*

Slightly west of the museums is the usually crowded **Japanese
Tea Garden** (daily 8am–6pm; $3 admission charged 9am–5pm).
Built in 1894 for the California Midwinter Exposition, the garden was
beautifully landscaped by the Japanese Hagiwara family, who looked
after the garden until World War II, when, along with other Japanese
Americans, they were sent to internment camps. A massive bronze
Buddha dominates the garden, and all around are the bridges, foot-
paths, pools filled with shiny carp, bonsai and cherry trees that – but

for the busloads of tourists that pour in regularly throughout the day – lend a peaceful feel. The best way to enjoy the garden is to get there around 8am when it first opens and have a breakfast of tea and fortune cookies in the tea house.

Considering the abundance of flowers throughout the park in general, it would seem that an enormous exhibition space for them was unnecessary, but the **Conservatory of Flowers** on John F Kennedy Drive (daily 10am–5pm; free), a huge Victorian glass palace modelled on the Palm House at Kew Gardens, has an impressive collection of tropical plants and flowers. Still, it seems a bit foolish to endure the heat of this giant greenhouse when you can stroll the park, free of crowds, and see more or less the same thing. Two of the hundreds of flower gardens are particularly lovely: **Rhododendron Dell**, where John F Kennedy Drive meets Sixth Avenue, is a twenty-acre memorial to John McLaren, filled with over 500 species of his favorite flower, as well as statues of McLaren and his favorite poet, Robert Burns. The **Shakespeare Garden**, where Middle Drive meets Martin Luther King Jr Drive, has every flower or plant ever mentioned in the writer's plays.

The best things to do at the park are outdoors and free. On Sundays, in the central space near the museums, **music** can be heard for free at the **Music Pavilion** bandstand; to enjoy the quieter corners of the park head west through the many flower gardens and eucalyptus groves towards the ocean. Although most people head for the western end of the park to do nothing whatsoever, activities are many, and quite cheap, if you're feeling energetic. **Boat rental** on the beautiful, vast and marshy **Stow Lake** costs around $10 per hour, and is most enjoyable midweek when the place is almost deserted. In the middle of the lake, the large artificial mountain of **Strawberry Hill** is perfect for a picnic and a laze in the sunshine.

Perhaps the most unusual thing you'll see in the park is the substantial herd of bison, roaming around the **Buffalo Paddock** off JFK Drive near 38th Avenue; you can get closest to these shaggy giants at their feeding area, at the far west end. Moving towards the edge of the park at Ocean Beach, passing a tulip garden and large windmill, you'll come to the **Beach Chalet** facing the Great Highway. This two-storey, white-pillared structure designed by Willis Polk is home to some of San Francisco's lesser-known public art. A series of frescoes painted in the 1930s depict the growth of the city and the creation of Golden Gate Park.

Baker Beach and China Beach

Partly due to the weather, partly due to the people, **beach** culture doesn't exist in San Francisco the way it does in Southern California and people here tend to watch the surf rather than ride it. Powerful currents and very cold water make it almost impossible to swim

Baker Beach and China Beach

comfortably and with any degree of confidence outside high summer (though people *do* swim all year round) and more often than not nude sunbathing is as adventurous as it gets. As a result, San Francisco's beaches are blissfully uncrowded, free from parading dollies and the surf mobs they follow.

Baker Beach extends for almost a mile along the jagged cliffs below the Presidio, great for walking or fishing but not recommended for swimming. *Muni* bus #29 will bring you here, but if you're driving or cycling, approach from the Golden Gate Bridge: it's a breathtaking route along winding and cypress-shaded Lincoln Boulevard, with the green hills of the Presidio to your left and the crashing Pacific Ocean to your right. Far from being a pleasure zone, Baker Beach was originally used as the hiding place for an enormous 95,000-pound cannon that the army placed in an underground concrete bunker just above the strand in 1905 to protect the bay from intruders. When aircraft began to replace the army's land defences, the cannon was decreed obsolete and after World War II was melted for scrap, having never seen a day's active service in its forty-year career. A replacement cannon (for exhibition purposes only) was set up on the site in 1977, and at weekends the rangers give a brief demonstration of how the huge thing would have been aimed and fired. Most people who come here seem quite happy to ignore the massive lump of iron and steel, preferring to laze about taking in the fantastic views of the ocean and bridge.

Southwest of Baker Beach, **China Beach** is a tiny cove nestling at the bottom of the exclusive Sea Cliff neighborhood. It takes its name from the 1870s, when Chinese fishermen camped along its crescent and fished its comparatively calm waters. Later, when the government slapped immigration restrictions on the Chinese, China Beach was supposedly used to smuggle people into San Francisco. During the 1920s there was much wrangling over developing the beach and the land above, but busy campaigning won the day and the beach remained in public hands. These days it is San Francisco's safest swimming beach, but despite this is seldom used, most people opting for the much larger and more easily accessible Baker Beach. During good weather, however, you should make the effort to get there – changing rooms, showers and a sundeck are all freely available, making it the best option if you want to spend a whole day sunning and swimming.

Lands End and the Palace of the Legion of Honor

Balanced precariously at the city's edge, **Lands End** is as wild and remote as its name implies. Situated on the tip of land that divides Baker and China from Ocean Beach to the south, this lonely bluff has hiking trails and a sublime lookout across the ocean. Beneath the jagged cliffs are the shells of ships which fell foul of the treacherous waters – when the tide is out you can see the wreckage. This is one of the few wilderness areas left in the city: ice-plant grows across the sandy cliffs and dazzling wild flowers appear in random clumps; catch it on a good sunset and the experience is quite humbling. A mile-long circular trail that snakes through the cypress groves and along the grassy cliffs is a popular cruising spot for gays, who favor the privacy it offers – but apart from a few lurkers, expect to be alone.

At the south end of the Lands End trail, the **Palace of the Legion of Honor** is a white-pillared twin of the more famous Légion d'Honneur in Paris. Arguably San Francisco's best museum, it is probably also its most beautifully located – the romantic setting, graceful architecture and colonnaded courtyard combining to lend a truly elegant impression. However, the building has for some years been undergoing an extensive process of remodelling, expansion and seismic strengthening; at the time this book went to press, the museum was scheduled to reopen in October 1995.

Built from a donation from the wealthy San Franciscan Spreckels family, the Legion of Honor was built in 1920 and dedicated on Abraham Lincoln's birthday in 1921. Its permanent collection includes a strong **Renaissance** contingent, represented with the works of Titian, El Greco and sculpture from Giambologna. Great canvasses by Rembrandt and Hals are highlights of the seventeenth-century Dutch and Flemish collection, as is Rubens' magnificent *Tribute Money*. The **impressionist** and **post-impressionist** galleries contain works by Courbet, Manet, Monet, Renoir, Degas and Cezanne, and there's also one of the world's finest assemblies of **Rodin** sculptures, with bronze, porcelain and stone pieces such as *The Athlete*, *Fugit Amor*, *The Severed Head of John the Baptist* and *Fallen Angel*, as well as a small cast of *The Kiss*.

There's another impressive Rodin collection in Stanford University's art museum – see p.163.

Cliff House, Sutro Baths and Seal Rocks

About a mile southwest along the coast from the tip of Lands End, the **Cliff House**, judging by the number of tour buses parked outside, is one of the top sightseeing spots in the city. At the edge of the Pacific Ocean where Geary Boulevard meets the Great Highway, the house itself is not spectacular (or even authentic), but its setting on a mammoth rock perched over the Pacific, with the broad strand of Ocean Beach stretching for miles to the south, is memorable. The original building on this site in the 1850s, Seal Rock House, was used by hiking and horse-riding San Franciscans as a rest-spot after the long journey from downtown. It closed at the end of the 1850s, but the idea for a seaside resort stuck, and with the completion of

Cliff House, Sutro Baths and Seal Rocks

the first road from the city to the beach, the first Cliff House was constructed, thriving for two decades as an exclusive resort for the leisured classes – the Stanfords, Crockers and Hearsts of late nineteenth-century San Francisco – and soon earning a reputation for gambling and prostitution. A Prussian immigrant, Adolph Sutro bought the original Cliff House, only to watch it burn to the foundations in 1894, and it was he who built the Cliff House that is best remembered today. A stunning Gothic monolith of glass and spires, it had dozens of dining rooms, an art gallery and twenty private luncheon rooms, enjoying a much celebrated existence until it, too, was destroyed by fire in 1907. Sadly, today's Cliff House can't compare – though the view from the bar at sunset makes it worth braving the hordes.

Adolph's other opulent creation, the **Sutro Baths**, was more enduring: a hundred thousand feet of stained glass covering over three acres of sculpted swimming pools and tanks of fresh and salt water. It came to be known as California's "Tropical Winter Garden", and for ten cents you could enter through a classical pillared entrance that led to gardens of fountains, flowers and trees, and swim all day amid sculptures, tapestries and ancient artefacts that Sutro had collected from around the world. It all got to be too expensive to maintain, and the baths crumbled elegantly until they were razed by a fire in 1966. Today, some very ancient-looking ruins remain, and if you can manage the clamber down the steep staircase down the cliff face, it makes for an interesting, if occasionally wet, trek through the old ramparts and tunnels. At night, when the surf really starts to crash, things can get a bit frightening here, but there's a certain romance, too, and on a rare warm evening it becomes one of the city's favorite snogging spots. By day, you'll get the best and closest view of **Seal Rocks**, the clump of boulders a little way out to sea that have been colored white by the hundreds of seagulls. The rocks take their name from the population of seals that for ever compete for the sunniest spots.

The Richmond, Sunset and Ocean Beach

Quite apart from being awkward destinations to reach on public transportation, the **Richmond** and **Sunset** districts, often referred to as "The Avenues", are disappointing. Large areas, populated for the most part by families, the neighborhoods are neat, clean, respectable – and terrifically dull. Divided by Golden Gate Park, they have many similarities: flat – and often fog-bound – orderly avenues surrounded by some great open spaces. Stretching north to the Presidio and south of the Golden Gate Park, they extend westwards for miles before ending abruptly at the ocean's edge.

The Richmond

Solidly middle class, **THE RICHMOND** was first settled by Russian
and Eastern European Jews after World War I. Later came the
Japanese and now, most predominantly, Chinese families are
moving their businesses here away from the overcrowding and noise
of Chinatown, lending the area the name "New Chinatown". It's a
vast neighborhood, divided into **inner** and **outer** districts, separated
by Park Presidio Boulevard (Hwy-1). The outer portion is only for
passing through on your way out to Sutro Baths and the Cliff House,
and assuming that you're going to bother with it at all, you should
confine your wanderings to the inner Richmond around **Clement
Street** between Arguello St and Eighth Ave. This is the neighborhood's commercial strip, with some good Asian restaurants, a
couple of cafés, a movie theater and some rowdy Irish pubs.

The Sunset and Ocean Beach

Few places in San Francisco could be termed unpleasant, but neighborhoods like **THE SUNSET** can certainly be described as monotonous – clean, quiet streets, spread out across a large area, and
leading eventually to **Ocean Beach**, the largest and least arresting
stretch of San Francisco's shoreline. Some surfing and fishing goes
on, but mostly the beach is the domain of dog-walkers and strollers
out for some fresh air. Strong undertow and unexpected riptides
render swimming out of the question, and the often grey color of
the sand makes sunbathing unappealing.

Like Golden Gate Park and the Richmond district, the Sunset
was once just windswept sand dunes until a massive FHA
programme after World War II paved over the area and put up
houses that then cost $5000 each. The same modest structures,
occupied largely by the original owners (the Sunset has the highest
population of residents over sixty), are reckoned to be fetching
around half a million at today's prices.

There's a build-up of stores and a few restaurants around the
area of Judah and Ninth Avenue, but nothing worth making an effort
for; indeed, if you never saw the neighborhood you wouldn't be
missing a thing.

The Zoo, Lake Merced and Fort Funston

There may be precious little to do in the Sunset, but if you journey a
short way **south** your options widen considerably. Some of the city's
prettiest green spaces are locked into a square bordered by Hwy-1
to the east, the San Francisco county line to the south and the best
part of Ocean Beach to the west. Take a picnic and spend a day
exploring San Francisco's least-visited attractions.

The Zoo, Lake Merced and Fort Funston

Where Sloat Boulevard meets the Pacific coast, just off the end of the *Muni* L Taraval trolley line, **San Francisco Zoo** (daily 10am–5pm; $6, under-12s free) is a small, but expertly designed institution, organized around the principle that the animals should be housed in an environment most closely resembling their natural habitat. Rather than the usual spectacle of animals listlessly slumped in their small cages, the thousand or so exotic beasts at San Francisco Zoo swing happily from trees, roam across fields and lounge on islands. One of the most innovative enclosures is the **Primate Discovery Center**, a complex of fenced-in atriums in which you can get intimate with sixteen playful varieties of primate. It also has an interactive computer facility where you can design a primate to your own specification. There are also the more standard exhibits of lions and tigers, a special **Children's Zoo** ($1) where the under-12s can go and feed a barnyard full of domestic animals, and a **Zebra Zephyr Train** that will take them on an informative tour of the entire zoo.

A little way east, where Sloat Blvd crosses Nineteenth Ave (Hwy-1), **Stern Grove** is a leafy ravine of eucalyptus, redwood and fir trees that shelters a natural amphitheater. For most of the year it's used by picnickers and schoolchildren on nature rambles, but during the summer between June and August, **free concerts** are held each Sunday at 2pm. An excellent assortment of programmes from classical to jazz are presented – take a picnic and get there early to be sure of a good spot.

For something more active, head south along Skyline Boulevard to **Lake Merced**. A standby reservoir for the city, this large freshwater lake is a peaceful, uncrowded spot to rent a rowing boat or have a picnic. The bar and restaurant at the **boathouse** offer a welcome opportunity to sit out on the deck overlooking the lake and have a cheap lunch while waiting for the fog to lift. Seldom used, it's a great place for the crowd-weary and those who need a large open space to let their children run wild.

Even if you skip all of the above, it's well worth making the effort to visit **Fort Funston**, at the southernmost point of the city's coastline and above its most windswept and beautiful stretch of beach, where wild flowers grow along the cliff-tops. On a sunny day, you can clamber down the cliff face, lie on the fine white sand, and gaze up at the hang-gliders as they leap off the cliffs to soar above the ocean's edge.

Hunter's Point and Candlestick Park

San Franciscans speak of **HUNTER'S POINT** with some trepidation. The neighborhood has the city's largest concentration of public housing, and is rife with the social problems that ail many such projects. Situated south of the SoMa docks on its own mini-peninsula, in the far southeast corner of San Francisco, it was chosen as the site of a major US Navy shipyard during World War II. The temporary housing that went up to shelter the 35,000 employees who came to work in the war effort is still in use, and this is perhaps the city's most isolated and forgotten corner. The entire area has a distinct air of neglect about it, plagues by unemployment, crime and drug abuse. Few outsiders ever venture into the neighborhood, and to be honest, as a visitor, there's little reason to come.

About the only occasion you're likely to pass through this part of town is if you're trying to beat the often blocked-up traffic on the Bayshore Freeway (US-101) – the main route to and from the airport – or if you're taking Third Street to a *Giants* or *49ers* game at **Candlestick Park**, just south of Hunter's Point. *Muni* puts on special buses on game days, and most take this route. It was here at Candlestick during the World Series that the big 1989 earthquake hit. The panic of the startled crowds in the shaking stadium was broadcast nationwide – hardly what they'd expected but certainly something they'll never forget.

A walk around **Candlestick Point State Park** reveals a fine example of the 1970s asphalting craze, when hitherto unkempt pieces of land were paved into fitness courses, with trails that lead you from push-up bench to pull-up bar, with markers for you to gauge your progress. Skip that and walk towards the pier at the easternmost point of the park where old men and young boys fish indolently and share the views over the quiet stretch of the bay. To describe the park as beautiful, or even attractive, would be pushing it, but it's a pleasant enough place to picnic or just lie about and enjoy the peace.

For tickets to see the 49ers, *call* ☎ *468-2249; for the* Giants, *call* ☎ *467-8000; and see also p.267.*

Hunter's Point and Candlestick Park

The Bay Area

Chapter 7

Introducing The Bay Area

Whil e San Francisco proper occupies only 48 hilly square miles at the tip of a slender peninsula, the metropolitan **Bay Area** sprawls out far beyond these narrow confines, north and east across the impressive Golden Gate and Bay bridges, and to the south along the peninsula. There's no doubt about the supporting role these places play in relation to San Francisco – always "The City" – but each contributes in its own way to making the Bay Area one of the country's most desirable places to live or visit.

Across the grey steel Bay Bridge, eight miles from downtown San Francisco, the **East Bay** – covered in our Chapter Eight – is the biggest and perhaps the most interesting segment of the bay, home to the lively, left-leaning cities of Oakland and Berkeley, which hold some of the best bookshops and restaurants, and most of the live music clubs, in the greater Bay Area. The weather's generally much sunnier and warmer here, too, and it's easy to reach by way of the space-age BART trains that race under the bay. The rest of the East Bay is filled out by Contra Costa County, which includes the short-lived early state capital of California – the near-ghost town of Benicia – as well as the homes of writers John Muir and Eugene O'Neill.

South of the city, and the focus of Chapter Nine, the **Peninsula** holds some of San Francisco's oldest and most upscale suburbs, reaching down into the computer belt of the Silicon Valley around San Jose – California's fastest-growing city – though apart from some fancy houses there's not a lot to see. The beaches are excellent, though – sandy, clean and surprisingly uncrowded – and a couple of youth hostels are set in old lighthouses at the edge of the Pacific.

For some of the most beautiful land-and-seascapes in California, cross the Golden Gate Bridge or ride a ferry across the bay to **Marin County**, explored in Chapter Ten. This mountainous peninsula is half wealthy suburbia and half unspoiled hiking country, holding the coastal wildernesses of Muir Woods and the Point Reyes National Seashore. The redwood forests that rise sheer out of the thundering ocean are separated from the yacht clubs and plush bay-view houses of Sausalito and Tiburon by a range of 2500-foot peaks.

Full listings of accommodation, restaurants and other facilities in the Bay Area are provided in Chapters Twelve to Seventeen.

North of Marin County, at the top of the bay, and still within an hour's drive of San Francisco, is the **Wine Country**. Dotted with hundreds of prestigious wineries, Napa Valley in particular provides dozens of places where you can sample fine wines, enjoy a four-star meal or simply soak your weary bones in one of the many local hot springs. Its neighbor, the Sonoma Valley, is more rural and informal, and together they make an excellent day or two away from the San Francisco hustle. Chapter Eleven suggests some possible itineraries.

Public **transportation** around the Bay Area is quite good by US standards, although it is primarily aimed at commuters, not visitors. Unless you have more time than money, you'll probably do best to rent a car; many of the best places are simply inaccessible without one.

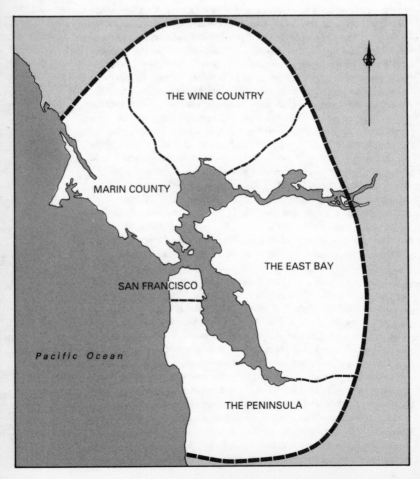

Chapter 8

The East Bay

The largest and most-travelled bridge in the US, the **Bay Bridge** heads east from downtown San Francisco, part graceful suspension bridge and part heavy-duty steel truss. Completed just a year after the more famous (and better-loved) Golden Gate, the Bay Bridge works a whole lot harder for a lot less respect: a hundred million vehicles cross the bridge each year, though you'd have to search hard to find a postcard of it. Indeed, its only claim to fame – apart from the much-broadcast videotape of its partial collapse during the 1989 earthquake – is that **Treasure Island**, where the two halves of the bridge meet, hosted the 1939 World's Fair. During World War II the island became a Navy base, which it remains, but just inside the gates there's a small museum (daily 10am–3pm; free) with pictures of the Fair amid maritime memorabilia. The island also offers great views of San Francisco and the Golden Gate.

The Bay Bridge – and the BART trains that run under the bay – finishes up in the heart of the East Bay in **Oakland**, a hard-working, blue-collar city that earns its livelihood from shipping and transport services, evidenced by the massive Port of Oakland whose huge cranes dominate the place, lit up at night like futuristic dinosaurs. Oakland spreads north along wooded foothills to **Berkeley**, an image-conscious college town that looks out across to the Golden Gate and collects a mixed bag of pin-striped Young Republicans, ageing 1960s radicals, and Nobel Prize-winning nuclear physicists in its many cafés and bookstores.

Berkeley and Oakland blend together so much as to be virtually the same city, and the hills above them are topped by a twenty-mile string of forested **regional parks**, providing much needed fresh air and quick relief from the concrete grids below. The rest of the East Bay is filled out by Contra Costa County, a huge area that contains some intriguing, historically important waterfront towns – well worth a detour if you're passing through on the way to the Wine Country region of the Napa and Sonoma valleys – as well as some of the Bay Area's most inward-looking suburban sprawl.

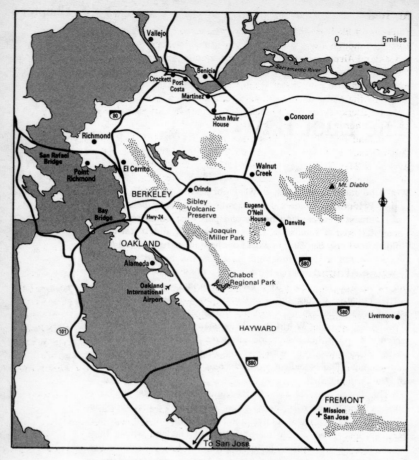

Curving around the **North Bay** from the heavy-industrial landscape of Richmond, and facing each other across the narrow **Carquinez Straits**, both Benicia and Port Costa were vitally important during California's first twenty years of existence, after the 1849 Gold Rush; they're now strikingly sited but little-visited ghost towns.

For East Bay accommodation, see Chapter 12; restaurants are on p.225; and cafés and bars on p.237.

In contrast, standing out from the soulless dormitory communities that fill up the often baking hot **inland valleys**, are the preserved homes of an unlikely pair of influential writers: the naturalist **John Muir**, who, when not out hiking around Yosemite and the High Sierra, lived most of his life near **Martinez**, and playwright **Eugene O'Neill**, who wrote many of his angst-ridden works at the foot of **Mount Diablo**, the Bay Area's most impressive peak.

Arrival

You're most likely to be staying in San Francisco when you visit the East Bay, though it is possible, and sometimes cheaper, to fly direct to **Oakland Airport**, particularly if you're coming from elsewhere in the US. It's an easy trip from the airport into town: take the *AirBART Shuttle* van (every 15min; $2) from outside the terminal direct to the Coliseum BART station, from where you can reach Oakland, Berkeley or San Francisco. In addition, various privately operated shuttle buses cost from $10.

Oakland's *Greyhound* **bus station** (☎510/834-3070) is in a dubious part of town, alongside the I-980 freeway on San Pablo Avenue at 21st Street. If you come to the Bay Area **by train**, the end of the line is the *Amtrak* station (☎510/645-4607) at 16th and Wood streets in the depths of West Oakland, though it's a better option to get off at Richmond and change there onto *BART*.

The most enjoyable way to arrive in the East Bay is to take the commuter **boat** ($3 each way) that sails every two hours from San Francisco's Ferry Building to Jack London Square.

Long-distance transportation connections to Oakland are detailed from p.8 onwards.

Getting Around

BART, the ultra-modern *Bay Area Rapid Transit* system, links San Francisco with the East Bay, via the underground transbay tube, between 6am and midnight, Monday to Saturday, 9am to midnight on Sundays. Three lines run from **Daly City** through San Francisco and on to Downtown Oakland, before diverging to service East Oakland out to **Fremont**, Berkeley and north to **Richmond**, and east into Contra Costa County as far as **Concord**. Fares range from 80¢ to $3, and the cost of each ride is deducted from the total value of the ticket, purchased from machines on the station concourse. If you're relying on *BART* to get around a lot, buy a **high-value ticket** ($5 or $10) to avoid having to stand in line to buy a new ticket each time you ride.

From East Bay *BART* stations, pick up a free transfer to save 35¢ off the $1.10 fares of *AC Transit* (☎510/839-2882), which provides a good bus service around the entire East Bay area, especially Oakland and Berkeley. *AC Transit* also runs buses on a number of routes to Oakland and Berkeley from the Transbay Terminal in San Francisco. These operate throughout the night, and are the only way of getting across the bay by public transit once *BART* has shut down. Excellent free **maps** of both *BART* and the bus system are available from any station.

Two smaller-scale bus companies can also prove useful. The *Contra Costa County Connection* (☎510/676-7500) runs buses to most of the inland areas, including the John Muir and Eugene O'Neill historic houses, while the *Benicia Bay Connection* (☎707/642-1168) operates between the Pleasant Hill *BART* station and downtown Benicia.

To phone BART from San Francisco dial ☎788-BART; from the East Bay it's ☎510/465-BART.

One of the best ways to get around is **by bike**; a fine cycle route follows Skyline and Grizzly Peak boulevards along the wooded crest of the hills between Berkeley and Lake Chabot. If you don't have your own, touring bikes are available for $15 a day (mountain bikes cost $25) from *Carl's Bikes* (☎510/835-8763), 2416 Telegraph Ave in Oakland, and from *Cal Adventures* (☎510/642-4000), at 2301 Bancroft Way on the UC Berkeley campus. For those interested in **walking tours**, the city of Oakland sponsors free "discovery tours" (☎510/273-3234) of various neighborhoods every Wednesday and Saturday at 10am.

If you're **driving**, allow plenty of time: the East Bay has some of California's worst traffic, with I-80 in particular jam-packed 16 hours per day.

East Bay Information

The **Oakland Convention and Visitors Bureau**, at 1000 Broadway near the 12th Street *BART* station downtown (Mon–Fri 8.30am–5pm; ☎510/839-9000), offers free maps and information, as does the **Berkeley Convention and Visitors Bureau**, 1834 University Ave (Mon–Fri 9am–4pm; ☎510/549-7040).

If you're spending any time at all in the Berkeley area, pick up a copy of *Berkeley Inside/Out* by Don Pitcher (*Heyday Books*, $12.95), an informative guide that'll tell you everything you ever wanted to know about the town and its inhabitants. For information on hiking or horse-riding in the many parks that top the Oakland and Berkeley hills, contact the **East Bay Regional Parks District**, 11500 Skyline Blvd (☎510/562-7275). The widely available (and free) *East Bay Express* – in many ways the best newspaper in the Bay Area – has the most comprehensive listings of **what's on** in the vibrant East Bay music and arts scene. The troubled daily *Oakland Tribune* (25¢) is also worth a look for its coverage of local politics and sporting events.

Oakland

A quick trip across the Bay Bridge or on *BART*, **OAKLAND** is a solidly working-class balance to upwardly mobile San Francisco: the workhorse of the Bay Area, one of the busiest ports on the West Coast and the western terminal of the railroad network. It's not all hard slog, though: the climate is rated the best in the US, often sunny and mild when San Francisco is cold and dreary, and, despite the 1991 fire that ravaged the area, there's great hiking around the redwood- and eucalyptus-covered hills above the city – and views right over the entire Bay Area.

Oakland is better served by historical and literary associations than important sights, of which it has very few. **Gertrude Stein** and **Jack London** both grew up in the city, at approximately the same

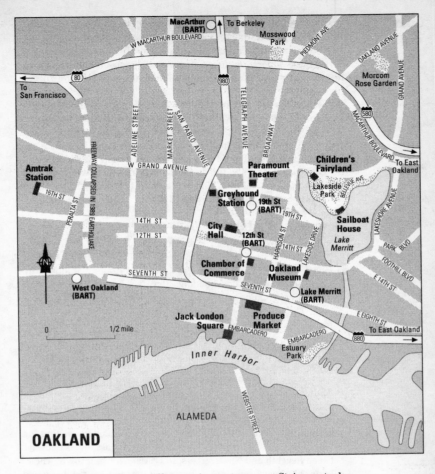

OAKLAND

time though in entirely different circumstances – Stein a stock-broker's daughter, London an orphaned delinquent. The macho and adventurous London is far better remembered – most of the water-front, where he used to steal oysters and lobsters, is now named in his memory – while Stein is all but ignored. Perhaps this is due to her book, *Everybody's Autobiography*, in which she wrote: "What was the use of me having come from Oakland, it was not natural for me to have come from there yes write about it if I like or anything if I like but not there, *there is no there there*" – a quote that has haunted Oakland ever since.

Jack London's mildly socialist leanings set a style for the city, and Oakland has been the breeding ground for some of America's most unabashedly revolutionary **political movements** in the years since. The 1960s saw the city's fifty-percent black population find a voice through the militant Black Panther movement, and in the 1970s Oakland was again on the nation's front pages when the Symbionese Liberation Army demanded a ransom for kidnapped heiress Patty Hearst in the form of free food distribution to the poor.

Oakland is still very much its own city, and it's worth taking the time to get a feel for its diversity and dynamism. A good place to start, if you're here in the spring, is at the annual Festival at the Lake, celebrated each June on the shores of Lake Merritt. Also, although civic pride has never fully recovered from the defection of the *Oakland Raiders* to the bright lights of Los Angeles a few years back, sports fans still rally behind the many-times American League and World Series champion *Oakland A's*.

Downtown Oakland

Coming by *BART* from San Francisco, get off at the 12th Street–Civic Center station and you're in **DOWNTOWN OAKLAND**, a compact district of spruced-up Victorian storefronts overlooked by modern hotels and office buildings that has been engulfed by an ambitious programme of restoration and redevelopment for over a decade. The project has been fraught with allegations of illegal dealings and incompetent planning, and so far it's less than a complete success. To make way for the moat-like I-980 freeway – now the main route through Oakland since the collapse of the Cypress Freeway in the 1989 earthquake – entire blocks were cleared of houses, some of which were saved and moved to **Preservation Park** at 12th Street and Martin Luther King Jr Way. The late nineteenth-century commercial center along Ninth Street west of Broadway, now tagged **Victorian Row**, underwent a major restoration some years ago, but many of the buildings are still boarded up waiting for tenants. By way of contrast, stroll a block east of Broadway, between Seventh and Ninth streets, to Oakland's **Chinatown**, whose bakeries and restaurants are as lively and bustling – if not as picturesque – as those of its more famous cousin across the Bay.

Oakland's restaurants are detailed on p.237.

Luckily not all of downtown Oakland has the look of a permanent building site. The city experienced its greatest period of growth in the early twentieth century, and many of the grand buildings of this era survive a few blocks north along Broadway, centered on the awkwardly imposing 1914 **City Hall** on 14th Street. Two blocks away, at 13th and Franklin, stands Oakland's most unmistakeable landmark, the chateau-esque lantern of the **Tribune Tower**, the 1920s-era home of the *Oakland Tribune* newspaper.

Further north, around the 19th Street *BART* station, are some of the Bay Area's finest early twentieth-century buildings, highlighted by the outstanding Art Deco interior of the 1931 **Paramount Theater** at 2025 Broadway (tours Sat at 10am; $5; ☎510/465-

4600), which shows Hollywood classics on selected Friday nights. Nearby buildings are equally exuberant in their decoration, ranging from the wafer-thin Gothic "flatiron" office tower of the **Cathedral Building** at Broadway and Telegraph, to the Hindu temple-like facade of the 3500-seat **Fox Oakland** on Telegraph at 19th – at the time it was built in 1928, the largest movie house west of Chicago – and, across the street, the 1931 **Floral Depot**, a group of small Moderne storefronts faced in black-and-blue terracotta tiles with shiny silver highlights.

West of Broadway, the area around the *Greyhound* bus station on San Pablo Avenue is fairly dubious. San Pablo used to be the main route in and out of Oakland before the freeways were built, but many of the roadside businesses are now derelict, especially around the industrial districts of **Emeryville**. Some of the old warehouses have been converted into artists' lofts and studios, though any gentrification there might be is diffused by the scenes on the street, where prostitutes and drug-dealers hang out under the neon signs of the dingy bars and gambling halls like the *Oaks Card Club*, owned by Oak Town rapper Hammer.

Lake Merritt and the Oakland Museum

Five blocks east of Broadway, the eastern third of downtown Oakland is made up of **Lake Merritt**, a three-mile-circumference tidal lagoon that was bridged and dammed in the 1860s to become the centerpiece of Oakland's most desirable neighborhood. All that remains of the many fine houses that once circled the lake is the elegant **Camron-Stanford House**, on the southwest shore at 1418 Lakeside Drive, a graceful Italianate mansion whose sumptuous interior is open for visits (Wed 11am–4pm, Sun 1–5pm; $2). The lake is also the nation's oldest wildlife refuge, and migrating flocks of ducks, geese and herons break their journeys here. The north shore is lined by **Lakeside Park**, where you can rent canoes and row boats ($4 per hour), and a range of sailboats and catamarans ($4–10 per hour) from the Sailboat House (daily 10am–5pm in summer, weekends only rest of year; ☎510/444-3807) – provided you can convince the staff you know how to sail. A miniature Mississippi riverboat makes half-hour lake cruises on weekend afternoons ($1), and kids will appreciate the puppet shows and pony rides at the Children's Fairyland (daily 10am–5.30pm, weekends only in winter; $1.50), along Grand Avenue on the northwest edge of the park. Every year, on the first weekend in June, the park comes to life during the **Festival at the Lake**, when all of Oakland gets together to enjoy non-stop music and performances from local bands and entertainers.

Two blocks south of the lake, or a block up Oak Street from the Lake Merritt *BART* station, the **Oakland Museum** (Wed–Sat 10am–5pm, Sun noon–7pm; free, $4 for special exhibitions) is perhaps a more worthwhile stop, not only for the exhibits but also for the superb modern building in which it's housed, topped by a terraced rooftop sculpture garden that gives great views out over the water and the city. The museum covers many diverse areas: there are displays on the **ecology** of California, including a simulated walk from the seaside through various natural habitats up to the 14,000-foot summits of the Sierra Nevada mountains; state **history** – ranging from old mining equipment to the guitar that Berkeley-born Country Joe MacDonald played at the Woodstock festival in 1969; and a broad survey of works by California artists and craftspeople, some highlights of which are pieces of turn-of-the-century **arts and crafts furniture**, and excellent **photography** by Edward Muybridge, Dorothea Lange and Imogen Cunningham. The museum also has a collector's gallery which loans and sells works by California artists.

The Waterfront, Alameda and West Oakland

Ferry services from San Francisco are detailed on p.135.

Half a mile down from Downtown Oakland on *AC Transit* bus #51A, at the foot of Broadway on the Waterfront, **Jack London Square** is Oakland's sole concession to the tourist trade. Also accessible by direct ferries from San Francisco, this somewhat soporific complex of boutiques and restaurants along the harbor was named after the self-taught writer who grew up pirating shellfish around here, but is about as distant from the spirit of the man as it's possible to get. Jack London's best story, *The Call of the Wild*, was written about his adventures in the Alaskan Yukon, where he carved his initials in a small cabin that has been reconstructed here; another survivor is *Heinhold's First and Last Chance Saloon*, a seedy bar where London spent much of his wayward youth.

No Jack London enthusiast should fail to visit his Sonoma Valley ranch – see p.192.

If you're not a keen fan of London, there are still a few worthwhile things to do here. One is to walk a few short blocks inland to the **Produce Market**, along Third and Fourth streets, where a couple of good places to eat and drink lurk among the railroad tracks (see p.226). This bustling warehouse district has fruit and vegetables by the forklift load, and is at its most lively early in the morning, from about 5am.

Alameda

AC Transit bus #51A continues from Broadway under the inner harbor to **Alameda**, a quiet and conservative island of Middle-America dominated by a large naval air station, where massive nuclear-powered aircraft carriers sometimes dock. Alameda, which has been hit very hard by post-Cold War military cutbacks, was severed from the Oakland mainland as part of a harbor improvement programme in 1902. The fine houses along the original shoreline on Clinton Street were part of the summer resort colony that flocked here to the *contra costa* or "opposite shore" from San Francisco, near the now-demolished Neptune Beach amusement park. The island has since been much enlarged by dredging and landfill, and 1960s apartment buildings now line the long, narrow shore of **Robert Crown Memorial Beach**, along the bay.

West Oakland

West Oakland – an industrial district of warehouses, railroad tracks, 1960s housing projects and decaying Victorian houses – may be the nearest East Bay *BART* stop to San Francisco, but it's light years away from that city's prosperity. Despite the obvious poverty, it's quite a safe and settled place, but the only time anyone pays it any attention is when something dramatic happens. Two examples are when Black Panther Huey Newton was gunned down here in a drugs-related revenge attack, and when the double decker I-880 freeway which divided the neighborhood from the rest of the city collapsed onto itself in the 1989 earthquake, killing dozens of commuters.

Local people have successfully resisted government plans to rebuild the old concrete eyesore (current plans call for it to be re-routed closer to the harbor); where the freeway used to run through is now the broad and potentially very attractive **Nelson Mandela Parkway**. But otherwise this remains one of the Bay Area's poorest and most neglected neighborhoods, and apart from a marvellous stock of turn-of-the-century houses there's little here to tempt tourists.

For a long time West Oakland was known as "the place where the trains stopped". It still is: take *Amtrak* to San Francisco and you'll arrive at the old **Southern Pacific Depot** at the end of 16th Street (from where buses run across the bay). The station is interesting for the interior alone, cut by huge blue-tinted arched windows and seemingly untouched for the last fifty years. However, since the structure was damaged in the 1989 'quake it may soon be demolished; in the meantime you can peer in and watch the colonies of feral cats who have taken over the lobby. Trains still use the platforms, and a temporary waiting room and ticket office have been built next door.

Half a mile south, near the West Oakland *BART* station, Seventh Street was the heart of the Bay Area's most vibrant entertainment district from the end of Prohibition in 1933 until the early 1970s, when many of the bars and nightclubs were torn down in the name of urban renewal. Seventh Street runs west between the docks and storage yards of the Oakland Army Base and the Naval Supply Depot, ending up at **Portview Park**, one of the best places to watch the huge cargo ships that cruise by. The small park stands on the site of the old transbay ferry landing, used by as many as forty million passengers per year at its peak in the 1930s before the Bay Bridge was completed. The park has officially been closed since the earthquake, but you can nip around the fence and join the people fishing from the small pier, or just enjoy the unmatched view of the San Francisco skyline framed by the Bay and Golden Gate bridges.

East Oakland

The bulk of Oakland spreads out along foothills and flatlands to the east of downtown, in neighborhoods obviously stratified along the main thoroughfares of Foothill and MacArthur boulevards. Gertrude Stein grew up in this area, though when she returned years later in search of her childhood home it had been torn down and replaced by a dozen Craftsman-style bungalows – the simple 1920s wooden houses that still cover most of **East Oakland**, each fronted by a patch of lawn and divided from its neighbor by a narrow concrete driveway.

A quick way out from the gridded streets and sidewalks of the city is to take *AC Transit* bus #15A from downtown east up into the hills to **Joaquin Miller Park**, the most easily accessible of Oakland's hilltop parks. The park stands on the former grounds of the home of the "Poet of the Sierras", Joaquin Miller, who made his name playing the eccentric frontier American in the literary salons of 1870s London. His poems weren't exactly acclaimed, although his prose account, *Life Amongst the Modocs*, documenting time spent with the Modoc Indians near Mount Shasta, does stand the test of time. It was more for his outrageous behavior that he became famous, wearing funny clothes and biting debutantes on the ankle. His house, a small white cabin called **The Abbey**, still survives, as do monuments he built to his friends Robert and Elizabeth Browning, and the thousands of trees he planted.

Perhaps Joaquin Miller's finest poetic achievement was to rhyme teeth with Goethe.

Perched in the hills at the foot of the park, the pointed towers of the **Mormon Temple** look like missile-launchers designed by the Wizard of Oz – unmissable by day or floodlit night. During the holiday season, speakers hidden in the landscaping make it seem as if the plants are singing Christmas carols. Though you can't go inside (unless you're a confirmed Mormon), there are great views out over the entire Bay Area, and a small museum explains the tenets of the faith (daily 9am–9pm; free).

Two miles east along Hwy-13 sits the attractive campus of **Mills College**. Founded in 1852 as a women-only seminary, and still decidedly female after a much-publicized recent struggle against plans to make it co-ed, Mills is renowned for its music school, considered one of the best and most innovative in the US, and worth a visit for its **museum** (Sept–June, Tues–Sun 10am–4pm; free), which has a fine collection of Chinese, Japanese and pre-Columbian ceramics. A broad stream meanders through the lushly landscaped grounds, and many of the buildings, notably the central campanile, were designed in solid California Mission style by Julia Morgan, architect of Hearst Castle as well as some 500 Bay Area structures. Further east, **Oakland Zoo** in Knowland Park is not worth the entry fee, but you can hire horses (☎510/569-4428) from the stables at 14600 Skyline Blvd, and ride around Lake Chabot in the forested hills above.

Along the bay south to San Jose stretch some twenty miles of tract house suburbs, and the only vaguely interesting area is around the end of the *BART* line in **FREMONT**, where the short-lived Essanay movie studios – the first studios on the West Coast – were based. Essanay made over 700 films in three years, including Charlie Chaplin's *The Tramp* in 1914. Not much remains from these pre-Hollywood days, however, and the only real sight is the **Mission San Jose de Guadalupe** on Mission Blvd south of the I-680 freeway (daily 10am–5pm; donations), which in the best traditions of Hollywood set design was completely rebuilt in Mission style only a few years ago.

North Oakland and Rockridge

The horrific October 1991 **Oakland fire**, which destroyed 3000 homes and killed 26 people, did most of its damage in the high-priced hills of **North Oakland**. It took the better part of two years, but most of the half-million dollar houses have been rebuilt, and though the lush vegetation that made the area so attractive will never be allowed to grow back, things are pretty much back to normal. Which is to say that these bayview homes, some of the Bay Area's most valuable real estate, look out across some of its poorest – the neglected flatlands below that in the 1960s were the proving grounds of Black Panthers Bobby Seale and Huey Newton.

Broadway is the dividing line between the two halves of North Oakland, and also gives access (via the handy *AC Transit* #51 bus) to most of what there is to see and do. The **Oakland Rose Garden**, on Oakland Avenue three blocks east of Broadway (daily April–Oct; free), repays a look if you do come during the day. One of Oakland's most neighborly streets, **Piedmont Avenue**, runs in between, lined by a number of small bookstores and cafés. At the north end of Piedmont Avenue, the **Mountain View Cemetery** was laid out in 1863 by Frederick Law Olmsted (designer of New York's Central Park) and holds the elaborate dynastic tombs of San Francisco's most powerful families – the Crockers, the Bechtels and the Ghirardellis. No one minds if you jog or ride a bike around the well-tended grounds.

Back on Broadway, just past College Avenue (see below), Broadway Terrace climbs up along the edge of the fire area to **Lake Temescal** – where you can swim in summer – and continues on up to the forested ridge at the **Robert Sibley Regional Preserve**, which includes the 1761-foot volcanic cone of Round Top Peak and panoramas of the entire Bay Area. Skyline Boulevard runs through the park and is popular with cyclists, who ride the twelve miles south to Lake Chabot or follow Grizzly Peak Boulevard five miles north to Tilden Park through the Berkeley Hills.

Most of the Broadway traffic, and the *AC Transit* #51 bus, cuts off onto College Avenue through Oakland's most upscale shopping

district, **Rockridge**. Spreading for half a mile on either side of the
Rockridge *BART* station, the quirky stores and restaurants here are,
despite their undeniably yuppie overtones, some of the best around
and make for a pleasant afternoon's wander. Both in geography and
in atmosphere it's as near as Oakland gets to the café society of
neighboring Berkeley.

Berkeley

*This Berkeley was like no somnolent Siwash out of her own
past at all, but more akin to those Far Eastern or Latin
American universities you read about, those autonomous
culture media where the most beloved of folklores may be
brought into doubt, cataclysmic of dissents voiced, suicidal of
commitments chosen – the sort that bring governments down.*

Thomas Pynchon, *The Crying of Lot 49*

More than any other American town, **BERKELEY** conjures up
images of dissent. During the Sixties and early Seventies, when
college campuses across the nation were protesting against the
Vietnam War, it was the students of the University of California,
Berkeley, who led the charge, gaining a name as the vanguard of
what was increasingly seen as a challenge to the authority of the
state. Full-scale battles were fought almost daily here at one point,
on the campus and on the streets of the surrounding town, and there
were times when Berkeley appeared to be almost on the brink of
revolution itself: students (and others) throwing stones and gas
bombs were met with tear-gas volleys and truncheons by National
Guard troops under the nominal command of then-Governor Ronald
Reagan.

Such activities were, of course, most inspired by the mood of the
time, and apart from several anti-apartheid rallies in the 1980s,
Berkeley politics are nowadays decidedly middle-of-the-road. But –
despite an influx of non-rebellious students, a thriving bedrock of
exclusive California Cuisine restaurants and the recent dismantling
of the city's rent control programme – the progressive legacy lingers,
noticeable in the many small bookstores and regular political demonstrations if not the agenda of the city council.

The **University of California** completely dominates Berkeley,
and, as it's right in the center of town, it makes a logical starting
point for a visit. Its many grand buildings and 30,000 students give
off a definite energy that spills down the raucous stretch of
Telegraph Avenue, which runs south from the campus and holds
most of the studenty hang-outs, including a dozen or so lively cafés,
as well as a number of Berkeley's many fine bookstores.

Older students, and a good percentage of the faculty, congregate
in the **Northside** area, popping down from their woodsy hillside
homes to partake of goodies from the "Gourmet Ghetto", a stretch of

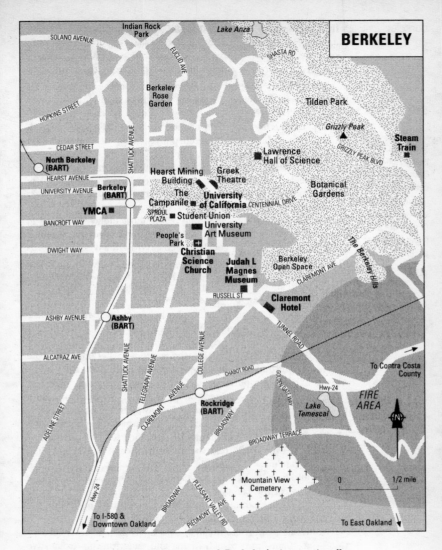

Shattuck Avenue that collects many of Berkeley's internationally renowned restaurants, delis, and bakeries.

Of quite distinct character are the flatlands that spread through **West Berkeley** down to the bay, a poorer but increasingly gentrified district that mixes old Victorian houses with builder's yards and light industrial premises. Along the bay itself is the **Berkeley Marina**, where you can rent sailboards and sailboats or just watch the sun set behind the Golden Gate.

The University of California

Caught up in the frantic crush of students who pack the **University of California** campus during the semesters, it's nearly impossible to imagine the bucolic learning environment envisaged by its high-minded founders. When the Reverend Henry Durant and other East Coast academics decided to set up shop here in the 1860s, these rolling foothills were still largely given over to dairy herds and wheatfields, the last remnants of the Peralta family's Spanish land-grant rancho which once stretched over most of the East Bay. Construction work on the two campus buildings – imaginatively named North Hall and South Hall – was still going on when the first 200 students, including 22 women, moved here from Oakland in 1873. Since then an increasing number of buildings has been squeezed into the half-mile-square main campus, and the state-funded university has become one of the most highly respected in America. Overcrowding aside, the beautifully landscaped campus, stepping down from the eucalyptus-covered Berkeley Hills towards the Golden Gate, is eminently strollable. With maps posted every-where, you'd have to try hard to get lost – though enthusiastic students will show you around on a free two-hour tour (Mon, Wed, Fri at 10am and 1pm; ☎510/642-5215).

There are so many Nobel laureates on the University faculty that it's said you have to win one just to get a parking permit.

A number of footpaths climb the hill from the Berkeley *BART* station on Shattuck Avenue, but the best way to get a feel for the place is to follow Strawberry Creek from the top of Center Street across the southeast corner of the campus, emerging from the groves of redwood and eucalyptus trees at **Sproul Plaza**. It's the newest and largest public space on campus, enlivened by street musicians playing for quarters on the steps of the **Student Union** building and conga drummers pounding away in the echoing court-yard below. **Sather Gate**, which bridges Strawberry Creek at the north end of Sproul Plaza, marks the entrance to the older part of the campus. Up the hill, past the imposing facade of Wheeler Hall, the 1914 landmark **Campanile** is modelled after the one in the Piazza San Marco in Venice; you can take an elevator to the top for a great view of the campus and the entire Bay Area (daily 10am–4pm; 25¢). At the foot of the tower stands red-brick **South Hall**, the sole survivor of the original pair of buildings.

Inside the plain white building next door, the **Bancroft Library** (Mon–Sat 10am–5pm) displays odds and ends from its exhaustive accumulation of artefacts and documents tracing the history of California, including a faked brass plaque supposedly left by Sir Francis Drake when he claimed all of the West Coast for Queen Elizabeth I. It also contains an internationally important collection of manuscripts and rare books, from Mark Twain to James Joyce – though you have to show some academic credentials if you want to see any of these. Around the corner and down the hill, just inside the arched main entrance to Doe Library, you'll find the **Morrison**

Berkeley's Bookstores

Berkeley's **bookstores** are as exhaustive as they are exhausting – not surprising for a college town. Perfect for browsing and taking your time, you won't be made to feel guilty or obliged to buy a book you've been poring over for ages.

Black Oak Books, 1491 Shattuck Ave. Some new books, some second-hand; also regular evening readings by internationally regarded authors. ☎510/486-0698.

Cody's Books, 2454 Telegraph Ave. The flagship of Berkeley booksellers, with an excellent selection of fiction, poetry and criticism. ☎510/845-7852.

Comics and Comix, 2461 Telegraph Ave. Great selection of comic books, both current and classic. ☎510/845-4091.

Easy Going, 1385 Shattuck Ave. Best travel bookstore in the Bay Area, with wide selection of guides and maps to California, the USA and the world. ☎510/843-3533.

The Holme's Book Company, 274 14th St, downtown Oakland. Not in Berkeley, but the largest new and second-hand bookstore in the Bay Area. Good local history selection. ☎510/893-6860.

Moe's Books, 2476 Telegraph Ave. The biggest (and most expensive) of Berkeley's bookstores, selling second-hand books at new book prices; there's an excellent art section on the top floor though. ☎510/849-2087.

Serendipity Books, 1201 University Ave. Damp and disorganized, but with an incredible selection of first edition and out-of-print books. A must for collectors of first editions and obscure fiction and poetry. ☎510/841-7455.

Shakespeare and Company, 2499 Telegraph Ave. Crammed with quality second-hand books at reasonable prices. The best place to linger and scour the shelves for finds. ☎510/841-8916.

Reading Room, a great place to sit for a while and read foreign magazines and newspapers, listen to a CD or just ease down into one of the many comfy overstuffed chairs and unwind.

Also worth a look if you've got time to kill is the **Museum of Paleontology** in the nearby Earth Sciences Building, which details evolutionary concepts with hundreds of fossils, skeletons and geological maps displayed along the corridors on the lower floors. From here it's a quick walk to the collection of cafés and restaurants lining Euclid Avenue and Hearst Avenue and the beginning of Berkeley's Northside (see below).

The Hearst family name appears with disturbing regularity around the Berkeley campus, though in most instances this is due not to the notorious William Randolph Hearst but to his altruistic mother, Phoebe Apperson Hearst. Besides inviting the entire senior class to her home every spring for a giant picnic, she sponsored the architectural competition that came up with the original campus plan, and donated a good number of the campus buildings, including many that have since been destroyed. One of the finest that survives, the 1907 **Hearst Mining Building** (daily 8am–5pm) on the northeast edge of the campus, conceals a delicate metalwork lobby topped by three glass domes, above ageing exhibits on geology and mining – which is how the Hearst family fortune was originally made, long before scion William Randolph took up publishing. Another Hearst legacy is the **Greek Theatre**, an open-air amphitheater cut into the Berkeley Hills east of the campus, which hosts a summer season of rock concerts.

Higher up in the hills, above the 80,000-seat Memorial Stadium, is the lushly landscaped **Botanical Garden** (daily 9am–5pm; free), good for defeating on-campus claustrophobia with its thirty acres of plants and cacti. Near the crest, with great views out over the bay, a full-size fiberglass sculpture of a sei whale stretches out in front of the space-age **Lawrence Hall of Science** (daily 10am–4.30pm; $5, under-6 $2), an excellent museum and learning center that features earthquake simulations, model dinosaurs and a planetarium, plus a number of hands-on exhibits for kids in the Wizard's Lab. Both the gardens and the Lawrence Hall of Science are accessible on weekdays via the free *UC Berkeley Shuttle* bus from the campus or the Berkeley *BART* station.

In the southeast corner of the campus, the **Hearst Museum of Anthropology** in Kroeber Hall (Thurs–Tues 10am–4pm; $2, free Thurs) holds a variety of changing exhibits as well as an intriguing display of artefacts made by Ishi, the last surviving Yahi Indian, who was found near Mount Lassen in Northern California in 1911. Anthropologist Alfred Kroeber brought Ishi to the museum (then located on the UC San Francisco campus), where he lived under the scrutiny of scientists and journalists – in effect, in a state of captivity – until his death from tuberculosis a few years later. Also in Kroeber Hall, the Worth Ryder Art Gallery in room 116 shows varying degrees of quality in the work of Berkeley's art students.

Alfred Kroeber was also the father of writer Ursula K Le Guin.

The brutally modern, angular concrete of the **University Art Museum** across Bancroft Way (Wed–Sun 11am–5pm; $5, free Thurs 11am–noon) is in stark contrast to the campus's older buildings. Its skylit, open-plan galleries hold works by Picasso, Cezanne, Rubens and other notables, but the star of the show is the collection of Fifties American painter Hans Hofmann's energetic and colorful abstract paintings, on the top floor. The museum is renowned for its cutting-edge, changing exhibitions: the main space hosts a range of major shows – such as Robert Mapplethorpe's controversial photographs – while the Matrix Gallery focuses on lesser known, generally local artists. Works on paper are shown downstairs outside the **Pacific Film Archive**, which shares the building, showing new films from around the world that you won't see elsewhere, as well as revivals from its extensive library.

There's more on the Pacific Film Archive *on p.251.*

Telegraph Avenue and South Berkeley

Downtown Berkeley – basically two department stores, a few banks, a post office and the City Hall building – lies west of the university campus, around the Berkeley *BART* station on Shattuck Avenue, but the real activity centers on **Telegraph Avenue**, which runs south of the university from Sproul Plaza. This thoroughfare saw some of the worst of the Sixties riots and is still a frenetic bustle, especially the four short blocks closest to the university, which are packed to the gills with cafés and second-hand bookstores. Sidewalk vendors hawk hand-made jewellery and brilliantly colored T-shirts, while down-and-outs hustle for spare change and spout psychotic poetry.

People's Park, now a seedy and overgrown plot of land half a block up from Telegraph between Haste Street and Dwight Way, was another battleground in the late Sixties, when organized and spirited resistance to the university's plans to develop the site into dormitories brought out the troops, who shot dead an onlooker by mistake. To many, the fact that the park is still a community-controlled open space (and outdoor dosshouse for Berkeley's homeless legions) is a small victory in the battle against the Establishment, though it's not a pleasant or even very safe place to hang about, especially after dark. A mural along Haste Street remembers some of the reasons why the battles were fought, in the words of student leader Mario Savio: "There's a time when the operation of the machine becomes so odious, makes you so sick at heart, that you can't take part, you can't even tacitly take part. And you've got to put your bodies upon the gears and upon the wheels, upon the levers, upon all the apparatus, and you've got to make it stop" – ideals that can't help but be undermined by the state of the place these days. Recent efforts by the university to reclaim the space with volleyball and basketball courts were met with short-lived but violent protests – rioters thrashed Telegraph Avenue storefronts, and a 19-year-old woman was shot dead by police while trying to assassinate the Chancellor.

Directly across Bowditch Street from People's Park stands one of the finest buildings in the Bay Area, Bernard Maybeck's **Christian Science Church**. Built in 1910, it's an eclectic but thoroughly modern structure, laid out in a simple Greek cross floorplan and spanned by a massive redwood truss with carved Gothic tracery and Byzantine painted decoration. The interior is only open on Sundays for worship and for tours afterwards at 11am, but the outside is worth lingering over, its cascade of many gently pitched roofs and porticoes carrying the eye from one hand-crafted detail to another. It's a clever building in many ways: while the overall image is one of tradition and craftsmanship, Maybeck also succeeded in inconspicuously incorporating such unlikely materials as industrial metal windows, concrete walls and asbestos tiles into the structure – thereby cutting down costs.

Many of the largely residential neighborhoods elsewhere in **South Berkeley** ("Southside") – especially the Elmwood and Claremont districts around College Avenue – are worth a wander, with a couple of specific sights to search out. One of these is the **Judah L Magnes Museum**, a few blocks south of the campus at

2911 Russell St (Sun–Fri 10am–4pm; free). Located in a rambling old mansion, it has California's largest repository of Judaica, and exhibits detail the history of Jewish life from ancient times to the present day. The other Southside attraction is much harder to miss, towering as it does over the Berkeley–Oakland border. The half-timbered castle imagery of the *Claremont Hotel* gives a fairly clear hint as to what's inside – it's now one of the Bay Area's plushest resort hotels, with the three-storey Tower Suite going for a cool $750 per night. Built in 1914, just in time for San Francisco's Panama-Pacific Exposition, the *Claremont* was designed to encourage day-trippers out across the bay in the hope that they'd be so taken with the area they'd want to live here. The ploy worked, and the hotel's owners (who incidentally also owned the streetcar system that brought people here, and all the surrounding land) made a packet.

North Berkeley

North Berkeley, also called "Northside," is a subdued neighborhood of professors and postgraduates, its steep, twisting streets climbing up the lushly overgrown hills north of the campus. At the foot of the hills, some of the Bay Area's finest restaurants and delicatessens – most famously *Chez Panisse*, started and run by Alice Waters, the acclaimed inventor of California Cuisine – have sprung up along Shattuck Avenue to form the so-called "Gourmet Ghetto", a great place to pick up the makings of a tasty al fresco lunch.

The restaurants of the Gourmet Ghetto are detailed on p.226.

Above the Gourmet Ghetto on Euclid Avenue (if you want to avoid the fairly steep walk, take bus #65 from Shattuck Avenue), there can be few more pleasant places for a picnic than the **Berkeley Rose Garden**, a terraced amphitheater filled with some three thousand varietal roses and looking out across the bay to San Francisco. Built as part of a WPA job-creation scheme during the Depression, a wooden pergola rings the top, stepping down to a small spring. Opposite the Rose Garden, through a pedestrian tunnel, is **Codornices Park**, a broad expanse of manicured lawn edged by a baseball diamond, basketball courts and lots of play equipment, the best of which is a long concrete helter-skelter that's good fun to hurtle down, and not only for kids. A footpath leads up from the park along Codornices Creek, burbling with small waterfalls after a good rain.

Though the hills are steep, the homes here – built in an eclectic range of styles, designed to meld seamlessly into the wooded landscape – are some of the finest and most impressively sited in the Bay Area. All repay many times over the effort it takes to see them, if only for their marvellous setting. Many were constructed by members of the Hillside Club, a slightly bohemian group of turn-of-the-century Berkeleyans who also laid out many of the pedestrian paths that climb the hills. Perhaps the single most striking of these hillside homes, the **Rowell House** – a half-timbered chalet built in 1914 by architect John Hudson Thomas – stands alone at the top of the path up from Codornices Park, where it crosses Tamalpais Road. Many of the other houses nearby were designed and built by Bernard Maybeck, architect of the Palace of Fine Arts, Christian Science Church, and other notable Bay Area buildings; the homes he built for himself and his family still stand around the junction of Buena Vista Way and La Loma Avenue, a hundred yards south.

A number of enticing parks, all with great views over the bay, complement the picturesque houses of the Berkeley Hills. The largest and highest of these, **Tilden Park**, spreads along the crest of the hills, encompassing some 2065 acres of near wilderness. You can get there from downtown Berkeley via *AC Transit* #65 bus, then go for a hike or swim in Lake Anza, ride the carved-wood horses of the old carousel, or take a miniature steam train through the redwood trees.

Nearer to town, at the north end of Shattuck Avenue and close by the stores and cafés along Solano Avenue, the gray basalt knob of **Indian Rock** stands out from the foot of the hills, challenging rock-climbers who hone their skills on its forty-foot vertical faces. There are steps around its back for those who just want to appreciate the extraordinary view and, carved into similarly hard volcanic stone across the street, mortar holes which native Ohlone Indians used to grind acorns into flour. In between, and in stark contrast, stands the rusting hulk of a Cold War air-raid siren.

West Berkeley and the Waterfront

From downtown Berkeley and the UC campus, **University Avenue** runs downhill towards the bay, lined by increasingly shabby frontages of motels and massage parlors. The liveliest part of this **West Berkeley** area is around the intersection of University Avenue and San Pablo Avenue – the pre-freeway main highway north – where a community of recent immigrants from India has set up shops and markets and restaurants that serve some of the best of the Bay Area's rare curries.

The area between San Pablo Avenue and the bay is the oldest part of Berkeley, and a handful of hundred-year-old houses and churches – such as the two white-spired Gothic Revival ones on Hearst Avenue – survive from the days when this district was a separate city, known as Ocean View. The neighborhood also holds remnants of Berkeley's industrial past, and many of the old warehouses and factory premises have been converted into living and working spaces for artists, craftspeople and computer software companies. Along similar lines are the cafés, workshops and galleries built in the late 1970s along **Fourth Street** north of University Avenue, which have since become somewhat yuppified but are still good places to wander in search of handicrafts and household gadgets.

One of the few places you can visit here is the **Takara Sake Tasting Room**, just off Fourth Street south of University Ave at 708 Addison St (daily noon–6pm; free). Owned and operated by one of Japan's largest producers, this plant is responsible for more than a third of all sake drunk in the US. You can sample any of the five varieties of California strain sake (brewed from California rice), best drunk warm and swallowed sharply. Though no tours are offered, they will show you a slide presentation of the art of sake brewing.

Berkeley Marina

The I-80 freeway, and the still-used railroad tracks that run alongside it, pretty well manage to cut Berkeley off from its waterfront. The best way to get there is to take *AC Transit* bus #51M, which runs regularly down University Avenue. Once a major hub for the transbay ferry services – to shorten journey times, a three-mile-long pier was constructed, much of which still sticks out into the bay – the **Berkeley Marina** is now one of the prime spots on the bay for leisure activities, especially windsurfing. If you're interested in having a go on the water, contact the *Cal Sailing Club* (see p.268 for details). The surrounding area, all of which is landfill largely owned by the Southern Pacific railroad, has long been the subject of heated battles between developers and the environmentalists who want to preserve it as a shoreline park. For the moment, the winds off the bay make it a good place to fly a kite, and there are some short hiking trails.

The North Bay and Inland Valleys

Compared to the urbanized bayfront cities of Oakland and Berkeley, the rest of the East Bay is sparsely populated, and places of interest are few and far between. The **North Bay** is home to some of the Bay Area's heaviest industry – oil refineries and chemical plants dominate the landscape – but also holds a few remarkably unchanged waterfront towns that merit a side trip if you're passing by. Away from the bay, the **inland valleys** are a whole other world, of dry rolling hills dominated by the towering peak of Mount Diablo. Dozens of tract house developments have made commuter suburbs out of what were once cattle ranches and farms, but so far the region has been able to absorb the numbers and still feels rural, despite having doubled in population in the past twenty years.

The North Bay

North of Berkeley there's not a whole lot to see or do. In **Albany**, *Golden Gate Fields* has horse-racing from October to June, and **El Cerrito**'s main contribution to world culture was the band Creedence Clearwater Revival, who did most of their *Born on the*

Bayou publicity photography in the wilds of Tilden Park in the hills above; El Cerrito is still home to one of the best record stores in the USA, *Down Home Music* (see p.263 for details). **Richmond**, at the top of the bay, was once a boomtown, building ships during World War II at the Kaiser Shipyards, which employed 100,000 workers between 1940 and its closure in 1945. Now it's the proud home of the gigantic Standard Oil refinery, the center of which you drive through before crossing the **Richmond–San Rafael Bridge** ($1) to Marin County. About the only reason to stop in Richmond is that the city marks the north end of the *BART* line, and the adjacent *Amtrak* station is a better terminal for journeys to and from San Francisco than the end of the line in West Oakland.

The North Bay and Inland Valleys

Amtrak *services to the San Francisco area are detailed on p.10.*

Though not really worth a trip in itself, if you're heading from the East Bay to Marin County **Point Richmond** repays a look. A cozy little town tucked away at the foot of the bridge between the refinery and the bay, its many Victorian houses are rapidly becoming commuter territory for upwardly mobile professionals from San Francisco. Through the narrow tunnel that cuts under the hill stands the most obvious sign of this potential gentrification: "Brickyard Landing", an East Bay docklands development, with modern bay-view condos, a private yacht harbor and a token gesture to the area's industrial past – disused brick kilns, hulking next to the tennis courts on the front lawn. The rest of the waterfront is taken up by the broad and usually deserted strand of **Keller Beach**, which stretches for half a mile along the sometimes windy shoreline.

The Carquinez Straits

At the top of the bay some 25 miles north of Oakland, the land along the **Carquinez Straits** is a bit off the beaten track, but it's an area of some natural beauty and much historic interest. The still-small towns along the waterfront seem worlds away from the bustle of the rest of the Bay Area, but how long they'll be able to resist the pressure of the expanding commuter belt is anybody's guess. *AC Transit* bus #70 runs every hour from Richmond *BART* north to **Crockett** at the west end of the narrow straits – a tiny town cut into the steep hillsides above the water that seems entirely dependent upon the massive C&H Sugar factory at its foot, whose giant neon sign lights up the town and the adjacent Carquinez Bridge.

From Crockett the narrow **Carquinez Straits Scenic Drive**, an excellent cycling route, heads east along the Sacramento River. A turn two miles along drops down to **Port Costa**, a small town that was dependent upon ferry traffic across the straits to Benicia until it lost its livelihood when the bridge was built at Crockett. It's still a nice enough place to watch the huge ships pass by on their way to and from the inland ports of Sacramento and Stockton. If you don't have a bike (or a car), you can enjoy the view from the window of an *Amtrak* train, which runs alongside the water from Oakland and Richmond, not stopping until Martinez at the eastern end of the straits, two miles north of the John Muir house (see below).

Benicia

On the north side of the Straits, and hard to get to without a car (see p.29), BENICIA is the most substantial of the historic waterfront towns, but one that has definitely seen better days. Founded in 1847, it initially rivalled San Francisco as the major Bay Area port, and was even the state capital for a time; but despite Benicia's better weather and fine deep-water harbor, San Francisco eventually became the main transportation point for the fortunes of the Gold Rush, and the town very nearly faded away altogether. Examples of Benicia's efforts to become a major city stand poignantly around the very compact downtown area, most conspicuously the 1852 Greek Revival building that was used as the **first State Capitol** for just thirteen months. The building has been restored as a museum (daily except Tues & Wed 10am–5pm; $2), furnished in the legislative style of the time, with top hats on the tables and shining spitoons every few feet.

A walking tour map of Benicia's many intact Victorian houses and churches is available from the **tourist office** at 831 First St (☎707/745-2120), including on its itinerary the steeply pitched roofs and gingerbread eaves of the **Frisbie-Walsh house** at 235 East L St – a prefabricated Gothic Revival building that was shipped in pieces from Boston in 1849. Across the City Hall park, the arched ceiling beams of **St Paul's Episcopal Church** look like an upturned ship's hull; it was built by shipwrights from the Pacific Mail Steamship Company, one of Benicia's many successful nineteenth-century shipyards. Half a dozen former brothels and saloons stand in various stages of decay and restoration along First Street down near the waterfront, from where the world's largest train ferries used to ply the waters between Benicia and Port Costa until 1930.

An identical house was erected by General Vallejo in Sonoma; see p.192.

In recent years Benicia has attracted a number of artists and craftspeople, and you can watch glass-blowers and furniture-makers at work in the **Yuba Complex**, at 670 East H St (Mon–Fri 10am–4pm). Judy Chicago is among those who work in converted studios and modern light industrial parks around the sprawling fortifications of the old **Benicia Arsenal** east of the downtown area, whose thickly walled sandstone buildings formed the main Army storage facility for weapons and ammunition from 1851 up through the Korean War. One of the oddest parts of the complex is the **Camel Barn** (Sat & Sun 1–4pm, also Fri in summer; free), now a museum of local history, but formerly used to house camels that the Army imported in 1856 to transport supplies across the deserts of the Southwestern US. The experiment failed, and the camels were kept here until they were sold off in 1864.

Vallejo and Marine World/Africa USA

Across the Carquinez Bridge from Crockett, the biggest and most
boring of the North Bay towns – VALLEJO – was, like Benicia, an
early capital of California, though it now lacks any sign of its historical significance. In contrast to most of the other Gold Rush-era
towns that line the Straits, Vallejo has remained economically vital,
largely because of the massive military presence here at the **Mare
Island Naval Shipyard**, a sprawling, relentlessly grey complex that
covers an area twice the size of Golden Gate Park. Its less than
glamorous history – the yard builds and maintains supply ships and
the like, not carriers or battleships – is recounted in a small
museum in the old city hall building at 734 Mare St (Tues–Fri
10am–4.30pm; $1), where the highlight is a working periscope that
looks out across the bay. Though no great thrill, it merits a quick
stop; it's right on Hwy-29, the main route from the East Bay to the
Wine Country, in the center of town.

The best reason to come to Vallejo is **Marine World/Africa USA**
(daily 9.30am–6.30pm; adults $22.95, 12-and-unders $16.95, under-
3s free; ☎707/643-6722), five miles north of Vallejo off I-80 at the
Marine World Parkway (Hwy-37) exit. Operated by a non-profit
educational group, it offers a well above average range of performing
sea lions, dolphins and killer whales kept in approximations of their
natural habitats, as well as water-ski stunt shows and the like. It can
be a fun day out, especially for children, and it's not bad as these
things go: the animals seem very well cared for, their quarters are
clean and spacious, and the shows are fun for all but the most jaded.
The new shark exhibit lets you walk (through a transparent tunnel)
alongside twenty-foot Great Whites, and the tropical butterfly aviary
is truly amazing – nearly worth the price of admission.

The most enjoyable way to get to Marine World from San
Francisco is to take one of the *Red and White Fleet* **catamaran
ferry** boats from Fisherman's Wharf, which take an hour each way
and add another $12 to the admission price.

The Inland Valleys

Most of the inland East Bay area is made up of rolling hills covered
by grasslands, slowly yielding to suburban housing developments
and office complexes, as more and more businesses abandon the
pricey real estate of San Francisco. The great peak of **Mount Diablo**
which dominates the region is twice as high as any other Bay Area
summit and surrounded by acres of campgrounds and hiking trails;
other attractions include two historic homes that serve as memorials
to their literate and influential ex-residents, John Muir and Eugene
O'Neill.

BART tunnels from Oakland through the Berkeley Hills to the
leafy-green stockbroker settlement of **Orinda**, continuing east
through the increasingly hot and dry landscape to the end of the line

at **Concord**, site of chemical plants and oil refineries and a controversial nuclear weapons depot. A few years ago, a peaceful, civilly
disobedient blockade here ended in protestor Brian Willson losing
his legs under the wheels of a slow-moving munitions train. The
event raised public awareness – before it happened few people knew
of the depot's existence – but otherwise it's still business as usual.

Martinez and John Muir's House

From Pleasant Hill *BART*, one stop before the end of the line,
Contra Costa County Connection bus #116 leaves every half hour
for **MARTINEZ**, the seat of county government, passing the
preserved home of naturalist **John Muir** (daily 10am–4.30pm; $1),
just off Hwy-4, two miles south of Martinez. Muir, an articulate,
persuasive Scot whose writings and political activism were of vital
importance in the preservation of America's wilderness, spent much
of his life exploring and writing about the majestic Sierra Nevada
mountains, particularly Yosemite. He was also one of the founders
of the **Sierra Club** – a wilderness lobby and education organization
still active today. Anyone who is familiar with the image of this thin,
bearded man wandering the mountains with his knapsack, notebook
and packet of tea might be surprised to see his very conventional,
upper-class Victorian home, now restored to its appearance when
Muir died in 1914. The house was built by Muir's father-in-law, and
only those parts Muir added to it himself reflect much of the person-
ality of the man, such as the massive, rustic fireplace he had built in
the East Parlor so he could have a "real mountain campfire". The
bulk of Muir's personal belongings and artefacts are displayed in his
study, on the upper floor, and in the adjacent room an exhibition
documents the history of the Sierra Club and Muir's battles to
protect America's wilderness.

Behind the bell-towered main house is a large, still productive
orchard where Muir cultivated grapes, pears and cherries to earn
the money to finance his explorations (you can sample the fruits
free of charge, pre-picked by staff gardeners). Beyond the orchard
is the 1849 **Martinez Adobe**, homestead of the original Spanish
land-grant settlers and now a small **museum** of Mexican colonial
culture. It's worth a look if you're out here, if only for the contrast
between Mexican and American cultures in early California; also,
the building's two-foot-thick walls keep it refreshingly cool on a
typically hot summer day.

Eugene O'Neill and Mount Diablo

At the foot of Mount Diablo, fifteen miles south, playwright **Eugene
O'Neill** used the money he got for winning the Nobel Prize for
Literature in 1936 to build a home and sanctuary for himself, which
he named **Tao House**. It was here, before 1944 when he was struck
down with Parkinson's Disease, that he wrote many of his best-

known plays: *The Iceman Cometh, A Moon for the Misbegotten* and *Long Day's Journey into Night*. Readings and performances of his works are sometimes given in the house, which is open to visitors, though you must reserve a place on one of the free guided tours (Wed–Sun at 10am & 12.30pm; ☎510/838-0249). There's no parking on site, so the tours pick you up in the town of **Danville**.

As for **Mount Diablo** itself, it rises up from the rolling ranchlands at its foot to a height of nearly 4000 feet, its summit and flanks preserved within **Mount Diablo State Park** ($5 parking; ☎510/837-2525). The main road through the park reaches within 100m of the top, so it's a popular place for an outing, and you're unlikely to be alone to enjoy the marvellous view: on a clear day you can see over 200 miles in every direction. The 15,000 acres of parkland surrounding the peak offer many miles of hiking and some of the only **camping** in the East Bay.

Two main entrances lead into the park, both well marked off I-680. The one from the southwest by way of Danville passes by the **ranger station**, where you can pick up a trail map ($1) which lists the best day-hikes. The other runs from the northwest by way of Walnut Creek, and the routes join together five miles from the summit. March and April, when the wild flowers are out, are the best times to be here, and since mornings are ideal for getting the clearest view, you should drive to the top first and then head back down to a trailhead for a hike, or to one of the many picnic spots for a leisurely lunch. In summer it can get desperately hot and dry, so much so that parts of the park are closed because of fire danger.

Livermore and Altamont

Fifteen miles southeast of Mount Diablo, on the main road out of the Bay Area (I-580), the rolling hills around **Livermore** are covered with thousands of shining, spinning, high-tech **windmills**, placed here by a private power company to take advantage of the nearly constant winds. It's the largest wind-farm in the world, and you'll probably have seen it used in a number of TV ads, as a space-age backdrop to hype flashy new cars or sexy perfumes. Though the Federal government provides no funding for this non-polluting, renewable source of energy, it spends billions of dollars every year designing and building nuclear weapons and other sinister applications of modern technology at the nearby **Lawrence Livermore Laboratories**, where most of the research and development of the nuclear arsenal takes place. A small **visitor center** holds hands-on exhibits showing off various scientific phenomena and devices, two miles south of I-580 on Greenville Road (Mon–Fri 9am–4.30pm, Sat & Sun noon–5pm; free).

Up and over the hills to the east, where I-580 joins I-5 for the 400-mile route south through the Central Valley to Los Angeles, stand the remains of **Altamont Speedway**, site of a nightmarish

No public transportation serves the park, but the Sierra Club *sometimes organizes day trips.*

The North Bay and Inland Valleys

Rolling Stones concert in December 1969. The free concert, which was captured in the film *Gimme Shelter*, was intended to be a sort of second Woodstock, staged in order to counter allegations that the Stones had ripped off their fans during a long US tour. In the event it was a complete fiasco: three people died, one of whom was kicked and stabbed to death by the Hell's Angels "security guards" – in full view of the cameras – after pointing a gun at Mick Jagger while he sang *Sympathy for the Devil*. Needless to say, no historical plaque marks the site.

Chapter 9

The Peninsula

The city of San Francisco sits at the tip of a five-mile-wide **Peninsula**. Home of old money and new technology, this stretches south from San Francisco along the bay for fifty miles of relentless suburbia, past the wealthy enclaves of Hillsborough and Atherton, to wind up in the futuristic roadside landscape of the "Silicon Valley" near **San Jose** – though your only glimpse of the area may be on the trip between San Francisco and the airport. There was a time when the region was covered with orange groves and fig trees, but the concentration of academic interest around Stanford University in Palo Alto and the continuing boom in computers – since the 1970s the biggest local industry – has buried any chances of it hanging on to its agricultural past.

Surprisingly, most of the land along the **coast** – separated from the bayfront sprawl by a ridge of redwood-covered peaks – remains rural and undeveloped; it also contains some of the best **beaches** in the Bay Area and a couple of affably down-to-earth farming communities, all well served by public transit.

Getting Around and Information

BART only travels down the Peninsula as far as **Daly City**, from where you can catch *SamTrans* (☎761-7000) buses south to Palo Alto or along the coast to Half Moon Bay. For longer distances, *Caltrain* (☎557-8661) offers an hourly rail service from its terminal at Fourth and Townsend in downtown San Francisco, stopping at most bayside towns between the city and San Jose, for between $1 and $5; *Greyhound* runs regular buses along US-101 to and from their San Jose terminal at 70 S Almaden (☎408/297-8890) as well. *Santa Clara County Transit* (*SCCT*) (☎408/287-4210) runs buses and modern trolleys around metropolitan San Jose. If you're going to be spending most of your time down here, it's possible to fly direct into **San Jose International Airport** (SJO), alarmingly close to downtown San Jose.

The **Palo Alto Chamber of Commerce**, 325 Forest Ave (Mon–Fri 9am–noon & 1–5pm; ☎324-3121), has lists of local restaurants

Peninsula accommodation options are listed in Chapter 12; restaurants are on p.228; and cafés and bars on p.238.

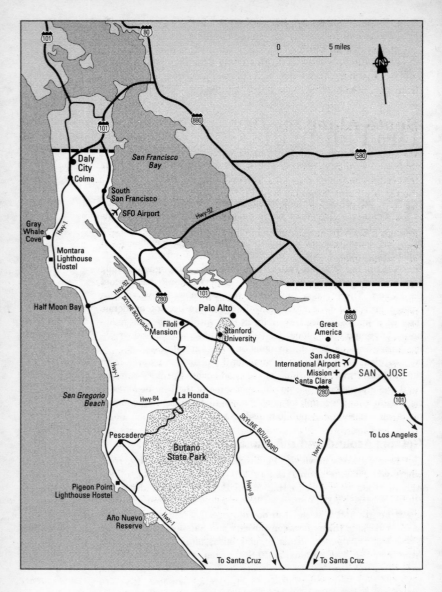

and cycle routes; for information on nearby Stanford University phone ☎ 723-2560. To find out what's on and where, pick up a free copy of the *Palo Alto Weekly*, available at most local shops.

At the southern end of the bay, the **San Jose Convention and Visitors' Bureau**, 333 W San Carlos St, Suite 1000 (Mon–Sat 9am–

5pm; ☎408/295-9600 or 1-800/SAN-JOSE), is the best bet for tourist information; for local news and events pick up a copy of the excellent *San Jose Mercury* newspaper or the free weekly *Metro*.

Along the coast, the **Half Moon Bay Chamber of Commerce** gives out walking tour maps and information on accommodation from a restored railroad car at 225 S Cabrillo Hwy (☎726-5202).

South Along the Bay

US-101 runs south from San Francisco along the bay through over fifty miles of unmitigated sprawl to San Jose, lined by light industrial estates and shopping malls. The only place worth stopping at is the **Coyote Point Museum** (Wed–Fri 9am–5pm, Sat & Sun 1–5pm; free), four miles south of the airport off Poplar Avenue in a large bayfront park, where examples of the natural life of the San Francisco Bay – from tidal insects to birds of prey – are exhibited in engaging and informative displays, enhanced by interactive computers and documentary films.

A more pleasant drive is via **I-280**, the newest and most expensive freeway in California, which runs parallel to US-101 but avoids the worst of the bayside mess by cutting through wooded valleys down the center of the Peninsula. Just beyond the San Francisco city limit the road passes through **Colma**, a unique place made up entirely of cemeteries, which are prohibited within San Francisco. Besides the expected roll-call of deceased San Franciscans luminaries are a few surprises, such as Wild West gunman Wyatt Earp.

Beyond Colma the scenery improves quickly as I-280 continues past the **Crystal Springs Reservoir**, an artificial lake which holds the water supply for San Francisco – pumped here all the way from Yosemite. Surrounded by twenty square miles of parkland, hiking trails lead up to the ridge from which San Francisco Bay was first spotted by eighteenth-century Spanish explorers; it now overlooks the airport to the east, but there are good views out over the Pacific coast, two miles distant.

At the south end of the reservoir, just off I-280 on Canada Road in the well-heeled town of **Woodside**, luscious gardens surround the palatial **Filoli Estate** (tours Tues–Sat 10.30am & 1pm; $8; ☎364-2880). The 45-room mansion, designed in 1915 in neo-Palladian style by architect Willis Polk, may seem familiar – it was used in the TV series *Dynasty* as the Denver home of the Carrington clan. It's the only one of the many huge houses around here that you can actually visit, although the gardens are what make it worth coming, especially in the spring when everything's in bloom.

Palo Alto and Stanford University

PALO ALTO, just south and three miles east between I-280 and US-101, is a small, leafy community with all the contrived atmosphere you'd expect to find in a college town but little of the vigor of its northern counterpart, Berkeley. Though a visit doesn't really merit the expense of a night's accommodation, you could spend a lazy day in the bookstores and cafés that line University Avenue, the town's main drag. Or, if you're feeling energetic, try cycling around the town's many well-marked bike routes; a range of bikes is available for $12–25 a day from *The Effortless Bike* at 401 High Street (☎328-3180), near the *Caltrain* station a block west of University Avenue. Be aware, however, that **East Palo Alto**, on the bay side of US-101, has a well-deserved reputation for gang and drug-related violence, with one of the highest per capita murder rates of any US city. Founded in the 1920s as the utopian Runnymeade colony, an agricultural, poultry-raising cooperative – the local historical society (☎329-0294) can point out the surviving sites – East Palo Alto, which is also where Grateful Dead guitarist Jerry Garcia grew up, is about as far as you can get off the SF tourist trail.

Stanford University, spreading out from the west end of University Avenue, is by contrast one of the tamest places you could hope for. The university is among the best – and most expensive – in America, though when it opened in 1891, founded by railroad magnate Leland Stanford in memory of his dead son, it offered free tuition. Ridiculed by East Coast academics, who felt that there was as much need for a second West Coast university (after UC Berkeley) as there was for "an asylum for decayed sea captains in Switzerland", Stanford was defiantly built anyway, in a hybrid of Mission and Romanesque buildings on a huge campus that covers an area larger than the whole of downtown San Francisco.

Stanford's reputation as an arch-conservative think-tank was enhanced by Ronald Reagan's offer to donate his video library to the school – which Stanford politely declined. It hasn't always been an entirely boring place, though you wouldn't know it to walk among the preppy future-lawyers-of-America that seem to comprise ninety percent of the student body. Ken Kesey came here from Oregon in 1958 on a writing fellowship, working nights as an orderly on the psychiatric ward of one local hospital, and getting paid $75 a day to test experimental drugs (LSD among them) in another. Drawing on both experiences, Kesey wrote *One Flew over the Cuckoo's Nest* in 1960 and quickly became a counter-culture hero. These days Stanford attracts a more prosaic body of students, preferring to bolster its departments in medicine, science and engineering.

Approaching from the Palo Alto *Caltrain* and *SamTrans* bus station, which acts as a buffer between the town and the university, you enter the campus via a half-mile-long, palm-tree-lined boulevard which deposits you at its heart, the **Quadrangle**, bordered by the phallic Hoover Tower and the colorful gold-leaf mosaics of the Memorial Church. Free hour-long walking tours of the campus leave from here daily at 11am and 2pm, though it's fairly big and is best seen by car or bike.

The one place worth devoting some attention to, the **Stanford Museum of Art** between "the Quad" and the town, recently reopened after being damaged by the 1989 earthquake (Tues–Fri 10am–5pm, Sat & Sun 1–5pm; $3). Have a laugh at the insipid mosaics that decorate its upper storey, then step inside to check out the Asian art and Egyptian sculpture. It says a lot about the collection that pride of place is given to the golden spike apocryphally driven by Leland Stanford to join the two halves of the Transcontinental Railroad in 1869: Stanford made his fortune from the railroad monopoly he and his Southern Pacific Railroad colleagues exerted over most of the western US. For now, the best reason to come here is to have a look at the distinguished collection of **Rodin sculpture**, including a *Gates of Hell* flanked by a shamed *Adam and Eve*, displayed in an attractive outdoor setting on the museum's south side. Also, if you keep up on the latest trends in sub-atomic behavior, you won't want to miss the **Stanford Linear Accelerator** (Mon–Fri by appointment only; ☎854-3300), a mile west of the central campus on Sand Hill Road, where infinitesimally small particles are crashed into one another at very high speeds to see what happens.

San Jose

The fastest-growing major city in America's fastest-growing state, **SAN JOSE** is not strong on identity – save the odd Burt Bacharach song – though in area and population it's close to twice the size of San Francisco. Sitting at the southern end of the Peninsula, located almost exactly in the center of the state, an abundance of cheap land brought developers and businessmen into the area in the 1960s, hoping to draw from the concentration of talent in the commerce-orientated halls of Stanford University. Fuelled by the success of computer firms such as Apple, Intel and Hewlett-Packard, in the past 25 years San Jose has emerged as the civic heart of **Silicon Valley**, surrounded by miles of faceless high-tech industrial parks where the next generations of computers are designed and crafted.

Ironically enough, San Jose is one of the oldest settlements in California, though the only sign of that is at the late eighteenth-century **Mission Santa Clara de Asis**. On the grounds of the Jesuit-run University of Santa Clara, two miles northwest of the *Caltrain* station, the **de Saisset Museum** (Tues–Fri 10am–5pm, Sat & Sun 1–5pm; $1) holds a permanent display of objects from the Mission era along with changing shows of contemporary art. Otherwise there are only a couple of good reasons to subject yourself to San Jose's relentlessly boring cityscape. The main attraction is the **Rosicrucian Museum**, 1342 Naglee Ave (daily 9am–5pm; $4). Languishing in the suburbs, this grand structure contains a brilliant collection of

Assyrian and Babylonian artefacts, with displays of mummies, amulets, a replica of a tomb and ancient jewellery. Right downtown, at 145 W San Carlos St, is a more modern magnet, the **Tech Museum of Innovation** (Tues–Sun 10am–5pm; $6), with hands-on displays of high-tech devices.

You could also stop off at the **Winchester Mystery House**, 525 S Winchester Blvd, just off I-280 near Hwy-17 (daily 9.30am–4.30pm; $15.95). Sarah Winchester, heir to the Winchester rifle fortune, was convinced by an occultist upon her husband's death that he had been taken by the spirits of men killed with Winchester rifles. She was told that unless a room was built for each of the spirits and the sound of hammers never ceased, the same fate would befall her. Work on the mansion went on 24 hours per day for the next thirty years, with results that need to be seen to be believed – stairs lead nowhere, windows open on to solid brick, and so on. It is, however, a shameless tourist trap, and you have to run a gauntlet of ghastly gift stores and soda stands to get in or out.

One other Peninsula place might exercise a certain attraction, particularly to those fond of roller coasters, log rides and all-American family fun: **Great America** (daily 10am–10pm in summer, weekends only in winter; $23.95, under-6s $16.95). This huge, 100-acre amusement park on the edge of San Francisco Bay, just off US-101 north of San Jose, is not in the same league as Disneyland, but doesn't suffer from the same crowds and lengthy lines, and the range of high-speed thrills and chills – from the loop-the-looping "Demon" to "The Edge", where you free-fall in a steel cage for over 100 feet – is worth the entry fee, especially on weekdays when you may well have the place to yourself. The whole park is laid out into such heritage-themed areas as "Hometown Square", "Yankee Harbor", and "County Fair", each filled with all sorts of sideshow attractions and funfair games.

The Coast

The **coastline** of the Peninsula south from San Francisco is more appealing than what's on offer inland – relatively undeveloped, with very few buildings, let alone towns, along the 75 miles of coves and beaches that extend down to the resort city of **Santa Cruz**. Bluffs protect the many nudist beaches from prying eyes and make a popular launching pad for hang-glider pilots, particularly at **Burton Beach** and **Fort Funston**, a mile south of the San Francisco Zoo – also the point where the earthquake-causing San Andreas Fault enters the sea, not to surface again until Point Reyes. **Skyline Boulevard** follows the coast from here past the repetitious tracts of proverbial ticky-tacky houses that make up **Daly City**, where it is joined by Hwy-1 (and *SamTrans* bus #1A) for the rest of the journey.

San Pedro Point, a popular surfing beach fifteen miles south of the city proper, marks the southern extent of San Francisco's suburban sprawl. The old **Ocean Shore Railroad Depot** here, now a private residence among the handful of shops in the beachfront town, is one of the few surviving remnants of an ill-advised train line between San Francisco and Santa Cruz. The line was wiped out during the 1906 earthquake, but was in any case never more than a third complete. Its few patrons had to transfer back and forth by ferry to connect the stretches of track that were built, the traces of which you can still see scarring the face of the bluffs. The continually eroding cliffs don't take very well to being built on, as evidenced a mile south by the **Devil's Slide**, where the highway is washed away with some regularity in winter storms. The slide area was also a popular dumping spot for corpses of those who'd fallen foul of rum-runners during Prohibition, and features under various names in many of Dashiell Hammett's detective stories.

Just south of the Devil's Slide, the sands of **Gray Whale Cove State Beach** (daily dawn–dusk; $5 to park) are clothing-optional. Despite the name it's not an especially great place to look for migrating grey whales, but there is a stairway from the bus stop down to a fine beach. Two miles south, the red-roofed buildings of the *Montara Lighthouse*, set among the windswept Monterey pines at the top of a steep cliff, have been converted into a youth hostel. There are a few good places to stop for a drink or a bite to eat in the town of **Moss Beach**, across Hwy-1.

For details of the Montara Lighthouse hostel, see p.208.

South of the lighthouse, the **James Fitzgerald Marine Reserve** strings along the shore, a two-mile shelf of flat, slippery rocks that make excellent tidal pools. The ranger often gives guided interpretive walks through the reserve at low tide, the best time to explore. At the south end of the reserve, **Pillar Point** juts out into the Pacific; just to the east, along Hwy-1, fishing boats dock at **Pillar Point Harbor**. In the faintly touristy, ramshackle town adjacent to the waterfront, **Princeton-by-the-Sea**, a couple of bay-view restaurants sell fish and chips, sometimes freshly caught. Further along, the best of the local surfing areas is just offshore from **Miramar Beach**; after a day in the water or on the beach, the place to head for is the beachfront *Bach Dancing and Dynamite Society*, an informal jazz club and beer bar that faces the sands.

Half Moon Bay

HALF MOON BAY, twenty miles south of the city and the only town of any size between San Francisco and Santa Cruz, takes its name from the crescent-shaped bay formed by Pillar Point. Lined by miles of sandy beaches, the town is surprisingly rural considering its proximity to San Francisco and Silicon Valley, and sports a number of ornate Victorian wooden houses around its center. The oldest of these is at the north end of Main Street: built in 1849, it's just across a little stone bridge over Pillarcitos Creek. The **Chamber of Commerce** on Hwy-1 (see p.000) has free walking tour maps of the town, and information on the two annual festivals for which the place is well known. These are the **Holy Ghost and Pentecost Festival**, a parade and barbecue held on the sixth Sunday after Easter, and the **Pumpkin Festival**, celebrating the harvest of the area's many pumpkin farms, just in time for Halloween, when the fields around town are full of families searching for the perfect jack-o'-lantern to greet the hordes of trick-or-treaters. There are free, primitive campgrounds all along the coast in **Half Moon Bay State Park**, half a mile west of the town.

Half Moon Bay is also the southern end of the *SamTrans* bus #1A route; to continue south, transfer here to route #90C, which runs every three hours to Waddell Creek, twenty miles south. **San Gregorio State Beach**, ten miles south of Half Moon Bay, is at its best in the spring, after the winter storms, when flotsam architects construct a range of driftwood shelters along the wide beach south of the parking area. In summer the beach is packed with well-oiled bodies; the sands around the bluffs to the north are quieter, and clothing-optional.

The Butano Redwoods and the Año Nuevo State Reserve

If you've got a car and it's not a great day for the beach, head up into the hills above, where the thousands of acres of the **Butano redwood forest** feel at their most ancient and primeval in the greyest and gloomiest weather. About half the land between San Jose and the coast is protected from development in a variety of state and county parks, all of which are virtually deserted despite being within a half-hour's drive of the Silicon Valley sprawl. Any one of a dozen roads heads through endless stands of untouched forest, and even the briefest of walks will take you seemingly miles from any sign of civilization. Hwy-84 climbs up from San Gregorio through the Sam McDonald County Park to the hamlet of **La Honda**, from where you can continue on to Palo Alto or, better, loop back to the coast via Pescadero Road. A mile before you reach the quaint town of **Pescadero**, Cloverdale Road heads south to **Butano State Park**, where you can hike and camp overlooking the Pacific.

Pescadero has two of the best places to eat on the Peninsula – Duarte's *and* Dinelli's Café. *See p.228 for reviews.*

Back on Hwy-1, five miles south of Pescadero is another great place to spend the night, sleeping in the old lighthouse keeper's quarters or soaking your bones in a marvellous hot tub at the **Pigeon Point Lighthouse Hostel**. If you're here in December or January, continue south another five miles to the **Año Nuevo State Reserve** for a chance to see one of nature's most bizarre spectacles – the mating rituals of the northern elephant seal. These massive, ungainly creatures, fifteen feet long and weighing up to three tons, were once found all along the coast, but were nearly hunted to extinction by whalers in the last century. During the mating season the beach is literally a seething mass of blubbery bodies, with the trunk-nosed males fighting it out for the right to sire as many as fifty pups in a season. At any time of the year you're likely to see a half dozen or so dozing in the sands. The reserve is also good for bird-watching, and in March there's a chance of getting a good look at migrating grey whales.

The slowly resurgent Año Nuevo seal population is still carefully protected, and during the breeding season the obligatory guided tours – designed to protect spectators as much as to give the seals some privacy – are often oversubscribed (hourly 8am–4pm; ☎879-0227). Otherwise tickets are usually made available to people staying at the Pigeon Point Hostel, and *SamTrans* (☎348-SEAL) sometimes runs charter bus tours from the town of **San Mateo** on the bay side of the Peninsula.

The Coast

For more information on the Pigeon Point Lighthouse hostel, see p.208.

Chapter 10

Marin County

Across the Golden Gate from San Francisco, **Marin County** (pronounced *Ma-RINN*) provides an unabashed introduction to Californian self-indulgence: an elitist pleasure-zone of conspicuous luxury and abundant natural beauty, with sunshine, sandy beaches, high mountains and thick redwood forests. Often ranked as the wealthiest county in the US, Marin's swanky waterside towns have attracted a sizeable contingent of northern California's wealthiest young professionals, many of whom grew up during the Flower Power years of the 1960s and lend the place its New Age feel and reputation. Locals have their shiitake-mushroom pizzas delivered in Porsches and think nothing of spending $1000 to see the Grateful Dead play at the Pyramids. Though many of the cocaine-and-hot-tub devotees who populated the place in the 1970s have traded their drug habits for mountain bikes, life in Marin still centers around personal pleasure, and the throngs you see hiking and cycling at weekends, not to mention the hundreds of esoteric self-help practitioners – Rolfing, Re-Birthing and soul-travel therapists fill up the want ads of the local papers – prove that Marinites work hard to maintain their easy air of physical and mental well-being.

Flashy modern ferry boats, appointed with fully stocked bars, sail across the bay from San Francisco and give a good initial view of the county: as you head past desolate Alcatraz Island, curvaceous **Mount Tamalpais** looms larger until you land at its foot in one of the chic bayside settlements of **Sausalito** or Tiburon. **Angel Island**, in the middle of the bay but accessible most easily from Tiburon, provides relief from the excessive style-consciousness of both towns, retaining a wild untouched feeling among the eerie ruins of derelict military fortifications.

Sausalito and Tiburon, and the lifestyles that go with them, are only a small part of Marin. The bulk of the county rests on the slopes of the ridge of peaks that divides the peninsula down the middle, separating the sophisticated harborside towns in the east from the untrammelled wilderness of the Pacific coast to the west. The **Marin Headlands**, just across the Golden Gate Bridge, hold

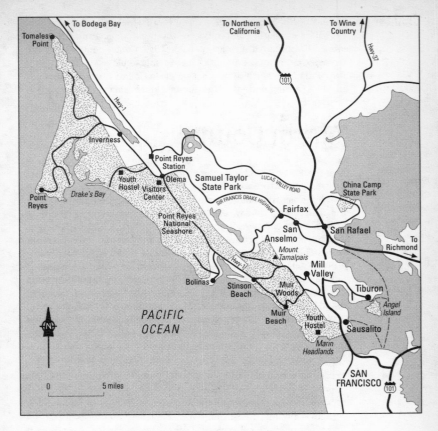

time-warped old battlements and gun emplacements that once protected San Francisco's harbor from would-be invaders, and now overlook surfers and backpackers enjoying the acres of open space. Along the coastline that stretches north, the broad shore of **Stinson Beach** is the Bay Area's finest and widest stretch of sand, beyond which Hwy-1 clings to the coast past the rural village of **Bolinas** to the seascapes of **Point Reyes**, where Sir Francis Drake landed in 1579 and claimed all of California for England.

Inland, the heights of Mount Tamalpais, and specifically **Muir Woods**, are a magnet to sightseers and nature-lovers, who come to wander through one of the few surviving stands of the native coastal redwood trees. Such trees once covered most of Marin, before they were chopped down to build and rebuild the dainty wooden houses of San Francisco. The long-vanished lumber mills of the rustic town of **Mill Valley**, overlooking the bay from the slopes of "Mount Tam", bear the guilt for much of this destruction; the oldest town in Marin County is now home to an eclectic bunch of art galleries and cafés.

Further north, Marin's largest town, **San Rafael**, is best passed by, though its outskirts contain two of the most unusual places in the county: **Frank Lloyd Wright**'s peculiar Civic Center complex and the preserved remnants of an old Chinese fishing village in **China Camp State Park**. The northern reaches of Marin County border the bountiful wine-growing regions of the Sonoma and Napa valleys, detailed in Chapter 11.

Arrival and Getting Around

Marin County accommodation listings are in Chapter 12; restaurants are covered on p.228; and cafés and bars on p.238.

Just getting to Marin County can be a great start to a day out from San Francisco. *Golden Gate Transit* **ferries** (☎322-6600) leave from the Ferry Building on the Embarcadero, crossing the bay past Alcatraz Island to **Sausalito** and **Larkspur**; they run from 5.30am until 8pm, approximately every half hour during the rush hour, less often the rest of the day, and every two hours at weekends and holidays. Tickets cost $3.50 one way to Sausalito, $2.20 to Larkspur Monday to Friday ($3 weekends). Refreshments are served on board. The more expensive *Red and White Ferries* ($9 round trip; ☎546-2805) sail from Pier 43½ at Fisherman's Wharf to **Sausalito** and to **Tiburon** – from where the *Angel Island Ferry* ($5 round trip, plus $1 per bicycle; ☎435-2131) nips back and forth to **Angel Island State Park** daily in summer, weekends only in the winter.

Golden Gate Transit also runs a comprehensive **bus service** around Marin County and across the Golden Gate Bridge from the Transbay Terminal in San Francisco (in Marin County, call ☎453-2100), and publishes a helpful and free system map and timetable, including all ferry services. Bus fares range from $1 to $3, depending on the distance travelled. Basic *GGT* bus routes run every half hour throughout the day, and once an hour late at night. *GGT* commuter services, which run only during the morning and evening rush hours, can be the only way to get to some places. Also, San Francisco's *Muni* bus #76 runs hourly from San Francisco direct to the Marin Headlands on Sundays only.

The only services between Marin County and the East Bay are offered by *Traveler's Transit* (☎457-7080) minivans, running between the Richmond *BART* station and downtown San Rafael for $2 a trip.

Marin County Bus Services

#10: San Francisco–Sausalito–Marin City–Mill Valley–Tiburon.

#20: San Francisco–Marin City–Larkspur–San Anselmo–San Rafael.

#50: San Francisco–Sausalito–Marin City–San Rafael.

#24: San Francisco–San Anselmo–Fairfax–Point Reyes Station; once a day at 5.40pm, weekdays only.

#63: Marin City–Stinson Beach; weekends and holidays only at 8.45, 9.45 and 10.45am.

#65: San Rafael–Point Reyes; 9am and 4pm weekends only.

If you'd rather avoid the hassle of bus connections, *Gray Line* (☎896-5915; $37.50) offers four-hour **guided bus tours** from San Francisco, taking in Sausalito and Muir Woods, daily at 9am, 11am and 1.30pm; the *Red and White* ferry fleet also has a boat-and-bus trip to Muir Woods, via Tiburon.

One of the best ways to get around Marin is by **bike**, particularly using a mountain bike to cruise the many trails that criss-cross the county. If you want to ride on the road, **Sir Francis Drake Highway** – from Larkspur to Point Reyes – makes a good route, though it's best to avoid weekends, when the roads can get clogged up with cars. All ferry services (except Alcatraz) allow bicycles.

Marin County Information

Three main on-the-spot sources can provide further information on Marin County: the **Marin County Visitors Bureau**, 30 N San Pedro Rd, San Rafael (Mon–Fri 9am–5pm; ☎472-7470); the **Sausalito Chamber of Commerce**, at 333 Caledonia St (Mon–Fri 9am–5pm; ☎332-0505); and the **Mill Valley Chamber of Commerce**, 85 Throckmorton Ave (Mon–Fri 9.30am–4pm; ☎388-9700), in the center of the town.

For information on **hiking** and **camping** in the wilderness and beach areas, depending on where you're heading, contact the Golden Gate National Recreation Area, Building 201, Fort Mason Center (daily 9am–4pm; ☎556-0560), Mount Tamalpais State Park, 801 Panoramic Highway, Mill Valley (daily 9am–5pm; ☎388-2070), or the Point Reyes National Seashore, Bear Valley, Point Reyes (daily 9am–5pm; ☎663-1092). Information on **what's on** in Marin can be found in the widely available local freesheets, such as the down-to-earth *Coastal Post* or the New-Agey *Pacific Sun*.

Across the Golden Gate: Marin Headlands and Sausalito

The headlands across the Golden Gate from San Francisco afford
impressive views of the bridge and the city behind. Take the first turn
past the bridge, and follow the road up the hill into the **Marin
Headlands** section of the Golden Gate National Recreation Area –
largely undeveloped land, except for the concrete remains of old
forts and gun emplacements standing guard over the entrance to the
bay. The coastline here is much more rugged than it is on the San
Francisco side, and though it makes a great place for an aimless cliff-
top scramble, or a walk along the beach, it's impossible not to be at
least a little sobered by the presence of so many military relics – even
if none was ever fired in anger. The oldest of these artillery batteries
dates from the Civil War, while the newest was built to protect
against a Japanese invasion during World War II, but even though
the huge guns have been replaced by picnic tables and brass plaques
– one of the concrete bunkers has even been painted to make a
trompe-l'oeil Greek temple – you can't overlook their violent intent.
Battery Wallace, the largest and most impressive of the artillery
sites, is cut through a hillside above the southwestern tip, and the
clean-cut military geometry survives to frame views of the Pacific
Ocean and Golden Gate Bridge. If you're interested in such things,
come along on the first Sunday of the month and take a guided tour
of an abandoned 1950s ballistic missile launchpad, complete with
disarmed nuclear missiles. The one non-military thing to see, the
Point Bonita Lighthouse, stands at the very end of the Headlands,
where it's open for tours at weekends, except during the winter.

Most of what there is to do out here is concentrated half a mile
to the north, around the rocky cliffs and islets of the point. Adjacent
to the **Marin Headlands Visitor Center** (daily 8.30am–4.30pm;
☎331-1450) – also the end of the *Muni* bus #76 route from San
Francisco on Sundays and holidays – a wide sandy beach fronts the
chilly ocean and marshy warm water of **Rodeo Lagoon**. Swimming

is prohibited here, in order to protect the nesting seabirds. Next to the center, the **Marine Mammal Center** rescues and rehabilitates injured and orphaned sea creatures, which you can visit while they recover; there's also a series of displays on the marine ecosystem and a bookstore that sells T-shirts and posters. The largest of the old army officers' quarters in the adjacent **Fort Barry**, half a mile to the east, has been converted into the spacious and homey **Golden Gate Youth Hostel**, an excellent base for more extended explorations of the inland ridges and valleys.

Sausalito

SAUSALITO, along the bay below US-101, is a pretty, smug little town of exclusive restaurants and pricey boutiques along a picturesque waterfront promenade. Very expensive, quirkily designed

Full details of the Golden Gate Youth Hostel can be found on p.208.

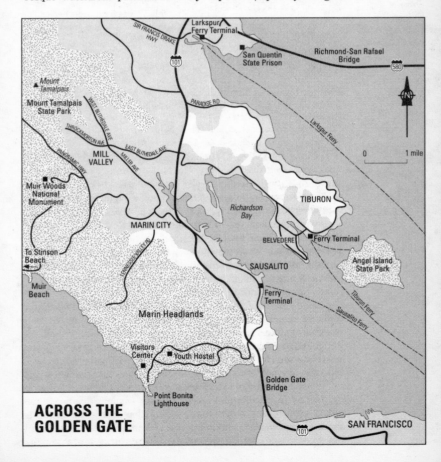

houses climb the overgrown cliffs above **Bridgeway Avenue**, the main road and bus route through town. Sausalito used to be a fairly gritty community of fishermen and sea-traders, full of bars and bordellos, and despite its upscale modern face it still makes a fun day out from San Francisco by ferry, the boats arriving next to the Sausalito Yacht Club in the center of town. Hang out for a while in one of the waterfront bars and watch the crowds strolling along the esplanade, or climb the stairways above Bridgeway and amble around the leafy hills.

Fifty years ago, Sausalito's waterfront served as one of the settings for Orson Welles' murder mystery, The Lady from Shanghai.

The old working wharves and warehouses that made Sausalito a haven for smugglers and Prohibition-era rum-runners are long gone; most have been taken over by dull steakhouses such as the *Charthouse*. However, some stretches of it have, for the moment at least, survived the tourist onslaught. Half a mile north of the town center along Bridgeway Avenue, an ad hoc community of exotic barges and houseboats, some of which have been moored here since the 1950s, is being threatened with eviction to make room for yet another luxury marina and bay-view office development. In the meantime many of the boats – one looks like a South Pacific island, another like the Taj Mahal – can be viewed from the marina behind the large brown shed that houses the Army Corps of Engineers museum (Mon–Sat 9am–4pm; free), which features a massive working model of San Francisco Bay, simulating changing tides and powerful currents.

The Marin County Coast to Bolinas

The **Shoreline Highway**, Hwy-1, cuts off west from US-101 just north of Sausalito, following the old main highway towards Mill Valley (see below). The first turn on the left, Tennessee Valley Road, leads up to the less-visited northern expanses of the Golden Gate National Recreation Area. You can make a beautiful three-mile hike from the parking lot at the end of the road, heading down along the secluded and lushly green **Tennessee Valley** to a small beach along a rocky cove; or you can take a guided tour on horseback from *Miwok Livery* ($15 per hr; ☎383-8048).

Hwy-1 twists up the canyon to a crest, where **Panoramic Highway** spears off to the right, following the ridge north to Muir Woods and Mount Tamalpais (see below); *Golden Gate Transit* bus #63 to Stinson Beach follows this route every hour on weekends and holidays only. Two miles down from the crest, a small unpaved road cuts off to the left, dropping down to the bottom of the broad canyon to the **Green Gulch Farm and Zen Center** (☎383-3134), an organic farm and Buddhist retreat, with an authentic Japanese tea house and a simple but refined prayer hall. On Sunday mornings the center is opened for a public meditation period and an informal discussion of Zen Buddhist practice, after which you can stroll down to Muir

Beach. If you already have some experience of Zen, enquire about the center's Guest Student Program, which enables initiates to stay from three days to several weeks at a time (it costs about $10 a night). If you just want a weekend's retreat, you can also stay overnight in the attached *Lindisfarne Guest House* for about $50 a night including meals, and take part as you choose in the communal life. Residents of the center rise well before dawn for meditation and prayer, then work much of the day in the gardens, tending the vegetables that are eventually served in many of the Bay Area's finest restaurants (notably *Greens*, in San Francisco's Fort Mason Center – see p.218).

The Marin County Coast to Bolinas

You'll find further details about the Lindisfarne Guest House *on p.205.*

Beyond the Zen Center, the road down from Muir Woods rejoins Hwy-1 at **Muir Beach**, surprisingly dark and usually uncrowded, around a semicircular cove. Three miles north, **Steep Ravine** drops sharply down the cliffs to a small beach, past very rustic $20-a-night cabins and a $6-a-night campground, bookable through Mount Tamalpais State Park (see above for details). A mile on is the small and lovely **Red Rocks** nudist beach, down a steep trail from a parking area along the highway. **Stinson Beach**, which is bigger, and more popular despite the rather cold water (it's packed at weekends in summer, when the traffic can be nightmarish), is a mile further. You can rent boogie boards and wetsuits for $10 a day from the *Livewater Surf Shop* (☎868-0333), along the highway at the south end of a short block of stores.

Bolinas and Southern Point Reyes

At the tip of the headland, due west from Stinson Beach, is the village of **BOLINAS**, though you may have a hard time finding it – locals tend to remove road signs marking the turnoff from Hwy-1 as soon as they're put up, in the hope of keeping the place to themselves. The campaign may have backfired, though, since press coverage of the "sign war" has done more to publicize the town than any road sign ever did; to get there, take the first left beyond the estuary and follow the road to the end. The village itself is a small colony of artists and writers (the late trout-fishing author Richard Brautigan and basketball diarist Jim Carroll among them), and there's not a lot to see – though you can get a feel for the place (and pick up a tasty sandwich and bags of fresh fruit and vegetables) at the *Bolinas People's Store* in the block-long village center.

Beyond Bolinas there's a rocky beach at the end of Wharf Road west of the village; and **Duxbury Reef Nature Reserve**, half a mile west at the end of Elm Road, is well worth a look for its tidal pools, full of starfish, crabs and sea anemones. Otherwise, Mesa Road heads north from Bolinas past the **Point Reyes Bird Observatory** (☎868-0655) – open for informal tours all day, though best visited in the morning. The first bird observatory in the US, this is still an important research and study center: if you time it right you may be able to watch, or even help, the staff as they put colored bands on the birds to keep track of them. Beyond here the road is no longer paved and leads on to the **Palomarin Trailhead**, the southern access into the Point Reyes National Seashore (see below). The best of the many beautiful hikes around the area leads past a number of small lakes and meadows for three miles to **Alamere Falls**, which throughout the winter and spring cascade down the cliffs onto Wildcat Beach.

Mount Tamalpais and Muir Woods

If you plan to follow the Californian coast, The Rough Guide To California is an invaluable companion.

Mount Tamalpais dominates the skyline of the Marin peninsula, hulking over the cool canyons of the rest of the county in a crisp yet voluptuous silhouette and dividing the county into two distinct parts: the wild western slopes above the Pacific coast and the increasingly suburban communities along the calmer bay frontage. Panoramic Highway branches off from Hwy-1 along the crest through the center of **Mount Tamalpais State Park**, which has some thirty miles of hiking trails and many campgrounds, though most of the redwood trees that once covered its slopes have long since been chopped down to form the posts and beams of San Francisco's Victorian houses. One grove of these towering trees does remain, however, protected as the **Muir Woods National Monument** (daily 8am–sunset; free), a mile down Muir Woods Road from Panoramic Highway. It's a tranquil and majestic spot, with sunlight filtering through the 300-foot trees down to the laurel- and fern-covered canyon below. The canyon's steep sides are what saved it from Mill Valley's lumbermen, and today this is one of the few first-growth redwood groves between San Francisco and the fantastic forests of Redwood National Park, up the coast near the Oregon border.

Being so close to San Francisco, Muir Woods is a popular target. The trails nearest the parking lot have been paved and are often packed with bus-tour hordes. However, if you visit during the week, or outside midsummer, it's easy enough to leave the crowds behind, especially if you're willing to head off up the steep trails that climb the canyon sides. Winter is a particularly good time to come, as the streams are gurgling – the main creek reaches down to Muir Beach, and salmon have been known to spawn in it – and the forest creatures are more likely to be seen going about their business. Keep an eye out especially for the various species of salamanders and newts that thrive in this damp environment; be warned, though, that some are poisonous and will bite if harassed. Other colorful Muir Woods denizens include the colonies of ladybugs that spend their winter huddling in the rich undergrowth.

One way to avoid the crowds, and the only way to get here on public transportation, is to enter the woods from the top, by way of a two-mile hike from the **Pan Toll Ranger Station** (☎388-2070) on Panoramic Highway – which is a stop on the *Golden Gate Transit*

#63 bus route. As the state park headquarters, the station has maps and information on hiking and camping, and rangers can suggest hikes to suit your mood and interests. From here the **Pan Toll Road** turns off to the right along the ridge to within a hundred yards of the 2571-foot summit of Mount Tamalpais, from where there are breathtaking views of the distant Sierra Nevada and close-ups of red-necked turkey vultures, listlessly circling the peak.

Mill Valley

From the East Peak of Mount Tamalpais, a quick two-mile hike downhill follows the **Temelpa Trail** through velvety shrubs of chaparral to the town of **MILL VALLEY**. The oldest and most enticing of the inland towns of Marin County is also accessible every half hour by *Golden Gate Transit* bus #10 from San Francisco and Sausalito. Originally a logging center, it was from here that the destruction of the surrounding redwoods was organized, though for many years the town has made a healthy living out of tourism. The **Mill Valley and Mount Tamalpais Scenic Railroad** – "the crookedest railroad in the world", as the blurb has it – was cut into the slopes above the town in 1896, twisting up through nearly three hundred tight curves in under eight miles. The trip proved so popular with tourists that the line was extended into Muir Woods in 1907, though road-building and fire combined to put an end to the railroad by 1930. You can, however, follow its route from the end of Summit Avenue in Mill Valley, a popular trip with daredevils on all-terrain bikes. More sport goes on here each June, when runners and assorted masochists come together for the **Dipsea**, a fiercely competitive seven-mile cross-country race over the mountains through Muir Woods to Stinson Beach.

Though much of Mill Valley's attraction lies in its easy access to hiking and mountain bike trails up Mount Tam, its compact yet relaxed center collects a number of cafés and some surprisingly good shops and galleries. The *Book Depot and Cafe* is an especially popular bookstore, café and meeting place on Throckmorton and Miller (daily 7am–10pm). The **Chamber of Commerce** (Mon–Sat 9am–5pm; ☎388-9700), next door, has maps and restaurant listings, as well as information on the wide range of local entertainments, including summer plays in the outdoor *Mountain Theater* and a world-class film festival in October.

All-terrain or "mountain" bikes were, incidentally, invented in Mill Valley.

Tiburon and Angel Island

TIBURON, at the tip of a narrow peninsula three miles east of US-101, is, like Sausalito, a ritzy harborside village to which hundreds of people come each weekend, many of them via direct *Red and White Fleet* ferries from Pier 41½ in San Francisco's Fisherman's Wharf.

Mill Valley

Despite the occasional throngs it's a relaxed place, less touristy than Sausalito, and if you're in the mood to take it easy and watch the boats sail across the bay, sitting out on the sunny deck of one of many cafés and bars can be idyllic. There are few specific sights to look out for, but it's quite pleasant just to wander around, calling into the odd gallery or antique store. The best of these are grouped together in **Ark Row**, at the west end of Main Street: the quirky buildings are actually old houseboats that were beached here early in the century. On a hill above the town stands **Old St Hilary's Church** (tours Wed & Sun 4–6pm), a Carpenter Gothic beauty that should be visited in the spring, when the surrounding fields are covered with multicolored buckwheat, flax and paintbrush.

If you're feeling energetic, rent a bicycle from *Ken's Bikes*, 94 Main St (☎465-1683), and cruise around the many plush houses of **Belvedere Island**, just across the Beach Road Bridge from the west end of Main Street, enjoying the fine views of the bay and Golden Gate Bridge. More ambitious cyclists can continue along the waterfront bike path, which winds from the bijou stores and galleries three miles west along undeveloped Richardson Bay frontage to a bird sanctuary at **Greenwood Cove**. The pristine Victorian house here is now the western headquarters of the National Audubon Society and open for tours on Sundays (10am–4pm); there's also a small interpretive center with displays on local and migratory birds and wildlife.

Another fine ride heads east from Tiburon along winding Paradise Road, around the mostly undeveloped headland three and a half miles to **Paradise Beach**, a county park with a fishing pier and close-up views of passing oil tankers heading for the refinery across the bay in Richmond. If you want to make a full circuit, Trestle Glen Boulevard cuts up and over the peninsula from near Greenwood Cove, linking with Paradise Road two miles northwest of Paradise Beach.

Angel Island

The pleasures of Tiburon are swiftly exhausted, and you'd be well advised to take the hourly *Angel Island Ferry* a mile offshore ($5 round trip, plus $1 per bicycle; ☎435-2131) to the largest island in the San Francisco Bay, ten times the size of Alcatraz. **Angel Island** is now officially a state park, but over the years it's served a variety of purposes, everything from a home for Miwok Native Americans to a World War II prisoner-of-war camp. It's full of ghostly ruins of old military installations and, with oak and eucalyptus trees and sagebrush covering the hills above rocky coves and sandy beaches, feels quite apart from the mainland. It's another excellent place to cycle: a five-mile road rings the island, and an unpaved track (plus assorted hiking trails) leads up to the 800-foot hump of **Mount Livermore**, which gives a panoramic view of the Bay Area.

The ferry arrives at **Ayala Cove**, where a small snack bar selling hot dogs and cold drinks provides the only sustenance available on the island – bring a picnic if you plan to spend the day here. The nearby **visitor center** (daily 9am–4pm; ☎435-1915) has displays on the island's history, in an old building that was built as a quarantine facility for soldiers returning from the Philippines after the Spanish-American War. Around the point on the northwest corner of the island the **North Garrison**, built in 1905, was the site of a prisoner-of-war camp during World War II, while the larger **East Garrison**, on the bay a half mile beyond, was the major transfer point for soldiers bound for the South Pacific.

Quarry Beach around the point is the best on the island, a clean sandy shore that's protected from the winds blowing in through the Golden Gate; it's also a popular landing spot for kayakers and canoeists who paddle across the bay from Berkeley.

Sir Francis Drake Boulevard and Central Marin County

The quickest route to the wilds of the Point Reyes National Seashore, and the only way to get there on public transportation, is by way of **Sir Francis Drake Boulevard**, which cuts across central Marin County through the inland towns of **San Anselmo** and **Fairfax**, reaching the coast thirty miles west at a crescent-shaped bay where, in 1579, Drake landed and claimed all of what he called Nova Albion for England. The route makes an excellent day-long cycling tour, and there are good beaches, a youth hostel and some tasty restaurants at the end of the road.

The *Larkspur Golden Gate Transit* **ferry**, which leaves from the Ferry Building in San Francisco, is the longest and, surprisingly, least expensive of the bay crossings. Primarily a commuter route, it docks at the modern space-frame terminal at Larkspur Landing. The monolithic, red-tile-roofed complex you see on the bayfront a mile east is the maximum-security **San Quentin State Prison**, which houses California's most violent and notorious criminals; a museum details the prison's history, and a small gallery displays and sells art and crafts created by men held inside.

San Anselmo, Fairfax and Point Reyes Station

San Anselmo, set in a broad valley two miles north of Mount Tam, calls itself "the antiques capital of Northern California" and sports a tiny center of specialty shops, furniture stores and cafés that draws out many San Francisco shoppers at weekends. The ivy-covered **San Francisco Theological Seminary** dominates the town from the hill above, and the very green and leafy **Creek Park** follows the creek that winds through the town center, but otherwise there's not a lot

Sir Francis Drake Boulevard and Central Marin County

This area was the location for Alan Parker's tear-jerking saga of Marin County life, Shoot the Moon, *starring slobby Albert Finney as a philandering writer.*

to do but eat and drink – or browse through fine bookstores such as *Oliver's Books*, at 645 San Anselmo Ave.

Center Boulevard follows the tree-lined creek west for a mile to **Fairfax**, a much less ostentatiously hedonistic community than the harborside towns, though in many ways it still typifies Marin lifestyles, with an array of wholefood stores and bookstores geared to a thoughtfully mellow crowd. From Fairfax, the narrow Bolinas Road twists up and over the mountains to the coast at Stinson Beach, while Sir Francis Drake Boulevard winds through a pastoral landscape of ranch houses hidden away up oak-covered valleys.

Ten miles west of Fairfax along Sir Francis Drake Boulevard, **Samuel Taylor State Park** has excellent camping (see above for details); five miles more brings you to the coastal Hwy-1 and the town of Olema, a mile north of which sits the town of **Point Reyes Station**, a good place to stop off for a bite to eat or to pick up picnic supplies before heading off to enjoy the wide-open spaces of the Point Reyes National Seashore just beyond. *Point Reyes Bikes*, 11431 Hwy-1 at Main St (☎663-1768), rents mountain bikes for $20 per day – much the best way to get around.

The Point Reyes National Seashore

From Point Reyes Station, Sir Francis Drake Boulevard heads out to the westernmost tip of Marin County at Point Reyes through the **Point Reyes National Seashore**, a near-island of wilderness surrounded on three sides by more than fifty miles of isolated coastline – pine forests and sunny meadows bordered by rocky cliffs and sandy, windswept beaches. This wing-shaped landmass, something of an aberration along the generally straight coastline north of San Francisco, is in fact a rogue piece of the earth's crust that has been drifting slowly and steadily northwards along the San Andreas Fault, having started some six million years ago as a suburb of Los Angeles. When the great earthquake of 1906 shattered San Francisco, the land here at Point Reyes, the epicenter, shifted over sixteen feet in an instant, though damage was confined to a few skewed cattle fences.

The park's **visitor center** (daily 9am–5pm; ☎663-1092), two miles southwest of Point Reyes Station near Olema, just off Hwy-1 on Bear Valley Road, holds engaging displays on the geology and natural history of the region. Rangers can suggest good hiking and cycling routes, and have up-to-date information on the weather, which can change quickly and be cold and windy along the coast even when it's hot and sunny here, three miles inland. They also handle permits and reservations for the various **campgrounds** within the park. Nearby, a replica of a Miwok village has an authentic religious **roundhouse**, and a popular hike follows the Bear Valley Trail along Coast Creek four miles to **Arch Rock**, a large tunnel in the seaside cliffs that you can walk through at low tide.

North of the visitors' center, Limantour Road heads west six miles to the **Point Reyes Youth Hostel**, continuing on another two miles to the coast at **Limantour Beach**, one of the best swimming beaches and a good place to watch the seabirds in the adjacent estuary. Bear Valley Road rejoins Sir Francis Drake Boulevard just past Limantour Road, leading north along the Tomales Bay through the village of **Inverness**, so-named because the landscape reminded an early settler of his home in the Scottish Highlands. Eight miles west of Inverness, a turn leads down past **Johnson's Oyster Farm** (Tues–Sun 8am–4pm; ☎669-1149) – where you can buy bivalves for around $5 a dozen, less than half the price you'd pay in town – to **Drake's Beach**, the presumed landing spot of Sir Francis in 1579. Appropriately, the coastline here resembles the southern coast of England, often cold, wet and windy, with chalk-white cliffs rising above the wide sandy beach. The main road continues west another four miles to the very tip of **Point Reyes**, where a precariously sited **lighthouse** stands firm against the literally crashing surf. You can't tour the building itself, but you can climb the tiring 300 or so steps down the steep cliffs to reach it. Even without making the trek all the way out, the bluffs along here are excellent places to look out for sea lions and, in winter, migrating grey whales.

*For details of
the Point Reyes
Youth Hostel,
see p.208.*

The northern tip of the Point Reyes seashore, **Tomales Point**, is accessible via the Pierce Point Road, which turns off Sir Francis Drake Boulevard two miles north of Inverness. Jutting out into Tomales Bay, it's the least visited section of the park and a refuge for hefty **tule elk**; it's also a great place to admire the lupines, poppies and other wild flowers that appear in the spring. The best swimming (at least the warmest water) is at **Heart's Desire Beach**, a little way before the end of the road; also, down the bluffs from where the road comes to a dead end, there are excellent tidal pools at rocky **McClure's Beach**. North of Point Reyes Station, Hwy-1 continues along the coast, through Bodega Bay up to Mendocino and the northern California coast.

San Rafael and Northern Marin County

You may pass through **SAN RAFAEL** on your way north from San Francisco, but it has little worth stopping for. The county seat and the only big city in Marin County, it has none of the woodsy qualities that make the other towns special, though there are a couple of good restaurants and bars along Fourth Street, the main drag. Its one attraction is an old **Franciscan Mission** (daily 11am–4pm; free), in fact a 1949 replica that was built near the site of the 1817 original, on Fifth Avenue at A Street. The real points of interest are well on the outskirts: the Marin County Civic Center to the north and the little-known China Camp State Park along the bay to the east.

San Rafael and Northern Marin County

The **Marin County Civic Center** (Mon–Fri 9am–5pm; free; ☎472-3500), spanning the hills just east of US-101 a mile north of central San Rafael, is a strange, otherworldly complex of administrative offices, plus an excellent performance space that looks like a giant viaduct capped by a bright blue-tiled roof. These buildings were architect **Frank Lloyd Wright**'s one and only government project, and although the huge circus tents and amusement park at the core of the designer's conception were never built, it does have some interesting touches, such as the atrium lobbies that open directly to the outdoors.

From the Civic Center, North San Pedro Road loops around the headlands through **China Camp State Park** (☎456-0766), an expansive area of pastures and open spaces that's hard to reach without your own transport. It takes its name from the intact but long-abandoned Chinese shrimp-fishing village at the far eastern tip of the park, the sole survivor of the many small Chinese communities that once dotted the California coast. The ramshackle buildings, small wooden pier and old boats lying on the sand seem straight out of some John Steinbeck tale, the only recent addition being a chain-link fence to protect the site from vandals. At the weekend you can get beer and sandwiches from the old shack at the foot of the pier, but the atmosphere is best during the week, at sunset, when there's often no one around at all. There's a **campground** at the northern end of the park, about two miles from the end of the *Golden Gate Transit* bus #39 route.

Six miles north of San Rafael, the **Lucas Valley Road** turns off west, twisting across Marin to Point Reyes. Although he lives and works here, it was not named after *Star Wars* film-maker George Lucas, whose sprawling **Skywalker Ranch** studios are well hidden off the road. Hwy-37 cuts off east, eight miles north of San Rafael, heading around the top of the bay into the Wine Country of the Sonoma and Napa valleys (see Chapter 11).

The Wine Country

S an Francisco during the summer can be a shock – persistent fog and cool temperatures dog the city from May to September – but you only need to travel an hour north to find a warm and sunny climate among the rolling hills of the Napa and Sonoma valleys, known jointly as the **Wine Country**. With its cool, oak-tree shaded ravines climbing up along creeks and mineral springs to chaparral-covered ridges, it would be a lovely place to visit even without the vineyards, but as it is, the "wine country" tag dominates almost everything here, including many often overlooked points of historical and literary interest. The Wine Country area doesn't actually account for all that much wine – production is something like five percent of the California total, most of which is of the Gallo and Paul Masson jug-wine variety and comes from the Central Valley. But far and away the best wines in the country come from here. The region has been producing wines since the days of the Spanish missions, and though most of the vines withered during Prohibition, the growers have struggled back and these days manage to turn out premium vintages that satisfy wine snobs around the world. Not surprisingly, it's a wealthy region, and rather a smug one, thriving as much on its role as a vacation land for upper-crust San Franciscans as on the wine trade: designer restaurants (all with massive wine lists) and luxury inns line the narrow roads that, on summer weekends especially, are bumper-to-bumper with wine-tasting tourists.

By and large the **Napa Valley** is home to the larger concerns, but even here the emphasis is on quality rather than quantity, and the high-brow tones of the winery tour guides-cum-sales reps can get maddeningly pretentious. However, wineries are everywhere, and while the town of **Napa** is sprawling and quickly done with, the many small towns further up the valley, particularly **St Helena**, have retained enough of their turn-of-the-century homestead character to be a welcome relief. **Calistoga**, at the top of the valley, offers the best range of non-wine-related distractions – mostly various methods of soaking your bones in tubfuls of hot spring water.

On the western side of the dividing Mayacamas Mountains, the small backroads wineries of the **Sonoma Valley** reflect the more down-to-earth nature of the place, which is both more beautiful and less crowded than its neighbor to the east. The town of **Sonoma** itself is by far the most attractive of the Wine Country communities, retaining a number of fine Mission-era structures around its gracious central plaza. **Santa Rosa**, at the north end of the valley, is the region's sole urban center, handy for budget accommodation but otherwise unremarkable.

As it's only an hour from Union Square to the Wine Country, most people are content to come here for a long day, visiting a few of the wineries and maybe having a picnic or a meal before heading back to the city. This is fine if you have a car and are happy to spend most of the day on the road, but if you really want to absorb properly what the region has to offer, plan to spend at least one night here, pampering yourself in one of the many (generally

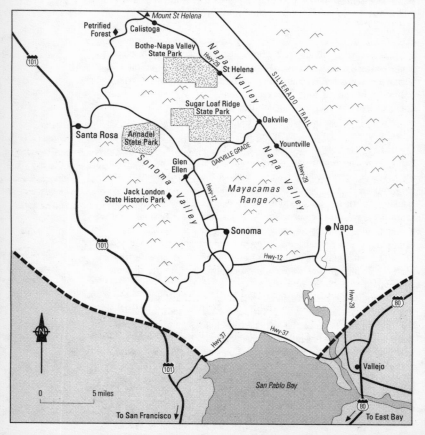

Cycling in the Wine Country

If you don't want to drive all day, **cycling** is a great way to get around. You can bring your own bike on *Greyhound* (though it costs $10, and the bike must be in a box), or rent one locally for around $20 a day from such outlets as *Bryan's Napa Valley Cyclery*, 4080 Byway East, Napa (☎707/255-3377); *St Helena Cyclery*, 1156 Main St, St Helena (☎707/963-7736); and *Sonoma Wheels*, 523 Broadway, Sonoma (☎707/935-1366).

Both valleys are generally flat, although the peaks in between are steep enough to challenge the hardest of hill-climbers. If the main roads through the valleys are packed out, as they are most summer weekends, try the smaller parallel routes: the **Silverado Trail** in Napa Valley, and the less evocatively named but nonetheless pretty **Arnold Drive** in Sonoma Valley. For would-be Kings of the Mountains, the **Oakville Grade** between Oakville in the Napa Valley and Glen Ellen in the Sonoma Valley has tested the world's finest riders: you can still make out traces of "Go Hinault!" and "C'mon LeMond!" daubed on the roadway for the *Coors Classic* tours many years ago.

If you feel like some company, or just want to be sure everything goes smoothly, a few local firms organize **tours**, providing bikes, helmets, food and sag wagons in case you get worn out. In Calistoga, *Cruisin' Jules* (☎707/942-0421) specializes in mountain bike downhill runs, and *Rob Mondavi's Napa Valley Biking Picnics* (☎707/252-1067) sets up more leisurely tours – highlighted by gourmet lunches – all over the Napa area. More ambitious (and quite expensive) overnight tours are run most weekends by *Backroads Bicycle Tours*, 1516 Fifth St, Berkeley (☎510/527-1555).

pricey) **hotels** and **bed and breakfast inns** that provide the bulk of the area's accommodation options. At peak times rooms of all descriptions can seem to be booked up, and if you have a hard time finding a place, avail yourself of one of the many **accommodation services** here – *Bed and Breakfast of Napa* (☎707/255-1280); *Inns of Sonoma Valley* (☎707/996-INNS); *Reservations Unlimited* (☎707/252-1985); or the *Napa Valley Tourist Bureau* (☎707/944-1557).

For Wine Country accommodation, see Chapter 12; restaurants are on p.229; and cafés and bars on p.238.

Arrival and Getting Around

The Wine Country region spreads north from the top of San Francisco Bay in two parallel, thirty-mile-long valleys, Napa and Sonoma, divided by the oak-covered Mayacamas Mountains. As long as you avoid the rush-hour traffic, it's about an hour's drive from the city along either of two main routes: from Marin County, via the Golden Gate Bridge and US-101, and from the East Bay, via the Bay Bridge and I-80.

As the Wine Country's attractions are spread over a fairly broad area, a **car** is pretty much essential. *Golden Gate Transit* (☎322-6600) runs commuter buses all day for the two-hour, $4.50 ride between the city and Santa Rosa which may be of use; *Greyhound* has only one bus a day to the Wine Country, leaving San Francisco at 12.45pm for Santa Rosa and costing $11. From Santa Rosa, *Sonoma County Transit* (☎707/576-RIDE) buses serve the entire Sonoma Valley on a comprehensive if less than frequent schedule. Another option for the car-less is to sign up for a *Gray Line* **guided bus tour** (☎558-9400) from San Francisco. These cost $42, and leave from the Transbay Terminal at 9am, visiting a winery in each valley, stopping for lunch in Yountville and returning to the city at about 6.30pm.

Much more exciting are the widely touted **hot-air balloon rides** over the Napa Valley. These usually lift off at dawn (hot air rises more strongly in the cold morning air) and last ninety magical minutes, winding up with a champagne brunch. The first and still the best of the operators is *Napa Valley Balloons* (☎707/253-2224), who fly out of Yountville. Others include *Balloons Above The Valley* (☎707/253-2222) and *Once in a Lifetime* (☎707/942-6541). The crunch comes when you realize the price – around $120 a head.

Wine Country Information

Not surprisingly for such a tourist-dependent area, the Wine Country has a well-developed network of **tourist information** outlets, though the rivalry between the two valleys makes it next to impossible to find out anything about Sonoma when you're in Napa, and vice versa. While the various small town **Chambers of Commerce** rarely do more than hand out useless brochures, both the **Napa Valley Visitors Bureau**, 1310 Napa Town Center off First St in downtown Napa (Mon–Fri 10am–5pm, Sat & Sun 11am–3pm; ☎707/226-7459), and the **Sonoma Valley Visitors Bureau**, 453 First St E (Mon–Sat 9am–4pm, Sun 9am–3pm; ☎707/996-1090), in Sonoma's central plaza, should be able to tell you all you need to know about their respective areas. If you're keen on **touring the wineries**, both the above places sell handy **maps** ($1) with the lowdown on the hundreds of producers.

The Napa Valley

A thirty-mile strip of gently landscaped corridors and lush hillsides, the **Napa Valley** looks more like southern France than a near-neighbor of the Pacific Ocean. In spring the valley floor is covered with brilliant wild flowers which mellow into autumnal shades by grape-harvest time. Local Native Americans named the fish-rich river which flows through the valley "Napa", meaning "plenty"; the name was adopted by Spanish missionaries in the early 1800s, but the Indians themselves were soon wiped out. The few ranchos the Spanish and Mexicans managed to establish were in turn taken over by Yankee traders, and by the 1850s, with California part of the US, the town of Napa had become a thriving river port, sending agricultural goods to San Francisco and serving as a supply point for farmers and ranchers. Before long Napa was bypassed by the railroads and unable to compete with other, deep-water Bay Area ports, but the area's fine climate saved it from oblivion, encouraging a variety of crops including the grape, which spawned the now super-lucrative wine industry.

NAPA itself, at the southern end of the valley, is still the local economic lynchpin, and the highway sprawl that greets travellers is fair warning of what the rest of the town has to offer. But for a proud courthouse, and some intriguingly decrepit old warehouses (ripe for gentrification) along the river, there's not much to see, though it's not bad for food, and the **visitors bureau** is the most helpful in the whole valley. YOUNTVILLE, the next town north, has similarly little to see, though it boasts the highest proportion of **places to eat** in the whole region.

St Helena

The first town really worth a stop – and it's not much more than a large village really – is pretty ST HELENA, 22 miles north of Napa. Its main street, Hwy-29, is lined by some of the Wine Country's finest old buildings, most of which have been restored to – or maintained in – prime condition. The town is also at the heart of the greatest concentration of wineries, as well as boasting some unlikely literary attractions.

The **Silverado Museum** (Tues–Sun noon–4pm; free), housed in St Helena's former Public Library building just off Main Street in the center of town, has a collection of over 8000 articles relating to Robert Louis Stevenson, who spent just under a year in the area, honeymooning and recovering from an illness. It's claimed to be the second most extensive collection of Stevenson artefacts in the US, though the only thing of interest to any but the most obsessed fan is a scribbled-on manuscript of *Dr Jekyll and Mr Hyde*. The other half of the building is taken up by the **Napa Valley Wine Library** (same hours), a briefly entertaining barrage of photos and clippings relating to the development of local viniculture. Another, more bizarre collection is on display on the north side of town at 1515 Main St, where the **Ambrose Bierce House** bed and breakfast inn is packed with memorabilia of the misanthropic ghost-story writer, who lived here for some fifteen years before heading off to die for Pancho Villa in the Mexican Revolution.

Calistoga

Beyond St Helena, towards the far northern end of the valley, the wineries become prettier and the traffic a little thinner. At the very tip of the valley, nestling at the foot of Mount St Helena, CALISTOGA is far and away the most enjoyable of the Napa towns, with a few good wineries but really better known for its mud baths

*Calistoga
accommodation
options are
listed on pages
202 and 206.*

and hot springs – and the mineral water which adorns every Californian supermarket shelf. Sam Brannan, the young Mormon entrepreneur who made a mint out of the Gold Rush, established a resort community here in 1860. In his groundbreaking speech he attempted to assert his desire to create the "Saratoga of California", modelled upon the Adirondack gem, but in the event got tongue-tied and coined the town's unique name.

Calistoga's main attraction, then as now, has nothing to do with wines, but rather with another pleasurable activity: soaking in the soothingly hot water that bubbles up here from deep inside the earth. It's a homey, health-conscious kind of place, with many spas and volcanic mud baths to draw jaded city-dwellers for the weekend. The extravagant might enjoy *Dr. Wilkinson's Hot Springs*, 1507 Lincoln Avenue (rooms and treatment from $100 per night; ☎707/ 942-4102): a legendary health spa and hotel whose heated mineral water and volcanic ash tension-relieving treatments have been featured on TV's *Lifestyles of the Rich & Famous*. If swaddled luxury is not what you're after, a number of more down-to-earth establishments spread along the mile-long main drag, Lincoln Avenue. *Nance's Hot Springs*, 1614 Lincoln Ave (☎707/942-6211), for example, offers a full mineral rub-down, blanket sweat, steam bath and massage for around $30.

Another sign of Calistoga's lively underground activity is the **Old Faithful Geyser** (daily 9am–5pm; $3), two miles north of town on Tubbs Lane, off Hwy-128, which spurts boiling water sixty feet into the air at fifty-minute intervals. The water source was discovered while drilling for oil here in the 1920s, when search equipment struck a force estimated to be up to a thousand pounds per square foot; the equipment was blown away and despite heroic efforts to control it, the geyser has continued to go off like clockwork ever since. Landowners finally realized that they'd never tame it and turned it into a high-yield tourist attraction.

A further local tourist trap is the **Petrified Forest** (daily 10am–5pm; $3), two miles west of Calistoga on the steep road over the hills to Santa Rosa – a forest that was toppled during an eruption of Mount St Helena some three million years ago. The entire redwood grove was petrified by the action of the silica-laden volcanic ash as it gradually seeped into the decomposing fibers of the uprooted trees.

Mount St Helena

The clearest sign of the local volcanic unrest is the massive conical mountain that marks the north end of the Napa Valley, **Mount St Helena**. The 4343-foot summit is worth a climb for its great views – on a very clear day you can see Point Reyes and the Pacific coast to the west, San Francisco to the south, the towering Sierra Nevada to the east and impressive Mount Shasta to the north. It is, however, a long hot climb (five steep miles each way) and you need to set off

Napa Valley Wineries

Almost all of the Napa Valley's more than a hundred **wineries** offer tastings, though comparatively few have tours. Since all produce wines of a very high standard, it's entirely a question of taste which ones you visit. The following selections, listed from south to north, are some long-standing favorites, plus a few lesser-known hopefuls. Keep in mind that the intention is for you to get a sense of a winery's product, and perhaps buy some, rather than get drunk on the stuff, so don't expect more than a sip or two of any one sort – though some wineries do sell wines by the glass. If you want to buy a bottle, particularly from the larger producers, you can in fact usually get it cheaper in supermarkets than at the wineries themselves.

Stag's Leap, 5766 Silverado Trail, east of Yountville; ☎707/944-2020. The winery that put Napa Valley on the international map by beating a bottle of Chateau Lafitte-Rothschild at a Paris tasting way back in 1976. Still quite highly rated. Tasting daily 10am–4pm; tours by appointment.

Robert Mondavi, 7801 St Helena Highway, Oakville; ☎707/963-9611. Long the standard-bearer for Napa Valley wines ("Bob Red" and "Bob White" are house wines at many California restaurants), they have the most informative and least hard-sell tours. Tours and tasting daily 9am–5pm, book ahead in summer. Free half-day tours are also available.

Berringer Brothers, 2000 Main St, St Helena; ☎707/963-7115. Napa Valley's most famous piece of architecture, the "Rhine House", modelled on an ancestral German Gothic mansion graces the cover of many a wine magazine. Expansive lawns and a grand tasting room, heavy on dark wood, make for a regal experience. Tours and tasting daily 10am–4pm; closed Aug.

Christian Brothers, 2555 Main St, St Helena; ☎707/963-0765. This was the world's largest winery when erected in 1889, but was a bit of a white elephant that kept changing hands until its present owners – oddly enough a Catholic education order – bought it in 1950, and it now turns out extremely popular sparkling wines. Tours and tasting daily 10am–4pm.

Conn Creek Winery, 8711 Silverado Trail, St Helena; ☎707/963-9100. A truly modern organization whose lightweight stone and steel building is worlds away from the cutesy old-stone image that's the norm in the rest of the valley. Tasting 10am–4pm daily; tours by appointment.

Clos Pegase, 1060 Dunaweal Rd, Calistoga; ☎707/942-4981. A flamboyant upstart at the north end of the valley, this high-profile winery emphasizes the links between fine wine and fine art, with a sculpture garden around buildings designed by post-modern architect Michael Graves. No tours, tastings daily 10.30am–4.30pm.

early in the morning to enjoy it – take plenty of water (and maybe a bottle of wine).

The mountain and most of the surrounding land is protected and preserved as the **Robert Louis Stevenson State Park** (daily 8am–sunset; $2) though the connection with him is fairly weak:

The Napa Valley

Stevenson spent his honeymoon here in 1880 in a bunkhouse with Fanny Osborne, recuperating from tuberculosis and exploring the valley. The bunkhouse remains, but little else about the park's winding roads and dense shrub-growth evokes its days of former notoriety, though it's a pretty enough place to take a break from the wineries and have a picnic. In Stevenson's novel, *Silverado Squatters*, he describes the highlight of the honeymoon as the day he managed to taste eighteen of local wine baron Jacob Schram's champagnes in one sitting. Quite an extravagance, especially when you consider that Schramsberg champagne is held in such high esteem that Richard Nixon took a few bottles when he went to visit Chairman Mao.

The Sonoma Valley

On looks alone the crescent-shaped Sonoma Valley beats Napa hands down. This smaller and altogether more rustic valley curves between oak-covered mountain ranges from Spanish colonial **Sonoma** a few miles north along Hwy-12 to **Glen Ellen**, to end up at the region's main city, **Santa Rosa**. The Sonoma Valley is also known as the "Valley of the Moon", after a Native American legend popularized by long-time resident Jack London that tells how, as you move through the valley, the moon seems to rise several times from behind the various peaks. Far smaller than Napa, most of the Sonoma Valley's wineries are informal, family-run businesses, many within walking distance of Sonoma itself, and with far fewer visitors – making it very much the stress-free alternative to the busy Napa Valley.

Sonoma

Behind a layer of somewhat touristy stores and restaurants, the small town of **SONOMA** retains a good deal of its Spanish and Mexican architecture. Set around a spacious plaza, the town has a welcoming feel that's refreshing after brash Napa, although as a popular retirement spot, with a median age of about fifty and a matching pace, it's not exactly bubbling with action. The **visitors' bureau** (see p.186), in the middle of the leafy central plaza, has walking-tour plans of the town and excellent free maps and guides to the wineries. What there is to see in the town itself will take no more than an hour: Sonoma is a place better known for its history than its sights.

It's hard to believe now that Sonoma was the site of a key event in West Coast history, but the so-called **Bear Flag Revolt** of 1846 was just that – at least as far as the flag-waving Fourth of July crowds who take over the central square are concerned. In this much-romanticized episode, American settlers in the region, who had long lived in uneasy peace under the Spanish and, later, Mexican rulers, were threatened with expulsion from California,

along with all other non-Mexican immigrants. In response, a band of
thirty armed settlers – some of whom came from as far away as
Sacramento – descended upon the disused and unguarded presidio
at Sonoma, taking the retired and much-respected commander,
Colonel Guadalupe Vallejo, as their prisoner. Ironically, Vallejo had
long advocated the American annexation of California and
supported the aims of his rebel captors, but he was nonetheless
bundled off to Sutter's Fort in Sacramento and held there for the
next two months while the militant settlers declared California an
independent republic. The Bear Flag, which served as the model for
the current state flag, was raised on Sonoma Plaza. A month later
the US declared war on Mexico, and without firing a shot took
possession of the entire Pacific coast.

In memory of all this, there's a monument to the Bear Flag revolutionaries in the middle of the plaza, and across the street to the
north, in **Sonoma State Historic Park**, there are some rusty old
cannons and the spooky-looking remains of the old Mexican presidio; the ragged flag is on display inside a small **museum** (daily
8am–5pm; $2). Next door, the restored **Mission San Francisco**

Sonoma Wineries

Fine **wineries** are scattered all over the Sonoma Valley, but there's a good
concentration in a well-signposted group a mile east of Sonoma Plaza,
down East Napa Street. Some are within walking distance, but often along
quirky back roads, so take a winery map from the tourist office and follow
the signs closely. If you're tired of chasing around, Sonoma also has the
handy *The Wine Exchange of Sonoma*, 452 First St E (☎707/938-1794),
a commercial tasting room where you can sample the best wines from all
over California.

Buena Vista Winery, 1800 Old
Winery Rd; ☎707/938-1266.
Oldest and grandest of the wineries, although the wine itself has a
reputation for being pretty mediocre, and the century-old stone
champagne cellars – the best thing
about the place – are being refash-
ioned into yet another pricey
restaurant. Tasting daily 10am–
5pm, tours daily at 2pm, Sat and
Sun also at 11.30am.

Hacienda Wine Cellars, 1000
Vineyard Lane; ☎707/938-3220. A
lavish Spanish colonialist building,
with some great topiary in the
gardens and extensive vineyards.
The wines are relatively
inexpensive, middle-of-the-range

vintages that appeal to the pocket
and palate alike; if you're looking
to buy a case, this one's a safe bet.
Tastings daily 10am–5pm, tours by
appointment.

Gundlach-Bundschu, 3775
Thornsberry Rd; ☎707/938-5277.
Set back about a mile away from
the main cluster, this is more
highly regarded for its wine,
having stealthily crept up from the
lower ranks of the wine league to
the point where it now regularly
steals from the big names. The
plain, functional building is
deceptive – this is premium stuff
and definitely not to be
overlooked. No tours, but tasting
daily 10am–5pm.

Solano de Sonoma (daily 10am–5pm; $1) was the northernmost and last of the California missions, and the only one established while California was under Mexican rule. Half a mile west of the plaza along Spain Street stands the ornate old home of General Vallejo, dominated by decorated filigreed eaves and slender Gothic arched windows. The chalet-style storehouse next door has been turned into a **museum** (daily 9am–5pm; free) of artefacts from the general's reign.

Glen Ellen and Jack London State Park

While the drive up the valley can be soothing, there's really very little to see north of Sonoma apart from a few small villages and the **Jack London State Park** (daily 8am–dusk; $3 per car) – just ten minutes from Sonoma on the London Ranch Road which curves sharply off Hwy-12 close to tiny **GLEN ELLEN** village. Jack London lived here with his wife for the last years of his short, unsettled life, on a 140-acre ranch in the hills above what he described as the "most beautiful, primitive land in California". A series of paths and walking trails leads through densely wooded groves to the remains of the Wolf House, where they lived until an arson attack reduced most of it to a pile of rubble in 1913, leaving only the huge stone chimney and fireplaces. London died three years later and is buried on a hill above the trail to the Wolf House. After his death London's wife Charmian built the more formal House of Happy Walls, which today serves as a small **museum** (daily 9am–4pm; free). Photographs and artefacts – including the desk where London cranked out his 2000 words a day – enliven the otherwise dry details of the writer's life and work.

Santa Rosa

Sixty miles due north of San Francisco on US-101, and about twenty miles from Sonoma, **SANTA ROSA**, the largest town in Sonoma County, sits at the top end of the Sonoma Valley and is more or less the hub of this part of the Wine Country. It's a very different world from the indulgence of other Wine Country towns, however; much of it is given over to shopping centers and roadside malls, and signs downtown ban teenagers from cruising the rarely packed but confusing system of one-way streets.

Probably the most interesting thing about Santa Rosa is that it was the home town of Raymond Chandler's fictional private eye Philip Marlowe; after that it's all downhill. The **Luther Burbank Home and Gardens** at the junction of Santa Rosa and Sonoma Avenues (April–Sept only Wed–Sun 10am–3.30pm; $1) may kill an hour or two: California's best-known turn-of-the-century horticulturalist is remembered here in the house where he lived and in the splendid gardens where he created some of his most unusual hybrids. If you're not into gardening, nip across the street to the

Ripley Museum, 492 Sonoma Ave (Wed–Sun 11am–4pm, March–Oct only; $1.50), where you might expend twenty minutes or so in one of the cartoonist Ripley's mediocre "Believe It or Not" chain of museums – Santa Rosa was Ripley's home town.

The Listings

Chapter 12

Accommodation

With over 50,000 hotel rooms in the greater metropolitan area, San Francisco isn't short on accommodation. Visitors are the city's number one business, and even during the peak summer months failure to phone ahead needn't result in getting stuck for a place to sleep. However, since room rates average around $100 per night, accommodation may prove to be the major expense of your stay. Fortunately, San Francisco has a number of options in all price ranges – from youth hostels to five-star luxury hotels – so it's well worth your while to shop around for something that suits both your taste and your bank balance.

Prices start at around $35 per night for a basic **motel** or **hotel** room – $70 a night is a good deal for something fairly decent and centrally located. The city's stock of **bed and breakfast** inns, starting at around $60 a night, can often be more pleasant and sometimes better value. A **dormitory bed** in a **hostel** will cost in the region of $13 a night, while **camping** is not really an option in San Francisco itself, as there are no sites within an hour's drive of the city.

We've listed our hotel and motel recommendations below, arranged by location; hostels and bed-and-breakfasts are listed separately, as are establishments catering specifically for gay men and lesbians. We've also included a short list of hotels near the airport, in case you're arriving or departing on a late night or early morning flight.

Rates are in all cases subject to change, and unless otherwise noted are for the cheapest double room in peak season; bear in mind, too, that all quoted room rates are subject to a **room tax** – currently 12 percent on top of your total bill. During the off season rates can drop considerably, and special deals are often available for guests who stay for longer periods.

Finally, if you do have trouble finding a place to stay, try contacting the ultra-efficient and friendly *San Francisco Reservations* (☎ 1-800/677-1550), who will find you a place somewhere in town without fail, though you should expect to spend upwards of $80 per night.

Hotels and Motels

San Francisco hotels and motels have an excellent reputation for comfort and cleanliness, and especially at the lower price ranges it can be hard to tell the difference between the two. The main distinction is that hotels tend to be more central, and to have better dining facilities, while motels are usually located on main roads and offer free parking – no small consideration in San Francisco, where parking is expensive ($15 a night) and hard to find.

Whichever sort of place you decide to stay at, you can expect a fairly uniform standard of comfort – double rooms with bathroom, color TV and phone – and on the whole you won't get much more by paying, say $75 for a night instead of $50. Over $75 and the room simply gets

Accommodation

larger and the fittings more luxurious. If you're prepared to pay over $100 per night, that will bring you into the decadent realms of the en-suite jacuzzi and round-the-clock room service.

Hotels in the slightly seedy South of Market and Tenderloin areas start at around $30 per night, $100 per week, though you shouldn't expect a private bath or even a toilet for that amount. In the glitzier areas around Union Square or atop Nob Hill it's hard to find anything at all for under $100 a night.

Wherever you stay, you'll be expected to pay in advance, at least for the first night and perhaps for further nights, too, particularly if it's high season. Some places also request a deposit of a night's room rate when you make your reservation and many will want a credit card number for security, which they will not hesitate to use for the cost of one night's stay should you fail to arrive; reservations are held until 5pm or 6pm unless you've told the hotel you'll be arriving late.

Payment in cash or US dollar travellers' checks is usually acceptable, though most places prefer to take a swipe of your credit card and have you sign for the full amount when you check out.

Downtown

Cartwright Hotel
524 Sutter St.
☎421-2865 or 1-800/227-3844.
Distinguishes itself from its rivals with little touches such as fresh flowers, afternoon tea and bend-over-backwards courtesy. Good location one block north of Union Square. ⑤.

Dakota Hotel
606 Post St. ☎931-7475.
Recently converted 1920s hotel, next door to the *Prescott* near Union Square. Low rates, thanks to the lack of luxury trimmings or fancy service, but all rooms have antique baths. ②.

Fairmont Hotel
950 Mason St. ☎772-5000.
Most famous of San Francisco's top-notch hotels, the *Fairmont* is an excessively decorated palace with seven restaurants, ten lounges and fantastic views from the rooms. ⑦–⑧.

Gates Hotel
140 Ellis St. ☎781-0430.
Super-cheap downtown location, with rooms of a predictable standard. ②.

Geary Hotel
610 Geary St. ☎673-9221.
Affordable, no frills Theater District hotel. ②–③.

Grant Plaza Hotel
465 Grant Ave. ☎434-3883.
Newly renovated hotel with clean rooms in the middle of Chinatown. ③.

Harbor Court Hotel
165 Steuart St.
☎882-1300 or 1-800/346-0555.
Plush rooms, offering the best bay views of any hotel in the city, and guests have free use of the excellent YMCA health club next door. ⑦.

Hotel Herbert
161 Powell St. ☎362-1600.
Slightly scruffy rooms, but they're very central and very inexpensive, especially by the week. ②.

Accommodation Price Codes

All the prices of hotels, motels and bed and breakfasts in this chapter have been graded with the symbols below, according to the cost of the least expensive double room throughout most of the year.

Bear in mind that you will have to pay **room tax** – currently 12 percent of the total bill – on top of these rates.

① 0–$30	⑤ $80–100
② $30–45	⑥ $100–130
③ $45–60	⑦ $130–180
④ $60–80	⑧ $180+

Hotel Mark Twain
345 Taylor St. ☎673-2332.
Elegantly decorated colonial-style hotel in the middle of the Theater District. ⑤.

Hotel Triton
342 Grant Ave.
☎394-0500 or 1-800/433-6611.
Very stylish, very comfortable and very central hotel, catering to design professionals and weekend shoppers. Across the street from the Chinatown Gateway, two blocks from Union Square. ⑥–⑦.

Huntington Hotel
1075 California St. ☎474-5400.
Understated and quietly elegant compared to its Nob Hill compatriots, this is the hotel for the wealthy who don't need to flash it about. Its bars are neither rooftop, nor revolving, but instead opt for simple dark-wood furnishings, a piano player and a very intimate atmosphere. The free limousine service makes it a must if going for the full luxury treatment. ⑧.

Hyde Plaza Hotel
835 Hyde St. ☎885-2987.
On the Tenderloin/Nob Hill border, this hotel offers unbelievably cheap accommodation. Small, clean and comfortable rooms with shared bath. ①–②.

Mandarin Oriental San Francisco
222 Sansome St. ☎885-0999.
You'll need silly amounts of money if you want to stay in what are reputedly San Francisco's most luxurious hotel rooms. Amenities include valet, concierge and 24hr room service. ⑧.

Pacific Bay Inn
520 Jones St.
☎673-0234, 1-800/343-0880 in CA, 1-800/445-2631 in rest of US.
Comfortable renovated hotel in busy downtown location, with a surprisingly high standard of service considering the relatively low rates. Discounted weekly rates available. ③.

Pan Pacific Hotel
500 Post St. ☎771-8600.
Sleek, modern hotel designed (but no longer owned) by John Portman. If slabs of granite, sparse furnishings and quietly attentive service are what you look for in a luxury hotel, it might just be for you. ⑧.

Prescott Hotel
545 Post St.
☎563-0303 or 1-800/283-7322.
The flagship of hotelier Bill Kimpton's San Francisco properties, this small Union Square hotel offers understated luxury, four-star comfort – and preferred seating at the city's most popular restaurant, *Postrio*, with which it shares space. ⑦–⑧.

Raphael Hotel
386 Geary St.
☎986-2000 or 1-800/821-5343.
Very popular Union Square hotel with spacious, good-value rooms and helpful, friendly staff. ⑤.

Ritz-Carlton San Francisco
600 Stockton St.
☎296-7465 or 1-800/241-3333.
The most luxurious hotel in San Francisco perched on the stylish slope of Nob Hill with gorgeously appointed rooms, a swimming pool, muti-million dollar art collection and one of the city's best hotel restaurants, the *Dining Room*. ⑧.

San Francisco Marriot
777 Market St. ☎777-2799.
Most people reckon this 1500-room mirrored monster, looming like a giant jukebox on the skyline, is the biggest blight on San Francisco's cityscape; but at least it has a certain surreal quality. ⑥–⑧.

Sheehan Hotel
620 Sutter St.
☎775-6500 or 1-800/848-1529.
Affordable and comfortable Union Square hotel. ③–⑤.

Temple Hotel
469 Pine St. ☎781-2565.
Plain and simple rooms at bargain rates, on fringes of Financial District. One of the better budget options. ②.

Westin St Francis
335 Powell St.
☎397-7000 or 1-800/228-3000.
Truly grand hotel with a sumptuous lobby, five restaurants, an elegant bar and disappointingly plain rooms. Its reputation far outstrips the reality of a stay here, but as long as you don't mind the throngs of tourists who pour in to gape at the lobby, you'll be happy. ⑦–⑧.

Accommodation

See p.211 for a review of the Dining Room *restaurant.*

See p.54 for more on the St Francis.

Accommodation

Specifically gay accommodation options are listed on p.206.

York Hotel
940 Sutter St.
☎885-6800 or 1-800/227-3608.
Quiet, older hotel on the western edge of downtown. Essential stop for Hitchcock fans: this is where the dramatic stairway scenes in *Vertigo* were filmed. ⑥.

North Beach and the Northern Waterfront

Bel Aire Travelodge
3201 Steiner St. ☎921-5162.
Good value Lombard Street motel. ③–④.

Days Inn
2358 Lombard St. ☎922-2010.
Simple, budget accommodation. ③–④.

Holiday Inn/Fisherman's Wharf
1300 Columbus Ave.
☎771-9000 or 1-800/465-4329.
Reliable if dull, with large clean rooms. ⑥.

Howard Johnson's Motor Lodge
580 Beach St. ☎775-3800.
Modern, standard motel. ⑤–⑥.

Hyde Park Suites
2655 Hyde St.
☎771-0200 or 1-800/227-3608.
Spacious suites, with kitchens, that are ideal family accommodation. Right on the Hyde Street cable car line, a short walk to Fisherman's Wharf. ⑦.

Marina Motel
2576 Lombard St.
☎921-9406 or 1-800/346-6118.
Among the least expensive of the Lombard Street motels. ③–④.

San Remo Hotel
2237 Mason St.
☎776-8688 or 1-800/352-7366.
Pleasant, old-fashioned rooms (i.e. you'll have to share a bathroom) in nicely preserved North Beach house. Friendly staff, and its own very good bar and restaurant. ④–⑤.

Sherman House
2160 Green St. ☎563-3600.
Rated the best in San Francisco by *Zagat* readers' guide, this small Cow Hollow hotel is one of the city's lesser-known jewels. ⑧.

Tuscan Inn
425 North Point.
☎561-1100 or 1-800/648-4626.
The most upmarket hotel on the waterfront, with afternoon wine tastings and free limo downtown. ⑦–⑧.

Van Ness Motel
2850 Van Ness Ave. ☎776-3220.
Large rooms, within walking distance of Fort Mason. ③–④.

Wharf Inn
2601 Mason St. ☎673-7411.
Comfortable, family-style hotel with free parking. ⑤–⑥.

Civic Center, South of Market and the Mission

Bay Bridge Inn
966 Harrison St. ☎397-0657.
Basic and somewhat noisy but perfectly sited for late nights in SoMa's clubland. ③.

Best Western Carriage Inn
140 Seventh St. ☎552-8600.
Clean, comfortable rooms in downmarket Civic Center area. Free parking. ⑤.

Embassy Motor Hotel
610 Polk St. ☎673-1404.
Bland, neat hotel close to Civic Center. ③.

Friendship Inn
860 Eddy St. ☎474-4374.
Newly renovated motel in slightly dodgy Tenderloin location. ③.

Golden City Inn
1554 Howard St. ☎431-9376.
Best of the inexpensive South of Market hotels, smack in the middle of the SoMa nightlife scene. Unbelievably good value. ①–②.

Grand Central Hotel
1412 Market St. ☎703-9988.
Very basic rooms with laundry facilities and gym in Civic Center. ②–③.

Mosser Victorian Hotel
54 Fourth St.
☎986-4400 or 1-800/227-3804.
Good SoMa location and clean no-frills accommodation. ④.

San Francisco Central Travelodge
1707 Market St. ☎621-6775.
Dependable chain motel with 24hr coffee shop. ④.

Travelodge Downtown
790 Ellis St. ☎775-7612.
Same as the above but in a slightly seed-
ier location. ④.

UN Plaza Hotel
Seventh and Market St. ☎626-4600.
Convenient location, opposite the Civic
Center. Glitzy lobby and large, comfy
rooms. ④.

The Central Neighborhoods

Beck's Motor Lodge
2222 Market St. ☎621-8212.
Good Castro location, with large, clean
rooms. See also "Gay Men's
Accommodation" on p.206. ④.

Best Western Miyako
1800 Sutter St.
☎921-4000 or 1-800/528-1234.
Immaculate Japan Center hotel, with quiet
rooms, some with steambaths. ⑤.

Metro Hotel
319 Divisadero St. ☎861-5364.
Homey, clean and comparatively inexpensive Lower Haight hotel. ④.

Queen Anne Hotel
1590 Sutter St.
☎441-2828 or 1-800/227-3970.
Very pretty and fairly pricey, but with full
amenities including valet service and free
afternoon tea and sherry. ⑥.

Stanyan Park Hotel
750 Stanyan St. ☎751-1000.
Gorgeous small Victorian hotel in a great
setting across from Golden Gate Park,

with friendly staff and free continental
breakfast. ⑤.

Golden Gate Park, the Beaches and Outlying Areas

Mar Oceanview Motel
4340 Judah St. ☎661-2300.
Good access for the park and zoo and
well-situated, right on the *Muni* N-Judah
line. ③.

Ocean Park Motel
2690 46th Ave. ☎566-7020.
A fair way from downtown (25 min
by Muni) this is nonetheless a great
Art Deco motel opposite the zoo and
the beach. ③.

Seal Rock Inn
545 Point Lobos Ave. ☎752-8000.
Modern motel a block from Point Lobos
and Sutro Baths. ④.

Sunset Motel
821 Taraval St. ☎681-3306.
One of the finest little motels in San
Francisco – clean, friendly and safe. ③.

East Bay

Claremont Hotel
41 Tunnel Rd at Ashby Ave on the
Oakland/Berkeley border.
☎510/843-3000.
At the top end of the scale, this
grand Victorian palace has panoramic
bay view rooms and all-inclusive "weekend breaks". ⑥–⑧.

*Price
categories:*
① *0–30*
② *$30–45*
③ *$45–60*
④ *$60–80*
⑤ *$80–100*
⑥ *$100–130*
⑦ *$130–180*
⑧ *$180+*

Airport Hotels

Best Western Grosvenor Hotel
380 South Airport Blvd ☎873-3200
Large comfortable hotel with pool, health
club and free shuttle service to the
airport. ④.

Best Western Lighthouse Hotel
105 Rockaway Beach Ave
Pacifica ☎355-6300
Far enough away from the airport to
ensure you get a good night's sleep, but
with a free shuttle service so you don't
miss your plane. ⑤.

La Quinta Inn
20 Airport Blvd ☎583-2223

Overnight laundry service and a pool
make this a comfortable stopover. Free
shuttle service to the airport. ④.

Radisson Inn San Francisco Airport
275 South Airport Blvd ☎873-3550
Great facilities include restaurant, pool,
jacuzzi, live music and a free shuttle to
the airport. ⑤.

Super 8 Lodge
111 Mitchell Ave
South San Francisco ☎877-0770
Plain, motel-style accomodations with
free laundry service, breakfast and
airport shuttle. ③–④.

Accommodation

*Price
categories:*
① *0–$30*
② *$30–45*
③ *$45–60*
④ *$60–80*
⑤ *$80–100*
⑥ *$100–130*
⑦ *$130–180*
⑧ *$180+*

French Hotel
1538 Shattuck Ave, North Berkeley.
☎510/548-9930.
Small and comfortable, in the heart of
Berkeley's Gourmet Ghetto. ⑤.

Golden Bear Motel
1620 San Pablo Ave, West Berkeley.
☎510/525-6770.
The most pleasant of the many motels in
the "flatlands" of West Berkeley, though
somewhat out of the way. ②–③.

Holiday Inn Bay Bridge
1800 Powell St, Emeryville.
☎510/658-9300.
Not outrageously pricey considering the
great views to be had from the upper
floors. Free parking. ⑤.

Hotel Durant
2600 Durant Ave, Berkeley.
☎510/845-8981.
Fairly plain but well worn and comfortable, and very handy for the UC Berkeley
campus. ⑤.

London Lodge
700 Broadway, downtown Oakland.
☎510/451-6316.
Spacious rooms, some of which have
kitchens, make this a good option for
families or groups. ③–④.

Shattuck Hotel
2086 Allston Way, Berkeley.
☎510/845-7300.
Very central and newly refurbished, near
Berkeley BART. ⑤.

Waterfront Plaza Hotel
21 Jack London Square, Oakland.
☎510/836-3800.
Newly redecorated hotel moored on the
best stretch of the Oakland waterfront. ⑦.

The Peninsula
Best Western Inn
455 S Second St, San Jose.
☎408/298-3500.
Right in downtown San Jose, with pool
and sauna. ④.

Best Western Stanford Park Hotel
100 El Camino Real, Menlo Park.
☎322-1234.
A better standard than the same money
would buy you downtown. ⑤.

Days Inn Palo Alto
4238 El Camino Real, Palo Alto.
☎493-4222 or 1-800/325-2525.
A mile from anywhere but the rooms are
particularly clean and well kept. ③–④.

Hotel California
2431 Ash St, Palo Alto. ☎322-7666.
Small, central with breakfast included. ⑤.

Stanford Terrace Inn
531 Stanford Ave, Palo Alto. ☎857-0333.
Big rooms and a small pool for not much
money. ⑤.

Valley Inn
2155 The Alameda, San Jose.
☎408/241-8500.
Standard motel not far from the
Rosicrucian Museum (see p.163). ③.

Marin County
Casa Madrona
801 Bridgeway, Sausalito. ☎332-0502.
Deluxe hideaway tucked into the hills
above the bay. ⑥–⑧.

Grand Hotel
15 Brighton Ave, Bolinas. ☎868-1757.
Budget rooms in comfortable old hotel. ③.

Ocean Court Motel
18 Arnold St, Stinson Beach. ☎868-0212.
Just a block from the beach, west of Hwy-
1. Large rooms with kitchens. ④.

San Rafael Inn
865 E Francisco Blvd, San Rafael.
☎454-9470.
Large roadside motel, just off US-101. ③.

Stinson Beach Motel
3416 Shoreline Highway, Stinson Beach.
☎868-1712.
Basic roadside motel right on Hwy-1, five
minutes' walk to the beach. ③.

Wine Country
Calistoga Inn
1250 Lincoln Ave, Calistoga.
☎707/942-4101.
Comfortable rooms in a landmark building. ④–⑤.

Comfort Inn
1865 Lincoln Ave, Calistoga.
☎707/942-9400.
Quiet, modern motel on the edge of
town. ③.

El Bonita Motel
195 Main St, St Helena. ☎707/963-3216.
Old roadside motel recently done up in
Art-Deco style. ④.

El Pueblo Motel
896 W Napa St, Sonoma.
☎707/996-3651.
Basic highway motel. ③.

Hillside Inn
2901 Fourth St, Santa Rosa.
☎707/546-9353.
Clean, attractive motel with swimming
pool. ③.

Hotel St Helena
1309 Main St, St Helena.
☎707/963-4388.
Opulently redecorated 1881 inn. ⑤.

Jack London Lodge
13740 Arnold Drive, Glen Ellen.
☎707/938-8510.
Modern motel near the Jack London State
Park (see p.192), with a good restaurant
and swimming pool. ④.

Magliulo's Pensione
691 Broadway, Sonoma.
☎707/996-1031.
Cosy accommodation with excellent
Italian restaurant attached. ④.

Motel 6
3380 Solano Ave, Napa.
☎707/226-1811.
Basic rooms, no frills. ②.

Mount View Hotel
1457 Lincoln Ave, Calistoga.
☎707/942-6877.
Lively Art-Deco-style hotel with nightly
jazz and an excellent restaurant. ④.

Sonoma Hotel
110 W Spain St, Sonoma.
☎707/996-2996.
Antique-filled rooms in an 1870 hotel just
off Sonoma Plaza. ④.

Vintage Inn
6541 Washington St, Yountville.
☎707/944-1112.
Huge luxury rooms – all with fireplaces –
plus swimming pool and free bike rental.
Handy for Yountville's many fine restaurants, and great for romantic getaways. ⑦.

White Sulphur Springs
3100 White Sulphur Springs Rd, west of
St Helena.
☎707/963-8588.
A relaxing retreat from the hyper-tourism
of the Napa Valley, unpretentious rooms
in a ramshackle old 300-acre hillside
resort. ④.

Accommodation

*Wine Country
restaurants are
listed on p.229*

Bed and Breakfast

Bed and breakfast around the Bay Area
is good-value luxury, offering a more
intimate and often more comfortable
alternative to the standard hotel or motel
experience. Europeans, accustomed to
shabby B&Bs in faded seaside resorts
and greasy bacon-and-eggs, may be

B&B Agencies

Bed and Breakfast Exchange
45 Entrata Drive
San Anselmo   ☎485-1971
Comfortable rooms private homes all
over Marin County from $55 a night for
two, ranging from courtyard hideaways
on the beach in Tiburon to houseboats in
Sausalito.

Bed and Breakfast International
PO Box 282910   ☎1-800/872-4500
San Francisco CA94128   or 696-1690
Self-catering apartments, home-stays
and small inns around the Bay Area and
California.

Bed and Breakfast San Francisco
PO Box 420009   ☎1-800/452-8249
San Francisco CA94142   or 479-1913
Private rooms and self-catering apart-
ments all over San Francisco and the
Bay Area, starting at $55 a night.

Colby International
139 Round Hey, Liverpool L28 1RG
England.
☎051/220-5848 in the UK.
☎703/551-5005 in the US.
Efficient and very reasonable English
accommodation agency, dealing in B&B
reservations and also self-catering
apartments.

Accommodation

Price categories:
① *0–$30*
② *$30–45*
③ *$45–60*
④ *$60–80*
⑤ *$80–100*
⑥ *$100–130*
⑦ *$130–180*
⑧ *$180+*

pleasantly surprised – though the rates of course are proportionately higher than in Europe.

Even the largest of establishments tend to have no more than ten rooms, with brass beds, plentiful flowers, stuffed cushions and an almost over-contrived homey atmosphere. Other places, most of which are bookable through the various specialist B&B agencies listed on the previous page, may consist merely of a couple of furnished rooms in someone's home, or an entire apartment where you won't even see your host. The latter makes particularly good sense for families or those travelling with small children.

While always including a huge and wholesome breakfast (ranging from granola, fresh fruit and scones to a full-blown pancakes, eggs and bacon fry-up), prices vary greatly: anything from $40 to $200 a night depending on location and season. Most of the ones listed below fall between $50 and $80 per night for two people sharing. Bear in mind, too, that being small, many places are booked up weeks in advance at peak times.

Downtown San Francisco

Adelaide Inn
5 Isadora Duncan Court.
☎441-2261.
Small bed-and-breakfast hotel between Geary and Post, with shared bathroom facilities. ②–③.

Alexander Inn
415 O'Farrell St. ☎928-6800.
Bright, well-equipped rooms in a great location, just off Union Square. ③–④.

Beresford Arms Hotel
701 Post St. ☎673-2600.
Luxury B&B in the heart of town, well worth the few extra dollars. ⑤.

Cornell Hotel
715 Bush St. ☎421-3154.
Pleasant Nob Hill/Union Square location with basic, clean rooms. ④.

Hotel David
480 Geary St.
☎771-1600 or 1-800/524-1888.

By no means the least expensive place in town, but a great Theater District location above San Francisco's largest and best Jewish delicatessen, where you get an all-you-can-eat breakfast. ⑤.

Nob Hill Inn
1000 Pine St. ☎673-6080.
Decorated by Anglophiles, this is a little bit of antique England for homesick Brits. Upmarket B&B with concierge and whirl-pool. ⑤–⑥.

Petite Auberge
863 Bush St. ☎928-6000.
One of two opulent downtown B&Bs, next to one another on Bush Street. ⑥.

White Swan Inn
845 Bush St. ☎775-1775.
The other Bush Street B&B, this one with a convincing English Manor-house theme: raging fireplaces, oak-panelled rooms and afternoon tea. ⑦.

North Beach and the Northern Waterfront

Art Center Bed and Breakfast
1902 Filbert St. ☎567-1526.
Quirky little inn that's a real home away from home. Painters come to sit in the grounds and attend the classes given by the owners. ④–⑤.

Bed and Breakfast Inn
4 Charlton Court, off Union St.
☎346-0424.
One of the first B&Bs to be established in the city, this lovely, sun-drenched Victorian house, tucked away down a quiet side street, offers some of San Francisco's most pleasant accommoda-tion. ⑤.

Edward II
3155 Scott St. ☎922-3000.
Large and comfortable inn-style accom-modation with free breakfast and after-noon sherry. ④–⑤.

Marina Inn
3110 Octavia St. ☎928-1000.
Comfortable, homey set-up, right off Lombard Street. ④.

Washington Square Inn
1660 Stockton St. ☎981-4220.
Cozy B&B bang on North Beach's lovely main square. Non-smokers only. ⑤–⑥.

Civic Center, South of Market and the Mission

Albion House Inn
135 Gough St. ☎621-0896.
Small and comfortable B&B above a fine restaurant. ⑤.

Amsterdam Hotel
749 Taylor St. ☎673-3277.
Midway between Union Square and City Hall, and halfway between a hotel and a B&B. ③–④.

Dolores Park Inn
3641 17th St. ☎621-0482.
Tiny but elegant boarding house with good access to Lower Haight and Castro districts. Non-smoking. ④–⑤.

Inn at the Opera
333 Fulton St. ☎863-8400.
Deluxe B&B with 24-hr room service and morning limo downtown. ⑥.

Pensione San Francisco
1668 Market St. ☎864-1271.
A good base near the Civic Center, walkably close to SoMa and the Castro. ②–③.

The Central Neighborhoods

Alamo Square Inn
719 Scott St. ☎922-2055.
A beautifully restored Victorian building. The rates aren't low, but guests get the use of a handsome dwelling, complete with fireplace and jacuzzi. ⑤–⑧.

Grove Inn
890 Grove St. ☎929-0780.
Nothing fancy, but good value and a fine location on Alamo Square. ③–④.

The Mansion
2220 Sacramento St. ☎929-9444.
Luxury-swaddled Victorian mansion, perched high up in the fancy reaches of Pacific Heights. ⑥–⑧.

Red Victorian Bed and Breakfast
1665 Haight St. ☎864-1978.
Bang in the middle of the Haight-Ashbury, a time-warped B&B with hippy art gallery and rooms with New Agey themes, courtesy of owner Sami Sunchild. ④–⑥.

East Bay

East Brother Light Station
117 Park Place in Point Richmond.
☎233-2385.

A handful of rooms in a converted lighthouse, on an island in the middle of the bay. Prices include highly rated gourmet dinners as well as breakfast. ⑧.

Elmwood House
2609 College Ave, Berkeley.
☎510/540-5123.
Attractive, turn-of-the-century house with B&B rooms not far from UC Berkeley. ④.

Gramma's
2740 Telegraph Ave, Berkeley.
☎549-2145.
Pleasant if slightly dull rooms, with fireplaces, in a pretty mock-Tudor mansion half a mile south of UC Berkeley. ⑤–⑥.

Peninsula

Old Thyme Inn
779 Main St, Half Moon Bay.
☎726-1616.
Half a dozen rooms, each with private bath, in lovely Victorian house surrounded by luxuriant herb and flower gardens. ⑤.

San Benito House
356 Main St, Half Moon Bay.
☎726-3425.
Twelve restful rooms in a 100-year-old building, just a mile from the beach. ⑤.

Marin County

Blue Heron Inn
11 Wharf Rd, Bolinas. ☎868-1102.
Lovely double rooms in an unbeatable locale. ⑤.

Lindisfarne Guest House
Green Gulch Zen Center, Muir Beach.
☎383-3036.
Restful rooms in a meditation retreat set in a secluded valley above Muir Beach. Price includes excellent vegetarian meals. ③.

Pelican Inn
10 Pacific Way, Muir Beach. ☎383-6000.
Very comfortable rooms in a pseudo-English country inn, with good bar and restaurant downstairs, ten minutes' walk from beautiful Muir Beach. ⑤.

Ten Inverness Way
10 Inverness Way, Inverness.
☎669-1648.
Quiet and restful in small village of good restaurants and bakeries on the fringes of Point Reyes. ⑤–⑥.

Accommodation

For more on the Green Gulch Zen Center, *see p.174.*

Accommodation

Our Wine Country chapter begins on p.183.

For more on Gay and Lesbian San Francisco, see p.35; gay bars are detailed on p.239.

Price categories:
① *0–$30*
② *$30–45*
③ *$45–60*
④ *$60–80*
⑤ *$80–100*
⑥ *$100–130*
⑦ *$130–180*
⑧ *$180+*

Wine Country

Calistoga Wine Way Inn
1019 Foothill Blvd, Calistoga.
☎707/942-0680 or 1-800/572-0679.
Small and friendly B&B with lovely garden and antique-filled rooms, a short walk from the center of town. ⑤–⑥.

Cinnamon Bear
1407 Kearney St, St Helena.
☎707/963-4388.
Quirky, sumptuously furnished inn. ⑤–⑥.

Gaige House Inn
13540 Arnold Drive, Glen Ellen.
☎707/935-0237.
Restored Victorian farmhouse in country setting. No children under 12. ⑤–⑥.

Thistle Dew Inn
171 W Spain St, Sonoma.
☎707/938-2909.
Newly restored rooms near Sonoma Plaza, plus full breakfast and free bike rental. ⑥.

Gay Accommodation

Not surprisingly, San Francisco has several accommodation options that cater specifically to gay and lesbian travellers. Most are geared towards men, although it's unlikely that lesbians would be turned away; see "Women's Accommodation", below, for more suitable alternatives. Information, up-to-date recommendations and referrals are available from a number of sources (see Basics, p.36, for details) and from the *International Gay Travel Association*, based in Key West, Florida, which has a lot of resources at its fingertips and can book ahead for you. You can call toll-free on ☎1-800/448-8550.

All of the places we've listed below are in San Francisco. In the rest of the Bay Area, gay travellers (including couples) rarely raise eyebrows, and your sexual orientation shouldn't be an issue.

Beck's Motor Lodge
2222 Market St. ☎621-8212.
Standard motel close to the Castro. ③.

Casa Loma Hotel
600 Fillmore St. ☎552-7100.
Mid-sized, friendly hotel with sauna, jacuzzi, sun deck and a lively bar. ③.

Gough Hayes Hotel
417 Gough St. ☎431-9131.
Informal, inexpensive Civic Center favourite – no private bathrooms but 24hr sauna and sun deck. ②.

Inn on Castro
321 Castro St. ☎861-0321.
A longstanding favorite with visiting gays, this luxury bed and breakfast doesn't come cheap, but is worth the price for the large rooms and good breakfasts. About two minutes' walk from the Castro. ⑤.

Leland Hotel
1315 Polk St. ☎441-5141.
Attractively decorated Polk Gulch hotel. ④.

Queen Anne Hotel
1590 Sutter St. ☎262-2663.
Very much a gay hotel with over-done decor, full valet service and complimentary afternoon tea and sherry. ⑤–⑥.

24 Henry
24 Henry St. ☎864-5686.
Intimate guesthouse in a quiet street just off the heart of the Castro. ③–④.

Twin Peaks Hotel
2160 Market St. ☎621-9467.
Set in the hills above, this is a quieter and prettier location not far from the Castro, even if the rooms are small and short on luxury. ②–③.

Women's Accommodation

Bock's Bed & Breakfast
1448 Willard St.
A basic, secure and friendly hotel for women. ②–③.

The Langtry
637 Steiner St. ☎863-0538.
Each room in this nineteenth-century mansion is dedicated to a famous woman in history. Hot tub, sundeck, views of the city. Fabulous but not cheap. ⑥–⑧.

Mary Elizabeth Inn
1040 Bush St. ☎673-6768.
Run by the United Methodist Church, so don't expect a swinging dyke scene. However, you can rely on a safe place to stay. ③–④.

642 Jones

642 Jones St. ☎775-1711.
Comfortable, secure building that is quite
safe despite being situated in the
unpleasant Tenderloin district. Weekly
rates are among the city's best deals:
singles $120 per week, doubles $170.
Men are allowed, though outnumbered
40 to 1. ②.

Hostels

At the bottom end of the price scale,
there are a number of **hostels** in San
Francisco and around the Bay Area,
some in very beautiful settings. Dormitory
beds go for around $13, and many
hostels also offer cut-rate single and
double rooms.

You can really expect little more from
a hostel than a clean safe bed and
somewhere to lock your valuables. Some
are livelier and more liberal than others,
though those with more regulations (i.e.
nightly curfews and bans on alcohol) also
tend to be the safest – for women
travelling alone they can often be good
places to feel secure and meet other
people. The hostels vary between
unofficial private establishments, where
things will in general be more relaxed,
and the **official AYH hostels**, which tend
to be cleaner and better equipped but
normally have some kind of curfew.

There are also a couple of **YMCAs**,
and a few rooms become available in
university dorms during the Summer
vacation – cheap hotels for younger
travellers, with single and double rooms
ranging from $25 right up to $75, and
good facilities including gyms and
swimming pools.

If you're planning to stay in a hostel,
it's always a good idea to **bring your
passport**, even if you're American – many
places will insist on seeing it before
renting you a bed. This is intended to
preserve the hostels for travellers; i.e. to
keep out local homeless people. For
similar reasons, many hostels also
impose a nominal maximum stay of 3 to
5 days, though this is generally enforced
only when demand for beds exceeds the
available supply.

San Francisco

AYH Hostel at Union Square

312 Mason St. ☎788-5604.
Large new downtown hostel with dorm
beds for $14 a night. No curfew. AYH
members only; day memberships cost $5.

European Guest House

761 Minna St. ☎861-6634.
Dormitory accommodation with communal kitchen and rooftop garden. No
curfew; secure lockers and laundry facilities. $12 per night per person, plus a
refundable $5 key deposit.

Interclub/Globe Hostel

10 Hallam Place. ☎431-0540.
Lively, recently redecorated South-of-
Market hostel with no curfew. $15 per
person, per night; doubles $25.

San Francisco International Guest House

2976 23rd St. ☎641-1411.
Very popular with European travellers. 4-
to-a-room dorms in the Mission plus a
few private rooms. $14 per person, 5-day
minimum stay, no curfew.

San Francisco International AYH-Hostel

Building 240, Fort Mason. ☎771-7277.
On the waterfront between the Golden
Gate Bridge and Fisherman's Wharf. One
of the most comfortable and convenient
hostels around. No curfew. 150 beds, free
parking. $13–15 per person.

San Francisco State University

800 Font Blvd. ☎338-2721.
Year-round dorms and summer-only
suites, near SF Zoo. Dorm beds with meals
$25 per night, rooms $40–75.

YMCA Central Branch

220 Golden Gate Ave. ☎885-0460.
Well equipped and centrally located, two
blocks from the Civic Center. Singles $27,
doubles $35, price includes a free conti-
nental breakfast and use of the gym,
swimming pool, squash courts and sauna.

East Bay

Berkeley YMCA

2001 Allston Way, Berkeley.
☎510/848-6800.
Ideal East Bay mixed-sex accommodation:
a block from the Berkeley *BART*, with
single rooms for $22, including use of gym
and swimming pool.

Accommodation

Accommodation

The Año Nuevo reserve is described on p.166.

University of California Housing Office
2400 Durant Ave, Berkeley.
☎510/642-5925.
Summer-only dorm rooms for $32 single, $42 double.

Peninsula

Hidden Villa AYH Hostel
26807 Moody Rd, Los Altos Hills.
☎408/941-6407.
Located on an 1800-acre ranch in the hills above the Silicon Valley. Closed in summer, and hard to reach without a car. $13 a night per person.

Pigeon Point Lighthouse AYH-Hostel
Hwy-1, just south of Pescadero.
☎879-0633.
Worth planning a trip around, this beauti-fully sited hostel, 50 miles south of San Francisco, is ideally placed for exploring the redwood forests in the hills above or for watching the wildlife in nearby Año Nuevo State Reserve. Outdoor hot tub. Office hours 7.30–9.30am & 4.30–9.30pm; doors locked 11pm. Members $9–11 per night, non-members $12–14; reservations essential in summer. Private rooms $30 a night.

Point Montara Lighthouse AYH-Hostel
16th St/Hwy-1, Montara.
☎728-7177.

Dorm rooms in a converted 1875 lighthouse, 25 miles south of San Francisco and accessible by bike or *SamTrans* bus (#1L; service operates until 5.50pm Mon–Fri, 6.15pm Sat). Outdoor hot tub. Office hours 7.30–9.30am & 4.30–9.30pm; doors locked 11pm. Members $9–11 per night, non-members $12–14; reservations essential in summer.

Marin County

Golden Gate AYH-Hostel
Building 941, Fort Barry, Marin Headlands.
☎331-2777.
Hard to get to without a car – it's near Rodeo Lagoon, five miles west of Sausalito – this cozy old army barracks has dorm beds for $9–11 a night. Office hours 7.30–9.30am & 4.30–11pm; doors locked 11pm.

Point Reyes AYH-Hostel
In the Point Reyes National Seashore.
☎663-8811.
An ideal stop on a cycling tour of Marin, surrounded by meadows and forests and just two miles from the beach. Eight miles from the nearest bus stop. Office hours 7.30–9.30am & 4.30–9.30pm; doors locked 11pm. Dorm beds in an old ranch-house cost $9–11 per night.

Chapter 13

Restaurants

It's not too much of an exaggeration to say that in San Francisco and the Bay Area you can eat whatever you want, whenever you want. Whether it's for basic daily sustenance or for a special social occasion, San Franciscans spend more per head on dining out than the inhabitants of any other US city – an average of $2500 each per year. The swarms of tourists inflate the figures, but that's enough to support a mass of restaurants, fast food places and coffee shops that line every main street.

Matters are further improved by the fact that California is one of the most agriculturally rich – and health-conscious – parts of the country. Junk food is noticeably less common than elsewhere in the US, and instead nutritious locally grown fruits and vegetables, abundant fish and seafood, and top-quality meat and dairy produce all find their way into Bay Area kitchens.

Breakfast

For a good-value and filling breakfast – costing around $3–6 – head to a **diner**, or, slightly smarter, a **café** or **coffee shop**, all of which serve breakfast until at least 11am (though diners sometimes offer it all day).

Thanks to California's love of light food, most offer the option of **fruit** – typically apple, banana, orange, pineapple or strawberry, wonderfully styled and served on their own or with pancakes. The only drawback is that it tends to cost as much as a full-blown fry-up.

Lunch, Fast Food and Soft Drinks

Most San Francisco workers take their **lunch break** between noon and 2.30pm. During those hours, many of the city's restaurants offer low cost, excellent value, **set menus**. Chinese restaurants, for example, frequently have rice and noodles or dim sum for $4–6, and many Japanese restaurants provide an opportunity to eat sushi at much lower prices ($7–10) than usual. Mexican restaurants are exceptionally well priced all the time, and you can get a good-sized lunch in one for $4–5.

One obvious inexpensive option is **pizza**; count on paying $5–7 for a basic two-person pizza, though you can usually buy it by the slice to take away. Most pizza chains and many mid-price restaurants have **salad bars**, where you can help yourself for a couple of dollars.

If you're just looking for a **quick snack**, many **delis** do ready-cooked meals for $3–5, as well as a range of **sandwiches** that can be meals in themselves, filled with a custom-built combination of meat, cheese, seafood, pasta and salad. In addition, San Francisco has its own local chain of burger bars, *Hot n Hunky*, serving up top-quality, tasty burgers that are as substantial as the name implies.

Free Food and Brunch

Some **bars**, particularly in downtown San Francisco, are used as much by diners as drinkers, who turn up in droves to fill up on the free **hors d'oeuvres** laid out

Downtown bars are listed on p.231.

Restaurants

between 5 and 7pm Monday to Friday – an attempt to nab the commuting classes before they head off to the suburbs. For the price of a drink you can stuff yourself silly on nachos, seafood or pasta.

Brunch is another deal to look out for, served between 11am and 2pm, and especially on Sundays. For a set price ($8 and up) you get a light meal and a variety of complimentary cocktails or champagne – perfect for daytime boozing, though rarely great value for money, especially if you don't drink.

Restaurants

Even if it often seems swamped by more fashionable regional and ethnic cuisines, traditional **American cooking** can be found all over the Bay Area.

California Cuisine in particular, geared towards health and aesthetics, is raved about by foodies – and rightly so, especially in Berkeley, its acknowledged birthplace and a not-to-be-missed gourmet ghetto. Basically a development of French *nouvelle cuisine*, utilizing the wide mix of fresh, locally available ingredients, California Cuisine is based on physiological efficiency – eating only what you need to and to what your body can process. Vegetables are harvested just before maturity and steamed to preserve a high concentration of vitamins, a strong flavor, and to look better on the plate; seafood comes from oyster farms and the catches of small-time fishermen;

and what little meat there is tends to be from animals reared on organic farms. The result is small but beautifully presented portions, and high, high prices – not unusually $50 a head for a full dinner with wine. The minimum you'll need for a sample is $15, which should buy a substantial portion. To whet your appetite, starters include such dishes as mussels in jalapeno and sesame vinaigrette, snails in puff pastry with mushroom puree, and, among main courses. roasted goat's cheese salad with walnuts, swordfish with herb butter, and tuna with cactus ratatouille.

Mexican food is so common it often seems like (and historically is) an indigenous cuisine. Certainly, in the Mission district you can't go more than a couple of doorways without encountering another Mexican restaurant. What's more, day or night, it's the least expensive type of food to eat: even a full dinner with a few drinks rarely costs over $10 anywhere except in the most upmarket establishment.

Other ethnic cuisines are plentiful too. **Chinese** food is everywhere, and can often cost as little as Mexican; **Japanese** is more expensive and more trendy, sushi being worshipped by some Californians.

Italian food is popular everywhere, above all in **North Beach**, but can be expensive once you leave the simple pastas and explore exotic pizza toppings or specialist regional cuisines. **French**

Mexican food – a Primer for Foreign Travellers

San Francisco's Mexican food – found all over the city, but especially in the Mission District – is different from that available in Mexico. Here more use is made of fresh vegetables and fruit, but the essentials are the same. Salsa, a spicy (sometimes very spicy) tomato, onion and cilantro sauce, is the key ingredient, backed by lots of rice and pinto beans, often served refried (ie boiled, mashed and fried in lard), with a **tortilla** – a thin maize dough pancake that comes in several ways. You can eat it as an accompaniment to your main dish; soft and wrapped around the food – a **burrito**; folded, fried and filled – a **taco**; filled, rolled and baked in a sauce – an **enchilada**; or baked flat and covered with a stack of food, known as a **tostada**. Another, less stodgy, option is the **chile relleno**, a green pepper stuffed with cheese, dipped in egg batter and fried. **El Salvadorean** and **Peruvian** food is often available in Mexican restaurants, with the emphasis on seafood, as in the delicious Peruvian dish *ceviche*, which consists of chunks of fish in a lime juice, onion and coriander marinade.

Restaurants

Downtown bars are listed on p.231.

food, too, is widely available, though always pricey, the cuisine of social climbers and power-lunchers. **Thai**, **Korean** and **Indonesian** food is similarly in vogue, though usually cheaper. **Indian** restaurants, on the other hand, are thin on the ground and often very expensive – although as Indian cooking catches on the situation is gradually changing for the better, with a sprinkling of moderately priced outlets, particularly in West Berkeley.

Not surprisingly, health-conscious San Francisco also has a wide range of **vegetarian** and **wholefood** restaurants, and it's rare to find a menu anywhere that doesn't have at least several meat-free items on the menu.

Finally, remember also that the vineyards of Napa and Sonoma Valley are on the city's doorstep and produce prize-fighting grapes that are good – and cheap – enough to make European wine growers nervous. Quality **wine** is a high profile and standard feature of most San Franciscan restaurants.

In the listings that follow, the **restaurants** are arranged primarily by neighborhood, and thereafter, when helpful, by ethnic type below.

Downtown
American

Bentley's Oyster Bar
185 Sutter St. ☎989-6895.
Extensive range of ultra-fresh oysters and other delicacies at the downstairs bar, grilled seafood and great desserts in the mezzanine dining area.

Bix
56 Gold St. ☎433-6300.
Jackson Square restaurant kitted out like a majestic ocean liner, with torch singer,

sax player and pianist – even if the food was rubbish you'd be enchanted with the place. Actually, the food is great – straightforward, classic dishes. Not surprisingly, a hot spot, where you'd be well advised to reserve in advance. Dinner for two should probably set you back around $80 with drinks, but if you're into elegant dining experiences you should definitely go.

Blondie's
63 Powell St. ☎282-6168.
Union Square pizzeria, usually packed out; they do well-topped pizzas for $1.50 a slice.

The Brasserie
In the basement of the *Fairmont Hotel,* Mason and California streets.
☎722-5000.
Plush and incredibly pricey, this is, however, the only place to satisfy a 4am craving for lobster thermidor.

David's Delicatessen
474 Geary St. ☎771-1600.
Kosher food in giant portions. Eat until you expire for around $10.

The Dining Room
Ritz Carlton Hotel, 600 Stockton at California. ☎296-7465.
The hotel's signature restaurant, run by celebrity chef Gary Danko, this is the perfect place for a special occasion. You'll be lucky to escape for under $80 a head with wine, but sometimes such extravagance is really worth it.

Fog City Diner
1300 Battery St. ☎982-2000.
Expensively done up to look like a top-class diner, this place errs on the pricey side, but provided you don't mind paying for your ambience, the food is pretty good.

The Fairmont *is reviewed on p.198*

Restaurants

Hard Rock Café
1699 Van Ness Ave. ☎885-1699.
Standard *Hard Rock* clone. Loud music,
rock'n'roll decor and attracting the sort
of crowd who don't mind waiting in
line for hours for the above-average
burgers.

John's Grill
63 Ellis St. ☎986-0069.
Straight out of the *Maltese Falcon*,
the menu at this steak-and-seafood
place hasn't changed since Dashiell
Hammett was a regular. The prices
have, but it's still reasonable, especially
for lunch.

Kuleto's
221 Powell St. ☎397-7720.
Very popular with the pre-theater crowds,
this upmarket Italianate bar and restaurant is a feast for the eyes as well as
the mouth. Decor focuses on a 100-
year-old hardwood bar, originally from
the landmark *Palace Hotel*; the food, especially the pastas and fresh breads, is very
good.

Maye's Original Oyster House
1233 Polk St. ☎474-7674.
In business since the 1860s, this is one of
the city's oldest restaurants, turning out
reasonably priced, well-cooked fish

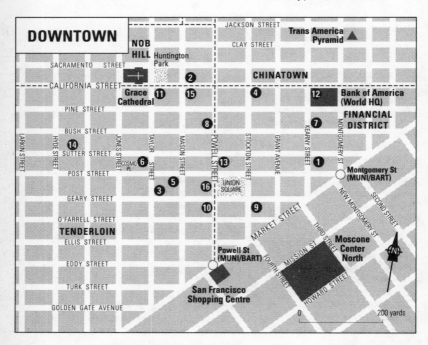

DOWNTOWN RESTAURANTS, BARS, CAFÉS AND CLUBS

Restaurants		
1 Bentley's Oyster Bar	6 Trader Vic's	11 The Big Four
2 The Brasserie	7 Le Candide	12 Carnelian Room
3 David's Delicatessen	8 Masa's	13 The Starlight Roof
4 The Dining Room	9 Rotunda	14 The Plush Room
5 Postrio	**Bars, Cafés and Clubs**	15 Top of the Mark
	10 Gold Dust Saloon	16 The Compass Rose

dishes. Oysters by the half-dozen with a beer at the bar for the budget conscious or less hungry.

Original Joe's
144 Taylor St. ☎775-4877.
Inexpensive American/Italian restaurant, good for steaks, ribs, salads and the like.

The Pine Crest
401 Geary St. ☎885-6407.
Every inch the greasy diner, but ideal for getting rid of your spare change and hunger at the same time.

Postrio
545 Post St. ☎776-7825.
Everybody's favorite top-notch San Francisco restaurant – come for breakfast if you can't score a dinner reservation – thanks to the high-style ambience and five-star reputation of chef Wolfgang Puck.

Sam's Grill
374 Bush St. ☎421-0594.
Moderately pricey seafood place, popular with Financial District types. As seen in *Hammett* and many other movies.

Scott's Seafood
3 Embarcadero Center. ☎981-0622.
Very good, very fresh oysters and other seafood dishes. Adjacent to the *Hyatt Regency*.

Seltzer City Café
680 Eighth St. ☎621-6001.
New York-style deli, ideal for large breakfasts and big sandwiches at lunchtime.

Splendido
4 Embarcadero Center. ☎986-3222.
Brash and lively Euro-Californian restaurant with fine bay views. A huge menu of Mediterranean specialties, plus wood-oven pizzas.

Tadich's
240 California St. ☎391-2373.
The oldest restaurant in California, and very much a San Francisco institution. Wood panelling, linen tableclothes, grilled fresh seafood and excellent desserts.

Tina's Restaurant
83 Eddy St. ☎982-3451.
Open from 6am for budget breakfasts.

Trader Vic's
20 Cosmo Place. ☎776-2232.
The restaurant of choice for San Francisco "society" for many years. Although the food has a slightly Polynesian/Indian bent, this is very much dining moneyed-American style. Ethnicity stops at the dinner plate.

French

Le Candide
301 Kearny St. ☎981-2213.
Reasonably priced, standard French food. You can rub shoulders with the well-dressed Financial District crowd.

Ernie's
847 Montgomery St. ☎397-5969.
Far from inexpensive, but a *haute cuisine* menu and a lovely Victorian interior, made famous by its role in Hitchcock's *Vertigo*. Dinner for two will cost you around $100, but the $15 *prix fixe*, three-course lunches are the city's best budget gourmet treat.

Masa's
648 Bush St. ☎989-7154.
Rated as one the best restaurants in the US, it's also among the most expensive: $75 per head *prix fixe*, plus wine starting at $35 a bottle. You get what you pay for, though, as chef Julian Serrano brings Spanish flair to traditional French cooking, presenting a tapas-like train of mouth-watering dishes and desserts.

Chinese and Indonesian

Benkay
Hotel Nikko, 222 Mason St. ☎394-1111.
Hi-tech, minimal and ultra-modern, *Benkay* is the Jean-Paul Gaultier of the restaurant biz. The theme is *Kaiseki*, a succession of many exquisite courses served by kimono-clad waitresses. If you've got around $100 to blow on dinner for two, you'll love it.

Harbor Village
4 Embarcadero Center. ☎781-8833.
Downtown's best dim sum, especially popular for Sunday lunch, with standard Cantonese dishes for dinner.

Indonesian Restaurant
678 Post St. ☎474-4026.
Small, unassuming and affordable place.

Restaurants

For another location used in Vertigo, see p.87

Restaurants

Tommy Toy's Cuisine Chinoise
655 Montgomery St. ☎ 397-4888.
Without rival the most elegant Chinese restaurant in San Francisco. Exotic variations on Cantonese favorites, prepared with a *nouvelle cuisine* emphasis on ultra fresh ingredients and served in a spacious candle-lit room, make for an enchanting dining experience. Power chow mein.

Wu Kong Restaurant
1 Rincon Center, 101 Spear St. ☎ 957-9300.
Popular with workers from the Financial District, the excellent Shanghai food here commands some pretty steep prices, but if you just nip in for dim sum you shouldn't be left penniless.

Yank Sing
427 Battery St. ☎ 362-1640.
Join the Financial District workers again as they lunch on dim sum in the fanciest of surroundings.

North Beach and the Northern Waterfront
American

Clown Alley
42 Columbus Ave. ☎ 421-2540.
Down-at-heel, with a dodgy clientele, but it does serve huge breakfasts and bargain burgers 24 hours per day.

Crustacean
Top of Chelsea Square, California and Polk. ☎ 776-CRAB.
Californian seafood with an Asian twist. Very interesting, innovative dishes, even if it's not what you could call a bargain feed.

Cypress Club
500 Jackson St. ☎ 296-8555.
Jackson Square hot spot famed for its delicately presented, inventive California Cuisine, served up in one of the most stylish dining rooms to be found in San Francisco – a cross between the *Ritz Carlton* and a Bedouin tent.

International House of Pancakes
2299 Lombard St. ☎ 921-4004.
Open 24 hours every day, for famous pancakes smothered with every conceivable topping.

You'll find details of restaurants that stay open 24 hours per day on p.218.

Johnny Love's
1500 Broadway at Polk. ☎ 931-6053.
Mainly a singles bar, this raunchy joint also has a large eating area where the food is probably too good to be wasted on the lurching drunks therein. If you like to have your dinner accompanied with booming rock music, look no further.

Johnny Rockets
2201 Chestnut St. ☎ 931-6258.
Fifties-style diner with juicy burgers and shakes thick enough to constitute a meal in themselves.

Le Petit Café
2164 Larkin St. ☎ 776-5356.
Small and friendly Russian Hill neighborhood bistro famed for its good-value, housemade pastas – and sumptuous Sunday brunch.

Liverpool Lil's
2942 Lyon St. ☎ 921-6664.
Modelled on an English pub, except that by serving great cocktails and good food it lacks the authenticity anyone familiar with real British pubs might expect. Opposite the Presidio gates, and a good place to collapse with a martini after an afternoon's walking.

Lou's Pier 47
300 Jefferson St. ☎ 771-0377.
Incongruously placed among the pricey seafood joints on the Wharf. Not just one of the best places to hear live R'n'B in the city, it also serves fresh, inexpensive seafood. A must for dinner, a few beers and great music.

Moose's
1652 Stockton St. ☎ 987-7800.
Run by the fomer proprietors of the *Washington Square Bar & Grill*, who have taken many of their old clients and become the latest word in power lunching for the media-politico crowd. Headphone-clad chefs (another gimmick) cook great food from the open kitchen.

Rendezvous Café
1760 Polk St. ☎ 441-CAFE.
The perfect spot just to sit, eat and read the paper. Classic diner serving breakfast lunch and dinner. Modern food at old-fashioned prices.

Washington Square Bar and Grill

1707 Powell St. ☎ 982-8123.
It may have lost a little of its cachet since the owners sold it and opened *Moose's* across the square (see above), but this is still the place to slip down smart cocktails at the bar and sample the food, cooked to rich and heavy perfection. If you want to catch the upper echelons of San Francisco society power lunching, this is your scene.

Italian

Allegro Ristorant Italiano

1701 Jones St. ☎ 982-4002.

Russian Hill hangout popular with those in the know. If you want to join such enlightened company, perhaps you won't mind paying for it.

Café Pescatore

2455 Mason at North Point. ☎ 561-1111.
Newish Fisherman's Wharf restaurant, with an open kitchen serving up very good, housemade pastas and wood-fired pizzas.

Calzone's

430 Columbus Ave. ☎ 397-3600.
Busy bar and restaurant right at the heart of North Beach, serving lush pizzas and calzones.

Restaurants

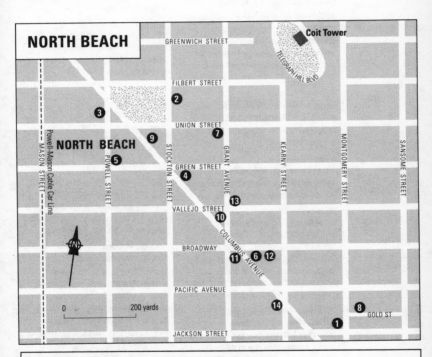

NORTH BEACH RESTAURANTS, BARS, CAFÉS AND CLUBS

Restaurants

1 Cypress Club
2 Moose's
3 Washington Square Bar and Grill
4 Calzone's
5 Capp's Corner

6 Little Joe's
7 North Beach Pizza
8 Bix

Bars, Cafés and Clubs

9 Bohemian Cigar Store

10 Café Trieste
11 Vesuvio's
12 Tosca's
13 The Saloon
14 San Francisco
     Brewing Co

Restaurants

Capp's Corner
1600 Powell St. ☎989-2589.
Funky, family-style restaurant, where fashionable clients line up for the big portions.

Frascati's
1901 Hyde St. ☎928-1406.
Attractive Russian Hill venue for delicious pastas and seafood. Like many of the city's newer restaurants, it operates a strict no-smoking policy.

Golden Boy
542 Grant Ave. ☎982-9738.
Good venue to sample exotic pizza by the slice. Mix'n'match your flavors.

Gold Spike
527 Columbus Ave. ☎986-9747.
More like a museum than a restaurant with enough photographs, mooseheads and war souvenirs to keep you occupied during what can be a long wait for the excellent-value $15 six-course dinner.

Green Valley Restaurant
510 Green St. ☎788-9384.
Good, hearty meals in a basic but busy place full of local North Beach families and birthday celebrants. Eat till you drop for around $12.

Il Fornaio
1265 Battery St. ☎986-0100.
Very popular Italian restaurant with sunny terrace, just a block from the waterfront on Levi Strauss Plaza.

Il Pollaio
555 Columbus Ave. ☎362-7727.
You'd be hard pushed to spend more than $10 for a blow-out meal in this postage stamp restaurant, where the sheer value for money of the food on offer more than makes up for the lack of elbow room.

Little Joe's
523 Broadway. ☎433-4343.
"Rain or shine, there's always a line . . .", but the inexpensive, enormous portions of well-cooked food in this North Beach institution are well worth waiting for.

North Beach Pizza
1499 Grant Ave at Union. ☎433-2444.
Good location in the middle of one of the best bar-hopping areas in the city. Tasty and low priced, it's just the ticket for a drink-induced munchie.

North Beach Restaurant
1512 Stockton St. ☎392-1587.
Extensive, moderately priced menu, plus great cocktails.

Ristorant Firenze
1421 Stockton St. ☎421-5813.
Modern decor, traditional food, quick service – always an attractive combination.

The Stinking Rose
325 Columbus Ave. ☎781-7673.
Subtitled "A Garlic Restaurant", and they're not kidding: everything they serve is steeped in garlic.

Chinese

Brandy Ho's Original Hunan
217 Columbus Ave. ☎788-7527.
Excellent, long-established Hunan restaurant. There's another, new branch at 450 Broadway.

Celadon
881 Clay St. ☎982-1168.
One of the fancier Cantonese restaurants in town. Not exactly bargain-basement food, but worth shelling out for the beautifully presented, fragrant dishes.

China Moon Café
639 Post St. ☎775-4789.
Standard Cantonese food, although the restaurant is particularly notable for its excellent budget dim sum lunches.

Empress of China
838 Grant Ave. ☎434-1345.
Without doubt, the poshest place in town to get to grips with Chinese cooking, with an incredible selection of dishes and amazing views over neighboring North Beach. You'll be lucky to pay less than $18 for a main course, but if you're in the mood for a blow-out it's quite the place to be decadent.

Jing Wah
1634 Bush St. ☎922-5279.
Highly rated Cantonese food, served at reasonable prices in very unpretentious surroundings right in the middle of Polk Gulch.

Restaurants

Afternoon Teas

One of the nicest ways to finish an afternoon of intense consuming in the downtown stores is to partake in the latest SF social custom – *afternoon tea* in one of the plush Union Square hotels. In true California style, the food is exquisite and you'll be offered the gamut from cucumber and watercress sandwiches to fresh fruit sorbets and scones with cream.

Campton Place
340 Stockton St.　　　☎781-5555
Tea served daily in the hotel bar, 2.30–4.30pm. Haunt of the weary shopper.

Four Seasons Clift Hotel
495 Geary St.　　　☎775-4700
A good post-matinée venue in the Theater District.

Garden Court
In the *Sheraton Palace*, 2 New Montgomery.　　　☎392-8600
The best thing about the recent renovation of this landmark hotel was the restoration of its exquisite lobby, where you can sip fine teas while enjoying the soothing live harp music.

King George Hotel
334 Mason St.　　　☎781-5050
A Laura Ashley nightmare, where customers nibble at finger sandwiches in mock-British cottage surroundings. Horribly twee, the sort of place that only the most desperate Anglophile could get a kick out of.

Mandarin Oriental
222 Sansome St.　　　☎885-0999
This is more like it; cakes galore, under millions of dollars worth of Austrian crystal chandeliers, with soft piano music.

Mark Hopkins
999 California St.　　　☎392-3434
Standard high teas served on lovely Wedgwood china.

Neiman Marcus
150 Stockton St.　　　☎362-3900
A personal favorite: tea is served in the glorious *Rotunda* restaurant at the top of the store. Watch the rich social-X-rays nibble fearfully at the calorie-laden food.

Ritz Carlton
600 Stockton St.　　　☎296-7465
The fanciest of them all, this is the place to slurp tea to the accompaniment of classical piano.

The Mandarin
Ghirardelli Square, Fisherman's Wharf. ☎673-8812.
Stylish conversion of industrial space stuffed with oriental antiques. The Chinese food is excellent but pricey – ideal for a special night out.

New Asia
722 Pacific Ave. ☎391-6666.
Considering Chinatown is so pressed for space, it's amazing that a place this big survives. It serves some of the most authentic dim sum in town, with waitresses pushing carts down the aisles, shouting out their wares as they pass.

Pot Sticker
150 Waverly Place. ☎397-9985.
Extensive menu offering Szechuan and Hunan dishes in this inexpensive and often crowded Chinatown favorite.

Sam Woh's
813 Washington St. ☎982-0596.
Much tamer since the death of the hilariously surly waiter Edsel Ford Fong some years ago, this basic late-night (until 3am) restaurant still attracts the North Beach crowds when the bars turn out. You have to climb dodgy old steps through the kitchen to reach the eating area.

Woey Loey Goey Café
699 Jackson St. ☎982-0137.
Like *Sam Woh's*, this is very much an after hours place and is similarly priced – it also serves wine for around $1 per glass.

Yuet Lee
1300 Stockton St. ☎982-6020.
Cheap and cheerful Chinese restaurant with a good seafood menu and enthusiastic crowds of diners. No alcohol, but you can bring your own beer and wine.

Chinatown is described in detail on p.63

Restaurants

Vegetarian Restaurants

Amazing Grace
216 Church St. ☎626-6411
Rated highly by local vegetarians, with a standard menu starting at around $5 a dish.

Green's
Building A, Fort Mason Center
Fort Mason. ☎771-6222
A converted army supply warehouse that's now San Francisco's only Zen Buddhist restaurant, serving unusual and delicious macrobiotic and vegetarian food to an eager clientele. Always busy, so book in advance and count on spending around $30 a head for a five-course dinner.

Marty's
508 Natoma St. ☎621-0751
Stuck down a little alley, this isn't the sort of place you'd stumble over, but if you're into macrobiotic food, you should definitely make the effort.

Real Good Karma
501 Dolores St at 18th. ☎621-4112
Hearty and nutritious portions of vegetarian and wholefood dishes in informal surroundings.

Japanese

Osome
923 Fillmore St. ☎346-2311.
Smart, popular restaurant which is renowned for its highly rated sushi and seafood.

Indian

Gaylord
Ghirardelli Square, 900 North Point, Fisherman's Wharf. ☎771-8822.
One of the very few Indian restaurants in San Francisco and probably the best, though you should expect to pay around $18 for a main course. Still, if you're dying for a curry . . .

India House
350 Jackson St. ☎392-0744.
Far from being inexpensive, but lavish decoration and extraordinarily punctilious service help to soften the blow when the bill arrives.

Middle Eastern

The Golden Turtle
2211 Van Ness Ave. ☎441-4419.
Though primarily a Vietnamese restaurant, this Russian Hill venue serves up an extensive selection of kebabs and other Middle Eastern dishes, all of which cost under $10.

Helmand
430 Broadway. ☎362-0641.
Excellent, inexpensive Afghani food. Exotic, unique and very popular.

Pasha's
1516 Broadway. ☎885-4477.
An extraordinary dining experience. Moroccan and Middle Eastern dishes served while you sit on the floor watching belly dancers gyrate past your table, proffering their cleavage for you to insert dollar bills. Go with a group of rowdy drunks, or not at all.

Civic Center, SoMa and Mission

American

Brain Wash Laundromat/Café
1122 Folsom St. ☎861-3663.
If you don't mind watching people pile their dirties into the machines, this is a surprisingly good venue for well-prepared, simple sandwiches, pizzas and salad. A boisterous SoMa hangout, providing a good opportunity to check out the locals.

The Connecticut Yankee
100 Connecticut St. ☎552-4440.
Pricey Potrero Hill restaurant, serving great weekend brunches accompanied by generous cocktails.

The Grubstake
1525 Pine St at Van Ness. ☎673-8268.
Converted 1920s railroad dining car, with some of the city's best late-night burgers.

Fringale
570 Fourth St. ☎543-0573.
Trendy but inexpensive bistro, open for lunch and dinner Mon–Fri.

Hamburger Mary's
1582 Folsom St. ☎626-1985.
Boisterous South-of-Market burger bar,
with punky waiting staff and good range
of vegetarian options. Inexpensive, and
open late for the club-going crowds.

Hamburger Nancy's
2001 17th St. ☎863-6777.
Not wildly different from the above, but
appealing more to the office worker
crowd with its bargain happy hour.

Ivy's
398 Hayes St. ☎626-3930.
Very popular Civic Center restaurant A
great spot for lunch, or for a late dinner
after the opera-going crowds – who pack
the place in the early evening – have
moved on. Stylish but not expensive.

Julie's Supper Club
1123 Folsom St. ☎861-0707.
The cuisine, both at the bar and in the
back-room restaurant, defies definition

Restaurants

*SoMa bars are
listed on p.239*

SOMA RESTAURANTS, BARS, CAFÉS AND CLUBS

Restaurants
1   Limbo
2   Lulu's
3   Julie's Supper Club
4   Spike's
5   Up & Down Club

6   Manora's Thai Cuisine
7   Hamburger Mary's
8   Appam
9   Café do Brasil

Bars, Cafés and Clubs
10   Brainwash

11   Paradise Lounge
12   The Stud
13   Rawhide
14   The Eagle
15   Slim's

Restaurants

and can only be described as eclectic. The decor however, is straight out of a B-52's/Jetsons dream. Worth a look, especially for the free live jazz in the evenings.

Limbo
299 Ninth St. ☎255-9945.
Super-inexpensive and ultra-trendy venue, where you can be sure that you won't be alone. Stodgy wholefood dishes and burgers from under $5.

LuLu's
816 Folsom St. ☎495-5775.
The latest in chic mastication, *LuLu's* has an international/Californian menu and visible chefs in open kitchens wearing headphones. Such obviously studied catering should not put you off the food, however, which is excellent. The restaurant that everybody is talking about. Until the next one comes along . . .

Mission Rock Resort
817 China Basin. ☎621-5538.
Good bargain breakfasts and lunches, which you can eat on the wharf when the weather's good.

Miss Pearl's Jam House
601 Eddy St. ☎775-5267.
The cooking may be Caribbean but the experience is definitely Californian. Run in conjunction with the *Phoenix* motel that shares the site, *Miss Pearl's* is full of muso types who come to look for their peers and enjoy the nightly live reggae and down-home atmosphere. Seated at the tables surrounding the pool, you really feel as though you're having a resort holiday in the middle of town. The menu, particularly the fish dishes, is outstanding and not bank-breaking. Highly recommended.

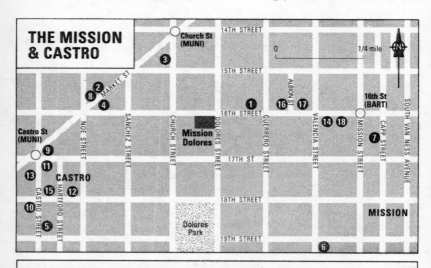

THE MISSION & CASTRO

THE MISSION AND CASTRO RESTAURANTS, BARS, CAFÉS AND CLUBS

Restaurants	Bars, Cafés and Clubs	
1 Bangkok 16	6 The Chatterbox	12 Uncle Bert's Place
2 Café du Nord	7 The Uptown	13 The Phoenix
3 Sparky's Diner	8 Café Flor	14 La India Bonita
4 Bagdad Café	9 Café San Marcos	15 Midnight Sun
5 Patio Café	10 Elephant Walk	16 Albion
	11 Esta Noche	17 Paula's Clubhouse

Restaurants

24-Hour Eating

Bagdad Café
2295 Market St. ☎621-4434

The Brasserie
In the basement of the *Fairmont Hotel*,
950 Mason St. ☎772-5000

Clown Alley
42 Columbus Ave. ☎421-2540

International House of Pancakes
2299 Lombard St. ☎921-4004

Lori's Diner
336 Mason St. ☎392-8646

Orphan Andy's
3991 17th St. ☎864-9795

The Pine Crest
401 Geary. ☎885-6407

Sparky's Diner
240 Church St. ☎621-6001

Zim's 1498 Market St. ☎431-0600
Also at 1090 Van Ness Ave. ☎885-2620
and 3473 California. ☎387-7771

Pauline's Pizza Pie
260 Valencia St. ☎552-2050.
Something of a truck stop as far as decor
goes, but widely esteemed for serving
inventive combinations, in big portions, at
good prices.

Primo Restaurant
214 Townsend St. ☎957-1129.
An interesting mix of grilled fish, tapas
and fresh pastas, this is the new
California/International style cuisine at its
innovative best.

Spike's
139 Eighth St. ☎255-1392.
Sixties-style diner, serving big breakfasts
and budget lunches. Watch out for the
discount coupons that appear regularly in
the local press.

Star's
150 Redwood Alley, near Van Ness and
Golden Gate. ☎861-7827.
Quite the place to be seen for oysters
and cocktails before – or a full-blown
meal after – the opera or symphony.
Expensive, but the food is exquisite, the
fixtures and fittings opulent, and the
clientele inevitably high-class.

Swan's Oyster Depot
1517 Polk St. ☎673-1101.
You wouldn't know it by the simple
decor, but this is one of the city's best
and oldest seafood places – take a seat
at the bar (there are no tables) for half a
dozen fresh-shucked West Coast oysters,
washed down with a glass of ice-cold
Anchor Steam beer.

Up & Down Club
1151 Folsom St. ☎626-2388.
Better known for its excellent live jazz
upstairs, the *Up & Down* also has a
perfectly respectable bistro downstairs.
Better for light snacking than serious
dining.

Vicolo Pizzeria
201 Ivy St off Franklin. ☎863-2382.
Popular Civic Center spot with very good
and not expensive designer pizzas and
salads.

Zim's
1498 Market St. ☎431-0600.
Classic San Francisco coffee shop, serving
breakfasts, burgers, steaks and salads 24
hours per day. Branches all over town.

Zuni Café
1658 Market St. ☎552-2522.
This has been the chic place to see and
be seen for the last five years. Californian
nouvelle cuisine for around $30 a head
with a glass of wine.

French and Italian

Café Landais
489 Third St. ☎495-6944.
SoMa bistro that is about the least
expensive place in town to eat good
French food. Popular with connoisseurs
on a budget.

Enoteca Lanzone
Opera Plaza, 601 Van Ness St.
☎928-0400.
A favorite with opera-goers, where the
menu may be priced beyond most

Bars and Cafés
in the Mission
are reviewed
on p.234.

Restaurants

There's a list of vegetarian restaurants in San Francisco on p.218.

For more on Mexican food, see p.210.

budgets, but the "Grappa Room" offers 140 different varieties of the stuff.

La Traviata
2854 Mission St. ☎282-0500.
Friendly, noisy and inexpensive Italian Mission restaurant.

Le Trou
1007 Guerrero St. ☎550-8169.
A bit like the *Landais*, this is another reasonably priced, unpretentious site for well-cooked French food.

South Park Café
108 South Park. ☎495-7275.
Chic SoMa gathering place for afficionados of all things French, especially pastries and good brandy.

Greek and Middle Eastern

Asimakopoulos Café
288 Connecticut St. ☎552-8789.
Upscale Greek cooking although you get the feeling you're paying for the decor rather than the food.

Mamounia
441 Balboa St. ☎752-6565.
Eat Moroccan food with your fingers and pay through the nose for the privilege. Tastes good through.

Steve the Greek
1431 Polk St. No phone.
Authentic Greek (including plastic tablecloths) and ultra-low-priced spot close to Civic Center.

Chinese, Japanese and Thai

Bangkok 16
3214 16th St. ☎431-5838.
Moderately priced Thai restaurant down in the Mission, with a great selection for vegetarians. For meat eaters they do a mean lamb satay.

Cloisonne
601 Van Ness Ave. ☎441-2232.
First-class Cantonese food, moderately priced and served in luxurious surroundings. Draws most of its business from the opera crowd, so it tends to be quite formal. You won't be refused if you turn up in jeans, but you might feel out of place.

Manora's Thai Cuisine
1600 Folsom St. ☎861-6224.

Massively popular and you may have to wait, but it's worth it for the light, spicy and fragrant dishes at around $6 each.

Moshi Moshi
2092 Third St. ☎861-8285.
Obscure SoMa restaurant full of people who pride themselves on finding such an out-of-the-way gem. Excellent Japanese, sushi and seafood, moderately priced.

Indian

Appam
1261 Folsom St. ☎626-2798.
Great atmosphere, and the old Indian method of "Dum Pukht" cooking is employed. Dishes are prepared in large clay pots in an open kitchen where you can watch as nan breads and kulchas bake in the tandoori oven.

Sirtaj India Cuisine
48 Fifth St. ☎957-0140.
Quiet retreat from the madness of the surrounding downtown SoMa area, this is a lovely place to stop for the bargain 13-course buffet lunch for only $6.99.

Central and South American

Border Café and Cantina
1198 Folsom St. ☎626-6043.
Authentic Mexican lunches and dinners served in a lively, comfortable atmosphere.

Cadillac Bar
1 Holland Court, off Howard St.
☎543-8226.
By the standards of most Mexican restaurants, this one is fairly upmarket, and offers live guitar music to help your burritos go down.

Café do Brasil
104 Seventh St. ☎626-6432.
Great Brazilian tapas and international cuisine.

El Cubane
1432 Valencia St. ☎824-6655.
Big portions of Cuban food, with a Tues–Fri lunch special for $5.

El Nuevo Frutilandia
3077 24th St. ☎648-2958.
Mission District Cuban restaurant specializing in spicy seafood dishes.

El Tazumal
3522 20th St. ☎550-0935.
Interesting Salvadorean restaurant where
you can try tripe, tongue and spicy rice
dishes for around $6 for lunch and $10
for dinner. Small but lively with a very
interesting mixed crowd.

El Toro
3071 16th St. ☎431-3351.
There are always crowds outside waiting
for the massive burritos.

Ensenada Restaurant
2976 Mission St. ☎826-4160.
One of the more cheerful looking of the
Mission's inexpensive restaurants with
Mexican art on the walls and a standard
menu with full meals for around $5.

Las Guitarras
3200 24th St. ☎285-2684.
Noisy Mexican favored by the locals.
Don't expect a fine dining experience, but
you can count on a good hearty dinner.

La Tacqueria
2889 Mission St. ☎285-7717.
Always busy with locals, which is as good
a recommendation as any for its fairly
standard Mexican menu.

La Victoria
1205 Alabama St. ☎550-9309.
Small, intimate South American cafeteria
run by two old women. Service is slow,
but the food is fresh and delicious.

Line Up
398 Seventh St. ☎861-2887.
Most people come and queue for great
take-outs, though if you don't mind over-
head neon, you can eat in.

Mission Villa Restaurant
2391 Mission St. ☎826-0454.
Enormous burritos and tacos for about $3.

Mom's Cooking
1192 Geneva St. ☎585-7000.
Small and crowded on the fringes of the
Mission district. You may have to wait for
a table, but it's well worth it for the super-
inexpensive fresh Mexican food.

New Central Restaurant
301 South Van Ness Ave. ☎431-8587.
Small, family-run restaurant serving
moderately priced, hearty dishes to a
ravenous crowd.

Central Neighborhoods
American
Bagdad Café
2295 Market St. ☎621-4434.
Good, hearty breakfasts and burgers
served 24 hours per day.

Café du Nord
2170 Market St. ☎861-5016.
Recently revamped as an inexpensive
supper club, this is great for entertainment
while you eat the good, inexpensive
dishes. On Wednesday evenings, *Ellington
Supper Club* features jazz music.

Café Majestic
Majestic Hotel, 1500 Sutter St.
☎776-6400.
Totally out of place in the Japantown
neighborhood, but nonetheless a lovely
place for dinner. The full-on classical
decor includes high ceiling and columns,
and the food is exquisite.

Homeboy's Barbeque
1117 Fillmore St. ☎563-3020.
Western Addition restaurant serving up
steak, ribs and chicken American-style –
LARGE. Good way to load up your protein
(and cholesterol levels).

Hot n Hunky
4039 18th St. ☎621-6365.
As the name suggests, the burgers are on
the large side, masses of red meat strain-
ing under their buns, in what is generally
considered San Francisco's best burger
joint. The atmosphere is negligible, but an
average serving can feed a family of four.

Noe Valley Pizza
3898 24th St. ☎647-1664.
If you love garlic, this is your place – every
pizza is loaded with it.

Oppenheimer
2050 Divisadero St. ☎563-0444.
Upscale delicatessen with a full range of
kosher foods.

Orphan Andy's
3991 17th St. ☎864-9795.
Favorite Castro hang-out, serving 24-hour
burgers, omelettes and breakfasts.

Patio Café
531 Castro St. ☎621-4640.
Casual terrace restaurant, great for wholesome food – mostly grilled meats and

Restaurants

*Our Central
Neighborhoods
chapter begins
on p.103.*

Restaurants

pasta dishes – and good-value weekend brunches where you can sling back inexpensive cocktails.

Pazzaz
3296 22nd St. ☎824-8080.
American food with a Chinese twist. Inexpensive and usually crowded.

Spaghetti Western
576 Haight St. ☎864-8461.
Best breakfasts for miles and a lively Lower Haight crowd to look at while you chow down.

Sparky's Diner
240 Church St. ☎621-6001.
24-hour diner cooking up burgers, pastas and pizzas plus breakfasts including a very good Eggs Florentine. Beer and wine too.

Japanese

Asuka Brasserie
Miyako Hotel, 1625 Post St. ☎922-3200.
Very flash indeed. Great Japanese food in beautiful surroundings, priced beyond the means of most. For special occasions only.

Elka's
1611 Post St. ☎922-7788.
Latest word in seafood with a Japanese twist. State of the art fish by celebrity chef Elka Gilmore. Take a bankroll.

Isuzu
1582 Webster St. ☎922-2290.
Fashionable Japan Center restaurant with separate sushi and tempura bars. Rub shoulders with those in the know.

Ma Tante Sumi
4243 18th St. ☎552-6663.
Interesting one this; Japanese with a French twist, producing innovative combinations of dishes ranging from the very light to the incredibly rich. A popular Castro dining spot.

Mifune
1737 Post St. ☎922-0337.
Moderately priced seafood and Japanese specialties to take away.

Miyota
1855 Post St. ☎563-2156.
Inexpensive sushi and seafood served from a bar where you sit on cushions. The adjoining bar has singers and is an excellent place to warm up before dinner.

Sanppo
1702 Post St. ☎346-3486.
Small, busy and unpretentious Japantown restaurant – the decor might be negligible but the food is low priced and first rate.

Sushi Bar
1800 Divisadero. No phone.
Bright, inexpensive and quick.

Yoshida Ya
2909 Webster St. ☎346-3431.
San Francisco has countless sushi bars, but not many where you can actually kick off your shoes and eat at low tables on futoned floors. This is just such a place; expect to pay around $25 per head for a good selection of sushi and a few drinks.

Korean and Thai

Mun's
401 Balboa St. ☎668-6007.
Western Addition venue serving inexpensive, simple Korean dishes.

Thep Phanom Restaurant
400 Waller St. ☎431-2526.
Simple, delicate decor and beautifully prepared Thai dishes make this Lower Haight restaurant seem more expensive than it really is. Expect to pay no more than $8 for main course dishes, but also expect to queue.

Golden Gate Park, the Beaches and Outlying Areas

Alejandro's Sociedad Gastronomica
1840 Clement St. ☎668-1184.
Tasty tapas and great South American seafood dishes, including SF's best paella, plus fairly standard Mexican food.

Bill's Place
2315 Clement St. ☎221-5262.
Very popular Richmond District burger joint. Dozens of different combinations are named for SF celebs and politicos.

The Boat House
1 Harding Blvd (on Lake Merced).
☎681-2727.
Great views turn this otherwise uninspiring sports bar into a great place to stop for lunch; basic menu of burgers, nachos, stuffed potato skins and buffalo wings.

Café Riggio
4112 Geary Blvd. ☎221-2114.
Out in the Richmond, this is the original
Italian bistro, a genuinely earthy haunt
that serves solid if unexceptional food
and the lowest-priced Italian wine in
town.

Ebisu
1283 Ninth Ave. ☎566-1770.
Authentic Japanese menu includes
seafoods, steak and sushi with 18-seat
sushi bar.

The Grapeleaf
4031 Balboa St. ☎668-1515.
Small Lebanese bistro serving unusual
and spicy food, and enlivened by belly
dancers shimmying around the tables.

La Marmite
2415 Clement St. ☎666-3781.
Cheerful Richmond District bistro with very
good, inexpensive country French
cooking.

Louis' Restaurant
902 Point Lobos Ave. ☎387-6330.
1940s-era diner serving great burgers and
sandwiches. Overlooking Sutro Baths,
with a marvellous sunset view.

Mel's Drive-In
3355 Geary Blvd at Stanyan. ☎387-2244.
Straight out of *American Grafitti*, with
burgers (including very good veggie
burgers), fries and milkshakes. No longer
a drive-in, but open late – after midnight
every night, till 3am on weekends.

New Village
4828 Geary Blvd. ☎668-3678.
Richmond restaurant that serves good-
value set meals, with barbeque short ribs,
chicken or seafood plus half a dozen
Korean specialties for around $10.

Owl & Monkey Café
1336 Ninth Ave. ☎665-4840.
Huge salads and other healthy foods.

Pig & Whistle Pub
2801 Geary Blvd. ☎885-4779.
The only true-to-life English pub in San
Francisco – home away from home
for INS-dodging British contingent.
Massive plates of fish'n'chips for $6.

Silver Moon
2301 Clement St. ☎386-7852.

Seafood and vegetarian Japanese dishes.
Very light, healthy food.

South Pacific
2500 Noriega Ave. ☎564-3363.
Seafood, tropical cocktails, live music and
hula dancers on weekends. Every bit the
novelty eatery.

Stoyanof's
1240 Ninth Ave near Irving. ☎664-3664.
Worth a streetcar ride (Muni's N-Judah
stops a block away), this Sunset District
Greek place has some of the best food
this side of Golden Gate Park.

Straits Café
3300 Geary Blvd. ☎668-1783.
Affordable Singaporean dishes in authentic surroundings.

East Bay
Budget Food: Diners and Delis
Barney's
4162 Piedmont Ave, Oakland.
☎510/655-7180.
Also at 5819 College Ave in Rockridge
(☎510/601-0444) and 1591 Solano Ave
in Berkeley (☎510/526-8185).
Barney's serves the East Bay's most
popular burgers – smothered in
dozens of different toppings – plus
grilled chicken and fresh salads.

Bette's Ocean View Diner
1807 Fourth St. ☎510/548-9494.
Named for the neighborhood, not for
the vista, but serving up some of the
Bay Area's best breakfasts and lunches.
Very popular on weekends, when you
may have to wait an hour for a table,
so come during the week.

Flint's Barbecue
3314 San Pablo Ave, Oakland.
☎510/658-9912.
Also at 6609 Shattuck Ave
(☎510/653-0593).
Open until the early hours of the
morning for some of the best ribs
and sausage links west of Chicago.

Lois the Pie Queen
851 60th St at Adeline, Oakland.
☎510/658-5616.
Famous around the bay for their
southern-style sweet potato and

Restaurants

*There's a list of
vegetarian
restaurants in
San Francisco
on p.218.*

*Bay Area bars
are listed on
p.237.*

Restaurants

A walking tour of Berkeley is described on p.144 onwards.

fresh fruit pies, this cozy diner also serves massive, down-home breakfasts and Sunday dinners that'll keep you full for a week.

Mabel's Café
635 First St, Benicia. ☎707/746-7068
Tiny but timeless all-American diner, serving fresh and healthy breakfasts and lunches.

Rick & Ann's
2922 Domingo Ave, Berkeley.
☎510/649-8538.
Across the street from the *Claremont Hotel*, this homey diner pulls in the crowds for its moderately priced "comfort food" – meat loaf and mashed potatoes, pork chops, pastas and fresh fish.

Rockridge Café
5492 College Ave, Rockridge.
☎510/653-1567.
Chrome-and-lino breakfast and burger bar with good desserts. Opens at 7am every day.

Saul's Deli
1475 Shattuck Ave, Berkeley.
☎510/848-DELI.
For pastrami, corned beef, kreplach or knishes, this is the place. Great sandwiches and picnic fixings to take away, plus a full range of sit-down evening meals.

Tea Spot Café
2072 San Pablo Ave, Berkeley.
☎510/848-7376.
Excellent fresh-cooked American diner food in popular, lesbian-run café near University Ave.

Time to Eat
In Oakland's Produce Market at 325 Franklin St. ☎510/835-4455.
A Chinese bar and café that serves breakfasts from 5am. Cheap beer, plus a pool table – 25¢ per game.

Top Dog
2534 Durant St, Berkeley. No phone.
Not just a hotdog stand, it stays open late for such assorted goodies as bockwurst, bratwurst, kielbasas, Louisiana Hot Sausages and veggie dogs.

American

Bay Wolf Café
3853 Piedmont Ave, Oakland.
☎510/655-6004.
Comfortable restaurant serving grilled meat and fish dishes on an ever-changing, moderately expensive menu.

Chez Panisse
1517 Shattuck Ave, Berkeley.
☎510/548-5525.
The first and still the best of the California Cuisineries, serving multi-course meals of delectably fresh food for $35–65 *prix fixe*. It's less expensive, and less crowded, earlier in the week; if you haven't made the obligatory advance reservations, try the upstairs café, though that isn't nearly as special.

Gulf Coast Oyster Bar & Specialty Co
736 Washington St., downtown Oakland.
☎510/839-6950.
Popular and reasonably priced Cajun-flavored seafood restaurant.

Spenger's
1919 Fourth St, Berkeley.
☎510/845-7111.
About as far as you can get from the subtle charms of Berkeley's high-style restaurants, this is nonetheless a local institution: the largest restaurant in the whole Bay Area, serving up literally tons of seafood to thousands of clients every day.

Mexican and South American

Alvita's Restaurant
3522 Foothill Blvd, East Oakland.
☎510/536-7880.
Arguably the best Mexican restaurant in the Bay Area, with great chiles rellenos, carnitas, and a range of seafood dishes.

Cafe Oliveto
5655 College Ave, Rockridge.
☎510/547-5356.
Popular sidewalk tapas bar, where good-sized portions cost around $4 per plate. Upstairs is a pricey Italian restaurant.

Juan's Place
941 Carleton St, West Berkeley.
☎510/845-6904.
The original Berkeley Mexican restaurant, with great food (tons of it) and an interesting mix of people.

Mario's La Fiesta
2444 Telegraph Ave at Haste St, Berkeley.
☎ 510/540-9123.
Always crowded with students and other budget-minded souls, who flock here for the heaping portions of good, inexpensive Mexican food.

Picante
1328 Sixth St at Gilman St, West Berkeley. ☎ 510/525-3121.
Good, inexpensive tacos with fresh salsa, plus live jazz at weekends.

Tambo Café
1981 Shattuck Ave near University Ave, Berkeley. ☎ 510/841-6884.
Brilliant, reasonably priced Peruvian food-papas huacainas (potatoes in spicy cheese sauce) and empanadas (meat or vegetable pies), as well as marvellous ceviche, served up fresh and fast.

Taqueria Morelia
4481 E 14th St., East Oakland.
☎ 510/261-6360.
Excellent burritos and the more unusual but authentic tortas.

Pizzas
Blondie's Pizza
2340 Telegraph Ave, Berkeley.
☎ 510/548-1129.
Takeout New York-style pizza by the slice ($1.25, plus topping) or by the pie; stays open until late (2am), and always crowded with people.

Cheese Board Pizza
1512 Shattuck Ave, Berkeley.
☎ 510/549-3055.
Tiny storefront selling some of the world's best "designer pizza" at very reasonable prices: $1.50 a slice, with a different topping every day. Worth searching out, but be aware of their irregular hours; usually Tues–Sat 11.30am–2pm & 4.30–7pm.

Zachary's Pizza
5801 College Ave, Rockridge.
☎ 510/655-6385.
Also at 1853 Solano Ave, North Berkeley (☎ 510/525-5950).
Good salads, and arguably the best pizzas in the East Bay.

Asian and African
The Blue Nile
2525 Telegraph Ave, Berkeley.
☎ 510/540-6777.
Come with a group to share the giant platters of Ethiopian stewed meats and veggies, eaten by hand with pancake-like injera bread.

Bombay Cuisine
2006 Ninth St at University Ave, Berkeley.
☎ 510/843-9601.
Great Indian food at reasonable prices, tucked away in the back room of a spice shop.

Cha-Am
1543 Shattuck Ave, Berkeley.
☎ 510/848-9664.
Climb up the stairs to this unlikely-looking, always crowded small restaurant, for deliciously spicy Thai food at bargain prices.

Le Chevral
1414 Jefferson St, Oakland.
☎ 510/763-8495.
Huge quantities of top-quality Vietnamese food at rock-bottom prices: full lunches cost under $5.

Jade Villa
800 Broadway, downtown Oakland.
☎ 510/839-1688.
For dim sum lunches or traditional Cantonese meals, this is one of the best places in Oakland's thriving Chinatown.

Maharani
1025 University Ave, West Berkeley.
☎ 510/848-7777.
One of the best of the handful of restaurants that have sprung up here in Little India, and certainly the least expensive, with $6 lunchtime buffets on weekdays.

O Chame
1830 Fourth St, West Berkeley.
☎ 510/841-8783.
One of the very best Japanese restaurants in the US, with beautifully prepared sashimi and sushi as well as a full range of authentic Japanese specialties. A treat.

Sorabol
372 Grand Ave, Lake Merritt.
☎ 510/839-2288.
Excellent Korean restaurant, with addictive barbecued meats for around $8 per dish.

Restaurants

Berkeley bars and cafés are reviewed on p.237.

Restaurants

Two lighthouse hostels on the Peninsula coast are reviewed on p.208.

Steve's Barbeque
In the Durant Center, 2521 Durant Ave, Berkeley. ☎ 510/848-6166.
Excellent, low priced Korean food (kim chee to die for); other cafés in the center sell Mexican food, healthy sandwiches, deep-fried doughnuts and slices of pizza – not to mention bargain pitchers of beer.

The Peninsula

Abigail's Pub
265 N First St, San Jose.
☎ 408/294-4111.
Ersatz English tavern catering to Anglo-phile computer wizards, but serving good roast beef and Yorkshire puddings for around $12, and a wide range of beers.

Barrio Fiesta
909 Antoinette Lane, South San Francisco.
☎ 871-8703.
Hard to find amid the shopping malls of South City, but worth hunting out for the huge portions of beautifully presented, delicious Filipino dishes, especially seafood. Full meals cost around $15; bring your own wine or beer.

Dinelli's
1956 Pescadero Rd, Pescadero.
☎ 879-0106.
Probably the best roadside café in the known world, with great burgers and a house specialty, fried artichoke hearts, that lures customers from all over the Bay Area.

Duarte's
202 Stage Rd, Pescadero.
☎ 879-0464.
Platefuls of traditional American cooking for $10, plus wonderful fresh fruit pies.

Eulipia
374 S First St, San Jose.
☎ 408/280-6161.
Upscale and stylish spot featuring well-prepared versions of California Cuisine staples like grilled fish and fresh pastas. Full bar; dinner and drinks will set you back $15–25.

Fresco
3398 El Camino Real, Palo Alto.
☎ 493-3470.
Wide selection of pastas, pizzas, and a menu of salads with palpably fresh

ingredients in unusual combinations. Opens early.

Krung Thai Cuisine
1699 W San Carlos St, San Jose.
☎ 408/295-5508.
Delicious, unusual seafood dishes – start off with a po-tak soup of clams and crab legs in citrus broth – and excellent range of satays.

Little Garden
4127 El Camino Real, Palo Alto.
☎ 494-1230.
Simple, spicy, well-prepared Vietnamese food – fried chicken on a bed of cabbage, shrimp and hot peppers in peanut sauce – in unpretentious surroundings.

Original Joe's
301 S First St, San Jose.
☎ 408/292-7030.
Grab a stool at the counter or settle into one of the comfy booths and enjoy a burger and fries or a plate of pasta at this San Jose institution, where $10 goes a long way.

Pudley's Burger Saloon
255 University Ave, Palo Alto.
☎ 328-2021.
Burgers ($4) and beers ($1.50) in retro-American 1940s setting.

Marin County

The Cantina
651 E Blithedale Rd at Camino Alto, Mill Valley. ☎ 381-1070.
Some of the best Mexican food in Marin, spiced by what's certainly the hottest salsa for miles.

Casa Madrona
801 Bridgeway, Sausalito. ☎ 331-5888.
Mediterranean staples meet California Cuisine in this highly rated (and very expensive) hotel-restaurant which does excellent fresh seafood. Great view of the harbor, and service is anything but hurried.

Da Angelo
22 Miller Ave, Mill Valley. ☎ 388-2000.
Good salads and tasty pasta and pizzas, served up in a lively but comfortable room right off the downtown plaza.

Restaurants

Dipsea Café
1 El Paseo, Mill Valley. ☎381-0298.
Hearty diner food, especially good for
breakfast before a day out hiking on
Mount Tamalpais.

Greater Gatsby's
39 Caledonia St, Sausalito. ☎332-4500.
Handy, inexpensive pizza parlor a block
from the waterfront on the north side of
town.

Hilda's
639 San Anselmo Ave, San Anselmo.
☎457-9266.
Great breakfasts and lunches in this
down-home, cozy café.

Manka's
30 Calendar Way, Inverness.
☎669-1034.
Excellent Czechoslovakian food in a
homey dining room near the wilds of Point
Reyes.

Milly's
1613 Fourth St, San Rafael. ☎459-1601.
Extremely healthy, wide-ranging vegetarian dishes such as Thai vegetable curries
and jalapeno ravioli. Open evenings only.

Mountain Home Inn
810 Panoramic Highway, above Mill
Valley. ☎381-9000.
Another place that's as good for the
atmosphere as for the food, with broiled
meats and fish dishes served up in a rustic
lodge on the slopes of Mount Tam.

New Morning Café
1696 Tiburon Blvd, Tiburon. ☎435-4315.
Lots of healthy wholegrain sandwiches,
plus salads and omelettes.

Pelican Inn
Hwy-1, Muir Beach. ☎383-6000.
Great fish and chips ($8) or roast beef
and Yorkshire pudding ($15) in a coach-
ing-house atmosphere.

Rice Table
1617 Fourth St, San Rafael. ☎456-1808.
From the shrimp chips through the crab
pancakes and noodles on to the fried
plantain desserts, these fragrant and spicy
Indonesian dishes are worth planning a
day around. Dinners only, but excellent
value at around $15 a head for a very
filling meal.

Sam's Anchor Café
27 Main St, Tiburon. ☎435-2676.
Rough-hewn, amiable waterfront café and
bar. Good burgers, soups, and sandwiches, plus very popular Sunday
brunches.

Station House Café
11180 Hwy-1 (Main St), Point Reyes
Station. ☎663-1515.
Open daily for lunch and dinner, this
friendly local favorite entices diners from
miles around to sample their grilled
seafood and great steaks.

Stinson Beach Grill
Stinson Beach. ☎868-2002.
Somewhat pricey California Cuisine in a
beachfront setting – look out for the
bright blue building right in the heart of
town.

Viva Bien Café
225 Corte Madera Ave, Larkspur.
☎924-7940.
A bit hard to get to, on the main route
from Larkspur up to Mill Valley, but worth
it for terrific, mostly vegetarian food,
including great filled crepes, sandwiches,
and salads.

Wine Country

All Seasons
1400 Lincoln Ave, Calistoga.
☎707/942-9111.
This friendly bistro, serving up good-sized
portions of California Cuisine, is probably
best known locally for its massive wine
list, many of which are available by the
glass. Main dishes should cost between
$10 and $20.

Bosko's Ristorante
1403 Lincoln Ave, Calistoga.
☎707/942-9088.
Standard Italian restaurant preparing
good-value fresh pasta dishes. Cheap and
cheerful, and popular with families.

Calistoga Inn
1250 Lincoln Ave, Calistoga.
☎707/942-4101.
Very good seafood – spicy Cajun prawns,
or crispy crab cakes – plus wide range of
wines, microbrewed beers and excellent
desserts.

*Wine County
accommodation
is listed in
Chapter 12.*

Restaurants

Wine Country wineries are listed on p.189 and p.191.

Checkers Pizza
1414 Lincoln Ave, Calistoga.
☎707/942-9300.
Soups, salads, and sandwiches, plus adventurous pizzas and good pasta dishes.

The Diner
6476 Washington St, Yountville.
☎707/944-2626.
Start the day's wine-touring off right, with good strong coffee and brilliant breakfasts. Open until 3pm Tues–Fri, until 10pm at weekends for flavorsome Mexican dinners.

Grist Mill Restaurant
14301 Arnold Drive, Glen Ellen.
☎707/996-3077.
Creekside dining in a spacious converted mill. A large menu plus an extensive list of local wines.

La Boucane
1778 Second St, Napa.
☎707/253-1177.
Mouthwatering chunks of tender meat prepared in traditional but imaginative sauces, plus perfect fish (especially shellfish) and vegetables. Very expensive, dinner only.

La Casa
121 E Spain St, Sonoma.
☎707/996-3406.
Friendly, festive and inexpensive Mexican restaurant just across from Sonoma Mission. Excellent salsa – buy some to take away.

Mustards
7399 St Helena Highway (Hwy-29), Yountville. ☎707/944-2424.
Credited with starting the late 1980s trend toward "grazing" food, emphasizing tapas-like titbits rather than main meals. Reckon on spending $15–20 a head, and waiting for a table if you come on a weekend.

PJ's Café
1001 Second St, Napa. ☎707/224-0607.
A Napa institution, open 11am–10pm every day for pasta, pizzas, and sandwiches.

Regina's
110 W Spain St in the *Sonoma Hotel*, Sonoma. ☎707/938-0254.
Very good Italian-American food, right off Sonoma Plaza.

Tra Vigne
1050 Charter Oak Ave, St Helena.
☎707/963-4444.
Just north of town, but it feels as if you've been transported to Tuscany. Excellent food and fine wines, served up in a lovely vine-covered courtyard. They also have a small deli, where you can pick up picnic goodies.

Chapter 14

Bars and Cafés

San Francisco has for many years possessed a reputation as the consummate boozing town, and is still blessed with a huge range of bars and cafés.

However, the city's attitude to alcohol is increasingly going the way of the rest of California. It is no longer fashionable (or in some circles even acceptable) to drink. A faint whiff of sanctimony hovers over the social scene, and San Franciscans in their thousands are joining the massively popular "Clean and Sober Clubs" – places where people who have served their time in the AA go to be with other non-drinkers.

An enviable provision of excellent **cafés** serve first-rate coffees, teas, and soft drinks in addition to beer and wine. These often make good places to grab some lunch and while away a couple of hours during the day. Furthermore, many non-drinkers looking for social alternatives to bars are opting instead for the newest pastime, the old English tradition of **Afternoon Tea**. So far it has only taken off in the big hotels, but it's catching on fast and should spread to the neighborhood cafés very soon.

There are around two thousand **bars** in San Francisco alone, varying from seedy late night dives to rooftop piano lounges with glittering views; include the Bay Area and the figures become dizzying. Though spread fairly evenly over the city, they are particularly numerous in North Beach, the Haight, SoMa and Mission, with the former, where they literally line up one after the other, being your best bet for serious bar-hopping.

On the whole, most bars are rough-hewn, informal affairs, pretty true to the image of long dimly lit counters, with a few punters perched on stools before a bartender-cum-guru, and tables and booths for those who don't want to join in the drunken bar-side debates. There are however plenty of slicker places in the downtown area and Financial District.

To **buy and consume alcohol** on the West Coast, you have to be at least 21 years old, and you could well be asked for ID even if you look much older. **Licensing laws** are, however, among the most liberal in the country (though laws on drinking and driving are not): alcohol can be bought and drunk any time between 6am and 2am, seven days a week; this is surplus to the requirements of most but handy for travellers who keep strange hours.

Most bars open mid-morning and close around 2am, with after-hours drinking (once a standard feature of the small neighborhood bar) becoming increasingly uncommon.

In addition to the personal favorites that follow, you should also look at the listings in Chapter Fifteen, which include many good spots for a drink before things hot up later in the evening.

Downtown

The Big Four
Huntington Hotel, 1075 California St. Classy hotel bar, aimed squarely at the middle-aged set who want a good cocktail in civilized surroundings.

Bars and Cafés

For a map of downtown bars, cafés and restaurants see p.212.

Good spots to enjoy afternoon tea downtown are listed on p.217.

San Francisco Beer

Much American **beer** may be fizzy and tasteless, but the brews concocted by the San Francisco-based *Anchor Brewery* are well worth sampling. The tasty, medium-bodied *Anchor Steam* beer and the richer-flavored, creamy *Liberty Ale* are both available by the bottle in most bars and cafés, and on draught at better establishments. The widely available *Sierra Nevada Ale* is also tasty, as are the products of the dozens of small microbreweries popping up all over the West Coast; any good bar or liquor store should stock a range. Another recent development are the so-called **"brewpubs"**, serving a range of generally good beers brewed on the premises.

Expect to pay $2 for a small glass (just over half a pint) or around $3.50 a pint for draught beer, $2–3 for a bottle of imported beer.

Carnelian Room
555 California St.
The best of the rooftop cocktail lounges, 52 floors up in the Bank of America Building. A truly elegant spot for some smart cocktails; bring smart money.

Champagne Exchange
In *Nordstrom's*, 4th Floor, San Francisco Center, Fifth and Market.
Take a break from your shopping to quaff a bottle of bubbly, looking out over the Powell Street cable car turnaround. Besides the champers (5 types by the glass, plus another 30 by the bottle) they've got an assortment of ice-cold vodkas from around the world at $3.50 a shot.

Corona Bar and Grill
88 Cyril Magnin St.
Just off Market and Powell, this huge Mexican place has suitably huge margaritas which you can down at the 100-foot cherrywood bar. Tapas-like snacks and full meals also available.

Equinox
Hyatt Regency, The Embarcadero.
Good for the novelty value only, this rooftop cocktail lounge attracts crowds of tourists who ascend its dizzy spires just to look at the views. The whole thing revolves, so you get a 360° view of the city without ever leaving your seat. Serious drinkers wouldn't be caught dead in here – have a drink, revolve and leave.

Gordon Biersch Brewery
2 Harrison St.
Bayfront microbrewery housed in converted Hills Brothers coffee warehouse. Good bar food and some of the best beers in San Francisco bring out downtown's overpaid twenty-somethings.

Harry Denton's
161 Steuart St.
For the after-work Financial District crowd, this is San Francisco's prime place to cruise and be cruised. Fortunately, the fully stocked bar has enough rare bourbons and West Coast microbrews to make whiling away an evening very pleasant indeed, even if you're not on the prowl. Great interior.

Johnny Love's
1500 Broadway at Polk.
Straight pick-up scene on an industrial scale. Hormone-driven Young Republicans line up around the block nightly to get a piece of the action.

Li Po's Bar
916 Grant Ave.
Named after the Chinese poet, *Li Po's* is something of a literary hang-out among the Chinatown regulars. Enter through the false cavern front and sit at the very dimly lit bar where Wayne Wang filmed *Chang is Missing*.

The London Wine Bar
415 Sansome St.
Dubiously tagged as "America's first wine bar", this place is a suitably pretentious and expensive locale for the Financial District clones that flock here after work.

The Redwood Room
Clift Hotel, 495 Geary St.
Gorgeous redwood-panelled Art-Deco lounge, dulled only slightly by the wealthy geriatric hotel guests who frequent it.

The Starlight Roof
Top floor of the *Sir Francis Drake Hotel*,
450 Powell St.
Totally tacky, the *Starlight* is nonetheless
an experience worth seeking out.
Panoramic views of the city and free food
at happy hour make it a must for misers.

Tonga Room
Fairmont Hotel, Powell and Mason streets.
Outrageously lavish Polynesian theme bar
with waitresses in grass skirts, a native-
laden raft floating around the room, and
expensive cocktails. Fun if you like the
joke and are in the mood for camp
hilarity.

Top of the Mark
Mark Hopkins Hotel, California St at
Mason.
The most famous of the rooftop bars, its
reputation surpasses the actual experience of drinking up here, and generally it
only attracts tourists and hotel guests
who can't be bothered to find anywhere
else.

North Beach and the Northern Waterfront

Balboa Café
3199 Fillmore St.
A favorite with the young, upmarket
singles of the Marina. Very good food,
too.

Bohemian Cigar Store
566 Columbus Ave.
Small, informal North Beach hang-out for
sipping coffee or slinging beers.

Buena Vista Café
2765 Hyde St., Fisherman's Wharf.
If you like your coffee with a kick, this is
the place for you. Claims to be the home
of the world's first Irish coffee, which is
hard to believe, but who cares – it's
certainly the best in town and the crowds
who pack the place are testimony to the
generously laced coffee. Good, inexpensive food too, making it a decent stop-off
for a sightseeing lunch.

Café Francisco
2161 Powell St.
North Beach home of the ponderous
coffee drinker.

Café Roma
414 Columbus Ave.
Not big on atmosphere, but a quiet spot
to read the paper over a coffee, while
checking out the classical, cherub-
adorned murals and ornate decor.

Café Trieste
609 Vallejo St.
Noisy North Beach Italian café, popular
with a serious literary crowd who hang
out and listen to the opera classics which
boom from the jukebox. Saturday
lunchtimes are a treat – the family who
run it get up and sing. Get there by noon
if you want a seat.

Chestnut Street Grill
2331 Chestnut St.
A neighborhood bar and grill that is a fine
place for a well-made cocktail before
dinner.

Curtain Call
1980 Union St.
Quiet, relaxed piano bar. Not the sort of
place for rowdy partying.

Eagle Café
Pier 39, Fisherman's Wharf.
Cheap diner by day and venue for drinks
and free live music at night, this place
survives remarkably untarnished amid all
the waterfront tat at the Wharf.

Enrico's Sidewalk Café
504 Broadway.
Busy little place for listening to jazz and
having your milkshake spiked with the
liquor of your choice.

Harry's
2020 Fillmore St.
A bona fide saloon, this elegantly
decorated hang-out serves a mixed,
unpretentious crowd and makes for a
great night's drinking.

Moose's
1652 Stockton St.
North Beach's most recent addition,
Moose's is yet another upscale,
beautifully designed hang-out for the
glamorous and powerful. Although it's
ostensibly a restaurant, save yourself
money and just check out the bar scene
which features nightly jazz. See and be
seen.

Bars and Cafés

*The map on
p.215 shows the
locations of
many of the
North Beach
bars and cafés
listed here.*

Bars and Cafés

Pacific Heights Bar and Grill
Fillmore and Pine.
Overstuffed chairs make this the city's most comfortable bar, and it also has a good range of bar food, including fresh-shucked oysters.

Perry's
1944 Union St.
Sophisticated meat market, featured in Armistead Maupin's *Tales of the City* as the quintessential breeder bar.

The Saloon
1232 Grant Ave.
This bar has stood for over a hundred years and seen use as a whorehouse and Prohibition speakeasy. Today the old structure creaks nightly as blues bands and crowds of enthusiastic dancers do their thing.

San Francisco Brewing Co
155 Columbus Ave.
A must for beer fans who tire quickly of the insipid American variety, this North Beach hang-out makes its own full-flavored brews on the premises.

Savoy Tivoli
1434 Grant Ave.
Without a doubt, this place is North Beach's most attractively decorated and populated bar, also serving good, reasonably priced food – although the emphasis is definitely on liquid enjoyment.

Spec's
12 Adler St.
Long-standing North Beach bar where a jocular drinking crowd enjoys cocktail shakers full of martini for just $5. Particularly handy for women drinking alone: the barman will hand a card which reads "Sir, the lady is not interested in your company" to anyone who hassles you. A most civilized place to get ploughed.

Tosca's
242 Columbus Ave.
The theme here is opera, in time-worn but still stylish surroundings. Mingle with media people at the bar or slump into a comfy red leather booth – and pay through the nose for a drink.

Vesuvio's
255 Columbus Ave.
Legendary North Beach Beat haunt in the 1950s and still catering to an arty but friendly crowd who prop up the bar into the small hours. Situated next to *City Lights Bookstore*, it's a good place to peruse your new purchases over a drink.

Washington Square Bar & Grill
1707 Powell St.
Primarily a restaurant, but worth checking out for the great bar and the chance to spy on the media and literary crowd who have made this their second home. Some of the thunder has been stolen by *Moose's* across the square, but the regulars still flock here.

Civic Center, SoMa and Mission

Bouncer's Bar
64 Townsend St.
Old waterfront hang-out, with free live music and an earthy crowd (to put it mildly). Not for the easily intimidated.

Brainwash
1122 Folsom St.
Great idea – a café/bar and laundromat where you can have breakfast or a beer while you do your washing. Needless to say it's popular with the young and novelty-conscious.

Bull's Texas Café
25 Van Ness Ave.
Tacky Tex-Mex bar-cum-restaurant, but a great place to wolf down the free food at happy hour with your bucket of cheap frozen Margarita.

Café La Boheme
3138 24th St.
As the name suggests, a badly dressed crowd, but a staggering range of coffees keeps the Mission's caffeine addicts coming from sunup until late at night.

Café Picaro
3120 16th St.
Very popular, no-frills spot where you can get cheap lunches and browse through the hundreds of books that line the walls. Opposite the *Roxie* movie theater in the Mission.

The Chatterbox
853 Valencia St.
Mainly a night spot but good for drinking with the goth and leather mobs anytime.

The Dovre Club
3541 18th St.
Solid Irish bar, full of Gaelic charmers.

El Rio
3158 Mission St.
When it isn't staging one of its specials (samba on Sun, comedy on Wed and free oysters on the half shell and dancing on Fri), this is a great place for a quiet drink and a game on one of San Francisco's most handsome pool tables.

Julie's Supper Club
1123 Folsom St.
A popular restaurant, but best for sitting at the bar munching good-value Cajun snacks and listening to the free live jazz.

Max's Opera Café
Opera Plaza, Van Ness Ave.
Slightly sterile atmosphere, but very interesting people-watching when the dinner-suited opera, ballet and symphony fans pop in for a quick one before and after performances at the Civic Center venues.

Mission Rock Resort
817 China Basin. Scruffy, blue-collar bar down the old dockyards, great for a cheap beer and views of the bay.

Molloy's
1599 Howard St.
Favored by construction workers over fifty and the habitual drunk. The toughest of all the bars down this way.

Paradise Lounge
1501 Folsom St.
Cleverly constructed on two floors, you can suit your mood with a game of pool and a quiet drink upstairs or dance to live music downstairs.

The Ramp
855 China Basin.
Way out on the old docks, this is well worth the half-mile trek from downtown (you'll need a car unless you're a seasoned walker) to sit out on the patio and sip beers overlooking the abandoned piers and new boatyards. Free jazz on Sun afternoons.

Rockin Robin's
133 Beale St.
Fifties rock'n'roll music and lots of boys in leather. Good fun if you can stand to hear that much Elvis in one evening. Mon–Fri only.

South Park Café
108 South Park.
Chic SoMa rendezvous, where architects and other creative professionals meet their peers to drink in tasteful surroundings.

The Up & Down Club
1151 Folsom St.
Fast becoming the city's best jazz venue, this small club split across two floors serves great drinks and attracts a lively attractive crowd out for a good time.

The Uptown
200 Capp St.
Best of the Mission's neighborhood bars, embracing an eclectic clientele who shoot pool, drink like fiends and fall all over the scruffy leatherette upholstery. Some simply go to watch the ball game on TV . A more bizarre collection of characters would be hard to find. Don't miss it.

Zeitgeist
199 Valencia St.
A favorite in the Mission for bikers and those who like to dress in black. Comfortably scruffy.

The Central Neighborhoods

Achilles Heel
1601 Haight St.
Attractive, Victorian-style English pub in the Haight. Respectable, clean and quiet.

Café du Nord
2170 Market St.
A quiet neighborhood restaurant for years, this has recently become hyper-hip since it started its programme of nightly cabaret and jazz on Wed, reviving the old tradition of supper clubs. Quite the place for dinner and drinks, though it's OK just to have a beer at the bar if the budget won't stretch.

Bars and Cafés

For a map of SoMa bars, and cafés, see p.219.

Bars and cafés in the Mission and Castro districts are shown on the map on p.220.

Bars and Cafés

Clubs in the Castro are listed on p.247

Café Flor
2298 Market St.
Lively, mostly gay café near the Castro serving great breakfasts and lunch till 3pm. A popular cruising spot for the locals who come to string a coffee out for hours and be seen reading the latest in hip gay literature. Drown in a sea of newspapers and pretty faces.

Casa Loma Hotel
600 Fillmore St.
Very neighborly hang-out for a well-behaved young crowd. A must for the Lower Haight bar-hopping schedule.

Community Blend Café
233 Fillmore St.
Enjoy an excellent breakfast (served all day) or glass of wine in the contrived shabbiness of this Lower Haight gallery-cum-café, where groovy people come to write in their journals.

The Deluxe
1511 Haight St.
Formerly a hang-out for older gays, the *Deluxe* is now gaining a well-earned reputation as one of the better pool halls in town.

The First Inning Lounge
4026 24th St.
Home of the sports fan and rabble rouser, with a great jukebox.

The Gold Cane
1569 Haight St.
Beer for $1 and shots for $1.50 in what is admittedly a hang-out for senior citizens who have made a career out of drinking.

Ground Zero
783 Haight St.
Regular exhibits by local artists adorn the surreal walls of this Lower Haight café – worth the trip to check out the decor if not the menu.

Jack's Bailey Bar
26th and Church St.
Comfy neighborhood bar with proper armchairs, where you can really recline into a pint.

Jimmy's West Point
669 Haight St.
The joint is jumping most nights at this black neighborhood bar, where Philly soul and Motown blare out relentlessly from the jukebox. Sleazed to perfection in 1970s vinyl upholstery, this is perfect for one last shot before you stagger home.

The Mad Dog in the Fog
530 Haight St.
Aptly named by the two lads from Birmingham, England who own the joint, this is one of the Lower Haight's most loyally patronized bars with darts, English beer, copies of *The Sun* and a typical pub menu that includes bangers and mash, hearty ploughman's and the like. Amazingly, it is not the English, but the trend-conscious young blades of the Lower Haight who find it so groovy.

Noc Noc
557 Haight St.
Decorated like an Egyptian tomb. Draws a fashionable but informal young crowd in for new wave music and flasks of hot sake.

Noe's 1199 Church St.
Blue-collar sports bar; come here to catch a game on the giant video screen and have a jeer and cheer with the locals who can't take their eyes off it.

Orbit Room
Market St at Laguna.
The interior design is straight out of *Bladerunner*, and cyberpunk crowds flock here for the good coffees, great beers and ice-cold Blackthorn cider.

The Rat and the Raven
4054 24th St.
Friendly, hard-drinking neighborhood bar with pool, darts, and if you're into country music, a superb jukebox.

Toronado
547 Haight St.
With over twenty varieties on tap, this is definitely a beer drinker's haven. Mostly male, the crowd smacks of a leather-bound rugby reunion dinner.

Tropical Haight
582 Haight St.
Best decorated bar in the district; the theme is tropical, the crowd most definitely are not. Impromptu performances on Tuesdays provide the biggest laugh you're likely to have.

Golden Gate Park, the Beaches and Outlying Areas

Blue Danube Café
306 Clement St.
Café society alive and well in the suburbs? Not quite, but about as alternative as you'll get in the Richmond.

Boathouse
1 Harding Blvd (on Lake Merced).
Popular sports bar, with a superb view of Lake Merced and occasional live music.

Last Day Saloon
406 Clement St.
Very lively bar in the Richmond with regular blues and soul acts; often no cover.

Pig & Whistle Pub
2801 Geary Blvd.
Good range of English and California microbrews, and the cheapest happy hour in SF – $2 pints of beer 4–7pm daily. Pool table and dartboards, plus very good pub food.

The Plough and Stars
116 Clement St.
Irish ex-pat bar with live music on alternate evenings.

The East Bay

Brennan's
Fourth St and University Ave, Berkeley.
☎510/841-0960.
Solidly blue-collar hang-out that's a great place for drinking inexpensive beers, watching a game on TV, or simply waiting for a train – *Amtrak* stops right outside.

Café Mediterraneum
2475 Telegraph Ave, Berkeley.
☎510/841-5634.
Berkeley's oldest café, straight out of the Beat archives: beards and berets optional, battered paperbacks *de rigeur*.

Café Milano
2522 Bancroft Way, Berkeley.
☎510/644-3100.
Airy, artsy café across from UC Berkeley.

Café Strada
2300 College Ave, Berkeley.
☎510/843-5282.
Upmarket, open-air café where art and architecture students cross paths with would-be lawyers and chess wizards.

Coffee Mill
3393 Grand Ave, Oakland.
☎510/465-4224.
Spacious room that doubles as an art gallery, and often hosts poetry readings.

Heinhold's First and Last Chance Saloon
56 Jack London Square, Oakland.
☎510/839-6761.
Authentic waterfront bar that's hardly changed since the turn of the century, when Jack London himself drank here.

The Kingfish
5227 Claremont Ave, Oakland.
☎510/655-7373.
Less a bar than a tumbledown shed, selling low-priced pitchers of cold beer to UC Berkeley rugby players and other headbangers.

Peet's Coffee
2124 Vine St, Berkeley. ☎510/841-0564.
Many other East Bay branches, including 2916 Domingo (☎510/843-1434) across from the *Claremont Hotel,* and 1825 Solano Ave in North Berkeley (☎510/526-9607).

Mostly for take-home brewers, the shop in Berkeley's Gourmet Ghetto is the original of what's now a Bay Area-wide chain. Massive cups of the world's best coffee cost under $1, and they've also got a great range of fresh-brewed tea.

Raleigh's
2438 Telegraph Ave, Berkeley.
☎510/848-8652.
Very popular studenty pub with wide range of West Coast microbrewed beers.

Starry Plough
3103 Shattuck Ave, Berkeley.
☎510/841-2082.
Very comfortable, politically charged Irish bar with Guinness on draft, Powers Whiskey on call and sporadic collections for the IRA. Very near Ashby *BART,* with live music most nights.

Bars and Cafés

East Bay restaurants are reviewed on p.225

Bars and Cafés

White Horse Inn

6560 Telegraph Ave at 66th St, Oakland.
☎510/652-3820.
Large, friendly mixed bar – it was one of
the first Bay Area bars openly to welcome
lesbians and gay men – with good drinks,
dancing and a pool table.

The Peninsula

Abigail's Pub

265 N First St, San Jose. ☎408/294-4111.
Ersatz English pub catering to beer-
drinking computer wizards.

Gordon Biersch Brewery

640 Emerson St, Palo Alto. ☎323-7723.
Also in SF (see p.232) and in downtown
San Jose at 33 E San Fernando St (☎408/
294-6785).
Among the first and still the best of the
Bay Area's microbrewery-cum-restaurants.

Pudley's Saloon

255 University Ave, Palo Alto.
☎328-2021.
1940s-style retro-American beer-and-
burger bar.

Marin County

Book Depot and Café

87 Throckmorton Ave, Mill Valley.
☎383-2665.
Lively café in an old train station, which it
shares with a bookstore and newsstand.

Café Trieste

1000 Bridgeway, Sausalito. ☎332-7770.
This distant relative of the North Beach
institution (see p.233) serves good coffee,
a wide menu of pastas and salads, and
great gelati.

Caffe Nuvo

556 San Anselmo Ave, San Anselmo.
☎454-4530.
Great coffee and pastries, with a large
balcony overhanging a creek, plus poetry
readings and live music most nights

Marin Brewing Company

1809 Larkspur Landing, Larkspur.
☎461-4677.
Lively pub opposite the Larkspur ferry
terminal, with half a dozen tasty ales – try
the malty Albion Amber or the creamy St
Brendan's Irish Red – all brewed on site.

Mill Valley Coffee Roasters

2 Miller Ave, Mill Valley. ☎383-2912.
Boisterous, always crowded coffee house
right in the center of town.

no name bar

757 Bridgeway, Sausalito. ☎332-1392.
A thriving ex-haunt of the Beats which
still hosts poetry readings and evening
jam sessions.

Patrick's Bookshop and Café

9 Bolinas Rd, Fairfax. ☎454-2428.
Coffees, teas, tasty soups and sandwiches,
in this low-key hippie holdout; good selection of books and mags, too.

Pelican Inn

Hwy-1, Muir Beach. ☎383-6000.
Fair selection of traditional English and
modern Californian ales, plus fish'n'chips
(and rooms if you overdo it).

Sam's Anchor Café

27 Main St, Tiburon. ☎435-2676.
Slightly posey hang-out for Marin's yacht-
club brigades. Right on the water, it's
packed on weekends – when you can
still get a drink or two (or brunch; see
p.229 for more info) while waiting for the
ferry back to SF.

Sweetwater

153 Throckmorton Ave, Mill Valley.
☎388-3820.
Large open room full of beer-drinking
locals that after dark evolves into Marin's
prime live music venue (see p.000).

Wine Country

Ana's Cantina

1205 Main St, St Helena. ☎963-4921.
Long-standing unpretentious saloon and
Mexican restaurant.

Joe Frogger's

527 Fourth Ave, Santa Rosa.
☎707/526-0539.
Lively bar with free live music most
nights.

Sonoma Saloon

110 W Spain St, Sonoma.
☎707/996-2996.
Funky old saloon that's a hundred years
old and still going strong; the adjoining
dining room focuses on local cheeses
and baked goods.

Wine Exchange of Sonoma
452 E First St, Sonoma.
☎707/938-1794.
Right on Sonoma's main plaza, with an extensive range of California wines by the glass and by the bottle, this handy shop saves you having to tramp around dozens of far-flung wineries.

Gay and Lesbian Bars

San Francisco's gay bars are many and varied, though in the last few years every single lesbian bar (never more than a couple anyway) has disappeared. If you want exclusively female company you'll have to check the *Nightlife* section for lists of clubs that have lesbian nights, or venture over to the East Bay, which has traditionally catered rather better to gay women. Bear in mind, however, that the increasingly integrated nature of the gay scene means that formerly exclusively male bars now have a sizeable lesbian contingent.

Options for the boys are as lively as ever though, and though the scene is not quite as wild as it was at its zenith in the 1970s, you can still find establishments that range from the cozy cocktail bar to full no-holds-barred leather and chain affairs. It's hard to imagine a city that could rival San Francisco for gay entertainment.

The Castro, traditional home of the gay bar, has matured in recent years and you'll need to visit **SoMa** or **Polk Street** – or to a lesser extent the **Mission** – for anything outside the mainstream. Take note that places we've listed as bars may switch on some music later on and transform into a club; we've listed the better ones that do this in the following chapter, *Nightlife*.

Finally, remember that the vast majority of places welcome straight customers too (if only for their own amusement), especially in the Castro, and if you can't decide where to head for just ask: gays in San Francisco are on the whole a friendly and communicative lot and will normally be glad to point you to the kind of thing you're looking for. There's no shortage of printed matter to give you ideas either:

check out *The Sentinel, Bay Times* and *Bay Area Reporter*. Alternatively, if you don't mind forking out the $7 for a copy, a must-have for every visiting gay with a sense of humor is *Betty & Pansy's Severe Queer Review*, listing everything from the best place to eat upscale food to the best cruising alleys.

The Bear
440 Castro St.
Friendly neighborhood bar that draws a chatty, non-cruisy crowd – nice patio out back.

Black Rose
335 Jones St.
Raunchy Tenderloin bar popular with transvestites and transexuals. Good cabarets.

Café Flor
2298 Market St.
Very much the in spot before dark. Attractive café, with matching clientele and leafy outdoor area, and no shortage of people eyeing each other up. Very mixed, lots of women.

Café San Marcos
2367 Market St.
A Castro institution always referred to as "The café", this place has gone from being a gay bar to a lesbian bar and is now mixed with a little more emphasis on women. Restaurant downstairs and bar and pool tables upstairs. Bit of a couples' place, though it gets cruisier at weekends.

The Castro Station
456 Castro St.
Noisy disco bar that manages to pack 'em in even in the middle of the day. Very much the die-hard scene of the 1970's, with a fair number in their leather trousers.

The Cinch
1723 Polk St.
Rowdy bar with pool tables and a rough-ish crowd.

The Corral
2140 Market St.
Country and western bar with large dance floor and a cheerful crowd. Dolly Parton fans alight here.

Bars and Cafés

Castro bars are shown on the map on p.220

Bars and Cafés

Deluxe
1151 Haight St.
Large comfy bar with pool tables and a slightly older gay crowd, but getting a reputation as a good pool hall and drawing an increasingly mixed crowd.

The Eagle
12th and Harrison St.
Easily the best known leather bar in San Francisco. Large outdoor area with stage. Best time for a visit is for the $8 Sunday brunch.

Elephant Walk
500 Castro St.
Recently reopened after a devastating fire, it has lost none of its former glory, serving light lunches and snacks by day and civilized cocktails by night.

El Rio
3158 Mission St.
Mixed crowds gather for cabaret on Wednesdays, but on most nights this is an exclusively gay bar popular with Hispanics from the local Mission district. Live Samba on a Sunday afternoon draws a mostly female gay crowd.

Empress Lily
4 Valencia at Market.
Formerly an old, little-frequented drive known as the *Travel Lounge*, this bar has had a big revival of its fortunes since the gay community got hold of it and turned it into one of the liveliest venues for drag shows for miles. Draws a good, mixed crowd.

La India Bonita
3089 16th St.
Family-run, lighthearted drag-queen bar. Mostly for Hispanics; there were no English speakers at the last visit. Highly recommended.

Midnight Sun
4067 18th St.
Young, white boys dressed to the nines and cruising like maniacs in this noisy Castro video bar.

The Mint
1942 Market St.
Relaxed piano bar with occasional acts and mellow crowd. Nice, civilized middle-aged, well-dressed, well-behaved scene.

Moby Dick
4049 18th St.
Cruisy black men and their admirers. Pool tables and TV screens for the shy.

The Phoenix
482 Castro St.
The Castro's only dance bar, it not surprisingly draws a large, exuberant crowd.

Rawhide
280 Seventh St.
If men in chaps are your scene, go no further than this dimly lit SoMa landmark that plays country and western and bluegrass music to a jovial mixed crowd. Definitely recommended.

The Stud
399 Ninth St.
A favorite dancing spot with a mixed but mostly gay crowd. No cover charge and some raucous times and shameless freaking out on the dancefloor. A San Francisco institution, highly recommended.

Twin Peaks
17th and Castro St.
The Castro's first blatantly gay bar, with large see-through windows to make the point. Draws a low-key older crowd who gather for quiet drinks and conversation.

Uncle Bert's Place
4086 18th St.
Lives up to its name – a cozy neighborhood bar.

Chapter 15

Nightlife

Compared to New York or Los Angeles, where you need money and attitude in equal amounts, San Francisco's nightlife demands little of either.

This is no 24-hour city, and the approach to socializing is often surprisingly low-key, with little of the pandering to fads and fashions that goes on elsewhere. The casualness is contagious, and manifest in a **club scene** that – far as it is from the cutting edge of hip – is encouragingly inexpensive compared to other cities. Thirty dollars can buy you a decent night out, including cover charge, a few drinks and maybe even a taxi home.

The **live music** scene is similarly economical – and, frankly, what the city does best: San Franciscans may be relatively unconcerned with fashion, but there are some excellent rock, jazz or folk venues all over town, many entertaining you for no more than the price of a drink.

San Francisco has a somewhat better reputation for **opera** and **classical music**. Its orchestra and opera association are among the most highly regarded in the country. **Theater** is more accessible and much less costly, with discount tickets available, but most of the mainstream downtown venues – barring a couple of exceptions – are mediocre, forever staging Broadway reruns, and you'd do better to take some time to explore the infinitely more interesting fringe circuit.

Cabaret and comedy are also lively: some excellent clubs host an increasingly healthy and varied diet of good comedians. **Film**, too, is almost as big an obsession as eating in San Francisco, and you may well be surprised by the sheer number of movie theaters – repertory and current release – that flourish in the small city.

Live Music: Rock, Jazz and Folk

San Francisco's **music scene** reflects the character of the city as a whole: laid-back, eclectic, and not a little nostalgic. The options for catching **live**

Listings and Ticket Information

Apart from the flyers posted up around town, the *Sunday Chronicle*'s "Pink Pages" supplement is about the best source of **listings and what's on information**; you might also check the free weekly *Bay Guardian*, the *San Francisco Weekly*, and a host of other more specific publications listed below under the relevant sections.

For **tickets**, *BASS* (☎ 776-1999 or 510/762-2277), the *Bay Area Seating Service*, is the major Bay Area booking agency. You can either reserve with a credit card on these numbers, or in person at one of their many branches in record stores such as *Tower Records* or *Wherehouse*. **Theater tickets** are also on sale at the *Tix* ticket booth on Union Square; see "Theater" below for details.

Nightlife

music are wide and the scene is consistently progressive, charcterized by the frequent emergence of good young bands.

However, San Francisco has never recaptured its crucial Sixties role, and these days is principally renowned as a venue for good R&B, psychedelia, folk and rock standards, as well as country and western and Latin American bands. **Jazz** is also very good and not just confined to the city proper: the East Bay in particular is very strong on jazz/funk/blues bands.

Live bands are extremely easy to catch. As well as the big names, for whom the Bay Area is an essential stop on nationwide tours, many restaurants offer live music, so you can eat, drink and dance all at once and often with no cover charge; ordinary neighborhood bars regularly host groups, often for free; and there are any number of good and inexpensive small venues.

Although clubs tend to be concentrated in the South of Market area, live music venues are spread out across the city. Few fall into any particular camp, with most varying their bill throughout the week, and it can be hard to specify which of them cater to a certain music style. Many also double as clubs, hosting some kind of disco after the live music has stopped.

What follows is a pretty comprehensive list of established venues, but be sure to check the music press, the best of which is the free *BAM* (*Bay Area Music*). Available in most record stores, it carries exhaustive listings of events in the city and Bay Area as a whole.

The Large Performance Venues

The easiest way to book seats for the following venues is through *BASS*, either with a major credit card several weeks in advance, or at one of their record store branches; either way you'll have to pay a service charge of around $3. Bear in mind that some of the Bay Area's best large-scale venues, where the big names tend to play, are actually across the bay in Oakland and Berkeley.

Great American Music Hall
859 O'Farrell St.
☎885-0750.
Civic Center venue, too small for major names but too large for local yokels, and hosting a range of musical styles from balladeers to thrash bands. The lovely interior – it used to be a burlesque house and upscale bordello – makes for a great night out.

Oakland Coliseum Complex
Coliseum *BART*, near Oakland Airport.
☎510/639-7700.
Stadium rock – inside the 17,000 seat Arena, or outside in the 60,000 seat Coliseum.

The Warfield
982 Market St. ☎775-7722.
The Warfield can usually be relied upon to stage major rock crowd-pullers. Chart bands, big-name indie groups and popular old-timers keep the place packed.

Zellerbach Hall
UC Berkeley.
☎510/642-9988.
Together with the outdoor Greek Theater, two of the prime spots for catching touring big names in the Bay Area.

Rock, Folk and Country

Albion
3139 16th St. ☎552-8558.
Primarily just a Mission neighborhood bar, which occasionally hosts local bands on its tiny stage. Small, inexpensive and intimate, it's ideal for a night out on the cheap. No cover.

Babylon
2260 Van Ness. ☎567-1222.
Although this attractive Russian Hill, tomb-like venue is ostensibly for eating, most of the randy young singles are there to down cocktails and attract attention by dancing vigorously.

Bouncers Bar
64 Townsend St. ☎397-2480.
Hardcore drinkers' bar that stages obscure country, blues and R&B bands. Near the SoMa waterfront, this was originally a rowdy sailors' hang-out.; the sailors may be gone, but the rowdiness lives on.

Kennel Club
628 Divisadero St. ☎ 931-1914.
Mostly used as a one-off club venue, the
Kennel sometimes hosts live rock/blues,
appropriate to the roomy interior and
enormous circular bar.

Last Day Saloon
406 Clement St. ☎ 387-6343.
A bit out of the way, but if you find yourself in the Richmond and you're wonder-
ing where to find some action, this is the
best the area has to offer. Mostly soul,
blues and R&B. Cover $3–6.

Lost and Found Saloon
1353 Grant St. ☎ 397-3751.
Informal North Beach hang-out with a
catch-all selection of music styles.

Lou's
300 Jefferson St. ☎ 771-0377.
Country/rock and blues bar down on
Fisherman's Wharf that hosts some good
local bands. Weekend lunchtimes are a
good time to check out the lesser-
knowns in relative peace. Come nightfall
it's madness. No cover before 9pm.

Nightbreak
1821 Haight St. ☎ 221-9008.
Slightly shabby, small Haight venue
where new wave and goth bands play to
a matching crowd. Very dark, very loud,
and very crowded.

Olive Oyl's Bar & Grill
295 China Basin. ☎ 495-3099.
Great waterfront venue down at the old
SoMa docks. A fine spot for a good steak,
strong drink and a variety of nightly music
styles. Informal, comfortable and free.

Paradise Lounge
1501 Folsom St at 11th St. ☎ 861-6906.
Good SoMa venue to see up-and-coming
rock bands (usually three per night), or
take a break for a game of pool upstairs.
On Tuesday nights, don't miss the
Fabulous Bud E Love performing his inimi-
table Las Vegas lounge act. Cover varies
from free to $10; 21 and over only.

The Plough and Stars
116 Clement St. ☎ 751-1122.
Quite a way from downtown but worth
the trip if you're into Irish folk music. Very
much the haunt of the Irish ex-pat
community.

Saloon
1232 Grant St. ☎ 397-3751.
Always packed to the gills, this is
undeniably North Beach's best spot for
some rowdy R&B.

Slim's
333 11th St. ☎ 621-3330.
Slick but reliable showcase for mid-range
rock and R&B. Expensive by SF standards,
but often hosting internationally known
bands.

Sweetwater
153 Throckmorton Ave, Mill Valley.
☎ 388-3820.
Well worth a trip north of Marin, this
comfortable saloon brings in some of the
biggest names in music, from jazz and
blues all-stars to Jefferson Airplane
survivors.

Jazz and Latin American

Bahia Tropical
1600 Market St. ☎ 861-8657.
High-energy hang-out and supper club
with good Brazilian and samba bands –
attracts a skilled dancing crowd who can
shake it with a vengeance. 21 and over
only.

Bajone's
3140 Mission St. ☎ 648-6641.
Unusual – and refreshing – age-mix for
San Francisco, ranging from 25 to 65.
Excellent Latin jazz nightly. Casual,
unpretentious and genuine. $6 cover at
weekends.

Café du Nord
2170 Market St. ☎ 861-5016.
Excellent, friendly and affordable
venue to catch nightly live music
while you sample the food on offer
or just drink at the bar. Mostly jazz with
some mambo and salsa thrown in.
Recommended.

The Compass Rose
Lobby of the *St Francis Hotel*, Union
Square. ☎ 397-7000.
With the promise of a string quartet at
cocktail hour and a jazz trio in the
evenings, this is quite the place to sit in
deluxe surroundings and sip expensive
drinks.

Nightlife

*Many of the
clubs listed here
are shown on
the district
maps in our
Restaurants
chapter.*

Nightlife

Gold Dust Saloon
247 Powell St. ☎397-1697.
So close to Union Square it's a bit of a
tourist hang-out, but good for a sing-song
and old-time Dixieland jazz. No cover.

Jack's
1601 Fillmore St. ☎567-3227.
Small, intimate bar with jazz and blues
seven nights a week.

Kimball's
300 Grove St. ☎861-5585.
Slick establishment jazz-club-cum-
restaurant with a clientele bordering on
middle age. Luckily, you don't have to eat,
which is handy as the cover tends to be
high. Open daily until 3am.

Kimball's East
4800 Shellmound, Emeryville.
☎510/658-2555.
Very comfortable, intimate room hosting
some of the world's best jazz and blues
performers. Cover $15-20.

Miss Pearl's Jam House
601 Eddy St. ☎775-JAMS.
Attached to the super-hip *Phoenix* motel
– see p.220 – this Caribbean restaurant
features some great reggae.

Pasand Lounge
1875 Union St. ☎922-4498.
Unusual club where you can come to eat
Indian food and listen to very mellow jazz
in the comfortaable lounge.

Pearl's
256 Columbus Ave. ☎291-8255.
Cozy North Beach supper club, where you
enjoy jazz while sitting down with a good
meal. No cover, but you must eat or drink.

The Plush Room
York Hotel, 940 Sutter St. ☎885-2800.
Newly revived San Francisco institution,
which has successfully recreated its
former glory and on a good night attracts
a very glamorous crowd. Tickets around
$20; 21 and over only.

The Ramp
855 China Basin. ☎621-2378.
Informal bar and café, putting on live jazz
on the outside patio. Sunday lunch is a
definite live music fixture; mid-week
performances are not so regular, so you
should check the press for listings.

The Rite Spot Café
2099 Folsom St. ☎552-6066.
Informal, café-style club with jazz and
R&B bands. Open Mon–Sat, and serving
snacks, drinks and coffee until 1am. Small
cover at weekends.

The Tonga Room
Basement of the *Fairmont Hotel*, 950
Mason St. ☎772-5000.
An absolute must for fans of the ludicrous
or just the very drunk. The whole place is
decked out as a Polynesian village,
complete with pond and simulated rain-
storms, and a grass-skirted band play
terrible jazz and pop covers on a raft in
the middle of the water.

The Up & Down Club
1151 Folsom St. ☎626-2388.
San Francisco's newest and best addition
to the live music circuit. The *Up & Down*
is a small, comfortably styled bar full of
grown-up people enjoying top-notch jazz
and knocking back well-made drinks.

Clubbing

Still trading on a reputation earned
decades ago, San Francisco's **nightclubs**
in fact trail light years behind those of
other large American cities. That said, the
compensations are manifold – no waiting
for hours, or high cover charges, ridicu-
lously priced drinks and feverish posing.
Instead you'll find a diverse range of small
to medium-sized affordable clubs in which
leather-clad goths rub shoulders with the
bearded and beaded, alongside a number
of gay hang-outs still rocking to the
sounds of high-energy funk and Motown.

The greatest concentration of clubs is in
SoMa, especially the area around 11th
Street and Folsom, though the **Mission** is
similarly well provided with bars and small
live music venues – not to mention a
couple of outrageous drag bars – of
almost exclusively Latin origin.

Unlike most other cities, where the
action never gets going until after
midnight, many San Francisco **clubs** have
to close at 2am during the week, so you
can usually be sure of finding things well
under way by 11.30pm. At weekends,
most places stay open until 3 or 4am. San

Francisco isn't really big or club-orientated enough to sport a serious attitude towards weekend out-of-towners; in fact some places are more exciting at the weekend.

Very few venues operate any kind of restrictive admission policy, and only on very busy nights are you likely to have to wait. It's usually entirely acceptable to wander in and out of any club, so long as you have the regulation hand-stamp.

Note that many **gay clubs**, particularly those listed under "Mixed", are by no means no-go areas for straight people – indeed many rank among the city's best nightspots, whatever your sexuality.

Several places charge no **cover** at all and only the most chi-chi of clubs will charge a fortune for drinks. The entry age to most clubs, as with all bars, is 21, and it's a good idea to carry **ID** with you at all times: as a general rule, if you look under thirty you'll definitely need it.

The Clubs

Chatterbox
853 Valencia St. ☎821-1891.
Open daily until 2am for good no-nonsense rock'n'roll in a room resembling a pool hall. Mixed, beer-drinking biker crowd; cover around $5.

Covered Wagon Saloon
917 Folsom St. ☎974-5906.
Definitely one of the better SoMa places, especially on Thursday's *Love Shack* hi-tech psychedelic night, and on Saturday for hip-hop. Cover $4–6.

One excellent way to get the flavor of San Francisco's clubs when you first arrive is to experience the *Three Babes and a Bus* tour (☎552-2582) of various hot spots around town. For $30 the three women who organize the tours will drag you around on their bus for an evening visiting clubs and throwing in the odd drink. In between visits there is much carousing and game-playing on board; your companions are likely to be other gawky tourists, but you can always ditch them between rides

DNA Lounge
375 11th St. ☎626-1409.
Club which changes its music style nightly but draws the same young hipsters. Large dance floor downstairs and when the dancing gets too much you can lounge around in comfy sofas on the mezzanine. Cover $7. Tues–Sun 9pm–4am.

DV8
540 Howard St. ☎777-1419.
Huge, ornate and fashionable, this is the closest San Francisco comes to rivalling the big clubs of New York and Los Angeles, decorated by Keith Haring pop-art and playing high-energy funk and house music. It also has a nice members-only bar that's worth blagging your way into if you can. About the only club in town worth dressing up for. Cover $10. Wed–Sat.

El Rio
3158 Mission St. ☎282-3325.
Latin, jazz and samba are the specialty here, with live bands on Sunday, dancing to modern funk on Friday, and cabaret on Wednesday in a friendly, anything-goes atmosphere. Open 3pm–2am during the week, and 3pm–6am at weekends. No cover. See also "Comedy Clubs", p.250.

The End Up
Harrison and Sixth St. ☎495-9550.
A mostly gay crowd, but recently discovered by the weekend clubbers, and a good place for the hard-core party animal. Open continuously from 6am on Sat morning until 2am Mon. Small cover.

Holy Cow
1535 Folsom St. ☎621-6087.
Young club fiends trying hard to be cool, but a good rave once it warms up. A huge plastic cow hangs outside, you can't miss it. Usually no cover. Tues–Sun.

Kennel Club
628 Divisadero St. ☎931-9858.
Most popular on Thursday for the *Box* club, and, for the gay crowd, on Saturday. Friday is *Club Q* for women, and Sunday sees reggae and worldbeat music. Good fun, mixed crowd. Cover $6-10.

Nightlife

Many of the clubs listed here are shown on the district maps in our Restaurants chapter.

Nightlife

Klub Komotion
2779 16th St.
The latest rave joint; its one-nighters pull in a good cross section and set of styles.

The New Martini Empire
1015 Folsom St. ☎626-2899.
Club with an international bent where you'll be able to hear some of the more unconventional sounds of Brazilian, salsa, Arabic, African and soca. Cover $4. Fri–Sun.

Nightbreak
1821 Haight St. ☎221-9008.
Small Haight club that tags itself with the slogan "All the funk that's fit to pump". House, hip-hop and funk most nights, except for Wednesday when it becomes *Female Trouble*, lesbian dance night. Small cover at weekends.

The Palladium
1031 Kearny St. ☎434-1308.
Cavernous nightclub with three dance floors, flashing lights and disco – serious under-21 crowd. Cover $7. Thurs–Sun until 6am.

Paula's Clubhouse
3160 16th St. ☎621-1617.
Not to be missed, a bar/club with the broadest cross section of music styles and clientele that you're likely to find. Always energetic dancing – a definite party place. Relaxed, informal crowd and pool tables for those not into dancing. $3 cover at weekends.

Pierce Street Annex
3138 Fillmore St. ☎567-1400.
The archetypal singles hang-out, known as the "Bermuda Triangle" for its ability to make people disappear overnight with one another. DJs nightly, no cover.

Rock & Bowl
1855 Haight St. ☎752-2366.
Try this one for a change – a bowling alley that turns up the music at weekends so that you can dance while you bowl. Definitely good fun if you're in a group.

Townsend
177 Townsend St. ☎974-6020.
A must for house fans, this place really cranks up the bass and keeps it blaring. Thurs–Sat. Cover $5.

The Underground Club
201 Ninth St. ☎552-3466.
About the only place that you might have trouble getting into. It prides itself on its exclusivity, and there's a long line of well-dressed clubbers outside. Thurs–Sun, open until 8am Fri and Sat. $10 cover.

Gay and Lesbian Clubs
Many **gay and lesbian clubs** are bars that host various club nights at least once a week. Pleasingly unpretentious, the city's gay clubs rank among the city's best, and although a number are purely male affairs, with women-only discos few and far between, the majority welcome gay people of both sexes.

Bear in mind that there's a fine line between gay bars and **gay clubs**, and many gay bars convert to discos in the evening. Because all the lesbian bars seem to have disappeared, the women now usually share space with gay bars and host one-night affairs from various venues; check for details in the local press.

For gay men there is no better companion to exploring the penthouses and pavements of queer SF than *Betty & Pansy's Severe Queer Review*, which gives unashamedly explicit advice on getting the most out of your visit.

Mixed

The Box
At the *Kennel Club*, 628 Divisadero St. ☎931-9858.
Very popular dance club that plays a good selection of funk and house music. Currently the hot favorite for dance-serious men and women. Thurs & Sat.

Crystal Pistol
842 Valencia St. ☎695-7887.
One of the newer clubs and as such enjoying a very healthy patronage. Good dancing and a young, well-turned-out set make for a lively evening.

El Rio
3158 Mission St. ☎282-3325.
Mixed crowds gather for dancing to live samba on Sundays in the open-air court-yard, funk on Fridays and cabaret Wednesdays. Not to be missed. $4.

The End Up

Sixth St at Harrison. ☎495-9550.
Changes its bill weekly, but most nights
are gay or mixed, with girls-only dancing
on Saturdays and Sundays (see below).

Mainly for men

Esta Noche

3079 16th St. ☎861-5757.
Discomania Latin-style. Young men
and their pursuers dance to a high-
energy disco beat reminiscent of the
1970s.

La India Bonita

3089 16th St. ☎621-9294.
Family-run drag queen bar. Latin high-
jinks and revelry.

Lily's

4 Valencia at Market. ☎864-7028.
Bar with separate room for drag shows.
Draws a very mixed crowd.

My Place

1225 Folsom St. ☎863-2329.
Back with a vengeance after a fire that
put it out of action for a while, *My Place*
is a Seventies-style joint, with heavy cruising, heavy drinking and heavy petting.
Cheap drinks help the entertainment right
along.

Rawhide

280 Seventh St. ☎621-1197.
Country and western dance hall.
Hysterical good fun if you're into square
dancing and the like.

The Stud

399 Ninth St. ☎863-6623.
An oldie but a goodie. Has been popular
for years for its energetic, uninhibited
dancing and good times.

Mainly for Women

The Café

Market at 17th St.
On Friday nights this popular Castro
venue becomes the local lesbian lounge.

Club Q

At the *Kennel Club*, 628 Divisadero St.
☎931-9858.
Friday disco patronized by a young, ethni-
cally mixed group of women. Always
packed.

The Elephant Walk

18th & Castro.
Monday night is women's night, with the
slogan "Be one . . . bring one . . . or just
look like one". A lively and convivial place
for drinks and good music.

The End Up

Sixth St at Harrison.
Sunday evenings kick off with a tea
dance at 6pm, moving onto harder
grooves as the night progresses.

Feed

At the *Stud*, 399 Ninth St.
Sunday evening's top dykey-dancing spot.

The Garage

174 King St at Third.
Saturday night's best all-female rave. A
good mix of ages and styles, and a lot of
uninhibited gyrating round the dance
floor.

Girl Spot

Sixth St at Harrison.
Saturday night is girls only for upbeat
dancing. Very young leather crowd.

Paula's Clubhouse

3160 16th St.
Queer video fest on Thursday evenings
followed by dance night *Junk*, a frolicking
night out.

Pussycat Lounge

At the *Albion*, 3139 16th St.
Wednesday evenings are packed with
women watching Russ Meyer's *Faster
Pussycat* and shrieking. A strange experience and slightly mad.

Rapture

1484 Market St. No phone.
Saturday night dance club for women.
Tends to draw the younger, well-dressed
lipstick-lesbian crowd.

Nightlife

*See p.220 for a
map showing
clubs in the
Castro and
Mission
districts.*

Classical Music, Opera and Dance

Though the San Francisco arts scene has
to fight against a reputation for provincialism, this is the only city on the West
Coast to boast its own professional
symphony, **ballet** and **opera** companies,
each of which has a thriving upper-crust
social support scene, wining and dining
its way through fund raisers and the like.

Nightlife

Louise M Davies Symphony Hall

201 Van Ness Ave. ☎ 431-5400.
The permanent home of the San Francisco Symphony, which offers a year-round season of classical music and sometimes performances by other, often offbeat musical and touring groups. Established in 1909 as a small musical group, the symphony rose to international prominence in the 1950s when it started touring and recording. Without exactly being world beaters, they've scooped up several awards on the international circuit. Non-stop recording work has included sixteen symphonies and the soundtracks for *Amadeus* and *The Unbearable Lightness of Being*. Prices obviously depend on the performance, but are marginally lower than either the opera or ballet, with the least expensive seats going for around $20.

War Memorial Opera House

301 Van Ness Ave.
Ticket and schedule information ☎ 864-3330.
A night at the opera in San Francisco is no small-time affair. The Opera House, designed by architect Arthur Brown Jr, the creator of City Hall and Coit Tower, makes a very opulent venue for both the San Francisco Opera Association – which has been performing here since the building opened in 1932 – and the ballet.

By far the strongest of San Francisco's cultural trio, the Opera Association has won critical acclaim for its performances of the classics as well as obscure Russian productions that other companies prefer not to tackle. The SF Opera carries considerable international weight and pulls in big names like Placido Domingo and Kiri Te Kanawa on a regular basis. Its main season runs from the end of September for thirteen weeks, and its opening night

> During the summer months, look out for the **free concerts in Stern Grove** (at 19th Avenue and Sloat Blvd) where the symphony, opera and ballet give open-air performances for ten successive Sundays (starting in June).

is one of the principal social events on the West Coast. Sporadically, they also have a summer season during June and July. Tickets cost upwards of $40 – for which you do at least get supertitles with the foreign-language operas. **Standing room** costs a bargain $8, and 300 tickets are available (one per person) at 10.30am on the day of performance.

The San Francisco Ballet

☎ 893-2277.
The city's ballet company, the oldest and third largest in the US, puts on an ambitious annual six-month – January to June – programme of both classical and contemporary dance. Founded in 1933, the ballet was the first American company to stage full-length productions of *Swan Lake* and *Nutcracker*. They've won Emmys, broadcast, toured and generally earned themselves a reputation for ambition: overreach drove them toward bankruptcy in the 1970s and they seemed to be sliding until 1985, when the Icelandic Helgi Tomasson, "premier danseur" of the New York City Ballet, stepped in as artistic director. Since his appointment, the company can seem to do no wrong and some proud San Franciscans consider it "America's premier ballet company". Critical opinion hasn't quite concurred as yet, but the tickets (which cost upwards of $30) are by no means overpriced.

Theater

The majority of San Francisco's **theaters** congregate downtown around the Theater District. Most aren't especially innovative (although a handful of more inventive fringe places are scattered in other parts of town, notably SoMa), but tickets are reasonably inexpensive – up to $30 a seat – and there's usually good availability.

Tickets can be bought direct from the theater box offices, or, using a credit card, through *BASS* (☎ 776-1999 or 510/762-2277). The *Tix Bay Area* ticket booth on the Stockton Street side of Union Square regularly has last-minute tickets for as much as half off the marked price (Mon–Sat 11am–6pm; ☎ 433-7717).

Downtown

American Conservatory Theater
Geary Theater, 450 Geary St. ☎749-2228.
The Bay Area's leading resident theater
group. Despite suffering the wholesale
destruction of their theater in the 1989
earthquake, they have managed to
bounce back and today continue to
stage San Francisco's most impressive
plays from their newly restored
auditorium.

Curran Theater
445 Geary St. ☎474-3800.
Tackles bigger productions and musicals
of the Andrew Lloyd-Webber genre.

Golden Gate Theater
1 Taylor St. ☎474-3800.
Originally constructed during the 1920s
and recently restored to its former
splendor, the *Golden Gate* is San
Francisco's most elegant theater, with
marble flooring, rococo ceilings and
gilt trimmings. It's a pity that the
programs don't live up to the
surroundings – generally a mainstream
diet of Broadway musicals on their
latest rerun, although they occasionally
manage to pull a big name out of the
bag for a one-man Vegas-type show.

Lorraine Hansberry Theater
620 Sutter St. ☎474-8800.
Radical young group of black performers
whose work covers traditional theater as
well as more contemporary political
pieces and jazz/blues musical reviews.
Impressive.

The Orpheum
1192 Market St. ☎474-3800.
Showtime, song and dance performances
and "light" cabaret-style theater.

Stage Door Theater
420 Mason St. ☎749-2228.
Attractive, medium-sized
turn-of-the-century theater, run by the
American Conservatory Theater group.

Theater On The Square
450 Post St. ☎433-9500.
Converted Gothic theater with drama,
musicals, comedy and mainstream
theater pieces.

Elsewhere

Beach Blanket Babylon Series
Club Fugazi Cabaret, 678 Green St.
☎421-4222.
One of the few musts for theater-goers
in the city, its formality smacks of a
Royal Command Performance, but the
shows themselves are zany and
fast-paced cabarets of jazz singers,
dance routines and comedy very slickly
put together.

Climate Theater
252 Ninth St. ☎626-9196.
Small, reputable SoMa theater, specializing in fringe/alternative productions.
Cheaper and probably a lot more stimu-
lating than some of the downtown
efforts.

Intersection for the Arts
446 Valencia St. ☎626-3311.
Well-meaning, community-based group
that tackle interesting productions in inadequate facilities. Dance, comedy and
straight theater, alternating with art exhibitions and lectures.

The Lab
1805 Divisadero St. ☎346-4063.
Mixed media center with gallery and
changing exhibitions downstairs, and a
small theater for drama and dance
upstairs. Usually something locally based
and interesting going on.

The Magic Theater
Fort Mason Center, Building D.
☎441-8822.
The busiest and largest company after the
ACT, and probably the most exciting, the
Magic Theater specializes in the works of
contemporary playwrights and emerging
new talent: Sam Shepard traditionally
premieres his work here. They have been
described as the "most adventuresome
company in the West".

Mission Cultural Center
2868 Mission St. ☎821-1155.
An organization dedicated to preserving
and developing Latin culture, staging
small but worthy productions using the
wealth of talented but underrated
performers in San Francisco's Latin
community.

Nightlife

*The Theater
District is
described on
p.54*

Nightlife

Phoenix Theater
301 Eighth St. ☎621-4423.
Small SoMa playhouse that specializes in readings, one-act plays and sketches.

Theater Artaud
450 Florida St. ☎621-7797.
Very modern theater in a converted warehouse that tackles the obscure and abstract: visiting performers, both dance and theatrical. Always something interesting.

Theater Rhinoceros
2926 16th St. ☎861-5079.
San Francisco's only uniquely gay theater group, this company, not surprisingly, tackles productions that confront gay issues, as well as lighter, humorous productions.

Comedy

Comedians have always found a welcoming audience in San Francisco, but recently the alternative **comedy and cabaret scene** has been reborn. Some new, excellent venues have opened up, and while many may be smartening up beyond the tastes of some, they will undoubtedly be able to draw bigger names to the city.

Few of the comedians are likely to be familiar: as with any cabaret you take your chances, and whether you consider a particular club to be good will depend on who happens to be playing the week you go. You can expect to pay roughly the same kind of cover in most of the clubs ($7–15), and two-drink minimums are common. There are usually two shows per night, the first kicking off around 8pm and a late show starting at around 11pm. For bargains, check the press for "Open Mike" nights when unknowns and members of the audience get up and have a go; there's rarely a cover charge for these evenings and, even if the acts are diabolical, it can be a fun night out.

Comedy clubs

Cobbs Comedy Club
The Cannery, 2801 Leavenworth. St ☎563-5157.
Small venue, popular on the cabaret circuit, where new performers often get the chance of their first live appearance.

El Rio
3158 Mission St. ☎282-3325.
Wednesday night comedy shows, with a choice of performers that is often a lot riskier than in the established clubs. Very alternative, and, more often than not, extremely funny.

Finocchio's
506 Broadway. ☎982-9388.
A San Francisco institution, *Finocchio's* presents a small cast of female impersonators who run through textbook routines, heavy on the sauciness. At one time it was considered outrageous; these days it's more than a little tame, good for cheap laughs and expensive drinks.

The Improv
401 Mason St. ☎441-7787.
The chain store of the comedy world, with a string of venues in different cities, the *Improv* draws some good established talent and also has an eye for up-and-coming acts. Monday is the least expensive and best night to go, when guest company *Theater of the Deranged* presents a completely improvised night's entertainment.

Josie's Cabaret and Juice Joint
3583 16th St. ☎861-7933.
A good all-rounder offering a mixed menu of cabaret, comedy, live music and dancing.

Morty's
1024 Kearny St. ☎986-6678.
Old North Beach club that evokes the Lenny Bruce era of comedy. None of the acts are quite up to that standard, but the club itself has a genuine feel that makes it worth the trip.

The Punch Line
444 Battery St. ☎397-7553.
Frontrunner of the city's "polished" cabaret venues, this place has an intimate, smoky feel that's ideal for downing expensive cocktails and laughing your head off. The club usually hosts the bigger names in the world of stand-up and is always packed.

Film

After eating, watching **films** is the favorite San Francisco pastime. For one thing it's inexpensive (rarely more than $7, sometimes as little as $3), and secondly there's a staggering assortment of current-release and repertory film houses, with programmes ranging from the latest general-release films to Hollywood classics, iconoclastic Sixties pieces, and a selection of foreign and art films that's usually as good as (if not better than) most European centers. Film-going in San Francisco is a pleasure: there are rarely queues, and the cinemas are often beautiful Spanish-revival and Art-Deco buildings that are in themselves a delight to behold.

The Alhambra
Polk St and Union. ☎775-2137.
One of the city's grandest movie theaters; a gorgeous, plush, Moorish interior. Shows a mix of current releases and reruns.

ATA-Artists Television Access
992 Valencia St at 21st St. ☎824-3890.
Non-profit media center that puts on the city's most challenging barrage of film and TV productions, often with a political or psycho-sexual bent.

The Castro Theater
429 Castro St. ☎621-6120.
Perhaps San Francisco's most beautiful movie house, offering a steady stream of reruns, Hollywood classics and (best of all) a Wurlitzer organ played between films by a man who rises up from the stage. A fond favorite with the gay community, it hosts the annual Gay and Lesbian Film Festival each June.

Cinematheque
at San Francisco Art Institute, 800 Chestnut St. ☎558-8129.
Adventurous international programme of vaguely alternative movies.

The Clay
2261 Fillmore St. ☎346-1123.
Small, elegant art house cinema.

Kabuki Cinemas
Post St and Fillmore. ☎931-9800.
Attractive, modern building in the Japan Center complex, where eight screens show mainly current-release movies.

The Lumiere
1572 California St. ☎885-3200.
Another opulent Spanish-revival art house, a bit run-down but often with an interesting programme of obscure art films as well as a select choice of current-release films.

Opera Plaza
601 Van Ness Ave. ☎771-0102.
Modern Civic Center complex where four theaters screen the better pick of current-release films.

Pacific Film Archive
2621 Durant Ave, Berkeley.
☎510/642-1412.
For the serious film fan, this is perhaps the best movie theater in California, with seasons of contemporary works from around the world plus revivals of otherwise forgotten classics.

The Red Vic
1727 Haight St. ☎282-0318.
Friendly collective, formerly housed in a room full of ancient couches where you could put your feet up, and now moved to smarter premises up the street. Same idea, though, showing popular reruns and cult films.

The Roxie
3117 16th St. ☎863-1087.
San Francisco's trendiest, independent rep house in the heart of the Mission, showing a steady diet of punk, new wave and political movies.

Nightlife

> **The San Francisco Film Festival** is held at various cinemas around the city, but usually centring on the *Kabuki* eight-screen theater (see above), in the first couple of weeks in May. It specializes in political and short films you wouldn't normally see. Tickets sell extremely fast and you'll need to book around four days in advance for all but the most obscure movies.
>
> Just as popular is the **Gay and Lesbian Film Festival**, held in June at the *Castro Theater*. If you know you're going to be in town for either, call ahead for programmes by contacting the theaters.

Nightlife

The Royal
1529 Polk St. ☎ 474-0353.
Once elegant, now a decaying old theater looking about a week away from demolition. Varied, innovative programming, though.

The Strand
1127 Market St. ☎ 621-2227.
Dark, appropriately scruffy surroundings for cult films and B-movies.

Chapter 16

Shops and Galleries

San Francisco may not have the big prestige department stores of New York or London, or even Los Angeles, but it excels instead in its range of smaller-scale outlets, great for picking up odd and unusual things you wouldn't find at home.

Though all the international names are displayed in downtown storefronts, the great majority of places are low-key and unpretentious. Not only does this mean slightly lower prices, but it also makes shopping a more pleasant, stress-free activity all round.

If you want to run the gauntlet of designer labels, or just watch the style brigades in all their consumer fury, **Union Square** is the place you should aim for. The heart of the city's shopping territory, it has a good selection of big-name and chic stores – unashamedly expensive, but very good for browsing, especially in the district's many art galleries.

For things that you can actually afford to buy, you'll have a less disheartening and more interesting time in neighborhoods like **Haight-Ashbury** and the **Mission**. These are home to a profusion of the second-hand, quirky and plain bizarre, fascinating to pick through if you're at a loose end or on the lookout for some kitsch and unique souvenirs; the Mission, especially, has some marvellous second-hand clothing stores. The Civic Center is also good: stores specializing in Art Deco and retro-Americana abound around

Market and Gough street, while the stretch of Hayes Street between Franklin and Laguna holds San Francisco's most unusual array of galleries and one-off stores.

The city, and the Bay Area in general, is home to a number of excellent **bookstores**, and its many independent **music stores** are unbeatable for rare birds to add to your collection.

Most places are open Monday to Saturday, from 9am until 6pm, with quite a number open on Sunday too, particularly for basic things like food and drink. Many **supermarkets** are open 24 hours a day, so you'll never have to go without.

Credit cards are accepted in most stores for purchases above a minimum of $15; **travellers' checks** are as good as cash, provided they're in US dollar denominations and that you have your passport or other photo ID.

Department Stores and Shopping Malls

If you want to pick up a variety of things in a hurry, without having to roam all over town, it's hard to beat the one-stop convenience of **department stores** or, increasingly, **shopping malls**. Though even San Francisco's most opulent stores aren't in the same league as *Harrods* or *Bloomingdales*, and the few urban shopping malls still feel as though they'd be happier in the suburbs, they are useful and can even be quite lively.

Shops And Galleries

Department Stores

Emporium
835 Market St, near Powell St.
☎764-2222.
San Francisco's largest general department store, with a very average range of merchandise – everything the suburban home could possibly need.

I Magnin
Geary and Stockton St. ☎362-2100.
A stylish, if rather conservative store that sells well-made clothes at not terribly outrageous prices. Top designer names.

Macy's
Stockton and O'Farrell St. ☎397-3333.
Probably the city's best-stocked store, and as such a good place for general shopping, even if it's not a patch on its New York counterpart. Nonetheless, brimming with trinkets of the consumer society, and a dangerous place to go with a wallet full of money. Beautifully presented merchandise is hawked noisily from all sides.

Nieman Marcus
150 Stockton St. ☎362-3900.
The sheer cheek of the pricing department has earned this store the nickname "Needless Mark-up". Undoubtedly Union Square's most beautiful department store, however, with its classic rotunda, and good for enjoyable browsing.

Nordstrom's
865 Market St. ☎243-8500.
Shoppers flock here for the high-quality fashions, as well as a chance to ride on the spiral escalators that climb the four-storey atrium.

Sak's Fifth Avenue
384 Post St. ☎986-4300.
Pathetic compared to its New York sister store. A dodgy selection geared towards the middle-aged shopaholic.

Shopping Malls

Crocker Galeria
Kearny and Post St. ☎392-5522.
The most recent in the new wave of shopping malls, this has been built to as modern and attractive a design as possible, and features some very pricey showcase boutiques. It's all very nice for a wander, but don't plan on spending money unless your reserves are bottomless.

Embarcadero Center
The Embarcadero, Market St. ☎772-0500.
Ugly, four-plaza shopping complex with almost 200 stores, distinguished from other anaesthetic shopping malls only by the occasional work of art and a reasonably carefully planned layout.

Ghirardelli Square
900 North Point. ☎775-5500.
This attractive turn-of-the-century building used to be a chocolate factory, but is now home to seventy stores and some great restaurants . . . the nicest way to drop dollars at the Wharf.

Japan Center
Three blocks, bounded by Post, Sutter, Laguna and Fillmore streets. ☎922-6776.
Surprisingly banal and characterless five-acre complex of stores, movie theaters and restaurants with a Japanese theme.

San Francisco Shopping Centre
Fifth & Market Streets. ☎495-5656.
A good-looking mall this one; glass, Italian marble, polished green granite and spiral escalators up and down its nine storeys all add to the seductive appeal of spending money with California-style panache.

Drugs, Beauty Products and Toiletries

Standard **drugstores** can be found in every San Francisco neighborhood. A few are open 24 hours a day, selling essentials like film and batteries for your Walkman, and all have a pharmacy that can dispense medications and fill prescriptions.

Walgreen is the largest chain pharmacy with numerous branches throughout the city, selling prescription drugs and general medical supplies, as well as cosmetics and toiletries. Most are open long hours (Mon–Sat 8am–10pm, Sun 9am–8pm); the most central is at 135 Powell St (☎391-4433).

Outlets for such indulgences as body oils and bubble bath tend to congregate in the pricier neighborhoods.

Drugstores

Embarcadero Center Pharmacy
1 Embarcadero Center. ☎788-4511.
Prescription drugs and general medical and toiletry supplies.

Fairmont Pharmacy
801 Powell St. ☎362-3000.
Huge pharmacy, perfumery and toiletry supply store that also has a good selection of maps and books on San Francisco.

Mandarin Pharmacy
895 Washington St. ☎989-9292.
This amiable, well-stocked drugstore is a sanctuary in the bustle of Chinatown.

Thrifty JR
2030 Market St. ☎626-7387.
Also at 2664 Mission St (☎282-8600) and 1449 Webster St (☎928-1856).
General prescription and non-prescription drug and medical needs.

Toiletries and Beauty Supplies

Beauty Supplies Store
3600 16th St. ☎861-2019.
Also at 1560 Haight St.
Make-up, hair dye and massage oils.

Body Time
2072 Union St. ☎922-4076.
Though they sold the original name to the UK-based *Body Shop*, they still put out a full range of aromatic natural bath oils, shampoos and skin creams.

Common Scents
3920 24th St. ☎826-1019.
Natural oils, cures, remedies and bath salts.

Crabtree and Evelyn
50 Post St, in the Crocker Galleria.
☎392-6111.
Anglophile toiletries store that is full of scented body care products and potpourri.

Clothes and Accessories

Perhaps more than anywhere else in the US, San Francisco's power-dressing **designer clothes** stores are distinct from the bulk of the city's clothing outfitters.

Though Ralph Lauren-chic definitely rules the Financial District, style elsewhere in the city is a much more open concept. Dozens of stores – *Esprit* and *The Gap* are two of the bigger names – sell very Californian **casual wear**, mainly jeans and polo-type shirts in pastel colors, but if you're feeling adventurous check out the countless **second-hand clothes** stores specializing in period costume, from Twenties gear to leftover hippy garb. Better still, explore the myriad of charitable **thrift stores**, where you can pick up high-quality cast-offs for next to nothing.

Designer Clothes

Betsey Johnson
2031 Fillmore St. ☎567-2726.
One of the few American designers who doesn't see women in business suits. Her clothes are stylish and have flair without being silly – and, by designer standards, they are also affordable.

Brooks Brothers
201 Post St. ☎397-4500.
The original preppy clothes store: traditional men's clothing, well tailored and conservative. This is where the Financial District clones go to get their clobber.

Bullock and Jones
340 Post St. ☎392-4243.
Much the same as *Brooks*, but if you have to buy suits and look the part, this is the better choice and even has its own barber's shop.

California
2343 Market St. ☎864-1534.
Castro women's clothing store: designer patterns, beautifully copied, well made and not overpriced.

Emporio Armani
1 Grant Ave. ☎677-9400.
Simple European chic comes to SF big time. This large store with its own restaurant is the perfect place to deck yourself out in style.

Shops And Galleries

Shops And Galleries

MAC (Modern Appealing Clothing)
812 Post St. ☎775-2515.
Showcase for up-and-coming contemporary designers such as Workers for Freedom. Where the young and beautiful go to get dressed and pay heartily for the pleasure.

Rolo
535 Castro St. ☎431-4545.
Tiny store, crammed with unusual and attractive one-offs by lesser-known designers. Moderately priced and well-made clothing.

Wilkes Bashford
375 Sutter St. ☎986-4380.
Five floors of fabulous designer finery for men. A fashion victim's fantasy.

Designer Accessories: Bags, Shoes, Hats, Jewellery

China Gem Co
500 Grant Ave. ☎397-5070.
Good place for jade, opals and gold.

The Coach Store
3 Embarcadero Center. ☎392-1772.
Well-made, simple and expensive handbags and luggage. Definitely worth the investment if you've got the money, *Coach* bags are timeless in their style and come with a lifetime guarantee.

Gucci
253 Post St. ☎392-2808.
Classic Italian shoes, bags and apparel that you need a trust fund to indulge in. Snoop around the store and be fascinated by the rich ladies who come in and say "I'll have one of those, two of those, one of those", etc.

Hats on Post
201 Post St. ☎392-3737.
Interesting, odd designs, very contemporary, but only worth shelling out for if you're *really* into hats.

Hermes
1 Union Square. ☎391-7200.
Classy French luggage and accessories for the super-rich. Again, good only for spying on those who can afford it.

Kenneth Cole
2078 Union St. ☎346-2121.
State-of-the-art boutique selling the well-designed shoes of this New York designer. His men's shoes are imaginative and funky, but the women's stuff is pretty mediocre.

Kenneth Lane
110 Geary St. No phone.
Beautiful copies of Van Cleef and Bulgari classics, but at the price you'd be better off spending a bit more on the originals.

Pearl of the Orient
Ghirardelli Square, Fisherman's Wharf. ☎441-2288.
Reputedly the largest stock of pearls in the Bay Area, and very nice too.

Shapur
245 Post St. ☎392-1200.
Unusual fittings for uniquely cut diamonds and various other gems; each piece is created individually.

Shreve & Co
200 Post St. ☎421-2600.
The oldest jewellers in town and quite possibly the best. Known for their fine silverware and flawless diamonds.

Tiffany
Union Square. ☎781-7000.
Luxurious new site on several floors where the extraordinarily courteous staff are happy to let you try the stuff on even if it's obvious that you can't afford it.

Casual Wear

Banana Republic
256 Grant Ave. ☎788-3087.
Stylish clothes for the travelling yuppie, in this main branch of the San Francisco-based nationwide chain.

Esprit
16th St at Illinois. ☎648-6900.
Warehouse-sized store in SoMa that is the flagship of the wildly successful international chain selling sporty "California-style" casual wear in ghastly colors. For basics, T-shirts, etc, it's pretty good.

The Gap
934 Market St. ☎397-2266.
Also at 1975 Market St, and all over the city.
Hugely successful chain store selling jeans, T-shirts and casual wear.

Groger's Western Wear
1445 Valencia St. ☎674-0700.
Mission store selling cowboy boots,
Stetson hats, boot tips and traditional
brand-name Western clothes. Fun
shopping.

North Beach Leather
190 Geary St. ☎362-8300.
Leather everything, and in some pretty
sickly colors, but for basic black jackets
and simple pieces, there are some pretty
well-made styles. Actually in the Union
Square district, despite the name.

Patagonia
770 North Point, Fisherman's Wharf.
☎771-2050.
Functional, outdoor clothing that has a
cult, semi-yuppie following.

Second-hand Clothes
Aardvarks Odd Ark
1501 Haight St. ☎621-3141.
Large second-hand clothing store in
Haight-Ashbury: some junk, but also
some priceless pieces and an infinite
supply of perfectly faded Levis.

American Rag Co
1305 Van Ness Ave. ☎474-5214.
As second-hand clothing stores go, this
one is expensive, but it's probably also
superior to most others in San Francisco.

Bargain Mart
1823 Divisadero St. ☎921-7380.
Downscale second-hand clothes that look
as though they're about to fall apart, but
are ideal if you need to get decked out
on the cheap.

Buffalo Exchange
1800 Polk St. ☎346-5726.
Also at 1555 Haight St (☎431-7733), and
2512 Telegraph Ave in Berkeley (☎510/
644-9202).
Cheap and occasionally tatty store, but if
you've got the patience to search through
the piles of clothing, you may turn up
some gems.

Mascara Club
1408 Haight St. ☎863-2837.
Vintage clothing in the heart of Haight-
Ashbury, heavy on the psychedelic and
more recently Wild Western garments.

Past Tense
665 Valencia St. ☎621-2987.
Mission district store selling 1930s to
1960s collectable vintage clothing. One of
the smarter second-hand stores.

Spellbound Vintage Clothing
1670 Haight St. ☎863-4930.
Not cheap, but truly classy rags from
yesteryear.

Third Hand Store
1839 Divisadero St. ☎567-7332.
As other stores cash in on the craze for
vintage clothing, this Western Addition
store keeps its prices reasonable and has
some interesting pieces.

The Way You Wore
1838 Divisadero St. ☎346-1386.
Directly opposite the *Third Hand Store*;
there isn't much to choose between
them, but a trip to the neighborhood will
double your chances of finding what
you're looking for.

Worn Out West
1850 Castro St. ☎431-6020.
Gay second-hand cowboy gear store – a
trip for browsing, but if you're serious
about getting some Wild West kit, this is
the least expensive place in town to pick
out a good pair of boots, stylish western
shirts and chaps.

Thrift Stores
Community Thrift
625 Valencia St. ☎861-4910.
Gay thrift store in the Mission with clothing, furniture and general junk. All
proceeds are ploughed back into gay
groups in the community.

Goodwill
2279 Mission St. ☎928-6200.
There are *Goodwill* outlets all over the
city; the Mission branch is their biggest
and best, stocking everything from handbags to three-piece suites.

Purple Heart
1855 Mission St. ☎621-2581.
Top quality junk and kitsch.

Recollections
17th and Valencia St. ☎626-3104.
Great Fifties furniture and household
goods. Not the least expensive in town
but perhaps the least tatty.

Shops And Galleries

Shops And Galleries

San Francisco Symphony Thrift Store
2223 Fillmore St. ☎563-3123.
Top-rate vintage clothing store in Pacific Heights, with flamboyant and original pieces going for top dollar.

St Vincent de Paul
1519 Haight St. ☎863-3615.
Also at 4452 Mission St in the Mission. Queen of the junk stores, *St Vinnies* will keep you amused for hours. You could spend money all day and still have change from $50.

Thrift Town
2101 Mission St. ☎861-1132.
Huge and well-displayed selection, with some of San Francisco's better quality trash as well as pretty stylish second-hand clothing bargains.

Food and Drink

Food faddists will have a field day in San Francisco's many **gourmet stores**, which are on a par with the city's restaurants for culinary quality and diversity. The simplest neighborhood deli will get your taste buds jumping, while the most sophisticated places are enough to make you swoon.

Be sure to try such **local specialties** as *Boudin*'s sourdough bread, *Gallo* salami and *Anchor Steam* beer. Bear in mind, too, that however overwhelming the food on offer in San Francisco itself may seem, some of the very best places are to be found across the bay in Berkeley. For more basic stocking up there are, of course, **supermarkets** all over the city (*Safeway* is probably the most widespread name), some of them open 24 hours per day.

Any of the above will sell you an array of beers, wines and spirits – provided you're over 21, and have a photo ID to prove it – but for the best selection head to a specialist retailer.

Delis and Groceries

Auntie Pasta
3101 Fillmore St. ☎921-7576.
Fresh pasta and sauces to heat and eat. Great if you don't want to dine out or cook.

Canton Market
1135 Stockton St. ☎982-8600.
One of the more exotic Chinatown delis. The decor may be a bit stark, and the store unbearably crowded, but the selection (and prices) makes it worth the effort.

Caravansaray
262 Sutter St. ☎922-2705.
Gourmet cheese and coffee store. Very expensive.

Casa Lucas
2934 24th St. ☎826-4334.
Mission store with an astonishing array of exotic fruits and vegetables that includes a dozen varieties of banana.

Cheese Board
1504 Shattuck Ave, Berkeley.
☎510/549-3183.
Collectively owned and operated since 1967, this was one of the first outposts in Berkeley's Gourmet Ghetto and is still going strong, offering over 200 varieties of cheese, fresh-baked bread and the Bay Area's best designer pizza – at a bargain $1.50 per slice.

The Cheesery
427 Castro St. ☎552-6676.
Reasonably priced coffees and cheeses from around the world.

David's
474 Geary Blvd. ☎771-1600.
The consummate Jewish deli, open until 1am. A downtown haven for the after-theater crowd and night owls.

La Ferme Beaujolaise
2000 Hyde St. ☎441-6913.
French country market-type store, with mouthwatering meats, cheeses, sausages, pastries and bread, as well as a good selection of imported wines.

Lucca Ravioli
1100 Valencia St. ☎647-5581.
Pasta factory that you can spy on through the big picture windows before you go in to the store.

Molinari's
373 Columbus Ave. ☎421-2337.
Bustling North Beach Italian deli, jammed to the rafters with goodies.

Rainbow Wholefoods
1899 Mission St. ☎863-0620.
Progressive politics and organic food in this Mission wholefood store.

San Francisco Health Store
333 Sutter St. ☎392-8477.
Dried fruits, juices and wholefood.

San Francisco Herb Company
215 14th St. ☎861-3108.
SoMa-based store with large quantities of fresh herbs at wholesale prices.

Sunrise Deli and Café
2115 Irving St. ☎664-8210.
Specialty Middle Eastern foodstuffs – stuffed vine leaves, aubergine and hummus.

Tokyo Fish Market
1908 Fillmore St. ☎931-4561.
Every type of fish. It's fun to look, even if you don't want to buy.

Williams Sonoma
576 Sutter St. ☎421-7900.
A few gourmet foods amid an incredible selection of cookware.

Bread, Pastries and Sweets

The Acropolis Bakery and Deli
5217 Geary Blvd. ☎751-9661.
Greek/Russian bakery selling unusual filo pastries and baklavas.

Bakers of Paris
449 Castro St; 3989 24th St. ☎626-4076.
Castro and Noe Valley bakeries that serve up mountains of baguettes and croissants.

Boudin
156 Jefferson St, Fisherman's Wharf. ☎928-1849.
They only make one thing – sourdough bread – but it's the best around.

Godiva Chocolates
50 Post St, in the Crocker Galleria. ☎982-6798.
Rich Belgian chocolates at around a dollar a nibble. Heaven for the chocoholic.

Liguria Bakery
1700 Stockton St, North Beach. ☎421-3786.
Marvellous old world Italian bakery, with deliciously fresh *focaccia*.

Tea, Coffee and Spices

Bombay Bazaar
548 Valencia St. ☎621-1717.
Exotic spices and tons of pulses, grains and other staples.

Freed, Teller & Freed
1326 Polk St. ☎673-0922.
Polk Gulch coffee, tea and spice emporium. Every conceivable legal addiction and all the paraphernalia to go with it.

Graffeo Coffee
733 Columbus Ave. ☎986-2420.
Huge sacks of coffee are piled up all around this North Beach store – you can smell the place from half a block away. Great coffees, reasonably priced.

Haig's Delicacies
642 Clement St. ☎752-6283.
Way out in the Richmond, but for Indian and Middle Eastern spices and delicacies, this is the place.

Peet's Coffee
1156 Chestnut St. ☎931-8302.
Russian Hill-based San Francisco flagship of this venerable Berkeley coffee roaster, offering some 25 different blends and roasts, and pint cups for 50¢ a go.

Wines and Spirits

California Wine Merchant
3237 Pierce St. ☎567-0646.
Before you set off for the Wine Country, pick up a sample selection at this Marina wine emporium so you know what to look out for.

Shops And Galleries

Shops And Galleries

Cannery Wine Cellars
The Cannery, Fisherman's Wharf.
☎673-0400.
An astounding selection of wines and imported beers, as well as Armagnac and Scotch, lines the walls.

Coit Liquors
585 Columbus Ave. ☎986-4036.
North Beach specialty wine store, with the accent on rare Italian vintages. Good stock of regular booze.

Connoisseur Wine Imports
462 Bryant St. ☎433-0825.
SoMa store that is the city's best place for French, Spanish, Italian, Portuguese or German wines if you tire of the Californian variety.

D & M Liquors
Fillmore and Sacramento St. ☎346-1325.
Great selection of Californian wines, but their specialty is champagne.

Marasco's
3821 24th St. ☎824-2300.
The dipsomaniac's dream – hundreds of wines and exotic spirits taking booze shopping to its zenith.

Books

Although San Francisco does boast some truly excellent **bookstores,** the range of reading material on offer is surprisingly small for a city with such a literary reputation.

The established focus for literature has long been in North Beach, in the area around the legendary *City Lights* bookstore, but increasingly the best spots, particularly for contemporary creative writing, are to be found in the lower-rent Mission district, which is home some of the city's more energized – and politicized – bookstores.

There are a few **second-hand booksellers** in the city itself (the best bargains are found in thrift stores; see above), but these can't compare with the diverse bunch across the bay in Oakland and Berkeley. Most bookstores tend to open every day, roughly 10am–8pm, though *City Lights* is open daily until midnight.

See p.147 for a full list of Berkeley bookstores

General Bookstores

The Booksmith
1644 Haight St. ☎863-8688.
Good general Haight-Ashbury bookstore with an excellent stock of political and foreign periodicals.

City Lights Bookstore
261 Columbus Ave. ☎362-8193.
America's first paperback bookstore, and still San Francisco's best, with a range of titles including *City Lights'* own publications (see p.70).

A Clean, Well Lighted Place for Books
Opera Plaza, 601 Van Ness Ave.
☎441-6670.
Good selection of the latest titles.

Crown Books
1245 Sutter St. ☎441-7479.
Also at 518 Castro St (☎552-5213).
San Francisco branches of the nationwide chain, selling new general books at discounted prices.

Doubleday Bookshop
The White House, 265 Sutter St.
☎989-3420.
Main San Francisco branch of this nationwide chain.

Philosopher's Stone Bookshop
3814 24th St.
General bookstore with a decent range of titles, though rather heavy on the New Age stuff.

Tillman Place Bookstore
8 Tillman Place, off Grant Ave, near Union Square. ☎392-4668.
Downtown's premier general bookstore and certainly one of the oldest, with a beautifully elegant feel.

Discount and Second-hand Bookstores

Around the World
1346 Polk St. ☎474-5568.
Musty, dusty and a bit of a mess, this is a great place to spend hours of poring over first editions, rare books and records.

Columbus Avenue Books
540 Broadway. ☎986-3872.
North Beach store with a good selection of new and used books, and a large guide and travel books section.

Hunter's Books
151 Powell St. ☎397-5955.
Desirable range of publishers' remainders and other bargain books, with a good line in travel guides.

Maelstrom Books
572 Valencia St. ☎863-9933.
One of the Mission's many second-hand bookstores; they trade almost anything. Could be useful for off-loading the paperbacks you finished on your travels.

Specialist Bookstores

About Music
375 Grove St. ☎647-3343.
Tiny, hole-in-the-wall place crammed with books on classical and contemporary music.

Bound Together Anarchist Collective Bookstore
1369 Haight St. ☎431-8355.
Haight-Ashbury store specializing in radical and progressive publications.

China Books
2929 24th St. ☎282-2994.
Mission bookstore dealing in books and periodicals from China, although they also stock a good number of publications on the history and politics of the Third World.

Fanning's Bookstore
Second Floor, Ghirardelli Square, Fisherman's Wharf.
Specialty bookstore that only offers the works of Northern Californian writers – Hammett, London, Twain and Steinbeck among others.

Field's Bookstore
1419 Polk St. ☎673-2027.
Metaphysical and New Age books.

Great Expectations
1512 Haight St. ☎863-5515.
Radical liberal bookstore with hundreds of T-shirts bearing political slogans, some funnier than others.

Greenpeace Shop
Ghirardelli Square, Fisherman's Wharf.
☎474-1870.
Books, posters and a small gallery document the activities of the environmental group.

Kinokuniya
Second floor, Japan Center, 1581 Webster St. ☎567-7625.
Large stock of Japanese and English-language books, but they really excel in art books.

Modern Times
968 Valencia St. ☎282-9246.
Largely radical feminist publications, but a hefty stock of Latin American literature and progressive political publications. The shop also stocks a good selection of gay and lesbian literature, and stages regular readings of authors' works.

Opera Shop
199 Grove St. ☎565-6414.
A must for opera fans, with good selections of recordings and T-shirts, as well as an exhaustive stock of everything ever written about the opera.

Rand McNally
595 Market St at Second. ☎777-3131.
Brand new store selling travel guides, maps and paraphernalia for the person on the move.

Revolution Books
1541 Grant Ave. No phone.
What it says.

Small Press Traffic
3599 24th St. ☎285-8394.
Situated down in the Mission, don't be misled by the unprepossessing storefront: this is San Francisco's prime outlet for independent, contemporary fiction and poetry, with an astounding range of books, chapbooks and literary magazines (and postcards too). It's also the best place, along with *City Lights*, to find out about readings and writing workshops.

William Stout Architectural Books
804 Montgomery St. ☎391-6757.
One of San Francisco's world-class booksellers, with an excellent range of books on architecture, building, and urban studies.

Gay and Lesbian Bookstores

Books Etc
538 Castro St. ☎621-8631.
Stocks the gamut of gay publishing, from psychology to soft-core porn.

Shops And Galleries

Shops And Galleries

A Different Light
489 Castro St. ☎431-0891.
Well stocked, diverse and usually crammed with people.

Music

San Francisco's **music stores** are of two types: massive, anodyne warehouses pushing all the latest releases, and impossibly small specialist stores crammed to the rafters with obscure discs.

The big places like *Tower Records* are more or less identical to those throughout the world, though foreign visitors tend to find the prices marginally cheaper than back home. More exciting is the large number of **independent** retailers and **second-hand and collectors' stores**, where you can track down anything you've ever wanted, especially in West Coast jazz or psychedelic rock.

New

Aquarius Music
3961 24th St. ☎647-2272.
Small neighborhood store with friendly, knowledgeable staff and a reluctance to stock CDs. Emphasis on indie rock, jazz and blues.

Discolandia
2964 24th St. ☎826-9446.
Join the snake-hipped groovers looking for the latest in salsa and Central American sounds in this Mission outlet.

Discoteca Habana
24th and Harrison St. No phone.
Caribbean and samba recordings.

Embarcadero Discs and Tapes
2 Embarcadero Center, the Embarcadero. ☎956-2204.
Up-to-the-minute CDs and tapes.

Magic Flute
756 Columbus Ave. ☎661-2547.
Fine classical music store with a smattering of rock, jazz and vocals.

Musica Latina/American Music Store
2388 Mission St. ☎647-2098.
Mission store selling music from all over the continent, including South America.

Rainbow Records
2222 Fillmore St. ☎922-4474.
Branches all over town, but this is the biggest and has the best stock of new rock and pop.

Reckless Records
1401 Haight St. ☎431-3434.
If you can't complete your Sixties collection here, you never will.

Record Finder
Noe and Market St. ☎431-4443.
One of the best independents, with a range as broad as it's absorbing. Take a wad and keep spending.

Record House
1550 California St. ☎474-0259.
Nob Hill archive library of over 25,000 Broadway and Hollywood soundtracks. Great record-finding service.

Record Rack
3987 18th St. ☎552-4990.
Castro emporium focusing mainly on 12" singles. The accent is definitely on stuff you can dance to.

Rough Trade
1529 Haight St. ☎621-4395.
Because of its London connections, this is the first place in town to get British imports. Good reggae department in particular and indie rock in general.

Streetlight Records
3979 24th St. ☎282-3550.
Also at 2350 Market St.
A great selection of used records, tapes and CDs. The perfect opportunity to beef up your collection on the cheap.

Tower Records
Columbus Ave and Bay St, Fisherman's Wharf. ☎885-0500.
Main San Francisco location of the multinational empire.

Wherehouse Records
2083 Union St. ☎346-0944.
Large, general store, with a wide range of new releases, etc.

Second-hand

Amoeba Music
2455 Telegraph Ave, Berkeley.
☎510/549-1125

The biggest and best selection of used records and CDs in the Bay Area, with an admirably liberal trade-in policy.

Bay Area Records and Tapes
1444 Polk St. ☎441-0777.
Well-rounded assortment of new and used recordings.

Butch Wax Records
4077 18th St. ☎431-0904.
A hangover from 1970s gay discomania, this Castro shop is the best place in town for hard to find 12" singles, rare grooves and Euro-beat.

Down Home Music
10341 San Pablo Ave, El Cerrito. ☎510/525-2129.
As you might guess from the name, the excellent selection of folk, blues and bluegrass music makes it well worth the trek across to the East Bay.

Groove Merchant Records
776 Haight St. ☎252-5766.
Very groovy Lower Haight soul and jazz shop.

Jack's Record Cellar
254 Scott St. ☎431-3047.
The city's best source for American music – R&B, jazz, country and rock & roll. They'll track down rare discs and offer the chance to listen before you buy.

The Jazz Quarter
1267 20th Ave near Irving. ☎661-2331.
A bit of a trek to get to, out in the Sunset District near Golden Gate Park, but if you're a jazz fiend on the lookout for rarities, it's worth the effort.

Kaleidoscope Records
575 Haight St (no phone).
Funky, new and used music store. Not a comprehensive collection, but a good one.

Let It Be Records
2434 Judah St. ☎681-2113.
Out in the Sunset, and selling Beatles memorabilia and rock rarities.

Recycled Records
1377 Haight St. ☎626-4075.
Good all-round store, that also stocks well as a good selection of music publications, American and imported.

Rocky Ricardo's
448 Haight St. ☎864-7526.
Formerly an exclusive purveyor of 45s, they've recently introduced a few albums, but the theme remains the same: 1960s and 1970s soul and funk. Brilliant.

Star Records,
551 Hayes St. ☎552-3017.
Rap, soul, jazz, gospel and reggae specialist, out in Western Addition. Any track ever cut by a black artist, you'll find here.

Shops And Galleries

Art Galleries

At first glance the low-profile San Francisco **art scene** seems provincial compared to the glamorous internationalism of New York and Los Angeles. And in many respects it is. But there is a scene of sorts, and it could be argued that artists here have the freedom to be more concerned with the quality of their own work than with the stylistic vagaries of the world art market.

Out-of-towners tend to find it difficult to get a sense of what's going on, as most younger artists shun **commercial galleries**, especially the mainstream ones around Union Square, and prefer to show their work in their favorite cafés and bars. That said, there is a core of relatively innovative galleries around the South of Market area – though even here the asking prices can be pretty steep.

Union Square and Around

The Allrich Gallery
251 Post St. ☎398-8896.
Contemporary painting and sculpture as well as textiles.

American Indian Contemporary Arts
685 Market St. ☎495-7600.
Non-profit gallery run by and for contemporary Native American artists.

Atelier Dore
771 Bush St. ☎391-2423.
Salon-style gallery hung floor-to-ceiling with top-quality paintings. Historical genre paintings from California, including WPA works, and about the only place that carries the work of nineteenth- and twentieth-century black American painters.

Shops And Galleries

John Berggruen Gallery
228 Grant Ave. ☎781-4629.
Ultra-trendy gallery on three floors, showing big-name American and international artists.

Caldwell Snyder Gallery
357 Geary St. ☎296-7896.
Contemporary graphics regularly featuring Andy Warhol, David Hockney and Jurgen Gorg. Expensive coveted stuff.

Circle Gallery
140 Maiden Lane. ☎989-2100.
Dull and overpriced contemporary art, ceramics and glassware, worth a look for the Frank Lloyd Wright building.

Japonesque
50 Post St. ☎398-8577.
Museum-quality Japanese art, including pottery, sculpture and watercolors.

Miller Brown Gallery
77 Geary St. ☎861-2082.
Mixed media includes photography, textiles, sculpture and paintings.

Modernism
685 Market St. ☎541-0461.
Futurism, Expressionism, Pop Art, Minimalism and American modern art.

Moss Gallery
55 Grant Ave. ☎433-7224.
Top-rate contemporary art and sculpture from Latin America.

Pascel de Sarthe Gallery
315 Sutter St. No phone.
Impressionist and twentieth-century masters.

John Pence Gallery
750 Post St. ☎441-1138.
Realist painting and sculpture.

Richard Thompson Gallery
80 Maiden Lane. ☎956-2114.
Twentieth-century American Impressionism with occasional European Impressionistic works.

Vorpal Gallery
393 Grove St. ☎397-9200.
Contemporary international work.

James Willis Gallery
109 Geary St. ☎989-4485.
Tribal artefacts from India, Africa and Indonesia. Unusual carvings and fabrics.

SoMa and Elsewhere

Art Lick Gallery
4147 19th St. ☎621-5131.
One of the few galleries to show work in all media: sculpture, paintings, photography, graphic art and furniture.

Artspace
Ninth and Folsom St. ☎626-9100.
Adventurous, avant-garde gallery that often exhibits video installations.

Joanne Chappel Gallery
625 Second St. ☎777-5711.
Works by nationally known and West Coast artists.

Joseph Chowning Art Gallery
1717 17th St. ☎626-7496.
Massive forum for humorous and bizarre art.

Contemporary Realists Gallery
506 Hayes St. ☎863-6556.
One of the more interesting galleries; the first in California to be dedicated to promoting current realist drawing.

Crown Point Press
871 Folsom St. ☎974-6273.
With a showcase that changes monthly, you never know what to expect from one of SoMa's most eclectic galleries.

Erickdon & Elins Fine Art
398 Kansas St. ☎861-1080.
Nineteenth- and twentieth-century fine art.

Folk Art International
Ghirardelli Square, Fisherman's Wharf. ☎441-6100.
African, Indian, Chinese and Mexican folk art.

New Langton Arts
1246 Folsom St. ☎626-5416.
Non-commercial gallery space showing cutting-edge works in all media, and hosting lectures, readings and performances.

San Francisco Art Institute
800 Chestnut St. ☎771-7020.
Local avant-garde contemporary art and student work.

SF MOMA Rental Gallery
Building A, Fort Mason. ☎441-4777.
Large space where over 500 artists try to break into the commercial art world.

William Sawyer Gallery
3045 Clay St. ☎921-1600.
New work in a variety of styles.

Six-oh-One
601 Minnesota St. No phone.
SoMa gallery known for its controversial
and alternative works.

Smile, A Gallery With Tongue In Chic
1750 Union St. ☎771-1909.
From the whimsical to the very serious,
this gallery is one of very few into it just
for the fun of it. They'll exhibit anything.

Bruce Velick Gallery
371 11th St. ☎626-9055.
Drawing, photography, printing and
sculpture.

Vision Gallery
1155 Mission St. ☎621-2107.
Photography by the well known and the
unknown.

Specialty Stores

In among the designer clothes stores and
art galleries of the Union Square area, a
handful of stores sell **antiques and other
treasurable objects**; though prohibitively
expensive, many repay a look-in at least.
We've also pulled together in this section
some of the city's odd shops specializing
in things you often need desperately but
never know where to find – stationery,
birthday cards, nuts and bolts, flowers,
camping gear, children's toys, etc . . .

Antiques and Collectables

Antonio's Antiques
701 Bryant St. ☎781-1737.
Three floors of antiques from around the
world. Good porcelain and sculpture.

Asakichi Japanese Antiques and Art
Japan Center, 1581 Webster St.
☎921-2147.
Lovely pieces, but definitely geared
towards the tourist dollar.

Biordi
412 Columbus Ave. ☎392-8096.
North Beach store selling lovely hand-
painted Italian dinnerware and orna-
ments. It's unlikely that you'd ever buy
this kind of stuff while travelling, but it
makes for very enjoyable browsing.

Genji Kimonos
1731 Buchanan St. ☎931-1616.
Expensive oddments and beautiful
wooden chests.

Gump's
250 Post St. ☎982-1616.
Famous for its jade, oriental rugs and
objects cast in crystal, silver and china.
More fuel for fantasies than genuine
consumption.

Heartland
1801 Fillmore St. No phone.
Pacific Heights store that stocks handicrafts from around the US, including lovely
granny-style patchwork quilts, baskets
and pottery.

J Canes
530 Folsom St. ☎495-3579.
Small store with interesting and reasonably priced collectables and antiques.

Originals of Nature
Ghirardelli Square, Fisherman's Wharf.
☎928-1592.
Unusual selection of minerals, fossils and
gems.

Primitivo
2241 Fillmore St. ☎563-0505.
Native and folk art from the US, Central
America and Brazil. Great stuff at prices
that may prove tempting.

Miscellaneous

Brooks Cameras
45 Kearny St. ☎392-1900.
Huge, high-quality camera store with full
repair department.

FAO Schwartz
180 Post St. ☎391-0100.
Mega-toystore, designed to turn children
into monsters.

Figoni Hardware
1351 Grant Ave. ☎392-4765.
Ancient-looking but incredibly well-
stocked North Beach hardware store.

Headlines
1217 Polk St. ☎776-4466.
Also at 838 Castro St (☎989-8240) and
557 Castro St (☎626-8061).
Good cheap clothes and huge range of
novelty gift items. Fun to browse, even if
you don't want to spend any money.

**Shops And
Galleries**

Shops And Galleries

Star Magic
4026 24th St. ☎641-8626.
Situated down in Noe Valley, this is the ultimate New Age store, full of crystals to cleanse your chakras and the like.

Union Street Papery
2162 Union St. ☎563-0200.
Excellent, pricey stationers selling fine writing paper and a range of cards and pens.

Chapter 17

Sports and Outdoor Activities

With such a mild climate and wide range of landscapes to choose from, it's not surprising that so many San Franciscans spend so much time outdoors. The fitness exuded by many locals is not the cosmetic "body-beautiful" kind that California, especially LA, is renowned for. Rather, people here just seem to lead more healthy lives. However, for all the outdoorsy windsurfers and hikers, there are equally many armchair sports fans who watch avidly but would collapse if forced to take part.

Spectator Sports

Although they're still reeling from the departure of 49ers quarterback Joe Montana, the dedication of San Franciscans to their professional sports teams can verge on the obsessive. Tickets for the big events sometimes sell out well in advance, though it's generally possible to take in a game if you show up on the day, and it needn't cost all that much: a seat in the sun-drenched "bleachers" (the outfield grandstand) to watch a baseball game goes for around $7, with seats closer in topping the scale at around $15.

Advance tickets for all Bay Area sports events are available through the BASS charge-by-phone ticket service (☎510/762-BASS), as well as from the teams themselves.

Baseball's **Oakland A's** play at the usually sunny Oakland Coliseum (☎510/638-0500), the **San Francisco Giants** at often cold and foggy Candlestick Park south of the city (☎467-8000).

Football's fabulous **San Francisco 49ers**, many-time Super Bowl champions, also appear at Candlestick Park (☎468-2249). It really can be hard to get hold of a ticket for their games; you may be lucky and get in for around $25, but you have to be prepared to fork out as much as $100 for a good seat.

The **Golden State Warriors** play basketball at Oakland Arena (☎638-6000). The Bay Area's newest sports team is ice hockey's **San Jose Sharks** (☎408/287-4275), based at their own brand-new arena in the South Bay.

Participant Sports

Cycling is quickly becoming San Francisco's favorite sporting pastime; almost every evening or weekend, bikes tend to outnumber motorists on the most popular routes. As well as enjoyable circuits in the East Bay and Marin County, a fine tour follows the crest of the coastal mountains from the city south down the Peninsula, looking out over the bay and the Pacific. For more ambitious, overnight tours, the Wine Country is hard to beat; see "Cycling in the Wine Country" on p.185 for further information and bike rental locations.

Sport and Outdoor Activities

The biggest boom has been the rise of **mountain biking**, which is said to have been invented on the steep slopes of Mount Tamalpais in Marin County, across the Golden Gate.

Local shops **rent** touring bikes with costs starting at about $15 per day, or mountain bikes starting from $25, and can usually suggest good routes. Outlets in San Francisco include *Park Cyclery*, 1865 Haight St (☎221-3777), and *Presidio Bicycles*, 5335 Geary Blvd (☎752-2453). In the East Bay, try *Cal Adventures*, 2301 Bancroft Way on the UC Berkeley campus (☎510/642-4000); in Tiburon, where you can cycle along the bayfront, *Ken's Bikes* is at 94 Main St (☎465-1683). *Point Reyes Bikes*, 11431 Hwy-1 in Point Reyes Station (☎663-1768), is also reliable.

Golden Gate Park and the Marina Green have become popular localities for **roller-blading**; if you want to have a go, rent skates from *Nuvo Colors*, 3108 Fillmore St (☎771-6886). To some extent, cycling and roller-blading have supplanted the Bay Area's former obsession, **jogging**, though you'll still see people running in the parks, and late May's **Bay-to-Breakers Race**, a distinctly San Franciscan institution, continues to thrive. Throngs of costumed joggers – waiters carrying wine glasses, giant centipedes and the like – follow a dozen world-class runners from the Embarcadero seven and a half miles across the city to Ocean Beach. If you're tempted to join in, call ☎777-2424 for details. In Marin County's much more serious **Dipsea** race, which takes place each June, several hundred runners race across the mountains from Mill Valley to Stinson Beach.

The water off the San Francisco coast tends to be pretty chilly, so **surfing** remains more of a Southern California phenomenon. However, wet-suited enthusiasts do get radical off most Bay Area **beaches**, particularly **Stinson Beach** in northern Marin County and along the Peninsula south of San Francisco – **Gray Whale Cove** and **San Gregorio** to name just two.

For simple suntanning or sandcastle-buiding, there are only two good beaches within the city itself: **Baker Beach**, just west of the Golden Gate Bridge, and **China Beach** near Lincoln Park.

Windsurfing is especially visible around Crissy Field and the Presidio, from where sailors race out and around the Golden Gate. At the Berkeley Marina, another center for windsurfers, you can also rent **sailboats** from the *Cal Sailing Club* (☎527-7245) and cruise around the bay.

Other Outdoor Activities

Besides the above, there's a whole range of considerably less athletic things to do in the great outdoors. If you're into gambling, you might fancy a day out at one of the two Bay Area **horse-racing** tracks: *Golden Gate Fields* in Albany in the East Bay (☎526-3020), or *Bay Meadows*, south of San Francisco down the Peninsula (☎547-7223). If you prefer to **ride** horses yourself, *Chabot Equestrian Center*, above East Oakland (☎569-4428), and *Miwok Livery* (☎383-8048) in Marin County both provide animals for trail-riding in fine locations. They charge around $35 for a three-hour ride.

Perhaps the most exceptional outdoor adventure available in the Bay Area is **whale-watching**, following herds of mighty California Gray Whales on their annual migration – generally between December and April – from Alaska to the Sea of Cortez. You can usually spot them from headlands (Point Reyes is one of the best), but to get a real sense of their size and might, you have to join them on the seas. The best local operator of boat trips is the non-profit *Oceanic Society*, Building E, Fort Mason Center (☎441-1104), who offer all-day trips out to the Farallon Islands, where even if it's not the right time of year for gray whales you'll see thousands of seabirds, including pelicans, cormorants and rarer creatures, and may possibly spy the world's largest mammal, the glorious blue whale.

Another possibility for wildlife-watchers (especially good for those prone to seasickness) happens around the same time as the whale migration – the mating season of the massive and grotesquely beautiful **Northern Elephant Seals**. These two-ton creatures spend most of January and February at Año Nuevo State Reserve, down the coast thirty miles south of San Francisco. If you fancy watching the trunk-nosed males as they battle it out for the right to make babies, see p.166 for details.

**Sport and
Outdoor
Activities**

The Contexts

A History of San Francisco

Though its recorded history may not stretch back very far by European standards, in its 150 years of existence San Francisco has more than made up for time. The city first came to life during the California Gold Rush of 1849, an adventure which set a tone for the place that it sustains to this day, both in its valuing of individual effort above corporate enterprise and in the often nonconformist policies that have given it perhaps the most liberal image of any US city. The following account is intended to give an overall view of the city's development; for a rundown of the figures – both past and present – who have helped to shape the city, see the "San Francisco People" glossary on p.297.

Native Peoples

For thousands of years prior to the arrival of Europeans, the **aboriginal peoples** of the Bay Area lived healthily and apparently fairly peacefully on the naturally abundant land. Numbering around 15,000, and grouped in small, tribal villages of a few hundred people, they supported themselves mainly by hunting and fishing rather than agriculture. Most belonged to the coastal **Miwok** tribe, who inhabited most of what is now Marin County, as well as the Sonoma and Napa valleys; the rest were **Ohlone**, who lived in smaller villages sprinkled around the bay and down the south coast of the peninsula.

Very few artefacts from the period survive, and most of what anthropologists have deduced is based on the observations of the early explorers, who were by and large impressed by the Indian way of life – if not their "heathen" religion. One of the first colonists characterized them as "constant in their good friendship, and gentle in their manners". Indian boats, fashioned from lengths of tule reed, were remarkably agile and seaworthy. Of the buildings, few of which were ever intended to last beyond the change of seasons, the most distinctive was the *temescal* or sweat lodge. Kule Loklo, a replica Miwok village in the Point Reyes National Seashore, provides a good sense of what their settlements might have looked like.

Since there was no political or social organization beyond the immediate tribal level, it did not take long for the colonizing Spaniards effectively to wipe them out, if more through epidemics than through outright genocide. Nowadays no Bay Area Native Americans survive on their aboriginal homelands.

Exploration and Conquest

Looking at the Golden Gate from almost any vantage point, it's hard to imagine that anyone might fail to notice such a remarkable opening to the Pacific. Nevertheless, dozens of **European explorers**, including some of the most legendary names of the New World conquest – Juan Cabrillo, Sir Francis Drake, Sebastian Vizcaino – managed to sail past for centuries, oblivious of the great harbor it protected. Admittedly, the passage is often obscured by fogs, and even on a clear day the Bay's islands, and the East Bay hills which rise up behind, do disguise the entrance to the point of invisibility.

The Englishman **Sir Francis Drake** came close to finding the Bay when he arrived in the *Golden Hind* in **1579**, taking a break from plundering Spanish vessels in order to make repairs. The "white bancks and cliffes" of his supposed landing spot – now called Drake's Bay, off Point Reyes north of San Francisco – reminded him of Dover. Upon going ashore, he was met by a band of Miwok, who greeted him with food and drink and placed a feathered crown upon his head; in return, he claimed all of their lands, which he called Nova Albion (New England), for Queen Elizabeth. Supposedly, he left behind a brass plaque; although this has been proved to be a fake, a copy remains on display in the Bancroft Library at the University of California in Berkeley.

Fifteen years later the Spanish galleon **San Augustín** – loaded to the gunwales with treasure from the Philippines – moored in the same spot, but met with tragically different results. After renaming Drake's Bay to honor their patron saint, San Francisco de Asis (Francis of Assisi), disaster struck: the ship was dashed against the rocks of Point Reyes and wrecked. The crew were able to salvage some of the cargo and enough of the ship to build a small lifeboat, on which they travelled south all the way to Acapulco, the Spanish base of operations in the Pacific, hugging the coast for the entire voyage and still sailing right past the Golden Gate. Indeed it was not until the end of 1769 that Western eyes set sight on the great body of water now called San Francisco Bay.

Colonization: The Mission Era

The **Spanish occupation** of the West Coast, which they called "Alta California", began in earnest in the late 1760s, following the Seven Years' War, partly due to military expediency (to prevent another power from gaining a foothold), and partly to Catholic missionary zeal to convert the heathen Indians. Early in **1769** a company of 300 soldiers and clergy set off from Mexico to establish an outpost at Monterey, half of them by ship, the other half overland. A number stopped to set up the first California mission at San Diego, while an advance party – made up of some sixty soldiers, mule skinners, priests and Indians, and led by Gaspàr de Portola – continued up the coast, blazing an overland route. It was hard going, especially with their inadequate maps, and not surprisingly they overshot their mark, ending up somewhere around Half Moon Bay.

Trying to regain their bearings, Portola sent out two scouting parties, one north along the coast and one east into the mountains. Both groups returned with extraordinary descriptions of the Golden Gate and the great bay, which they thought must be the same "Bahia de San Francisco" where the *San Agustín* had come to grief almost two centuries earlier. On November 4, 1769, the entire party gathered together on

the ridgetop, overwhelmed by the incredible sight: Father Crespi, their priest, wrote that the bay "could hold not only all the armadas of our Catholic Monarch, but also all those of Europe". Portola's band barely stayed long enough to gather up supplies before turning around and heading back to Monterey; that mission was to become the capital and commercial center of Spanish California.

It took the Spanish another six years to send an expedition 85 miles north to the bay Portola had discovered. In May **1775**, when he piloted the *San Carlos* through the Golden Gate, Juan Manuel de Ayala became the first European to sail into San Francisco Bay. The next year Captain **Juan Bautista de Anza** returned with some 200 soldiers and settlers to establish the **Presidio of San Francisco** overlooking the Golden Gate, as well as a mission three miles to the southeast, along a creek he named Nuestra Señora de Dolores – "Our Lady of Sorrows". From this came the mission's popular – and still current – name, **Mission Dolores**.

Over the coming years four other Bay Area **missions** were established. Santa Clara de Asis, forty miles south of Mission Dolores, was founded in 1777; San José de Guadalupe, set up in 1797 near today's Fremont, grew into the most successful of the lot. In 1817 the *asistencia*, or auxiliary mission San Rafael Arcangel was built in sunny Marin County as a convalescent hospital for priests and Indians who had been taken ill at Mission Dolores. The last, San Francisco Solano, built at Sonoma in 1823, was the only mission established under Mexican rule.

Each of the mission complexes was broadly similar, with a church and cloistered residence structure surrounded by irrigated fields, vineyards and more distant ranchlands, the whole protected by a small contingent of soldiers. Indian catechumens were put to work making soap and candles, but were treated as retarded children, often beaten and never educated. Objective facts about the missionaries' treatment of the Indians are hard to come by, though mission registries record twice as many deaths as they do births, and their cemeteries are packed with Indian dead. Many of the missions suffered from Indian raids; the now ubiquitous red-tiled roofs replaced the earlier thatch to resist fire.

To grow food for the missions and the forts or presidios, **towns** – called *pueblos* – were established, part of the ongoing effort to attract settlers to this distant and as yet undesirable territory. The first was laid out in 1777 at San José in a broad fertile valley south of the Mission Santa Clara. Though it was quite successful at growing crops, it had no more than a hundred inhabitants until well into the 1800s. Meanwhile, a small village – not sanctioned by the Spanish authorities – was beginning to emerge between Mission Dolores and the presidio, around the one deepwater landing spot, southeast of today's Telegraph Hill. Called **Yerba Buena**, "good grass", after the sweet-smelling minty herb that grew wild over the windswept hills, was little more than a collection of shacks and ramshackle jetties. Although the name San Francisco was not applied to it until the late 1840s, this tiny outpost formed the basis of today's metropolis.

The Mexican Revolutions and The Coming of the Americans

The emergence of an independent **Mexican state** in 1821 spelled the end of the mission era. Within a few years the new republic had secularized the missions and handed over their lands to the few powerful families of the "Californios" – mostly ex-soldiers who had settled here after completing their military service. The Mexican government exerted hardly any control over distant Yerba Buena, and was generally much more willing than the Spanish had been to allow foreigners to remain as they were, so long as they behaved themselves. A few trappers and adventurers had passed by in the early 1800s, and, beginning in the early 1820s, a number of British and Americans started arriving in the Bay Area, most of them sailors who jumped ship, but also including a few men of property. The most notable of these immigrants was **William Richardson**, an Englishman who arrived on a whaling ship in 1822 and stayed for the rest of his life, marrying the daughter of the Presidio commander and eventually coming to own most of southern Marin County, from where he started a profitable shipping company and ran the sole ferry service across the tricky bay waters. In Richardson's wake, dozens followed – almost without exception males who, like him, tended to fit in with the existing Mexican culture, often marrying into established families and converting to the Catholic faith.

As late as the mid-1840s, Monterey was still the only town of any size on the entire west coast, and tiny Yerba Buena (population 200 or

so) made its livelihood from supplying passing ships, mainly Boston-based whaling vessels and the fur traders of the English-owned **Hudson's Bay Company**. Though locals lived well, the Bay Area was not obviously rich in resources, and so was not by any means a major issue in international relations. However, from the 1830s onwards, the **US government** decided that it wanted to buy all of Mexico's lands north of the Rio Grande, California included, in order to fulfil the "Manifest Destiny" of the United States to cover the continent from coast to coast. Any negotiations were rendered unnecessary when, in June 1846, the Mexican–American War broke out in Texas, and US naval forces quickly took over the entire West Coast, capturing San Francisco's presidio on **July 9, 1846**.

A revealing – although historically insignificant – episode, which set the tone for the anarchic growth of the Bay Area over the next fifty years, took place around this time. An ambitious US Army captain, John C Fremont, had been working to encourage unhappy settlers to declare independence from Mexico, and to set himself up as their leader. By assembling an unofficial force of some sixty sharpshooting ex-soldiers, and by spreading rumors that war with Mexico was imminent and unstoppable, he managed to persuade settlers to take action: the **Bear Flag Revolt**. On June 14, some thirty farmers and trappers descended upon the abandoned presidio in Sonoma and took the retired commandant, Colonel Guadupe Vallejo, captive, raising a makeshift flag over the plaza and declaring California independent. The flag – which featured a roughly drawn grizzly bear above the words "California Republic" – was eventually adopted as the California state flag, but this "Republic" was short-lived. Three weeks after the disgruntled settlers hoisted their flag in Sonoma, it was replaced by the Stars and Stripes, and California was thereafter **US territory**. Ironically, just nine days before the Americans took formal control, **gold** was discovered on January 24, 1848, in the Sierra Nevada foothills a hundred miles east of the city – something that was to change the face of San Francisco forever.

The Gold Rush

At the time gold was discovered, the Bay Area had a total (non-native) population of around two thousand, about a quarter of whom lived in tiny **San Francisco**, which had only changed its name from Yerba Buena the year before. By the summer of 1848 rumors of the find attracted a trickle of gold seekers, and when news of their subsequent success filtered back to the coast (relayed by a local shopkeeper **Sam Brannan**, in Portsmouth Square), soldiers deserted and sailors jumped ship, and most towns were abandoned. Would-be settlers dropped everything to head for the gold fields. The first prospectors on the scene made fantastic fortunes – those working the richest "diggings" could extract more than an ounce every hour – but the real money was being made by merchants charging equally outrageous prices for essentials. Even the most basic supplies were hard to come by, and what little was available cost exorbitant amounts: a dozen eggs for $50, a shovel or pickaxe twice that. Exuberant miners willingly traded glasses of gold dust for an equal amount of whisky – something like $1000 a shot. Though it took some time for news of the riches to travel, soon men were flooding in to California from all over the globe to share the wealth, in the most madcap migration in world history. Within a year some 100,000 men – known collectively as the **Forty-Niners** – had arrived in California. About half of them came overland, after a three-month slog across the continent, and headed straight for the mines. The rest arrived by ship and landed at San Francisco, expecting to find a city where they could recuperate before continuing on the arduous journey. They must have been disappointed with what they found: hulks of abandoned ships formed the only solidly constructed buildings, rats overran the filthy streets, and drinking water was sparse and often contaminated.

Few of the new arrivals stayed very long in San Francisco, but, if anything, life in the mining camps proved even less hospitable. As thousands of moderately successful but worn-out miners returned to San Francisco, especially during the torrential rains of the **winter of 1849–50**, the shanty town settlement began to grow into a proper city. Ex-miners set up foundries and sawmills to provide those starting out with the tools of their trade, and traders arrived to profit from the miners' success, selling them clothing, food, drink and entertainment. The city where the successful miners came to blow their hard-earned cash was a place of luxury hotels and burlesque theaters, which featured the likes of Lola Montez, whose semi-clad "spider dance" enthralled legions of fans. Throughout the early

1850s immigrants continued to pour through the Golden Gate, and although the great majority hurried on to the mines, enough stayed around to bring the city's population up to around 35,000 by the end of 1853. Of these, more than half were from foreign parts – a wide-ranging mix of Mexicans, Germans, Chinese, Italians and others.

Within five years of the discovery of gold the easy pickings were all but gone, and as the free-wheeling mining camps evolved into increasingly large-scale, corporate operations, San Francisco swelled from frontier outpost into a substantial city, with a growing industrial base, a few newspapers, and even its own branch of the US Mint. When revenues from the gold fields ceased to expand in the late 1850s, the speculative base that had made so many fortunes quickly vanished. Lots that had been selling at a premium couldn't be given away, banks went bust, and San Francisco had to declare itself **bankrupt** as a result of years of corrupt dealings. The already volatile city descended into near-anarchy, with vigilante mobs roaming the streets enforcing their particular brand of justice. By the summer of 1856 the "Committee of Vigilance", led by William Coleman and the ever-present Sam Brannan and composed of the city's most successful businessmen, was the **de facto government** of the city, having taken over the state militia and installed themselves inside their "Fort Gunnybags" headquarters, outside which they regularly hanged petty criminals (admittedly after giving them a fair trial), to the amusement of gathered throngs. A few of the most radically minded vigilantes proposed secession from the US, but calmer heads prevailed, and the city was soon restored to more legitimate governance. The rest of the 1850s were comparatively uneventful, as San Francisco prepared for what was to become the biggest boom in the city's boom-and-bust cycle.

The Boom Years (1860–1900)

In the 1860s San Francisco enjoyed a bigger boom than that of the Gold Rush, following the discovery of an even more lucrative band of precious **silver ore** in the Great Basin mountains of western Nevada. Discovered just east of Reno in late 1859 and soon known as the **Comstock Lode**, it was one of the most fantastic deposits ever encountered: a single, solid vein of silver, mixed with gold, that ranged from ten to over a hundred feet wide and stretched a little over two miles long, most of it buried hundreds of feet underground. Mining here was in complete contrast to the freelance prospecting of the California gold fields, and required a scale of operations unimagined in the California mines. Many of San Francisco's great engineers, including George Hearst, Andrew Hallidie and Adolph Sutro, put their minds to the task.

As the mines had to go increasingly deeper to get at the valuable ore, the mining companies needed larger and larger amounts of capital, which they attracted by issuing shares dealt on the burgeoning San Francisco **Stock Exchange**. Speculation was rampant, and the value of shares could rise or fall by a factor of ten, depending on the day's rumors and forecasts; Mark Twain got his literary start publicizing, for a fee, various new "discoveries" in his employers' mines. Hundreds of thousands of dollars were made and lost in a day's trading, and the cagier players, like James Flood and James Fair, made millions.

While the Comstock silver enabled many San Franciscans to enjoy an unsurpassed prosperity throughout the 1860s, few people gave much thought to the decade's other major development, the building of the **transcontinental railroad**, completed in 1869 using imported Chinese laborers. Originally set up in Sacramento to build the western link, the **Central Pacific** and later **Southern Pacific** railroad soon expanded to cover most of the West, ensnaring San Francisco in its web. Wholly owned by the so-called **Big Four** – Charles Crocker, Collis P Huntington, Mark Hopkins and Leland Stanford – the Southern Pacific "octopus", as it was caricatured in the popular press, exercised an essential monopoly over transportation in the Bay Area. Besides controlling the long-distance railroads, they also owned San Francisco's streetcar system, the network of ferry boats that criss-crossed the bay, and even the cable car line that lifted them up California Street to their Nob Hill palaces (see p.64).

However, not everyone reaped the good fortune of the Nob Hill elite. The coming of the railroad usurped San Francisco's primacy as the West Coast's supply point, and products from the East began flooding in at prices well under anything local industry could manage. At the same time the Comstock mines ceased to produce such enormous fortunes, and depression began to set in. The lowering of economic

confidence was compounded by a series of droughts which wiped out agricultural harvests, and by the arrival in San Francisco of thousands of now unwanted **Chinese workers**. As unemployment rose throughout the late 1870s frustrated workers took out their aggression in racist assaults on the city's substantial Chinese population. While there were many instances of violent acts against individual Chinese people, most of the workers' displeasure was channelled into political activity. At mass demonstrations all over the city, thousands rallied behind the slogan "The Chinese must Go!"

Though San Francisco was popularly seen as being powered by ignoble motives and full of self-serving money-grabbers, there were a few exceptions, even among its wealthiest elite. **Adolph Sutro**, for example, was a German-born engineer who made one fortune in the Comstock mines and another buying up land in the city – in 1890 he was said to own ten percent of San Francisco, even more than the Big Four. But Sutro was an unlikely millionaire, as compassionate and public-spirited as the Big Four were ruthlessly single-minded; in fact, when the Southern Pacific tripled fares to a quarter on the trolley line out to Golden Gate Park, Sutro built a parallel line that charged a nickel. He also built the Sutro Baths and the Cliff House and in 1894 was elected mayor of San Francisco on the Populist Party ticket, campaigning on an anti-Southern Pacific manifesto which promised to rid San Francisco of "this horrible monster which is devouring our substance and debauching our people, and by its devilish instincts and criminal methods is every day more firmly grasping us in its tentacles". Sutro died in 1898, with the city still firmly in the grasp of the "octopus".

The Great Earthquake and After

San Francisco experienced another period of economic expansion in the **early years of the 1900s**, due in equal part to the Spanish–American War and the Klondike Gold Rush in Alaska. Both of these events increased ship traffic through the port, where dockworkers were beginning to organize themselves into **unions** on an unprecedented scale. The mighty longshoremen's association they formed was to become a political force to be reckoned with. The fight to win recognition and better wages was long and hard; unrest was virtually constant, and police were brought in to scare off strikers and prevent picket lines from shutting down the waterfront. But this economic instability was nothing compared to the one truly earth-shattering event of the time: the **Great Earthquake of 1906**.

The quake that hit San Francisco on the morning of April 18, 1906, was at 8.1 on the Richter Scale the most powerful ever to hit anywhere in the US, before or since (over ten times the force of the 1989 earthquake). It destroyed hundreds of buildings, but by far the worst destruction was wrought by the **post-earthquake conflagration** that followed, as ruptured gas mains exploded and chimneys toppled, starting fires that spread right across the city. It all but levelled the entire area from the waterfront, north and south of Market Street, west to Van Ness Avenue, whose grand mansions were dynamited to form a firebreak. Comparatively few people, around 500 in total, were killed, but about half of the population – some 100,000 people – were left homeless and fled the city. Many of those who stayed set up camp in the barren reaches of what's now Golden Gate Park, where soldiers from the Presidio undertook the mammoth task of establishing and maintaining a tent city for about 20,000 displaced San Franciscans.

During the ensuing ten years, San Francisco was rebuilt with a vengeance, reconstructing the city as it was and largely ignoring the grand plan drawn up by designer Daniel Burnham just a year before the disaster. The city council had given its approval to this plan, which would have replaced the rigid grid of streets with an eminently more sensible system of axial main boulevards filled in with curving avenues skirting the hills and smaller, residential streets climbing their heights. However, such was the power and influence of the city's vested interests that the status quo was quickly reinstated, despite the clear opportunity afforded by the earthquake.

To celebrate its recovery, and the opening of the Panama Canal – a project which had definite implications for San Francisco's trade-based economy – the city fathers set out to create the magnificent **1915 Panama Pacific International Exhibition**. Land was reclaimed from the bay for the exhibition and on it an elaborate complex of exotic buildings was constructed, including Bernard Maybeck's exquisite Palace of Fine Arts and centering on the 100-metre-high, gem-encrusted Tower of Jewels. Hundreds of thousands visited the fair, which lasted throughout the year, but when it ended all the buildings, save the Palace of Fine Arts, were torn down, and the land sold off for the houses that now make up the Marina district.

The great success of the exhibition proved to the world that San Francisco had recovered from the earthquake. But the newly recovered civic pride was tested the next year by one of the city's more disgraceful episodes. On the eve of America's involvement in **World War I**, a pro-war parade organized by San Francisco's business community was devastated by a **bomb attack** that killed ten marchers and severely wounded another forty. In their haste to find the culprit, the San Francisco police arrested half a dozen radical union agitators. With no evidence other than perjured testimony, activist **Tom Mooney** was convicted and sentenced to death, along with his alleged co-conspirator Warren Billings. Neither, fortunately, was executed, but both spent most of the rest of their lives in prison; Billings wasn't pardoned until 1961, 45 years after his fraudulent conviction.

The Roaring Twenties

The war years had little effect on San Francisco, but the period thereafter, the **Roaring Twenties**, was in many ways the city's finest era. Despite Prohibition, the jazz clubs and speakeasies of the Barbary Coast district were in full swing. San Francisco was still the premier artistic and cultural center of the West Coast, a role it would relinquish to Los Angeles by the next decade, and its status as an international financial hub (both major international credit card companies – today's *Visa* and *Access* – had their start here) was as yet unchallenged by the upstart southern megalopolis. The strength of San Francisco as a banking power was highlighted by the rise of the Bank of America – founded as the Bank of Italy in 1904 by A P Giannini in North Beach – into the largest bank in the world.

The buoyant 1920s gave way to the Depression of the 1930s, but, despite the sharp increases in unemployment, there was only one major battle on the industrial relations front. On **"Bloody Thursday"** – July 5, 1934 – police protecting strike-breakers from angry picketers fired into the crowd, wounding thirty and killing two longshoremen. The army was sent in to restore order, and in retaliation the unions called a **General Strike** that saw some 125,000 workers down tools, bringing the Bay Area economy to a halt for four days. Otherwise there was little unrest, and, thanks in part to **WPA sponsorship**, some of the city's finest monuments – Coit Tower for example, and most importantly the two great bridges – were built during this time. Before the **Bay and Golden Gate bridges** went up, in 1936 and 1937 respectively, links between the city and the surrounding towns of the Bay Area were provided by an impressive network of **ferry boats**, some of which were among the world's largest. In 1935, the ferries' peak year, some 100,000 commuters per day crossed the bay by boat; just five years later the last of the boats was withdrawn from service, unable to compete with the increasingly popular automobile.

World War II

The Japanese attack on Pearl Harbor and US involvement in **World War II** transformed the Bay Area into a massive war machine, its industry mobilizing quickly to provide weaponry and ships for the war effort. **Shipyards** opened all around the bay – the largest, the Kaiser Shipyards in Richmond, was employing over 100,000 workers on round-the-clock shifts just six months after its inception – and men and women flooded in to the region from all over the country to work in the lucrative concerns. Entire cities were constructed to house them, many of which survive – not least Hunter's Point, on the southern edge of the San Francisco waterfront, which was never intended to last beyond the end of hostilities but still houses some 15,000 of the city's poorest people. A more successful example is Marin City, a workers' housing community just north of Sausalito, which – surprisingly considering its present-day air of leisured affluence – was one of the most successful wartime shipyards, able to crank out a ship a day.

The Fifties

After the war, thousands of GIs returning from the South Pacific came home through San Francisco, and many decided to stay. The city spilled out into new districts, and, especially in suburbs like the Sunset, massive tracts of identical dwellings, subsidized by Federal loans and grants, were thrown up to house the returning heroes – many of whom still live here. The accompanying economic prosperity continued unabated well into the 1950s, and in order to accommodate increasing numbers of cars on the roads, huge **freeways** were constructed, cutting through the

city. The Embarcadero Freeway in particular formed an imposing barrier, perhaps appropriately dividing the increasingly office-orientated Financial District from the declining docks and warehouses of the waterfront, which for so long had been the heart of San Francisco's economy.

As the increasingly mobile and prosperous middle classes moved out from the inner city, new bands of literate but disenchanted middle-class youth began to move into the areas left behind, starting in the middle part of the decade, in the bars and cafés of North Beach, which swiftly changed from a staunch Italian neighborhood into the Greenwich Village of the West Coast. The **Beat Generation**, as they became known, reacted against what they saw as the empty materialism of 1950s America by losing themselves in a bohemian orgy of jazz, drugs and Buddhism, expressing their disillusionment with the status quo through a new, highly personal and expressive brand of fiction and poetry. The writer **Jack Kerouac**, whose *On the Road* became widely accepted as the handbook of the Beats, both for the style of writing (fast, passionate, unpunctuated), and the lifestyle it described, was in some ways the movement's main spokesman, and is credited with coining the term "Beat" – meaning beatific – to describe the group. Later, columnist Herb Caen somewhat derisively turned "beat" into beatnik, after Sputnik. San Francisco, and particularly the **City Lights Bookstore**, at the center of North Beach, became the main meeting point and focus of this diffuse group, though whatever impetus the movement had was gone by the early 1960s.

The Sixties

Though the long-term value of their writing is still debatable, there's no doubt that the Beats opened people's minds. However, it was an offshoot of the group, the **hippies**, that really took this task to heart. The term was originally a Beat put-down of the inexperienced but enthusiastic young people who followed in their hedonistic footsteps. The first hippies appeared in the early 1960s, in cafés and folk music clubs around the fringes of Bay Area university campuses. They, too, eschewed the materialism and the nine-to-five consumer world, but preferred an escapist fantasy of music and marijuana that became adapted as a half-baked political indictment of society and where it was going wrong.

The main difference between the Beats and the early hippies, besides the five years that elapsed, was that the hippies had discovered – and regularly experimented with – a new hallucinogenic drug called LSD, better known as **Acid**. Since its synthesis, LSD had been legally and readily available, mainly through psychologists who were interested in studying its possible therapeutic benefits. Other, less scientific research was also being done by a variety of people, many of whom, from around 1965 onwards, began to settle in the Haight-Ashbury district west of the city center, living communally in huge low-rent Victorian houses, in which they could take acid and "trip" in safe, controlled circumstances. **Music** was an integral part of the acid experience, and a number of bands – the Charlatans, Jefferson Airplane and the Grateful Dead – came together in San Francisco during the summer of 1966, playing open-ended dance music at such places as the Fillmore Auditorium and the Avalon Ballroom.

Things remained on a fairly small scale until the spring of **1967**, when a free concert in Golden Gate Park drew a crowd of 20,000 and, for the first time, media attention. Articles describing the hippies, most of which focused on their prolific appetites for sex and drugs, attracted a stream of newcomers to the Haight from all over the country, and within a few months the **"Summer of Love"** was well under way, with some 100,000 young people descending upon the district.

In contrast to the hippy indulgence of the Haight-Ashbury scene, across the bay in Berkeley and Oakland **revolutionary politics**, rather than drugs, were at the top of the agenda. While many of the hippies opted out of politics, the student radicals threw themselves into political activism, beginning with the Free Speech Movement at the University of California in 1964. The FSM, originally a reaction against the university's banning of on-campus political activity, laid the groundwork for the more passionate, **anti-Vietnam War** protests that rocked the entire country for the rest of the decade. The first of what turned out to be dozens of **riots** occurred in June 1968, when students marching down Telegraph Avenue in support of the Paris student uprising were met by a wall of police, leading to rioting that continued for the next few days. Probably the most famous event in Berkeley's radical history took place in **People's Park**, a plot of university-owned land that was taken over as

a community open space by local people. Four days later an army of police, under the command of Edwin Meese – who later headed the US Department of Justice in the Reagan years – teargassed and stormed the park, accidentally killing a bystander and seriously injuring over 100 others.

Probably the most extreme element of late 1960s San Francisco emerged out of the impoverished flatlands of Oakland – the **Black Panthers**, established by Bobby Seale, Huey Newton and Eldridge Cleaver in 1966. The Panthers were a heavily armed but numerically small band of militant black activists with an announced goal of securing self-determination for America's blacks. From their Oakland base they set up a nationwide organization, but the threat they posed, and the chances they were willing to take in pursuit of their cause, were too great. Thirty of their members died in gun battles with the police, and the surviving Panthers lost track of their aims: Eldridge Cleaver later became a right-wing Republican, while Huey Newton was killed over a drugs deal in West Oakland in 1989.

Contemporary San Francisco

The unrest of the 1960s continued into the **early 1970s**, if not at such a fever pitch. One last headline-grabber was the kidnapping in 1974 of heiress Patty Hearst from her Berkeley apartment by the *Symbionese Liberation Army*, or **SLA**, a hardcore bunch of revolutionaries who used their wealthy hostage to demand free food for Oakland's poor. Hearst later helped the gang to rob a San Francisco bank, wielding a submachine gun. Otherwise, certainly compared to the previous decade, the 1970s were quiet times, which saw the opening of the long-delayed *BART* high-speed transportation system, as well as the establishment of the **Golden Gate National Recreation Area** to protect and preserve 75,000 acres of open space on both sides of the Golden Gate Bridge.

Throughout the 1970s, it wasn't so much that San Francisco's rebellious thread had been broken, but rather that the battle lines were being drawn elsewhere. The most distinctive political voices were those of the city's large **gay and lesbian communities**. Inspired by the so-called Stonewall Riots in New York City in 1969, San Francisco's homosexuals began to organize themselves politically, demanding equal status with heterosexuals. Most importantly, gays and lesbians stepped out into the open and refused to hide their sexuality behind closed doors, giving rise to the gay liberation movement that has prospered worldwide. One of the leaders of the gay community in San Francisco, **Harvey Milk**, won a seat on the Board of Supervisors, becoming the first openly gay man to take public office. When Milk was **assassinated** in City Hall, along with Mayor George Moscone, by former Supervisor Dan White in 1978 – see p.108 – the whole city was shaken. The fact that White was found guilty of manslaughter, not murder, caused the gay community to erupt in riotous frustration, burning police cars and laying siege to City Hall.

The **1980s** have seen the city's gay community in retreat to some extent, with the advent of **AIDS** in the early part of the decade devastating the confidence of activists and toning down what was a very promiscuous scene. Now the community – in conjunction with City Hall – is fighting an impressive and dignified rearguard battle to deal with the disease.

Mayor **Diane Feinstein**, who took over after the death of Moscone, oversaw the construction of millions of square feet of office towers in downtown's Financial District, despite angry protests against the **Manhattanization** of the city. Although she dumped a tangled mess of financial worries in the lap of her successor, **Art Agnos**, Feinstein remains among the most prominent female politicians in America.

Many of the problems that face San Francisco – urban poverty, drug abuse, homelessness and of course the AIDS crisis – are much the same as those encountered by any major Western city. On top of this, the city was shaken by a major earthquake in October 1989, 7.1 on the Richter Scale – an event watched by 100 million people on nationwide TV since it hit during a World Series game between Bay Area rivals, the *San Francisco Giants* and the *Oakland A's*. That disaster, from which the city is still recovering, was followed two years later by a horrific fire in the Oakland hills, which killed 26 people and destroyed three thousand homes.

Midway through the 1990s, San Francisco finds itself grappling with fundamental questions. The city's liberal temperament is increasingly at odds with the behavior of current **Mayor Frank Jordan**, a former Chief of Police whose solution to homelessness has been to play Wild West lawman and give the homeless a one-way *BART* ticket out of town. Though such law-and-order tactics have not met with much public support, neither has there been much vocal opposition. Meanwhile, the effects of the ongoing economic downturn in California have been amplified in the Bay Area by post-Cold War military cut-backs, which have caused the closure of a number of military bases and cost 35,000 civilian jobs. Nonetheless, San Francisco remains a city few residents would forsake for anywhere else.

Writers on San Francisco

Writers seem to pull out all the stops trying to capture San Francisco's great beauty and unique energy. Some of the city's best writing has been in the form of journalism; the pieces below are essentially dispatches from various key points in its history.

Herb Caen

*The irascible, indefatigable **Herb Caen** has been giving the inside story of San Francisco people and places in his daily column for the San Francisco Chronicle since 1938. Although a fine satirist and good reporter of political happenings, he is best loved for daily dishing the dirt on San Francisco "society", and his 56 years of unstinting praise for the town he chose as home. The city's sole surviving upholder of politically incorrect journalism – we'll not see his like again. The two columns reproduced below are taken from The Best of Herb Caen, published by Chronicle Books.*

The Terrific Triangle

The clean old man was lounging against a wall at Taylor and Ellis, watching the new Hilton rise in all its sterile glory. "Well, that's it, kid," he said with a resigned smile. "That's the end of the Tenderloin."

As he spoke he was rhythmically flipping a $20 gold piece, that talisman of the old crowd. "Of course," he went on, "the Tenderloin has been dying for years. But that thing there" – he jabbed a finger at the monumental blockhouse – that's the gravestone." he chuckled without amusement. "Sort of looks like one, too."

I glanced around. There were more parking lots and fewer places to go. Nearby, a new jewellery shop was being installed. A streamlined branch of the world's biggest bank was already in business. A small hotel once noted for all-night revels has become a "residence" for "senior citizens", that irritating euphemism.

His purple-veined face shadowed under the pearl-gray fedora. The Clean Old man squinted into the late afternoon sun. Two hard-looking blondes in linty black slacks and high heels gave him a brief "Hi, baby" as they walked past. His eyes followed their rears down Ellis. "Won't see much of that any more," he said. "The old

Tenderloin is about to get as square as that hotel. Now tell me about the conventions Mr Hilton is gonna bring to town, and I'll ask you – where they gonna go for laughs when they get here?"

• • •

The old Tenderloin – the "Terrific Triangle" bounded by Jones, O'Farrell and Market. Tenderloin: a peculiarly American term, born in New York. The lexicographers aren't too sure about its origin; the most educated guess surmises that the cops on a certain beat in Manhattan were able to afford tenderloin steaks. In San Francisco, the juice was rich enough for filet mignons, sparkling burgundy, apartment houses and places in the country.

• • •

In the few blocks of the "Terrific Triangle," for a comparatively few years as a city's time is reckoned, there was more action than anywhere else in the country. There were fine restaurants: the Techau Tavern at 1 Powell, Newman's College Inn, the Bay City Grill, Herbert's Bachelor Grill. There were the "French" places – Blanco's, the St. Germain – with utter respectability on the ground floor, shady booths on the second, "riding academies" (as they were known) on the third.

You could drink till dawn in Dutch White's at 110 Eddy, and at Chad Milligan's Sport Club on Ellis. Franchon & Marco danced at Tait's Pavo Real on O'Farrell, where a kid named Rudolph Valentino was a busboy. Frank Shaw and Les Poe reigned at Coffee Dan's. It was unthinkable to miss a Sunday night at the old Orpheum, and if the bill there was a little weak (Jack Benny and Sophie Tucker), there was always the Tivoli, the Warfield, the Capitol, the Alcazar or Will King's Casino, with Will singing "I've got a girl who paints her cheeks, another with a voice that squeaks, they both ran away with a pair of Greeks – I wish I owned a restaurant!"

Girls, girls, girls. Every theater had a line, with Stage Door Johns to match. Every other small hotel was a house (the old Drexel alone had 30 girls). A doll with the marvelously San Francisco name of Dodie Valencia was a legend. Even the manicurists at Joe Ruben's barbershop were "as beautiful as Follies girls," the supreme accolade of the era.

* * *

But the lifeblood of the Old Tenderloin was gambling. The cars shuffled and the dice rattled through the smoky nights at the Menlo Club and the Kingston and at Chad Milligan's. The high rollers – Nick the Greek, Titanic Thompson, Joe "Silver Fox" Bernstein, Eddie Sahati – faded in and out with the foggy dawns. At Tom Kyne's in Opal Place, the cul-de-sac alongside the Warfield, you could bet on anything from the Mayor's race to the St Mary's–Santa Clara football game to how many passengers the ferries would carry the next day.

The gamblers were the kings of the Tenderloin, and their names rang true, straight out of Runyon and Lardner. Carnation Willie and Benny the Gent, Bones Remmer and Siggie Rosener, Freddy the Glut, and Jelly and Marty Breslauer. At 10 am – the end of the day that started at midnight – the bookies gathered at John's Grill on Ellis. Over the corned beef hash and the eggs sunnyside up they counted the cash and paid off the winners. Enough long green was scattered over the tables to carpet Ireland. Marty Breslauer alone packed $100,000, and one night a kid he'd befriended gunned him down for his roll.

But violence was rare. It was an underworld with class, a closed corporation. The cops, who were getting their share, kept it-that way, and the hoods of the Organization never had a chance to move in. When they arrived at Third and Townsend they were met by the two toughest Inspectors on the force, who put them right back on the train.

The cops knew a good thing, and they had it: The mother of a Captain on the Force was the biggest madam in the area. One day at Bay Meadows a rookie cop who didn't know the score told her: "One of these nights I'm gonna come into your place and close you down." "And when you do," she replied coolly, "you'll find your boss in the kitchen drinking coffee."

* * *

It was a world we'll never see again. Godliness and purity now reign – don't they? – and the final long shadow is being cast over the Tenderloin by the Rising Hilton. The section is about to become infinitely more respectable. And infinitely duller.

June 2, 1963

The View from the Heights

A reader writes: "As a newcomer to San Francisco, I am confused by the constant newspaper references to a district known as Pacific Heights, which I cannot find on any map of the city. Where – and what – is it?"

* * *

One is tempted to reply that Pacific Heights is a mythical faubourg that exists only in the minds of society editors, columnists and real estate agents, but that wouldn't be entirely accurate. For there really is a Pacific Heights, with its own peculiar view of San Francisco – perhaps the only view in town that looks inward rather than out.

Literally, Pacific Heights is a bit of a misnomer. Since it lies on the Northern flank of the city, it overlooks the Bay, not the Pacific. Physically, its boundaries are as loose as its restrictions are tight – let us say, from around Fillmore to Presidio, and from Clay to Union (westward from Presidio to about Arguello the section becomes Presidio Heights, with no marked difference in income or outlook).

However, as you may infer from these loose delineations, there is more to Pacific Heights than location, for many poor or socially unacceptable people live in the areas sketched above, and to be Really Pacific Heights you may not be either. But as long as you are neither, you may even live on Russian, Nob or Telegraph hills, and, in rare instances, Sea Cliff or even Jordan Park (VERY rare). Potrero Hill may make it yet, but never St Francis Wood.

A further salient of Pacific Heights juts down the Peninsula into parts of Burlingame, Hillsborough and Woodside, somehow avoiding Atherton almost completely. The late Mr Atherton would be astounded.

* * *

In sum, Pacific Heights is a point of view that points at itself with pride. Ideally, it is Old Money, which, as anybody knows, is much better than new, inflated stuff. It is Pucci pants, little Chanel suits, English bootmakers and an accent compounded of Ivy League schools, the proper upbringing and Old Forester.

Pacific Heights is "let's hop in the Jag and buzz down to Pebble for the weekend." It's knowing Paris much better than Los Angeles, New York better than Oakland, and the Right People in both. It's "couldn't be nicer, couldn't be more attractive, couldn't be more fun" and "couldn't have been duller," with or without the quotes. It's saying on long weekends, "Let's go away – EVERYBODY will be out of town anyway."

Pacific Heights is houseboys in white jackets walking poodles in clipped jackets, polished windows with shades drawn by polished butlers, indifferent dinners cooked by indifferent cooks ("good ones are SO hard to get"), surprisingly strong martinis and surprisingly bad wines. The houses are pleasant, whether done in Early Michael Taylor or Late Anthony Hail, and the mirrors are generally superior to, and looked at more often than, the pictures. As the finger bowls come, the ladies go to powder their noses.

Pacific Heights is an eternal cocktail party at which everybody knows everybody else, an endless bridge game involving the identical foursome, musical chairs to the same old tune, packages from Gump's, I Magnin, Pódesta and Laykin, Tuesday and Friday nights at the opera and a third-base box at Candlestick. If you're not With It, where are you?

Through all the changes it changes not. It is the city's power and sometimes glory, the Northern Lights and the Southern Cross, the day-and-night repository of all that is gilded and glamorous about San Francisco. It is Big Business and Big Pleasure, and it keeps a lot of money in circulation, occasionally its own. And if it sometimes appears to be out of touch with reality, weep not. Reality could very well be out of touch with Pacific Heights.

* * *

Without Pacific Heights – and let me stress again that I use the term loosely – San Francisco would not be what it is today, for better or worse. To the world of stylish travellers and slick magazine editors, it IS San Francisco – or at least the part of it that is thought of (and written about) as "sophisticated, gay and sparkling." When any distinguished visitor says, "I just adore San Francisco," you may be sure he isn't referring to picnics in Golden Gate Park or the English muffins at Foster's. He has been taken in by The Group, he has been given the Pacific Heights whirl, and this, forevermore, is San Francisco to him.

He is one of the fortunate few, for The Group is as clannish as its counterparts anywhere (visitors who say San Francisco is "cold" and "hard to get to know" didn't make it through the pearly gates). The cable cars, the bridges and Twin Peaks are fine to see, but if you haven't been invited into the hushed drawing rooms, where the minions of Thomas the Butler pass the

canapes, you haven't been inside the San Francisco where names are dropped and unlisted phone numbers picked up.

So I say hail to Pacific Heights, wherever it may be. As the city grows away from itself, it grows more deeply into itself, perhaps in self-protection. It is the last of the constants, where children still curtsy, manners are excellent, the ladies are lovely, and drinking a bit too much is not only acceptable but almost mandatory. Life may be equally pleasant in the Deep Mission or the Far Sunset, but Pacific Heights has the panache and the postiche, not to mention the Beluga and the Malassol, and the Aubusson underfoot.

Whatever high style still accrues to San Francisco lives on in this glorious Never-Never Land of three cars for every two-car garage and Chicken à la .Kiev in every pot. Long may it be preserved, sous cloche or on the rocks.

October 18, 1964

Hunter S Thompson

*One of America's most exciting and controversial essayists, **Hunter S Thompson** is a trouble-maker and muck-raker of the first order. Equally wild away from his typewriter, his experiences have included a spell with the Hell's Angels in San Francisco, about whom he wrote his first book. His later fascination with Richard Nixon reached its culmination in his long and consistently unforgiving book The Great Shark Hunt, from which the extract below is taken. After lying relatively low for a while at his Colorado ranch, he resurfaced in the 1980s to write a column for the San Francisco Examiner, pieces of which have been brought together in his latest collection of essays, Generation of Swine.*

The "Hashbury" Is the Capital of the Hippies

In 1965 Berkeley was the axis of what was just beginning to be called the "new left". Its leaders were radical, but they were also deeply committed to the society they wanted to change. A prestigious faculty committee said the Berkeley activists were the vanguard of "a moral revolution among the young," and many professors approved.

Now in 1967 there is not much doubt that Berkeley has gone through a revolution of some kind, but the end result is not exactly what the original leaders had in mind. Many one-time activists have forsaken politics entirely and turned to drugs. Others have even forsaken Berkeley.

During 1966, the hot center of revolutionary action on the coast began moving across the bay to San Francisco's Haight-Ashbury district, a run-down Victorian neighborhood of about forty square blocks between the Negro/Fillmore district and Golden Gate Park.

The "Hashbury" is the new capital of what is rapidly becoming a drug culture. Its denizens are not called radicals or beatniks, but "hippies" and perhaps as many as half are refugees from Berkeley and the old North Beach scene, the cradle and the casket of the so-called beat generation.

The other half of the hippy population is too young to identify with Jack Kerouac, or even with Mario Savio. Their average age is about twenty, and most are native Californians. The North Beach types of the late nineteen-fifties were not nearly as provincial as the Haight-Ashbury types are today. The majority of beatniks who flocked into San Francisco ten years ago were transients of the East and Midwest. The literary artistic nucleus – Kerouac, Ginsberg, et al – was a package deal from New York. San Francisco was only a stop on the big circuit: Tangier, Paris, Greenwich Village, Tokyo and India. The senior Beats had a pretty good idea what was going on in the world; they read newspapers, travelled constantly and had friends all over the globe.

The word "hip" translates roughly as "wise" or "tuned-in". A hippy is somebody who "knows" what's really happening, and who adjusts or grooves with it. Hippies despise phoniness; they want to be open, honest, loving, free. They reject the plastic pretence of twentieth-century America, preferring to go back to the "natural life", like Adam and Eve. They reject any kinship with the Beat Generation on the ground that "those cats were negative but our thing is positive". They also reject politics, which is "just another game". They don't like money, either, or any kind of aggressiveness.

A serious problem in writing about the Haight-Ashbury is that most of the people you have to talk to are involved, one way or another, in the drug traffic. They have good reason to be leery of strangers who ask questions. A twenty-two-year-old student was recently sentenced to two years in prison for telling an undercover narcotics agent where to buy some marijuana. "Love" is the password in the Haight-Ashbury, but paranoia is the style. Nobody wants to go to jail.

At the same time, marijuana is everywhere. People smoke it on the sidewalks, in doughnut shops, sitting in parked cars or lounging on the grass in Golden Gate Park. Nearly everyone on the streets between twenty and thirty is a "head", a user of either marijuana, LSD, or both. To refuse the proffered joint is to risk being labelled a "nark" – a narcotics agent – a threat and a menace to almost everybody.

With a few loud exceptions, it is only the younger hippies who see themselves as a new breed. "A completely new thing in this world, man." The ex-beatniks among them, many of whom are now making money off the new scene, incline to the view that hippies are, in fact, second generation beatniks and that everything genuine in the Haight-Ashbury is about to be swallowed – like North Beach and the Village – in a wave of publicity and commercialism.

Haight Street, the great white way of what the local papers call "hippieland", is already dotted with stores catering mainly to the tourist trade. Few hippies can afford a pair of $20 sandals or a "Mod outfit" for $67.50. Nor can they afford the $3.50 door charge at the Fillmore Auditorium and the Avalon Ballroom, the twin wombs of the "psychedelic, San Francisco, acid-rock sound". Both the Fillmore and the Avalon are jammed every weekend with borderline hippies who don't mind paying for the music and the light shows. There is always a sprinkling of genuine, bare-foot, freaked-out types on the dance floor, but few of them pay to get in. They arrive with the musicians or have other good connections.

Neither of the dance palaces is within walking distance of the Hashbury, especially if you're stoned, and since only a few of the hippies have contacts in the psychedelic power structure, most of them spend their weekend nights either drifting around on Haight Street or loading up on acid – LSD – in somebody's pad. Some of the rock bands play free concerts in Golden Gate Park for the benefit of those brethren who can't afford the dances. But beyond an occasional Happening in the park, the Haight-Ashbury scene is almost devoid of anything "to do" – at least by conventional standards. An at-home entertainment is nude parties at which celebrants paint designs on each other.

There are no hippy bars, for instance, and only one restaurant above the level of a diner or a lunch counter. This is a reflection of the drug culture which has no use for booze and regards food as a necessity to be acquired at the least possible expense. A "family" of hippies will work for hours over an exotic stew or curry in a communal kitchen, but the idea of paying $3 for a meal in a restaurant is out of the question.

Some hippies work, others live on money from home and many are full-time beggars. The post office is a major source of hippy income. Jobs like sorting mail don't require much thought or effort. A hippy named Admiral Love of the Psychedelic Rangers delivers special-delivery letters at night. The admiral is in his mid-twenties and makes enough money to support an apartmentful of younger hippies who depend on him for their daily bread.

There is also a hippy-run employment agency on Haight Street and anyone needing part-time labor or some kind of specialized work can call and order as many freaks as he needs; they might look a bit weird, but many are far more capable than most "temporary help", and vastly more interesting to have around.

Those hippies who don't work can easily pick up a few dollars a day panhandling along Haight Street. The fresh influx of curiosity-seekers has proved a great boon to the legion of psychedelic beggars. During several days of roaming around the area, I was touched so often that I began to keep a supply of quarters in my pocket so I wouldn't have to haggle over change. The panhandlers are usually barefoot, always young and never apologetic. They'll share what they collect anyway, so it seems entirely reasonable that strangers should share with them.

The best show on Haight Street is usually on the sidewalk in front of the Drog Store, a new coffee bar at the corner of Masonic Street. The Drog Store features an all-hippy revue that runs day and night. The acts change sporadically, but nobody cares. There will always be at least one man with long hair and sunglasses playing a wooden pipe of some kind. He will be wearing either a Dracula cape, a long Buddhist robe, or a Sioux Indian costume. There will also be a hairy blond fellow wearing a Black Bart cowboy hat and a spangled jacket that originally belonged to a drum major in the 1949 Rose Bowl parade. He will be playing the bongo drums. Next to the drummer will be a dazed-looking girl wearing a blouse (but no bra) and a plastic mini-skirt, slapping her thighs to the rhythm of it all.

These three will be the nucleus of the show. Backing them up will be an all-star cast of freaks,

every one of them stoned. They will be stretched out on the sidewalk, twitching and babbling in time to the music. Now and then somebody will fall out of the audience and join the revue; perhaps a Hell's Angel or some grubby, chain-draped impostor who never owned a motorcycle in his life. Or maybe a girl wrapped in gauze or a thin man with wild eyes who took an overdose of acid nine days ago and changed himself into a raven. For those on a quick tour of the Hashbury, the Drog-Store revue is a must.

Most of the local action is beyond the reach of anyone without access to drugs. There are four or five bars a nervous square might relax in, but one is a Lesbian place, another is a hangout for brutal-looking leather fetishists and the others are old neighborhood taverns full of brooding middle-aged drunks. Prior to the hippy era there were three good Negro-run jazz bars on Haight Street, but they soon went out of style. Who needs jazz, or even beer, when you can sit down on a public kerbstone, drop a pill on your mouth and hear fantastic music for hours at a time in your own head? A cap of good acid costs $5, and for that you can hear the Universal Symphony, with God singing solo and the Holy Ghost on drums.

Drugs have made formal entertainment obsolete in the Hashbury, but only until somebody comes up with something appropriate to the new style of the neighborhood. This summer will see the opening of the new Straight Theater, formerly the Haight Theater, featuring homosexual movies for the trade, meetings, concerts, dances. "It's going to be a kind of hippy community center", said Brent Dangerfield, a young radio engineer from Salt Lake City who stopped off in San Francisco on his way to a job in Hawaii and is now a partner in the Straight. When I asked him how old he was he had to think for a minute. "I'm twenty-two," he said finally, "but I used to be much older."

Another new divertissement, maybe, will be a hippy bus line running up and down Haight Street, housed in a 1930 Fagol bus – a huge, lumbering vehicle that might have been the world's first house trailer. I rode in it one afternoon with the driver, a young hippy named Tim Thibeau who proudly displayed a bathtub under one of the rear seats. The bus was a spectacle even on Haight Street: people stopped, stared and cheered as we rumbled by, going nowhere at all. Thibeau honked the horn and waved. He was from Chicago, he said, but when he got out of the Army he stopped in San Francisco and decided to stay. He was living, for the moment, on unemployment insurance, and his plans for the future were hazy. "I'm in no hurry", he said. "Right now I'm just taking it easy, just floating along." He smiled and reached for a beer can in the Fagol's icebox.

Dangerfield and Thibeau reflect the blind optimism of the younger hippy element. They see themselves as the vanguard of a new way of life in America – the psychedelic way – where love abounds and work is fun and people help each other. The young hippies are confident that things are going their way.

The older hippies are not so sure. They've been waiting a long time for the world to go their way, and those most involved in the hip scene are hedging their bets this time. "That back to nature scene is okay when you're twenty," said one. "But when you're looking at thirty-five you want to know something's happening to you."

Ed Denson, at twenty-seven, is an ex-beatnik, ex-Goldwaterite, ex-Berkeley radical and currently the manager of a successful rock band called Country Joe and the Fish. His home and headquarters is a complex of rooms above a liquor store in Berkeley. One room is an art studio, another is an office: there is also a kitchen, a bedroom and several sparsely furnished areas without definition.

Denson is deeply involved in the hippy music scene, but insists he's not a hippy. "I'm very pessimistic about where this thing is going," he said. "Right now it's good for a lot of people. It's still very open. But I have to look back at the Berkeley scene. There was a tremendous optimism there, too, but look where all that went. The beat generation? Where are they now? What about hula-hoops? Maybe this hippy thing is more than a fad; maybe the whole world is turning on but I'm not optimistic. Most of the hippies I know don't really understand what kind of a world they're living in. I get tired of hearing about what beautiful people we all are. If the hippies were more realistic they'd stand a better chance of surviving."

Lewis Lapham

Lewis Lapham comes from a firmly establishment San Francisco family: his grandfather was mayor of the city. Despite these top-notch connections, he grew completely disenchanted with the town and California as a whole, and headed East to become the editor of the highly respected Harpers Magazine. The following account describes what irks him about a city that so many people love so unquestioningly.

Lost Horizon

For the past six or seven weeks I have been answering angry questions about San Francisco. People who know that I was born in that city assume that I have access to confidential information, presumably at the highest levels of psychic consciousness. Their questions sound like accusations, as if they were demanding a statement about the poisoning of the reservoirs. Who were those people that the Reverend Jim Jones murdered in Guyana, and how did they get there? Why would anybody follow such a madman into the wilderness, and how did the Reverend Jones come by those letters from Vice-President Mondale and Mrs Rosalynn Carter? Why did the fireman kill the mayor of San Francisco and the homosexual city official? What has gone wrong in California, and who brought evil into paradise? Fortunately I don't know the answers to these questions; if I knew them, I would be bound to proclaim myself a god and return to San Francisco in search of followers, a mandala, and a storefront shrine. Anybody who would understand the enigma of San Francisco must first know something about the dreaming narcissism of the city, and rather than try to explain this in so many words, I offer into evidence the story of my last assignment for the *San Francisco Examiner*.

I had been employed on the paper for two years when, on a Saturday morning in December of 1959 reported for work to find the editors talking to one another in the hushed and self-important way that usually means that at least fifty people have been killed. I assumed that a ship had sunk or that a building had collapsed. The editors were not in the habit of taking me into their confidence, and I didn't expect to learn the terms of the calamity until I had a chance to read the AP wire. Much to my surprise, the city editor motioned impatiently in my direction, indicating that I should join the circle of people standing around his desk and turning slowing through the pages of the pictorial supplement that the paper was obliged to publish the next day. Aghast at what they saw, unable to stifle small cries of anguished disbelief, they were examining twelve pages of text and photographs arranged under the heading LOS ANGELES – THE ATHENS OF THE WEST. To readers unfamiliar with the ethos of San Francisco, I'm not sure that I can convey the full and terrible effect of this headline. Not only was it wrong, it was monstrous heresy. The residents of San Francisco dote on a romantic image of the city, and they imagine themselves living at a height of civilization accessible only to Erasmus or a nineteenth-century British peer. They flatter themselves on their sophistication, their exquisite sensibility, their devotion to the arts. Los Angeles represents the antithesis of these graces; it is the land of the Philistines, lying somewhere to the south in the midst of housing developments that stand as the embodiment of ugliness, vulgarity, and corruptions of the spirit.

Pity, then, the poor editors in San Francisco. In those days there was also a *Los Angeles Examiner,* and the same printing plant supplied supplements to both papers. The text and photographs intended for a Los Angeles audience had been printed in the Sunday pictorial bearing the imprimatur of the *San Francisco Examiner.* It was impossible to correct the mistake, and so the editors in San Francisco had no choice but to publish and give credence to despised anathema.

This so distressed them that they resolved to print a denial. The city editor, knowing that my grandfather had been mayor of San Francisco and that I had been raised in the city, assumed that he could count on my dedication to the parochial truth. He also knew that I had studied at Yale and Cambridge universities, and although on most days he made jokes about the future of a literary education, on this particular occasion he saw a use for it. What was the point of reading all those books if they didn't impart the skills of a sophist? He handed me the damnable pages and said that I had until five o'clock in the afternoon to refute them as false doctrine. The story was marked for page 1 and an eight-column headline. I was to spare no expense of adjectives.

The task was hopeless. Los Angeles at the time could claim the residence of Igor Stravinsky, Aldous Huxley, and Christopher Isherwood. Admittedly they had done their best work before coming west to ripen in the sun, but their names and photographs, together with those of a few well-known painters and a number of established authors temporarily engaged in the writing of screenplays, make for an impressive display in a newspaper. Even before I put through my first telephone call, to a poet in North Beach experimenting with random verse, I knew that cultural enterprise in San Francisco could not sustain the pretension of a comparison to New York or Chicago, much less to Periclean Athens.

Ernest Bloch had died, and Darius Milhaud taught at Mills College only during the odd years; Henry Miller lived 140 miles to the south at Big Sur, which placed him outside the city's penumbra of light. The Beat Generation had disbanded. Allen Ginsberg still could be seen brooding in the cellar of the City Lights Bookshop, but Kerouac had left town, and the tourists were occupying the best tables at Cassandra's, asking the waiters about psychedelic drugs and for connections to the Buddhist underground. Although I admired the work of Evan Connell and Lawrence Ferlinghetti, I doubted that they would say the kinds of things that the city editor wanted to hear. The San Francisco school of painting consisted of watercolor views of Sausalito and Fisherman's Wharf; there was no theater, and the opera was a means of setting wealth to music. The lack of art or energy in the city reflected the lassitude of a citizenry content to believe its own press notices. The circumference of the local interest extended no more than 150 miles in three directions – as far as Sonoma County and Bolinas in the north, to Woodside and Monterey in the south, and to Yosemite and Tahoe in the east. In a westerly direction the civic imagination didn't reach beyond the Golden Gate Bridge. Within this narrow arc the inhabitants of San Francisco entertained themselves with a passionate exchange of gossip.

At about three o'clock in the afternoon I gave up hope of writing a believable story. Queasy with embarrassment and apology, I informed the city editor that the thing couldn't be done, that if there was such a place as an Athens of the West – which was doubtful – then it probably was to be found on the back lot of a movie studio in Los Angeles. San Francisco might compare to a Greek colony on the coast of Asia Minor in the fourth century B.C., but that was the extent of it. The city editor heard me out, and then after an awful and incredulous silence, he rose from behind his desk and denounced me as a fool and an apostate. I had betrayed the city of my birth and the imperatives of the first edition. Never could I hope to succeed in the newspaper business. Perhaps I might find work in a drug-store chain, preferably somewhere east of St Louis, but even then he would find himself hard-pressed to recommend me as anything but a liar and an assassin. He assigned the story to an older and wiser reporter, who relied on the local authorities (Herb Caen, Barnaby Conrad, the presidents of department stores, the director of the film festival), and who found it easy enough to persuade them to say that San Francisco should be more appropriately compared to Mount Olympus.

I left San Francisco within a matter of weeks, depressed by the dreamlike torpor of the city. Although in the past eighteen years I often have thought of the city with feelings of sadness, as if in mourning for the beauty of the hills and the clarity of the light in September when the wind blows from the north, I have no wish to return. The atmosphere of unreality seems to me more palpable and oppressive in San Francisco than it does in New York. Apparently this has always been so. Few of the writers associated with the city stayed longer than a few seasons. Twain broke camp and moved on; so did Bierce and Bret Harte. In his novel *The Octopus*, Frank Norris describes the way in which the Southern Pacific Railroad in the 1890s forced the farmers of the San Joaquin Valley to become its serfs. The protagonist of the novel, hoping to stir the farmers to revolt and to an idea of liberty, looks for political allies among the high-minded citizens of San Francisco. He might as well have been looking for the civic conscience in a bordello. A character modelled after Collis Huntington, the most epicurean of the local robber barons, explains to him that San Francisco cannot conceive of such a thing as social justice. The conversation takes place in the bar at the Bohemian Club, and the financier gently says to Norris's hero that "San Francisco is not a city ... it is a midway plaisance".

The same thing can be said for San Francisco almost a hundred years later, except that in the modern idiom people talk about the city as "carnival." The somnambulism of the past has been joined with the androgynous frenzy of the present, and in the ensuing confusion who knows what's true and not true, or who's doing what to whom and for what reason? The wandering bedouin of the American desert traditionally migrate to California in hope of satisfying their hearts' desire under the palm tree of the national oasis. They seek to set themselves free, to rid themselves of all restraint, to find the Eden or the fountain of eternal youth withheld or concealed from them by the authorities (nurses, teachers, parents, caliphs) in the walled towns of the East. They desire simply to be, and they think of freedom as a banquet. Thus their unhappiness and despair when their journey proves to have been in vain. The miracle fails to take place, and things remain pretty much as they were in Buffalo or Indianapolis. Perhaps this explains the high rate of divorce, alcoholism, and suicide. The *San Francisco Examiner* kept a record of the people who jumped off the Golden Gate Bridge, and the headline always specified the number of the most recent victim as if adding up the expense of the sacrifice to the stone-faced gods of happiness.

Books

Travel/Impressions

Where the books we recommend below are published in both the USA and Britain, the US publisher is listed first.

Martin Amis *The Moronic Inferno and Other Visits to America* (Viking Penguin/Penguin). An assortment of essays that pull no punches in their dealings with American life and culture, including the moral majority, militarism and high-energy consumerism.

John Miller (ed) *San Francisco Stories* (Chronicle, US). Patchy collection of writings on the city with contributions from Lewis Lapham, Tom Wolfe, Dylan Thomas and Hunter S Thompson to name a few.

Czeslaw Milosz *Visions from San Francisco Bay* (Farrar, Straus & Giroux/Carcanet). Written in Berkeley during the unrest of 1968, these dense and somewhat ponderous essays show a European mind trying to come to grips with California's nascent Aquarian Age.

Mark Twain *Roughing It* (Signet/Penguin). Vivid tales of frontier California, particularly evocative of life in the silver mines of the 1860s Comstock Lode, where Twain got his start as a journalist and storyteller. His descriptions of San Francisco include a moment-by-moment description of an earthquake.

Tom Wolfe *The Electric Kool-Aid Acid Test* (Bantam/Black Swan). Tom Wolfe at his most expansive, riding with the Grateful Dead and Hell's Angels on the magic bus of Ken Kesey and the Merry Pranksters as they travel through the early 1960s, turning California on to LSD.

History, Politics and Society

Walton Bean *California: An Interpretive History* (McGraw-Hill, US). Blow-by-blow account of the history of California, including all the shady deals and back-room politicking, presented in accessible, anecdotal form.

Joan Didion *Slouching Towards Bethlehem* (Farrar, Straus & Giroux/Penguin). Selected essays from one of California's most renowned journalists, taking a critical look at the West Coast of the Sixties, including San Francisco's acid-culture and a profile of American hero John Wayne. In a similar style, *The White Album* (Penguin) traces the West Coast characters and events that shaped the Sixties and Seventies, including The Doors, Charles Manson and the Black Panthers.

Edmund Fawcett and Tony Thomas *America and the Americans* (Harper & Row/Fontana). A wide-ranging, up-to-the-minute and engagingly written rundown on the USA in all its aspects from politics to sport and religion. An essential beginner's guide to the nation.

Frances Fitzgerald *Cities on a Hill* (Touchstone Books/Picador). Intelligent, thorough and sympathetic exploration of four of the odder corners of American culture, including San Francisco's Castro district, the Rajneeshi community of Oregon, and TV evangelism.

Jamie Jensen *Built ·to Last – 25 Years of the Grateful Dead* (Penguin). Photo-filled history of San Francisco's psychedelic heroes from their early days in the Haight to their present near-divine stature, by one of the authors of this guide.

Charles Perry *The Haight-Ashbury* (Random House o/p, US). Curiously distant but detailed account of the Haight during the Flower Power years, written by an editor of *Rolling Stone*, a magazine that got its start there.

Mel Scott *The San Francisco Bay Area: A Metropolis in Perspective* (UC Press, US). Though somewhat dry and academic, this enormous tome will tell you all you ever wanted to know about the evolution of San Francisco and the Bay Area.

Jay Stevens *Storming Heaven: LSD and the American Dream* (Harper & Row/Heinemann). An engaging account of psychedelic drugs and their effect on American society through the Sixties, with an epilogue covering "designer drugs" – Venus, Ecstasy, Vitamin K and others – and the inner space they help some modern Californians to find.

Hunter S Thompson *The Great Shark Hunt* (Warner Books/Picador). Collection of often barbed and cynical essays on 1960s American life and politics – thought-provoking and hilarious. *Generation of Swine* (Random/Picador) is a more recent collection of caustic musings on the state of America and those who control it, assembled from his regular column in the *San Francisco Examiner*.

Tom Wolfe *Radical Chic & Mau Mauing the Flak Catchers* (Bantam, US). Wolfe's waspish account of Leonard Bernstein's fundraising party for the Black Panthers – a protracted exercise in character assassination – is coupled with an equally sharp analysis of white guilt and radical politics in City Hall, San Francisco. Often ideologically unsound, always very funny.

Specific Guides

Adab Bakalinsky *Stairway Walks in San Francisco* (Lexicos, US). Small, nicely illustrated guide detailing pretty back streets and stairways through San Francisco's hills. Excellent for turning up lesser-known spots on a walking tour.

California Coastal Commission *California Coastal Access Guide* (UC Press, US). The most useful and comprehensive plant and wildlife guide to the California coast, packed with maps and background information.

Don Herron *The Literary World of San Francisco* (City Lights, US). A walk through the San Francisco neighborhoods associated with authors who have lived in and written about the city. Detailed and well presented, it's an essential handbook for anyone interested in San Francisco's literary heritage.

Judith Kahn *Indulge Yourself* (Kahn, US). The ideal companion for the café animal, this book covers San Francisco's most famous and beautiful coffee spots, giving hints on when to go, what sort of people you'll see and what's on offer.

Karen Liberatore *The Complete Guide to the Golden Gate National Recreation Area* (Chronicle,

US). Easy-to-read book covering San Francisco's extensive waterfront areas and large green spaces, with historical perspective. Lots of photos.

Don and Betty Martin *The Best of San Francisco* (Chronicle, US). A lighthearted series of top-ten listings of the best that San Francisco has to offer. Categories range from the "Top Ten Seafood Restaurants" to the "Ten Naughtiest Things to do in San Francisco". More amusing than helpful, but some interesting pointers.

Grant Peterson *Roads to Ride* (Heyday Books, US). As its subtitle says, this is a bicyclist's topographic guide to the whole Bay Area, and is particularly good on the back roads of Marin County.

Don Pitcher *Berkeley Inside/Out* (Heyday Books, US). This is an extremely well-written, fully illustrated and encyclopedic guidebook to the most dynamic small town in the Bay Area.

Peggy Wayburn *Adventuring in the San Francisco Bay Area* (Sierra Club, US). If you are planning to spend any time hiking in the Bay Area's many fine wilderness regions, pick up this fact-filled guide, which also details a number of historic walks through the city's urban areas.

Fiction and Poetry

Ambrose Bierce *The Enlarged Devil's Dictionary* (Dover/Penguin). Spiteful but hilarious compilation of definitions (ie "Bore: a person who talks when you wish him to listen") by turn-of-the-century journalist. Bierce also wrote some great horror stories, including the stream-of-consciousness "An Occurrence at Owl Creek Bridge", collected in *Can Such Things Be* (Citadel, US) and his *Collected Works* (Citadel/Picador).

Richard Brautigan *The Hawkline Monster* (Pocket/Picador). Whimsical, surreal tales by noted Bay Area hippy writer.

Philip K Dick *The Man in the High Castle* (Berkeley Pub/Penguin). Long-time Berkeley- and Marin County-based science fiction author imagines an alternative San Francisco, following upon a Japanese victory in World War II. Of his dozens of other brilliant novels and short stories, *Bladerunner* (Balantine/Grafton) and *The Transmigration of Timothy Archer* (Pocket/Grafton) make good use of Bay Area locales.

John Dos Passos *USA* (Houghton Mifflin/Penguin). Massive, groundbreaking trilogy, combining fiction, poetry and reportage to tap the various strands of the American Experience. Much of the first part, *The 42nd Parallel*, takes place around Sutro Baths and Golden Gate Park.

Allen Ginsberg *Howl and Other Poems* (City Lights, US). The attempted banning of the title poem assured its fame; *Howl* itself is an angry rant that will often make you wince, but a Whitmanesque voice shines through in places.

Dashiell Hammett *The Four Great Novels* (Knopf/Picador). Seminal detective stories including *The Maltese Falcon* and starring Sam Spade, the private investigator working out of San Francisco. See also Diane Johnson's absorbing *The Life of Dashiell Hammet* (Fawcett/Picador).

Jack Kerouac *On the Road* (Signet/Penguin). The book that launched a generation with its "spontaneous bop prosody", it chronicles Beat life in a series of road adventures, featuring some of San Francisco and a lot of the rest of the US. His other books include *Lonesome Traveller* (Grove-Weidenfeld/Grafton), *The Dharma Bums* (Signet/Grafton) and *Desolation Angels* (Perigee/Grafton).

David Lodge *Changing Places* (Viking Penguin/Penguin). Thinly-disguised autobiographical tale of an English academic who spends a year teaching at UC Berkeley (renamed in the book) and finds himself bang in the middle of the late 1960s student upheaval.

Jack London *Martin Eden* (Airmont/Penguin). Jack Kerouac's favorite book; a semi-autobiographical account tracking the early years of this San Francisco-born, Oakland-bred adventure writer. The lengthy opus tells of his rise from waterfront hoodlum to high-brow intellectual, and of his subsequent disenchantment with the trappings of success.

Armistead Maupin *Tales of the City; Further Tales of the City; More Tales of the City; Babycakes; Significant Others; Sure of You* (Harper & Row/Black Swan). Six lively consecutive soap operas, wittily detailing the sexual and emotional antics of a select group of archetypal San Francisco

characters, taking them from the late 1970s to the end of the 1980s.

Seth Morgan *Homeboy* (Random/Chatto & Windus). Novel charting the sleazy San Francisco experiences of the former junkie boyfriend of Janis Joplin.)

Frank Norris *McTeague: A Story of San Francisco* (Viking Penguin/Penguin). Dramatic, extremely violent but engrossing saga of love and revenge in turn-of-the-century San Francisco; later filmed by Erich von Stroheim as *Greed*. Norris's *Octopus* (Penguin) tells the bitter tale of the Southern Pacific Railroad's stranglehold over the California economy.

Thomas Pynchon *The Crying of Lot 49* (Harper & Row/Picador). Follows the labyrinthine adventures of techno-freaks and pot-heads in 1960s California, revealing the sexy side of stamp collecting.

Vikram Seth *The Golden Gate* (Random/Faber). Slick novel in verse, tracing the complex social lives of a group of San Francisco yuppies, by the subsequent author of the spell-binding blockbuster *A Suitable Boy*.

Gary Snyder *Left Out in the Rain* (North Point Press, US). One of the original Beat writers, and the only one whose work ever matured, Snyder's poetry is direct and spare, yet manages to conjure up a deep animistic spirituality underlying everyday life.

Amy Tan *The Joy Luck Club* (Ivy Books/Minerva). Four Chinese-American women and their daughters gather together to look back over their lives. Moving story of immigrant struggle in the sweatshops of Chinatown.

William T Vollman *The Rainbow Stories* (Atheneum/ Andre Deutsch). Gut-level portraits of San Francisco street life: Tenderloin whores, Haight Street skinheads, beggars, junkies and homeless Vietnam Vets. Visceral and involving stuff.

San Francisco on Film

San Francisco is a favorite with Californian film-makers, the city's staggering range of settings and chameleon-like geography making an often economical choice for the director who needs sunny beaches, swirling fogs, urban decay and pastoral elegance all at once. Thrillers, in particular, seem to get good mileage out of the city; Hitchcock loved it, while the ridiculous gradients are almost ideally suited to the car chases that Hollywood loves so much. Below is a list of the obvious and not-so-obvious films made about or in California's most beautiful city.

An Eye for an Eye (Steve Carver 1981). Chuck Norris plays an undercover San Francisco narcotics officer who quits the force when his partner is set up and killed. Typical lone-wolf action flick, with Norris flexing his bulk through a series of violent acts on an Oriental drug ring until he nails the bad guy.

Barbary Coast (Howard Hawks 1935). Set in misty, fog-bound turn-of-the-century San Francisco, Edward G Robinson finds he has competition when he tries to seduce the exotic dancer played by Miriam Hopkins. A brawling adventure film that captures the spirit of a lawless San Francisco.

Basic Instinct (Paul Veerhoven 1992). Surprisingly conventional sex murder mystery that makes good use of San Francisco locales.

Bird Man of Alcatraz (John Frankenheimer 1962). Earnest but overlong study of real-life convicted killer Robert Stroud (Burt Lancaster) who becomes an authority on birds while kept in America's highest security prison.

The Birds (Alfred Hitchcock 1963). Some brilliant set-pieces in this allegory about our hostile feathered friends, set on the rugged coast just north of San Francisco.

Bullit (Peter Yates 1968). Steve McQueen gives an assured central performance in this over-praised but entertaining cop thriller, which contains the definitive San Francisco car chase.

Chan is Missing (Wayne Wang 1982). Low-budget sleeper hangs a thoroughly unpredictable study of San Francisco's Chinatown and the Chinese-American experience on a mystery-suspense peg. Often satirical, it shows a Chinatown the tourists don't usually see.

Common Threads: Stories from the Quilt (Robert Epstein 1989). The maker of *The Times of Harvey Milk* again focuses on gay San Francisco in his sensitive feature-length documentary about the Names Project Memorial Quilt. Talking to six bereaved partners of AIDS victims, it tackles the political and social impact of the disease as well as concentrating on the sacrifice of those involved.

The Conversation (Francis Ford Coppola 1974). This chilling character study of San Francisco surveillance expert Harry Caul (Gene Hackman at his finest) is one of the best films of the Watergate era. The key titular sequence is set in San Francisco's Union Square.

The Counsellor (Alberto De Martino 1973). Italian Mafia movie, dubbed into English and shot in San Francisco. Little more than a take-off of *Bullit* and *The Godfather*.

Crackers (Louis Malle 1983). Donald Sutherland rescues what is otherwise a limp art film about struggling on the back streets of San Francisco. One of a million films to romanticize being poor.

Dark Passage (Delmer Davies 1947). Classic thriller set in fog-bound San Francisco, where Humphrey Bogart, with Lauren Bacall's help, tries to clear his name of a murder of which he is wrongly accused. Beautifully shot, if unconvincing.

Days of Wine and Roses (Martin Manulis 1962). Jack Lemmon plays a likeable drunk who drags his wife into alcoholism, too, only to leave her there. once he's on the road to recovery. Smart satirical comedy that occasionally slips into melodrama.

The Dead Pool (Buddy Van Horn 1988). Clint Eastwood maintains his unflinching facial expression through this *Dirty Harry Part Five* as he stalks the streets of San Francisco's Chinatown looking for trouble. Repetitive rubbish.

Dim Sum (Wayne Wang 1985). Appealing little film about a more-or-less Westernized Chinese family in San Franciso. A treat.

Dirty Harry (Don Siegel 1971). Sleek and exciting sequel-spawning thriller casts Clint Eastwood in definitive role as neo-fascist San Francisco cop. Morally debatable, technically dynamic.

D.O.A. (Rudolph Mate 1949). Surprisingly involving suspense movie in which Edmond O'Brien tries to discover who poisoned him before he dies. Excellent use of LA and San Francisco locales.

The Enforcer (James Fargo 1976). *Dirty Harry Part Three* finds Clint Eastwood in typically aggressive mood, at odds with the liberal supervisors who want to stop him from killing every teenage delinquent on the streets of San Francisco. The predictability is relieved only slightly by the appearance of Tyne Daly, who plays a female police officer against ridiculous odds.

Escape From Alcatraz (Don Siegel 1979). Tense, well-crafted picture, based on a true story about an attempted escape from the infamous prison.

Experiment in Terror (Blake Edwards 1962). The inspiration for David Lynch's *Twin Peaks*, this entertaining Cold War period piece has dozens of FBI agents tying to track down an obscene phone caller in SF's Twin Peaks neighborhood.

Eye of the Cat (David Lowell Rich 1969). *Psycho*-esque thriller in which a man with a cat phobia goes to stay with an ageing aunt who has an army of them.

Family Plot (Alfred Hitchcock 1976). The master's last film is a lark about stolen jewels, kidnapping and psychic sleuthing in and around San Francisco.

Fillmore (Richard T Heffron 1972). Bad rock movie about San Francisco's famous music venue in the last week of its existence. Good footage of the Grateful Dead, Jefferson Airplane and Boz Scaggs, but Bill Graham's egomaniacal ranting between the acts soon becomes wearying.

Flower Drum Song (Ross Hunter 1961). Patronizing, remorselessly cute Rogers and Hammerstein musical about love dilemmas in San Francisco's Chinatown.

Fog over Frisco (William Dieterle 1934). A very young Bette Davis plays a wayward heiress who is kidnapped in this terse thriller.

48 Hours (Walter Hill 1982). Eddie Murphy puts in a slick comic performance as the criminal sidekick to Nick Nolte's tough-talking cop, who has 48 hours to wrap up a homicide case. Fantastic shots of San Francisco and quick-witted dialogue make this fast-paced comedy-thriller immensely entertaining.

Foul Play (Colin Higgins 1978). Entertaining comedy thriller in which Goldie Hawn plays against type as a dizzy blonde next to a similarly petite Dudley Moore. Chevy Chase is a great pot head.

Freebie and the Bean (Richard Rush 1974). Another San Francisco cop movie that tries to be at once achingly funny and disturbingly violent. James Caan does a credible job of playing one half of a wise-cracking duo, but overall it's a cheap, manipulative piece of tat.

The Frisco Kid (Samuel Bischoff 1935). James Cagney stars in this rough and tumble tale of a shanghaied sailor who rises to power amid the riff-raff of the 1860s Barbary Coast.

The Frisco Kid (Howard Koch Jr 1979). Implausible but amusing comedy about a rabbi who befriends an outlaw on his way to San Francisco. Silly and sentimental, it nonetheless has good comic performances from Gene Wilder and Harrison Ford.

Gentleman Jim (Raoul Walsh 1942). Rich evocation of 1880s San Francisco with Eroll Flynn playing the charming, social-climbing boxer, Gentleman Jim Corbett.

Gimme Shelter (David & Albert Maysles/Charlotte Zwerin 1970). Legendary film about the Rolling Stones' Altamont concert (see p.158). Lots of shots of Mick Jagger looking bemused during and after the notorious murder.

Greed (Erich von Stroheim 1924). Legendary, lengthy silent masterpiece based on Frank Norris's *McTeague* – see p.292 – detailing the squalid, ultimately tragic marriage between a blunt ex-miner with a dental practice on San Francisco's Polk Street, and a simple girl from nearby Oakland. Dated but nonetheless unforgettable, including the classic finale in Death Valley.

Guess Who's Coming to Dinner (Stanley Kramer 1967). Well-meaning but slightly flat interracial comedy in which Spencer Tracy and Katharine Hepburn playing the supposedly liberal but bewildered parents of a woman who brings home the black man (Sidney Poitier) she intends to marry.

Hammett (Wim Wenders 1982). The film that broke Coppola's *Zeotrope* production company, this is a rich tribute to Dashiell Hammett's search for fiction material in the back streets of San Francisco's Chinatown.

Harold and Maude (Hal Ashby 1971). Very funny black comedy about a death-obsessed teenager and the eighty-year-old woman he befriends at various funerals. A bizarre love story with kooky twists, it clarifies very little but manages to entertain thoroughly.

High Anxiety (Mel Brooks 1977). Juvenile but amusing spoof of Hitchcock's San Francisco-based thrillers – *Vertigo*, *The Birds* and *Spellbound*. Silly story based around a psychologist who works at the Institute for the Very Very Nervous.

I Remember Mama (George Stevens 1948). Sentimental, nostalgic tribute to family life *circa* 1910 for a group of Norwegian immigrants in San Francisco. Told through the memories of a now successful authoress, who dwells on her tough past and credits it with making her the woman she is. Enjoyable, if shamelessly romanticized, vision of poverty.

Invasion of the Body Snatchers (Phillip Kaufman 1978). Thanks largely to Donald Sutherland, a good re-make of the 1956 classic tale of extraterrestrial pod people erupting into and replacing humans.

It Came from beneath the Sea (Charles Schneer 1955). A giant octopus destroys San Francisco. Feeble monster movie with laughable special effects.

Jimi Plays Berkeley (Peter Pilafian 1971). The historic Memorial Day Jimi Hendrix concert in Berkeley, interspersed with lots of shots of rampaging students waving their peace signs. Hendrix ignores the peripheral action and just plays.

Joy Luck Club (Wayne Wang 1993). Amy Tan's bestselling novel, which chronicled the lives of four Chinatown women, faithfully translated to the screen with mixed results. Excellent performances in all roles.

The Killer Elite (Sam Peckinpah 1975). Familiar themes of betrayal and trust in this mostly straightforward action flick, built around the internal politics of an underground San Francisco company and a wounded agent (James Caan) who seeks revenge. Excellent set-pieces include a Chinatown shoot-out and siege.

The Lady from Shanghai (Orson Welles 1948). Orson Welles and Rita Hayworth star in this twisted and impossible plot about murder, mystery and sexual unease on board a cruise ship. Compelling, if rambling account of the relationship between a clever young man and beautiful older woman.

The Laughing Policeman (Stuart Rosenberg 1973). Walter Matthau and Bruce Dern pair up in yet another brutal San Francisco cop thriller, triggered by the gunning down of a busload of people in the Mission district. Queasy use of gay characters.

The Lenny Bruce Performance Film (John Magnuson 1967). A historical document of Lenny Bruce's penultimate performance at San Francisco's *Basin Street West* club, one of the few places he was still allowed to perform, during his lengthy obscenity trial. The film catches Bruce at his maniacal and scalding best, though the excerpts from his trial, which he reads obsessively, get to be exhausting.

The Lineup (Frank Cooper 1958). Film adaptation of the TV series *San Francisco Beat*, about the SFPD capturing a junkie-gunman. An unconvincing plot, but polished acting and fantastic shots of San Francisco.

Magnum Force (Ted Post 1973). Sequel to *Dirty Harry*, with more shots of Clint Eastwood looking tough and San Francisco looking spectacular. The storyline, detailing Harry's rejection of vigilante policing methods, is pathetically unbelievable.

The Maltese Falcon (John Huston 1941).

Diamond-hard candidate for the best-ever detective movie, with Humphrey Bogart as San Francisco private dick Sam Spade.

Out of the Past (Jacques Tourneur 1947). Definitive flashback *film noir* starring Robert Mitchum who has a rendezvous with death and his own past in the shape of Jane Greer. Beautiful and bewildering.

Pal Joey (Fred Kohlmar 1957). Frank Sinatra, Rita Hayworth and Kim Novak star in this slick musical about a lovable cad and rising nightclub entertainer. Begins well, but slides alarmingly into cheap sentiment.

Petulia (Richard Lester 1968). San Francisco surgeon George C Scott takes up with unhappily married kook Julie Christie in richly detailed, deliberately fragmentary comedy drama set in druggy, decadent society.

Play it Again Sam (Herbert Ross 1972). Woody Allen as (what else?) neurotic San Francisco film critic who has an affair with his best friend's wife, Diane Keaton.

Point Blank (John Boorman 1967). Lee Marvin plays a double-crossed gangster out for revenge on his cheating partner. Stands up well as a violent gang thriller, with good location shots of LA and San Francisco, but occasionally overreaches itself. Angie Dickinson plays a convincingly faithless wife.

The Presidio (Peter Hyams 1988). Crime thriller about a couple of ill-matched cops investigating the murder of a military policewoman. Sean Connery plays a by-the-book army man with conviction, but the story falls embarrassingly apart with inept handling of romance and father/daughter conflicts.

Psych Out (Richard Rush 1968). Pumped out quickly to capitalize on the "Summer of Love". Good performances from Jack Nicholson and Bruce Dern can't save what is basically a compendium of every hippy cliché in the book. That didn't stop it from quickly becoming a cult movie, though.

San Francisco (W S Van Dyke 1936). Elaborate, entertaining hokum about a Barbary Coast love triangle circa 1906. The script is upstaged by the climactic earthquake sequence.

Shoot the Moon (Alan Parker 1981). Albert Finney and Diane Keaton star in this strained tale of self-obsessed Marin County trauma and heartbreak. About as affecting as an episode of *Dallas*.

Skidoo (Otto Preminger 1968). By far the strangest of all the Flower Power-era films, this has an all-star cast – Carole Channing, Jackie Gleason, Slim Pickens et al – dropping Acid on Alcatraz and generally tripping out. Worth watching to see Groucho Marx, playing God, smoke a joint, and for the Harry Nilsson soundtrack.

Star Trek IV – The Voyage Home (Leonard Nimoy, 1986). Morality crusaders Kirk & Co return through time to San Francisco, to save the whales in the best of the *Star Trek* movies.

The Times of Harvey Milk (Robert Epstein 1984). Exemplary feature-length documentary about America's first openly gay politician, chronicling his career in San Francisco and the aftermath of his 1978 assassination.

They Call Me Mister Tibbs (Gordon Douglas 1970). Sidney Poitier plays Virgil Tibbs, the black San Francisco cop who sleuths his way to unravelling a murder mystery. Benign thriller.

Time after Time (Nicholas Meyer 1979). Courtesy of the Time Machine, Malcolm McDowell chases Jack the Ripper into twentieth-century San Francisco accompanied by a lot of cheap jokes and violence.

Towering Inferno (Irwin Allen 1974). Disaster film that opened the door for a whole decade of banal catastrophes, this one telling the tale of how the world's tallest building is destroyed by fire on the night of its inauguration. Verging on the ridiculous but saved by great special effects and a cast of stars that includes Steve McQueen, Paul Newman, Faye Dunaway and Fred Astaire.

Vertigo (Alfred Hitchcock 1958). A tragedy of obsession, stunningly set in San Francisco, in which detective (and lonely voyeur) James Stewart tracks down the long-dead Madeleine played by Kim Novak. Perhaps Hitchcock's most personal and psychologically revealing work.

What's Up Doc? (Peter Bogdanovich 1972). Wildly likeable screwball comedy pastiche, set in San Francisco and starring Barbra Streisand and Ryan O'Neal as a cook and a naive professor.

Glossaries

American cities have a jargon all their own, and none more so than San Francisco. Some of the listings here would be of use anywhere; others are specifically San Franciscan (or at least Californian), not least the gay slang section, very much a product of the city's Castro district. We've also included a rundown of San Franciscan personalities, past and present, which may both aid your reading of the main part of the guide, and help to decipher the city at ground level.

San Francisco People

AGNOS Art Former mayor of San Francisco, elected on a liberal platform in 1987 when Diane Feinstein stepped down to pursue her career in state politics.

BIERCE Ambrose Came to San Francisco on an army assignment, where he began his literary career as a journalist and went on to become the *San Francisco Examiner*'s most satirical and witty staff writer. Spent his old age writing ghost and detective stories, gathered together in his *Collected Works*.

BRANNAN Sam Founded a Mormon colony in the early years of the city and started San Francisco's first newspaper, *The California Star*. Most famous, however, as the man who brought the news of the discovery of gold in the Sierras, Brannan made a fortune in real estate before drinking his way into poverty and spending his last years alone and forgotten in Escondido, San Diego.

BRIDGES Harry Inspired by Jack London's fiction to leave his native Australia and come to San Francisco to work on sailing vessels, Bridges went on to become the militant leader of the International Longshoremen's Association, a career which brought him disciples and enemies in equal numbers as he led his union through major battles with the Pacific Coast shipowners in 1934, and again in 1971, when he came out of retirement on behalf of his longshoremen. A genuine working-class hero.

BROWER David California-born conservationist, Brower was long-time Director of the Sierra Club (1952–1969) and went on to help found Friends of the Earth.

BROWN Arthur (1874–1957). Oakland-born architect who built San Francisco's City Hall and Coit Tower.

BROWN Willie San Francisco's flamboyant and outspoken black Democrat politician, who has climbed the political ladder very quickly and was Jessie Jackson's campaign manager in the 1988 presidential race.

BRUBECK Dave Oakland-born pianist and jazz composer (notably of *Take Five*), Brubeck brought attention to so-called West Coast Jazz, achieving international celebrity status for himself as a jazz musician along the way.

BRUNDAGE Avery Michigan-born engineer, Brundage went on to become the president of the International Olympic Committee, but he is most famous for his enormous collection of Oriental art, donated to San Francisco's de Young Museum and now known as the Asian Art Museum.

BURNHAM Daniel Chicago architect who was invited by San Francisco's mayor, James D Phelan, to plan the city's development in the early twentieth century, giving rise to the Beaux Arts complex of Civic Center – though this was in fact only a small part of his ambitious scheme.

CAEN Herb San Francisco's most prominent columnist, Caen has been writing for the *San Francisco Chronicle* since the year dot. Though a touch overrated, he occasionally digs up good dirt on San Francisco's more prominent society figures. Worth reading for the indiscreet gossip. See p.282.

COIT Lillie Renowned for her unusual behavior, Lillie Coit came to San Francisco as a child and was reared in the best social circles. Married briefly to Howard Coit, on her death she left $100,000 to the city in order to build Coit Tower, Telegraph Hill's principal landmark, as a memorial to San Francisco's volunteer firefighters.

COOLBRITH Ina San Francisco poet who introduced Jack London to literature when working for the Oakland Public Library. Her poems are collected in the books *Singer of the Sea, A Perfect Day* and *Songs of the Golden Gate*. In recognition for her organization of the World Congress of Authors, for the Panama Pacific Exhibition in 1915, the legislature made her the state's first Poet Laureate.

COPPOLA Francis Ford San Francisco-based film-maker, whose works include *Apocalypse Now, The Conversation* and *One from the Heart*. He still lives in the city and is the owner of the Columbus Tower in North Beach.

DI MAGGIO Joe Began his baseball career in 1932 with the San Francisco Seals and went on to stardom as centerfielder with the New York Yankees. Married Marilyn Monroe in the 1950s.

FEINSTEIN Diane Ex-San Francisco mayor who stepped in when George Moscone and Harvey Milk were assassinated and is now a US Senator. Very much the career politician, rumors abound about her dealings with the big business corporations in the late 1970s that led to massive development in San Francisco's Financial District.

FERLINGHETTI Lawrence Founder and still owner of the *City Lights Bookstore*, America's first paper-back bookshop, Ferlinghetti became a prominent figure during the Beat movement of the 1950s and had close links with its major figures.

GARCIA Jerry Lead guitarist and vocalist for psychedelic rock gods, the Grateful Dead.

GINSBERG Allen Though born in New Jersey, Ginsberg is associated with San Francisco because of the controversial Beat poem *Howl*, which he wrote in North Beach.

GRAHAM Bill Rock music impresario Graham, who died in a helicopter accident in 1992, can in part be credited with the success of psychedelic music, which he promoted through the concerts he staged at the famous Fillmore Auditorium.

HALLIDIE Andrew English-born engineer who emigrated to California in the nineteenth century to work in the Comstock mines, in 1873 he invented the universally loved cable car, and thereby made travel over San Francisco's ridicu-lous gradients possible.

HAMMETT Dashiell Hammett , who travelled to San Francisco as a young man and worked for the Pinkerton Detective Agency, drawing on his experiences to write the hard-boiled detective stories that inspired Raymond Chandler and others. His most famous works include *The Maltese Falcon* and *The Thin Man*. In his later years, Hammett was involved in the Hollywood Ten McCarthy witchhunts concerning allegedly un-American activities, and was sent to prison for refusing to testify.

HEARST William Randolph Publishing magnate who as a young man worked on the *San Francisco Examiner* and went on to acquire a string of successful daily newspapers, motion picture companies and radio stations; he later served briefly as a congressman in New York. Famous for his lavish lifestyle and the incredible Hearst Castle at San Simeon, south of the city. Orson Welles' classic *Citizen Kane* was loosely based on his life.

HOBART Lewis P Missouri-born architect, who came to study at the University of California and went on to design the Bohemian Club, Grace Cathedral and the Steinhart Aquarium.

JOPLIN Janis Texas-born Joplin came to San Francisco at the age of eighteen, where she began her singing career with *Big Brother and the Holding Company*. A central figure in the psychedelic scene, her problem was not LSD but booze and heroin, an overdose of which finally killed her in 1970.

KEROUAC Jack A leading figure of the Beat move-ment in New York, Kerouac came out to San Francisco in the 1950s, where he drew on his experiences to write the Beats' bible *On The Road*. Spent much of his life returning to stay with his mother in Massachussetts and eventually drank himself into an early grave at the age of 46.

KESEY Ken Oregon-reared Kesey enrolled in a creative writing programme at Stanford University, during which time he became involved with psychiatric experiments with LSD – experiences which inspired him to write *One Flew Over the Cuckoo's Nest*. Important, too, for his involvement in San Francisco's psychedelic scene, Kesey toured the country with his busload of Merry Pranksters in the Sixties, a time richly chronicled in Tom Wolfe's *Electric Kool-Aid Acid Test*.

LONDON Jack London was an illegitimate child who grew up with little formal education but read books compulsively, a habit that was later to serve him well when he began his prolific writing career that produced *The Call of the Wild*.

MAYBECK Bernard Early modern architect responsible for some of the most beautiful buildings in the Bay Area, including the magnificent Palace of Fine Arts for the Panama Pacific Exhibition in 1915.

MIEGGS Henry Mieggs came to San Francisco at the beginning of the Gold Rush, and made a small fortune carrying lumber from upstate New York. He went on to become a civic leader and built Mieggs Wharf – today's Fisherman's Wharf. Later in life he was involved in a scandal concerning forged city treasury warrants and fled to South America.

MILK Harvey San Francisco's (and perhaps the world's) first openly gay politician, Milk played a key role in the gay emancipation of the 1970s, only to be assassinated at the height of his career and popularity by political rival, Dan White (see p.108).

MOONEY Tom Radical Socialist labor leader, charged with planting the bomb that killed ten people during a Preparedness Day Parade on San Francisco's Market Street in 1916. He was sentenced to hang for the killings, but the injustice of his conviction became a *cause célèbre* for years and in 1939 he was pardoned.

MONTGOMERY John B. Nineteenth-century naval captain in command of the *Portsmouth* during the Mexican War, who occupied San Francisco in 1846 and raised the American flag on the plaza that was the one-time waterfront.

MOSCONE George San Francisco's liberal mayor who was assassinated along with Harvey Milk in 1978.

NORRIS Frank (1870–1902). Highly respected writer, who studied at the University of California and went on to produce acclaimed works such as *McTeague*, *The Octopus* and *The Pit.*

NORTON Joshua Abraham "Emperor" London-born Norton came to be known as Emperor Norton after declaring himself "Norton I, Emperor of the United States" – a claim that was no doubt symptomatic of the insanity provoked by his bankruptcy in the rice market. He comported himself regally around San Francisco wearing a military suit and sword, usually accompanied by his two dogs, Bummer and Lazarus. His "loyal subjects" received him sympathetically and were tolerant of his various proclamations and commands, the most famous of which was a plan to build a bridge across the bay. Upon his death, the city conducted a formal civic funeral in honor of his services to the city.

POLK Willis (1865–1924). An architect, he came to San Francisco as a young man and became involved with a bohemian group known as Les Jeunes. He also headed Daniel Burnham's San Francisco office and worked on his city plan. Known for his elegant brown shingle designs.

SANTANA Carlos San Francisco-based guitar virtuoso renowned for his blending of Latin rhythms into pop music.

STANFORD Leland Made his fortune as one of the Big Four who constructed the Central Pacific Railroad. During a two-year term as governor he was a staunch union supporter, although he is perhaps best known now for the creation of the university in Palo Alto that bears his name.

SUTRO Adolph Prussian-born philanthropist who came to San Francisco and made his fortune in the Comstock silver bonanza. Heavy investment in San Francisco real estate led to his ownership of almost a twelfth of the entire city, to which he donated many developments, including the Cliff House, Sutro Baths and the Sutro Library.

TWAIN Mark (Samuel Langhorne Clemens) Spent his early years in Missouri before embarking on a journalistic career that brought him to San Francisco in 1864. A regular contributor to such publications as *The Golden Era*, *Californian* and *Territorial Enterprise*, he gained his biggest popularity after writing *Roughing It*, telling exaggerated tales of adventures in the Comstock mining era.

WHITE Dan The murderer of Harvey Milk and George Moscone, White was a disgruntled ex-policeman and city supervisor whose trial came to be known as the "Twinkie Defence" after his lawyer claimed that White was suffering from temporary insanity caused by harmful additives in fast food. After serving a controversially brief five-year sentence, White was released and committed suicide several months later.

Terms and Acronyms

Art Deco Style of decoration popular in the 1930s, characterized by elegant geometrical shapes and patterns.

Art Nouveau Art, architecture and design of the 1890s typified by stylized organic forms.

Atrium Enclosed, covered pedestrian space often forming the lobby of a corporate building.

The Avenues Catch-all term for the Richmond and Sunset neighborhoods.

BART (Bay Area Rapid Transit). The Bay Area's underground train system, linking San Francisco with Oakland, Berkeley and other parts of the East Bay.

Beaux Arts Style of Neoclassical architecture taught at the Ecole de Beaux Arts in Paris at the end of the last century, the best example of which in the Bay Area is Civic Center.

The Big Four Collis P Huntington, Mark Hopkins, Charles Crocker and Leland Stanford – the four railroad barons who made their fortune building the Central Pacific Railroad in the late 1800s.

Cal Nickname for University of California, Berkeley.

City Hall Not just the building, but also used to describe the local government as a whole.

Clapboard House covered with overlapping timber boards, in evidence throughout the city.

Colonial Dames of America Patriotic organization of women descended from worthy ancestors who became American residents before 1750.

Condo Short for condominium, an individually owned apartment within a building.

Co-op Not very common, but a form of apartment ownership in the city. A co-op differs from a condo in that you buy shares in the building in which the apartment is sited, rather than the apartment itself.

Federal National government, and as such not subject to state government – eg a federal housing programme would be one funded by Congress and not the state.

Loft Large open space usually at the top of an old warehouse, popular with artists because of the direct lighting.

Muni (San Francisco Municipal Railway). Not just a railway, but a system of buses, trolley buses, cable cars and streetcars that serves the city.

Plaza Wide open space that acts as a pedestrian forecourt to a skyscraper or set of buildings.

Project Council estate or blocks of public housing.

Skyscraper The word comes from the highest sail on a sailing ship, and hence refers to any high building.

WPA (Works Project Administration). Agency begun by Roosevelt in 1935 to create employment. As well as much construction work, the WPA art projects produced many murals in public buildings and a renowned set of guide-books to the entire country.

Index

You are
A STUDENT

You travel
THE WORLD

You want
TO SAVE MONEY

Here's how

The International
Student Identity Card

Available at Student Travel Offices Worldwide.

Entitles you to discounts and special services worldwide.

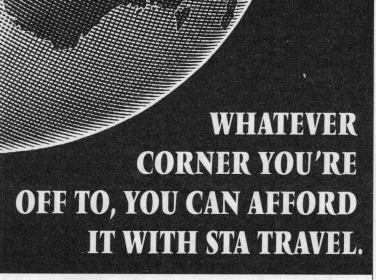